Fodor's

DENMARK
4TH EDITION

Where to Stay and Eat
for All Budgets

Must-See Sights
and Local Secrets

Ratings You Can Trust

Portions of this book appear in *Fodor's Scandinavia*

Fodor's Travel Publications   New York, Toronto, London, Sydney, Auckland
www.fodors.com

FODOR'S DENMARK

Editors: Nuha Ansari, Thomas Mercer

Editorial Production: Ira-Neil Dittersdorf
Editorial Contributors: Charles Ferro, Satu Hummasti, Eduardo López de Luzuriaga
Maps: David Lindroth, *cartographer;* Bob Blake and Rebecca Baer, *map editors*
Design: Fabrizio La Rocca, *creative director;* Guido Caroti, *art director;* Melanie Marin, *senior picture editor*
Production/Manufacturing: Colleen Ziemba
Cover Photo (Ærøskøbing): Bob Krist

SPECIAL SALES

Fodor's Travel Publications are available at special discounts for bulk purchases for sales promotions or premiums. Special editions, including personalized covers, excerpts of existing guides, and corporate imprints, can be created in large quantities for special needs. For more information, contact your local bookseller or write to Special Markets, Fodor's Travel Publications, 1745 Broadway, New York, New York 10019. Inquiries from Canada should be directed to your local Canadian bookseller or sent to Random House of Canada, Ltd., Marketing Department, 2775 Matheson Boulevard East, Mississauga, Ontario L4W 4P7. Inquiries from the United Kingdom should be sent to Fodor's Travel Publications, 20 Vauxhall Bridge Road, London SW1V 2SA, England.

AN IMPORTANT TIP & AN INVITATION

Although all prices, opening times, and other details in this book are based on information supplied to us at press time, changes occur all the time in the travel world, and Fodor's cannot accept responsibility for facts that become outdated or for inadvertent errors or omissions. So **always confirm information when it matters,** especially if you're making a detour to visit a specific place. Your experiences—positive and negative—matter to us. If we have missed or misstated something, **please write to us.** We follow up on all suggestions. Contact the Denmark editors at editors@fodors.com or c/o Fodor's at 1745 Broadway, New York, New York 10019.

DESTINATION DENMARK

The first thing you notice about Denmark is a contentment reflected in the faces of its people. It radiates almost blindingly on a fair summer's day, and it still shines through on a blustery, clammy November afternoon. The Danish attitude goes that life is only worth living if done so joyfully, selflessly, meticulously, and, most of all, aesthetically. When you walk through Danish cities and towns, notice how the city avenues conform perfectly to the harmony of the architecture, how elegant seating supplants cheap plastic chairs at outdoor cafés. On a larger scale, moats and well-groomed gardens surround the countryside's storybook castles, and shimmering lamps illuminate Copenhagen's Tivoli at night. With all the care they take, the Danes are sure to make you feel comfortable and at home, and you may find yourself donning that same contented look that seemed so foreign when you arrived. Whether you limit yourself to Copenhagen's canals or venture all the way to Greenland's arctic expanses, have a fabulous trip!

Karen Cure, Editorial Director

CONTENTS

On the Road with Fodor's *F9*
About this Book *F10*
What's Where *F12*
Great Itineraries *F14*
When to Go *F15*
On the Calendar *F16*
Pleasures & Pastimes *F18*
Fodor's Choice *F20*
Smart Travel Tips *F24*

1 Copenhagen 1

Exploring Copenhagen 2
Where to Eat 23
Where to Stay 33
Nightlife & the Arts 40
Sports & the Outdoors 47
Shopping 49
Side Trips from Copenhagen 54
Copenhagen A to Z 59

2 Sjælland & Its Islands 67

3 Fyn & the Central Islands 94

4 Jylland 117

5 Bornholm 144

6 The Faroe Islands 159

7 Greenland 172

Understanding Denmark 187

The Utterly Danish Pastries of
Denmark 188
The Feast Before the Fast 190
Books & Movies 192
Chronology 194
Vocabulary 198

Index 205

Maps

Scandinavia *F6–F7*

Denmark *F8*

Copenhagen *4–5*

Where to Eat in
Copenhagen *24–25*

Where to Stay in
Copenhagen *34–35*

Sjælland & Its Islands *70*

Fyn & the Central Islands *98*

Jylland *122*

Bornholm *150*

The Faroe Islands *163*

Greenland *177*

CloseUps

The Danish Royals *13*

Carlsberg Breweries: Ale &
Arty *21*

Denmark's Cinema Verité *45*

The Rise of Danish Design *53*

Sun, Sand & Waves *79*

Viking Victuals *82*

Jul-Tide in Denmark *135*

Faroese Flavors *168*

Scandinavia

COMMONWEALTH OF
INDEPENDENT STATES
(RUSSIA)

North Cape
TO
SVALBARD

Hammerfest
Alta
Karasjok
Kautokeino
Kilpisjärvi
Kirkenes
Utsjoki
Ivalo
Inari
Enontekiö
Muonio
Kittilä
Sodankylä
Posio
Kuusamo
Suomussalmi
Kuhmo
Nurmes

SUOMI
(FINLAND)

Puolanka
Kajaani
Otanmäki
Iisalmi
Pudasjärvi
Raahe
Oulu
Oulujärvi
Pulkkila
Kalajoki
Nivala
Haapajärvi
Kokkola
Syyjärvi

Kemijärvi
Rovaniemi
Kemi
Tornio
Tornea
Kalix
Torniojoki
Torneälv

Gulf of Bothnia

Kiruna
Jokkmokk
Piteå
Skellefteå
Umeå

Arvidsjaur
Arjeplog
Sorsele
Storuman
Lycksele
Ångermanälven
Strömsund
Meråker

SVERIGE
(SWEDEN)

200 miles
300 km

Tromsø
Harstad
Narvik
Fauske
Bodø
Mo i Rana
Mosjøen
Sandnessjøen
Brønnøysund
Namsos
Steinkjer
Trondheim
Kristiansund

Arctic Circle

LOFOTEN VESTERÅLEN
Vestfjorden

Norwegian
Sea

ATLANTIC
OCEAN

TO
ICELAND

ISLAND (ICELAND)

Arctic Circle

Raufarhöfn
Bakkaflói
Vopnafjörður
Egilsstaðir
Vopnafjörður
Neskaupstaður
Breiðdalsvík
Djúpivogur
Hornafjarðarós
Fagurhólsmyri
Kirkjubæjarklaustur

Skjálfandi
Tjörnes
Akureyri
Siglufjörður
Dalvík
Blönduós
Vatnajökull
Hofsjökull
Langjökull
Reykholt
Hveragerði
Hella
Vík
Westmann Islands

Vestfirðir
Breiðafjörður
Stykkishólmur
Faxaflói
Reykjavík
Hafnarfjörður

KEY

– – – Ferry lines

Faroe Islands (Denmark)

TO FAROE ISLANDS

NORGE (NORWAY)

DANMARK (DENMARK)

GERMANY

POLAND

LITHUANIA

LATVIA

ESTONIA

RUSSIA

North Sea

Baltic Sea

Gulf of Finland

Kattegat

Skagerrak

Oslofjord

Helsinki
St. Petersburg
Tallinn
Pskov
Joensuu
Kuopio
Varkaus
Savonlinna
Punkaharju
Imatra
Lappeenranta
Äänekoski
Mikkeli
Heinola
Kouvola
Kotka
Seinäjoki
Jyväskylä
Parkano
Tampere
Lahti
Porvoo
Vaasa
Pori
Rauma
Turku
Salo
Ekenäs
Hanko
Hiumaa
Saaremaa
Liepāja
Klaipeda
Mariehamn (Maarianhamina)
Uppsala
Stockholm
Slite
Visby
Gotland
Bornholm
Sundsvall
Hudiksvall
Bollnäs
Falun
Avesta
Borlänge
Fagersta
Nynäshamn
Norrköping
Linköping
Oskarshamn
Kalmar
Karlskrona
Kristianstad
Mora
Borlänge
Karlstad
Mellerud
Trollhättan
Borås
Falkenberg
Halmstad
Helsingborg
Malmö
Ystad
Idre
Koppang
Rena
Eidsvoll
Hamar
Lillehammer
Fredrikstad
Halden
Strömstad
Uddevalla
Skagen
Aalborg
Nakskov
Middelfart
Flensburg
Stören
Oppdal
Tynset
Dombås
Lake Mjøsa
Oslo
Drammen
Kongsberg
Porsgrunn
Larvik
Arendal
Kristiansand
Thisted
Silkeborg
Fredericia
Esbjerg
Ribe
Molde
Geiranger
Jostedalsbreen
Jotunheimen
Geilo
Evje
Grimstad
Mandal
Ringkøbing
Flora
Voss
Bergen
Haugesund
Stavanger
Sandnes
Österdalen
Ljusnan
Klarälven
Mälaren
Dalälven
Österdalen

North Sea

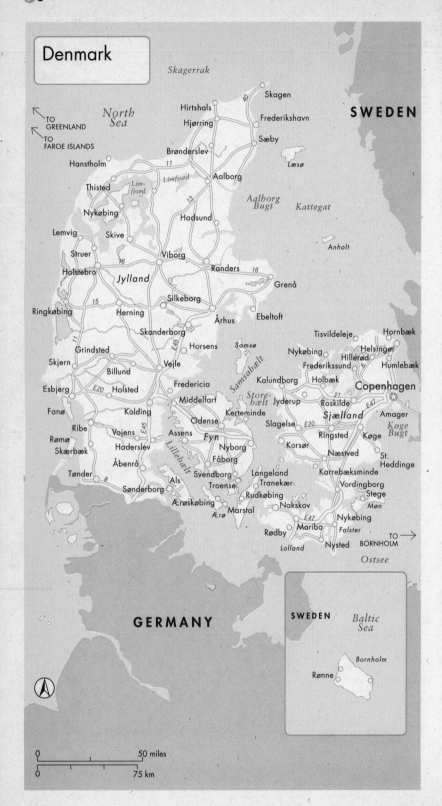

Denmark

Skagerrak

North Sea

TO GREENLAND
TO FAROE ISLANDS

Skagen
Hirtshals
Hjørring
Frederikshavn
Sæby
Brønderslev

SWEDEN

Hanstholm
Thisted
Lim-fjord
Limfjord
Aalborg
Læsø

Nykøbing
Hadsund
Aalborg Bugt
Kattegat

Lemvig
Skive
Struer
Viborg
Randers
Grenå
Holstebro
Jylland
Anholt

Ringkøbing
Herning
Silkeborg
Århus
Ebeltoft
Skanderborg

Grindsted
Horsens
Sømsø
Tisvildeleje
Hornbæk
Skjern
Vejle
Nykøbing
Helsingør
Billund
Fredericia
Kalundborg
Holbæk
Hillerød
Humlebæk
Esbjerg
Holsted
Middelfart
Storebælt
Jyderup
Roskilde
Copenhagen
Fanø
Kolding
Odense
Kerteminde
Slagelse
Ringsted
Amager
Ribe
Vojens
Assens
Fyn
Nyborg
Korsør
Køge
Køge Bugt
Rømø
Haderslev
Fåborg
Næstved
St. Heddinge
Skærbæk
Åbenrå
Svendborg
Langeland
Karrebæksminde
Tønder
Als
Troense
Rudkøbing
Vordingborg
Stege
Sønderborg
Ærøskøbing
Marstal
Nakskov
Møn
Ærø
Rødby
Maribo
Nykøbing
Falster
Lolland
Nysted
TO BORNHOLM

Samsøbælt
Lillebælt

Ostsee

GERMANY

SWEDEN
Baltic Sea

Bornholm
Rønne

0   50 miles
0   75 km

ON THE ROAD WITH FODOR'S

A trip takes you out of yourself. Concerns of life at home completely disappear, driven away by more immediate thoughts—about, say, what marvels will beguile the next day, or where you'll have dinner. That's where Fodor's comes in. We make sure that you know all your options, so that you don't miss something that's around the next bend just because you didn't know it was there. Because the best memories of your trip might well have nothing to do with what you came to Denmark to see, we guide you to sights large and small all over the region. You might set out to see Copenhagen's Tivoli at night, but back at home you find yourself unable to forget the glow of Skagen's supernatural light or your visit to one of Bornholm's traditional smokehouses. With Fodor's at your side, serendipitous discoveries are never far away.

Our success in showing you every corner of Denmark is a credit to our extraordinary writers. Although there's no substitute for travel advice from a good friend who knows your style, our contributors are the next best thing—the kind of people you would poll for travel advice if you knew them.

Greenland updater Charles Ferro, a freelance journalist, has lived in Copenhagen since 1977. A highlight of his journalism career was an interview with the late Danish comedian and pianist Victor Borge. He writes for travel and entertainment publications, as well as a number of consumer magazines, and edits the expatriate magazine *Abroad*. Charles is also the author of 14 books for teens.

After freelancing for several years in both Cologne, Germany, and London, our European Denmark and Smart Travel Tips updater Eduardo López de Luzuriaga moved to Copenhagen in 1997. He has worked regularly for the Spanish news agency EFE and is now editor of *Morada Internacional*, a magazine for Spanish-speaking expatriates in Denmark.

ABOUT THIS BOOK

There's no doubt that the best source for travel advice is a like-minded friend who's just been where you're headed. But with or without that friend, you'll have a better trip with a Fodor's guide in hand. Once you've learned to find your way around its pages, you'll be in great shape to find your way around your destination.

SELECTION

Our goal is to cover the best properties, sights, and activities in their category, as well as the most interesting communities to visit. We make a point of including local food-lovers' hot spots as well as neighborhood options, and we avoid all that's touristy unless it's really worth your time. You can go on the assumption that everything you read about in this book is recommended wholeheartedly by our writers and editors. Flip to On the Road with Fodor's to learn more about who they are. It goes without saying that no property mentioned in the book has paid to be included.

RATINGS

Orange stars ★ denote sights and properties that our editors and writers consider the very best in the area covered by the entire book. These, the best of the best, are listed in the Fodor's Choice section in the front of the book. Black stars ★ highlight the sights and properties we deem Highly Recommended, the don't-miss sights within any region. Fodor's Choice and Highly Recommended options in each region are usually listed on the title page of the chapter covering that region. Use the index to find complete descriptions. In cities, sights pinpointed with numbered map bullets ❶ in the margins tend to be more important than those without bullets.

SPECIAL SPOTS

Pleasures & Pastimes focuses on types of experiences that reveal the spirit of the destination. Watch for Off the Beaten Path sights. Some are out of the way, some are quirky, and all are worth your while. If the munchies hit while you're exploring, look for Need a Break? suggestions.

TIME IT RIGHT

Wondering when to go? Check On the Calendar up front and chapters' Timing sections for weather and crowd overviews and best days and times to visit.

SEE IT ALL

Use Fodor's exclusive Great Itineraries as a model for your trip. (For a good overview of the entire destination, follow those that begin the book, or mix regional itineraries from several chapters.) In cities, Good Walks guide you to important sights in each neighborhood; ☞ indicates the starting points of walks and itineraries in the text and on the map.

BUDGET WELL

Hotel and restaurant price categories from ¢ to $$$$ are defined in the opening pages of each chapter—expect to find a balanced selection for every budget. For attractions, we always give standard adult admission fees; reductions are usually available for children, students, and senior citizens. Look in Discounts & Deals in Smart Travel Tips for information on destination-wide ticket schemes. Want to pay with plastic? AE, D, DC, MC, V following restaurant and hotel listings indicate whether American Express, Discover, Diner's Club, MasterCard, or Visa are accepted.

BASIC INFO	Smart Travel Tips lists travel essentials for the entire area covered by the book; city- and region-specific basics end each chapter. To find the best way to get around, see the transportation section; see individual modes of travel ("Car Travel," "Train Travel") for details. We assume you'll check Web sites or call for particulars.
ON THE MAPS	Maps throughout the book show you what's where and help you find your way around. Black and orange numbered bullets ❶ ❶ in the text correlate to bullets on maps.
BACKGROUND	In general, we give background information within the chapters in the course of explaining sights as well as in CloseUp boxes and in Understanding Denmark at the end of the book. To get in the mood, review the suggestions in Books & Movies. The Vocabulary section can be invaluable.
FIND IT FAST	Within the book, chapters are arranged in a roughly east to west direction starting with Copenhagen. Each chapter covers one of Denmark's peninsulas or island clusters, within which towns are covered in logical geographical order; attractive routes and interesting places between towns are flagged as En Route. Heads at the top of each page help you find what you need within a chapter.
DON'T FORGET	Restaurants are open for lunch and dinner daily unless we state otherwise; we mention dress only when there's a specific requirement and reservations only when they're essential or not accepted—it's always best to book ahead. Hotels have private baths, phone, TVs, and air-conditioning and generally operate on the European Plan (meaning without meals). We always list facilities but not whether you'll be charged extra to use them, so when pricing accommodations, find out what's included.

SYMBOLS

Many Listings
- ★ Fodor's Choice
- ★ Highly recommended
- ⊠ Physical address
- ✛ Directions
- 🕮 Mailing address
- ☎ Telephone
- 🖷 Fax
- ⊕ On the Web
- ✎ E-mail
- ⊗ Open/closed times
- ⚑ Start of walk/itinerary
- Ⓜ Metro stations
- ▭ Credit cards

Outdoors
- 🏌 Golf
- ⛺ Camping

Hotels & Restaurants
- 🏨 Hotel
- ⮫ Number of rooms
- ⚲ Facilities
- ⑩ Meal plans
- ✕ Restaurant
- ⚲ Reservations
- 👖 Dress code
- ⚲ Smoking
- 🍺 BYOB
- ✕🏨 Hotel with restaurant that warrants a visit

Other
- ⚲ Family-friendly
- 🛈 Contact information
- ⇨ See also
- ⊠ Branch address
- ☞ Take note

WHAT'S WHERE

1 Copenhagen

The Danish capital is Scandinavia's largest city (population 1.5 million), incorporating the easternmost reaches of Sjælland and the northern part of adjacent Amager island. That Copenhagen occupies an extreme eastern post on the islands abutting Sweden, so far from the mainland peninsula of Jylland, explains as much about the embattled history of the Baltic port city as about the obvious differences between Copenhageners and the rest of the Danish population. Still, for almost 600 years Copenhagen has been the seat of the oldest kingdom in the world, and if coziness is a Danish trait, then Copenhagen is most certainly Danish. Bicycles roll alongside cars in the narrow streets, and a handful of skyscrapers are tucked away amid cafés, canals, and quaint old homes. But don't let the low-slung skyline fool you: downtown Copenhagen is a sophisticated cultural hub with a wealth of attractions. Strøget, Copenhagen's pedestrian shopping avenue, packs in the best in Danish design tastes from flowers to flatware and furs to furniture; street performers, sidewalk cafés, and pastry shops beckon outdoors. Formidable art collections hang at the Ny Carlsberg Glypotek and the Statens Museum for Kunst. Grandeur finds its expression in the city's royal residences, while the maritime neighborhood of Nyhavn teems with patio seating and harbors a modest fleet of old sailing vessels. The city's, if not Denmark's, best-known attraction is Tivoli Gardens, a bewitching blend of blooming gardens, funfair rides, pantomime theater, stylish restaurants, and concerts.

2 Sjælland & Its Islands

If it's necessary to "escape" from Copenhagen, then the island of Sjælland (Zealand), the largest of the Danish isles, is the country's most convenient and popular escape to the countryside. North of the city are royal castles (including Helsingør's Kronborg of Hamlet fame), ritzy beach towns, and top-notch museums. The modern-art museum Louisiana has a spectacular seaside perch on Sjælland's northeastern coast and a superb collection of modern European and American art, from Warhol to Giacometti. To the west, Roskilde holds relics of medieval Denmark; it also hosts Northern Europe's largest music festival, usually at the end of June, which draws over 75,000 revelers who come to groove to rock, pop, jazz, and folk music. And to the west and south, rural towns and farms edge up to beach communities and fine white beaches, often surrounded by forests. On the southeast island of Møn, 75-million-year-old chalk cliffs plunge dramatically to the sea.

3 Fyn & the Central Islands

Fyn (Funen), the smaller of the country's two main islands, is the site of Denmark's third-largest city, Odense, the birthplace of Hans Christian Andersen. It's no wonder this area inspired many fairy tales: 1,120 km (700 mi) of coastline and lush stretches of vegetable and flower gardens are punctuated by manor houses, beech glades, castles, swan ponds, and thatch-roof houses. In the south is the Egeskov Slot, a well-preserved Renaissance castle that even has a moat. Myriad islands speckle the sea south of Fyn, including verdant Ærø, called the Jewel of the Archipelago. In the island's friendly port town of Ærøskøbing, narrow cobbled streets wind among beautifully preserved half-timber houses.

4 Jylland

Jylland, Denmark's western peninsula, shares its southern border with Germany, its northern end jutting sharply toward the coast of Sweden.

At the northernmost point stands Skagen, a luminous, dune-covered site; marking even intervals to the south are Århus and Aalborg, two of Denmark's largest cities. Home to a large university, Århus pulsates with a lively nightlife and café scene that rivals Copenhagen's. Further south, in Billund, awaits the famed Legoland. Between outposts the heart of the peninsula, mostly lakeland and beech forests, is dotted with castles and parklands. Along the east coast, deep fjords are rimmed by forests. In the south marshlands surround Denmark's oldest town, Ribe, and its gabled houses. The western islands of Fanø and Rømø, with silky sand beaches wrinkled in windswept dunes, draw scores of vacationing Northern Europeans.

(5) Bornholm

The island of Bornholm, 177 km (110 mi) southeast of Sjælland, sits off the coast of Sweden and has a temperate climate that distinguishes it from the rest of Denmark. Its old-fashioned towns and exuberant natural beauty have earned it the title of Pearl of the Baltic. Gardens, forests, and dune grasses sprout up in a patchwork of verdure, and active cod and herring fisheries reap similar abundance from the surrounding Baltic waters.

(6) The Faroe Islands

The 18 Faroe Islands dot the North Atlantic north of Scotland and 1,300 km (812 mi) northwest of Denmark. Granted self-government in 1948, the native Faroese live by fishing and shepherding amid rugged pastureland that is home to over 120 migratory species of birds. Villages of thatch-roof houses nestle up to mossy hillsides and overlook rocky outcrops, and harbors bustle with the comings and goings of fishing boats.

(7) Greenland

Last but not least, there's Greenland, the second-largest island in the world (after the continent of Australia). Greenland's allure is its savage landscape of jagged fjords and gargantuan icebergs. Its wild and raw nature is the biggest and best sight of all. It's a land where tourism is still new and travel is limited to helicopters, coastal boats, or dogsleds that traverse the bright-white frozen plains. Greenland's second largest town, Sisimiut, is the center for winter tourism. Remember that Greenland is in the middle of the North Atlantic, and most visitors to the country will want to venture there on a separate trip!

Denmark is divided into three regions: the two major islands of Sjæl-land and Fyn, and the peninsula of Jylland. To the east, Sjælland is Den-mark's largest and most populated island, with Copenhagen its focal point. Denmark's second largest island, Fyn, is a pastoral, undulating land dotted with farms and summer-house beach villages, with Odense as its one major town. To the west, the relatively vast Jylland connects Denmark to the European continent; here you find the towns of Århus and Aalborg.

Denmark in 3 Days

Take at least two days to explore and enjoy **Copenhagen.** The third day, head north of the city, first to **Rungsted** to see Karen Blixen's manor house and the lush garden surrounding it, then to the Louisiana modern-art museum in **Humlebæk.**

Denmark in 5 Days

After two days and nights in **Copenhagen,** head north to **Rungsted** and **Humlebæk;** then spend the third night in **Helsingør.** The next day, visit the castles of Helsingør and **Hillerød,** and spend the night in medieval **Roskilde.** Day 5, venture southeast to enjoy the dramatic nature and his-tory of **Møn** and the villages and beaches of Lolland and Falster. An al-ternative last-day tour is to head west to Hans Christian Andersen's birthplace of **Odense,** on Fyn.

Denmark in 7 Days

In a week you can see Copenhagen and environs and explore Fyn and Jylland. Rent a car for the latter—it's the quickest way to make it from the historic cities of **Århus** and **Aalborg** to the blond beaches of **Skagen,** with time left over to meander through a couple of smaller villages. Keep in mind that to take in Greenland or the Faroe Islands in addition to seeing mainland Denmark, you'll need more than a week—ideally two.

°C		°F
100		212
40		105
37		98.6
30		90
25		80
20		70
15		60
10		50
5		40
0		32
−5		20
−10		10
−15		0
−20		

Summertime—when the lingering sun of June, July, and August brings out the best in the climate and the Danes—is the best time to visit. In July most Danes flee to their summer homes or go abroad. If you do go in winter, the weeks preceding Christmas are a prime time to explore Tivoli. Although the experience is radically different from the flower-filled summertime park, the winter park has a charm all its own. Much of Tivoli is closed during these weeks, but you can still experience some of the shops, restaurants, a handful of rides, an "elf house," and some Danish theater.

Climate

Mainland Denmark and its surrounding islands have a cool maritime climate with mild to warm summers and cold (but not frigid) winters. Late summer and early fall is the rainiest season, but even then, precipitation is rarely heavy. In summer, Bornholm tends to stay warmer and sunnier longer than elsewhere; this is also the best time to visit Greenland and the Faroe Islands. Winter is dark and misty, but it's a great time to visit museums, libraries, and the countless atmospheric meeting places in which the Danes take refuge.

Forecasts Weather Channel Connection ☎ 900/932–8437, 95¢ per minute from a Touch-Tone phone ⊕ www.weather.com.

COPENHAGEN

Jan.	36F	2C	May	61F	16C	Sept.	64F	18C
	28	− 2		46	8		52	11
Feb.	36F	2C	June	66F	19C	Oct.	54F	12C
	27	− 3		52	11		45	7
Mar.	41F	5C	July	72F	22C	Nov.	45F	7C
	30	− 1		57	14		37	3
Apr.	52F	11C	Aug.	70F	21C	Dec.	39F	4C
	37	3		57	14		34	1

ON THE CALENDAR

Denmark's top seasonal events are listed below, and any one of them could provide the stuff of lasting memories. You'll want to book tickets and plan ahead for the crowded Roskilde Festival. The summer jazz festivals in Copenhagen and Århus, as well as the early-fall Århus Festival, are also well-attended. The Danish Tourist Board's Web site, ⊕ www.visitdenmark.com, also has information about events.

WINTER	
Late Nov.–. Late Dec.	The Christmas Market at Tivoli Gardens has lots of decorations, gift ideas, and seasonal treats.

SPRING	
Mid-Mar.	The Snow Festival in Nuuk, Greenland, is best known for its demanding snow-sculpting contest, in which teams fashion their creations from a 3-meter cube of packed snow.
Late Mar.	The Arctic Circle Race is a grueling 160 km, three-day cross-country ski race that traverses the terrain surrounding Sisimiut, Greenland.
Late Mar.– Early Apr.	The Drambuie World Ice Golf Championship tees off in Uummannaq, Greenland, weather permitting. Its participants include some of the world's best.
April 16	The Queen's Birthday is celebrated with the royal guard in full ceremonial dress as the royal family appears before the public on the balcony of Amalienborg.
Mid-May	The Copenhagen Marathon leads 6,000 participants on a flat, fast course through the city streets.
Late May	The Aalborg Carnival draws 100,000 visitors to the Jylland city for two days of festivities, which include fireworks, outdoor concerts, and parades of costumed revelers.
Late May– Early June	The Copenhagen Carnival includes boat parades in Nyhavn and costumed revelers in the streets. Various musical and dance performances take place throughout the city.

SUMMER	
Early June	The Aalborg Jazz Festival, though not as large as its Copenhagen counterpart, fills the city with four days of indoor and outdoor concerts, many of them free.
Mid-June	The International Kite Festival in Fanø, an island off the western coast of Jylland, attracts thousands of kite enthusiasts who fill the skies above with their diving and soaring kites.
	The Riverboat Jazz Festival draws jazz fans to Silkeborg for the four-day celebration featuring local international bands.
	The Round Sjælland Regatta, one of the largest yachting events in the world, starts and ends in Helsingør.
June 21	On Midsummer's Night, Danes celebrate the longest day of the year with bonfires and picnics in the countryside.

Late June–Early July	The Roskilde Festival, the largest rock concert in northern Europe, attracts dozens of premier rock, pop, and hip-hop groups, and more than 75,000 fans.
Late June	The Skagen Festival, brings the northern tip of Jylland to its liveliest, showcasing international and local folk music.
July	The Copenhagen Jazz Festival, one of Europe's largest jazz-music events, gathers international and Scandinavian jazz greats for a week of concerts, many of them free.
July 4	The Fourth of July celebration in Rebild Park, near Aalborg, represents the only American Independence Day festivities outside the United States.
Mid-July	The Århus International Jazz Festival gathers world-renowned names for indoor and outdoor concerts.
	The family-friendly Samsø Festival gets underway on the island of Samsø, Jylland, with music performed by Danish and international acts.
Mid-Aug.	The Mermaid Pride Parade is a gay pride event that navigates the streets of Copenhagen, which has a sizeable gay and lesbian community.
Late Aug.	The Tønder Festival, held in this town in southern Jylland since 1974, brings in folk, bluegrass, and gospel artists, as well as folk music lovers from around the world.
FALL	
Early Sept.	The 10-day Århus Festival, Denmark's most comprehensive fête, fills the city with exhibits, concerts, sporting events, and theater.
September	The Golden Days Festival in Copenhagen celebrates Denmark's 19th-century cultural blossoming through exhibits, readings, and performances.
Late Oct.	On Culture Night in Copenhagen, which falls on the third Friday of October, the city's museums and cultural centers stay open, some by candlelight, into the wee hours of the morning. Over 100,000 Copenhageners and tourists take advantage of this opportunity to mill about the streets and check out the readings, exhibitions, and performances that take place at more than 700 venues.
November	The Musikhøst (Music Harvest) in Odense holds performances of new and avant-garde concert music throughout the city. The festival keeps to a different sub-genre each year.

PLEASURES & PASTIMES

Beaches In this country of islands, coastline, and water, beaches come in many breeds. In Sjælland, a series of chic strands stretches north and south of Copenhagen along Strandvejen—the old beach road—pinned down by a string of lovely old seaside towns; this is where the city's youth goes to strut and preen. Fyn's gentle, golden beaches are less a showplace than a quiet getaway for a largely northern European crowd. Windswept Jylland has the country's most expansive and dramatic shorelines—at its northern tip you can even see the line in the waves where the Kattegat meets the Skagerrak Sea. Even more remote, Bornholm's silky, white-sand beaches unfold against a backdrop of wild dunes along the southern edge of the island, while the rocky margins of the Faroe Archipelago are more suitable to distant admiration than leisurely recreation.

Biking Without a doubt, Denmark is one of the best destinations in the world for biking. More than half the population pedals along city streets that effectively coordinate public transportation and cycle traffic, and along the country paths laced through Jylland and the island of Bornholm. Be sure to contact local or central tourist offices to inquire about biking opportunities. Roughly half of all city streets have been adjusted to accommodate bike traffic and many country routes have bicycle paths running parallel to them. Visitors can plan shorter day trips, or longer itineraries with lodging along the way. Bicyclists must observe all traffic laws, meaning they must signal, stop at stop lights and signs, and use proper lighting from 20 minutes after sunset until 20 minutes before sunrise. The police fine bicyclists Dkr 500 for each traffic infraction.

Boating & Sailing Well-marked channels and nearby anchorages make sailing and boating easy and popular along the 7,300-km (4,500-mi) coastline. Waters range from the open seas of the Kattegat and the Baltic to Smålandshavet (between Sjælland, Lolland, and Falster) and the calm Limsfjord in Jylland. The country's calm streams are navigable for canoes and kayaks. In Copenhagen, the historic harbors of Christianshavn and Nyhavn and scores of marinas bristling with crisp, white sails are lined with old wooden houseboats, motorboats, yachts, and their colorful crews. And it's not only the well-heeled taking up this pastime: tousle-haired parents and babes, partying youths, and leathery pensioners tend to their boats and picnics, lending a festive, community spirit to the marinas.

Danish Design Danish design has earned an international reputation for form and function; you will probably recognize the Arne Jacobsen furniture and Bang & Olufsen audio equipment you encounter in Copenhagen's shop windows and designer hotels. The best sales take place after Christmas and last until February, and there you can snatch up glassware, stainless steel, pottery, ceramics, and fur at reasonable prices. Summer clearance sales usually begin at the end of July, but the best bargains pop up in mid-August. Danish antiques and silver are also much cheaper here than in the United States. For major purchases—Bang & Olufsen products, for example—check prices stateside first so you can spot a good buy.

Seafood, Smørrebrød & Spirits

From the hearty meals of Denmark's fishing heritage to the inspired creations of a new generation of chefs, Danish cuisine combines the best of tradition and novelty. Though the country has long looked to the French as a beacon of gastronomy, chefs have proudly returned to the Danish table, emphasizing fresh, local ingredients and combining them with fusion trends. Many of Denmark's young, up-and-coming chefs are fully homegrown, completing all their training locally at the country's expanding list of superb, internationally recognized restaurants. Sample fresh fish and seafood from the Baltic; beef and pork from Jylland; and more-exotic delicacies, such as reindeer, caribou, seal meat, and whale from Greenland. Denmark's famed dairy products—sweet butter and milk among them—as well as a burgeoning organic foods industry, contribute to the freshness of the modern Danish kitchen.

Lunchtime is reserved for *smørrebrød*. You'll find the best, most traditional sampling of these open-face sandwiches in modest family-run restaurants that focus on generous—though never excessive—portions and artful presentation. If you find yourself fixing your gaze on tender mounds of roast beef topped with pickles or baby shrimp piled high on a slice of French bread, you are experiencing a slice of authentic Danish culture. Another specialty is *wienerbrød*, a confection far superior to anything billed as "Danish pastry" elsewhere. The European flatfish plaice, which appears on many restaurant menus, is caught off the Scandinavian coast, and its mild meat goes well with many types of sauces (hence its popularity). All Scandinavian countries have versions of the cold table, but Danes claim that theirs, *det store kolde bord*, is the original and the best.

As for beer, the ubiquitous Carlsberg and Tuborg are facing international competition. But you can't do better than to stick with the Danish brands, which happily complement the traditional fare better than high-priced wine. For Christmas and Easter, Carlsberg and Tuborg release their perennially popular—and potent—Jul (Christmas) and Påske (Easter) brews. If you go for the harder stuff, try the famous *snaps*, the aquavit traditionally savored with cold food. For an evening tipple, have a taste of the uniquely Danish Gammel Dansk, a bitter that is consumed in small quantities.

FODOR'S CHOICE

LODGING

$$$$ D'Angleterre, Copenhagen. This grande dame has hosted everyone from royalty to rock stars. Victor Borge was a regular and stayed in a suite bearing his name. The prim and proper staff is renowned for its attentiveness.

$$$$ Hesselet, Nyborg, Fyn. Within the brick walls of this refined Anglo-Asian sanctuary, many rooms have a splendid view onto the nearby Storebæltsbro.

$$$$ Radisson SAS Royal, Copenhagen. Towering over the heart of Copenhagen, this luxury hotel was designed "right down to the door handles" by the legendary Arne Jacobsen in 1960; the light-filled rooms and high-ceiling lobby are living museums to Jacobsen's chairs, lamps, and other furnishings.

$$$–$$$$ Schackenborg Slotskro, Møgeltønder, Jylland. An intimate hotel with richly colored rooms, this is the official royal inn of nearby Schackenborg Castle, home to Prince Joachim and Princess Alexandra.

$$–$$$ Hotel Dagmar, Ribe, Jylland. Denmark's oldest hotel has 16th-century charm to spare; half-timber walls, sloping wooden floors, and stained-glass windows in the lobby lead to the antique canopy beds and chaise longues in the bedrooms.

BUDGET LODGING

$$ Skovshoved, Copenhagen. Some of the larger rooms overlook the sea at this art-filled inn in Charlottenlund, only a short drive north of the Danish capital.

$–$$ Den Gamle Arrest, Ribe, Jylland. This "Old Jail" served as Ribe's main prison from 1893 to 1989. The tiny cell windows and wrought iron gates have been preserved, but the rooms themselves have been creatively and comfortably refashioned.

$ Hotel Vallø Slotskro, Vallø, Sjælland. South of Køge, this rural inn has charming rooms and personable service only a short walk over a moat and through a manicured park from fairytale Vallø Slot.

¢   Hotel Ydes, Odense, Fyn. This hotel maintains comfortable rooms for travelers in town to see the Hans Christian Andersen sights.

¢   Skansin Guesthouse, Tórshavn, Faroe Islands. Faoerese hospitality reigns at this private home, which occupies a central location on the archipelago.

RESTAURANTS

$$$$ Falsled Kro, Millinge, Fyn. This former smuggler's hideaway is now an utterly romantic and elegant inn with a fabulous French-Danish restaurant. This is one of the most sought-after spots in the country and reservations are imperative.

$$$$ Kommandanten, Copenhagen. The ever-changing menu here is inventive and fresh with unusual combinations such as oxtail and lobster stew as well as pigeon on a bed of vegetables and fava beans.

$$$–$$$$ Marie Louise, Odense, Fyn. Renowned for its French cuisine, Marie Louise serves superb concoctions that include salmon scallop with bordelaise sauce and grilled veal with lobster-cream sauce.

$$–$$$$ Seafood, Århus, Jylland. This harborside seafood restaurant is famous for its bouillabaisse heaped with tiger prawns, squid, Norwegian lobster, and mussels. Aioli comes on the side.

$$$ Reinwalds, Copenhagen. Open, airy, and cozy, this spot serves fine neo-European food to equal some of the best spots in town, but at lower prices. Wines are superb, yet reasonable, and the service is envied by other eateries.

$$–$$$ Skipperhuset, Fredensborg, Sjælland. At this 18th-century former boathouse on the grounds of the queen's summer residence, meals eaten alfresco on the shore of Lake Esrum at sunset are a special delight. The wild Baltic salmon is a favorite for lunch and dinner.

$$ Ida Davidsen, Copenhagen. Over 100 years old, this Copenhagen institution serves an elaborate menu of smørrebrød that knows no rival. Ida herself, the fifth generation to run this family-owned restaurant, assembles the towering open-face sandwiches with such toppings as caviar, herring, smoked salmon, liver pâté, steak tartare, and egg yolks.

BUDGET RESTAURANTS

$$ Told & Snaps, Copenhagen. The long menu of Danish smørrebrød delights prices out more reasonably than at the iconic Ida Davidsen.

$–$$ Riz Raz, Copenhagen. This crowded Middle Eastern joint near Strøget maintains an inexpensive all-you-can-eat buffet full of spicy fare.

¢–$$ Bregninge Mølle, Tåsinge, Fyn. Although the traditional Danish dishes here are enjoyable, the real attraction is the 360-degree view of the surrounding sea, islands, and countryside from this converted windmill.

¢–$$ Bryggeriet Sct. Clemens, Århus, Jylland. This local haunt is primarily a watering hole, but food is served and this is a great place to meet some Århus residents and students.

CASTLES & CHURCHES

Christiansborg Slot, Copenhagen. The seat of Parliament, and once a year the queen of Denmark still receives guests in this 12th-century castle. Parts of the building are open to the public.

Domkirke, Roskilde, Sjælland. Once the capital of Denmark, Roskilde still has its magnificent 15th-century cathedral, where Danish royalty has been buried for the past half millennium.

Egeskov Slot, Kværndrup, Fyn. One of the best preserved island-castles in Europe, Egeskov Slot is topped with copper spires and ringed by lush Renaissance and baroque gardens. One of the world's largest mazes is also here.

Kronborg Slot, Helsingør, Sjælland. William Shakespeare never saw this castle, but that didn't stop him from using it as the setting for Hamlet. Don't miss the Flemish tapestries displayed in the "small room."

Østerlars Kirke, Bornholm. The largest of Bornholm's unique round churches—considered some of the finest specimens of Scandinavian medieval architecture—this whitewashed marvel was built of boulders and slabs of limestone.

Rosenborg Slot, Copenhagen. The only castle still owned by Denmark's royal family, Rosenborg Slot is home to the crown jewels and many other treasures. The castle is surrounded by the royal gardens, and delightful walks are offered in summer.

Tilsandede Kirke, Skagen, Jylland. Perched at Denmark's northernmost, wave-thrashed tip, the 18th-century Sand-Buried Church is covered by dunes.

Valdemars Slot, Troense, Fyn. One of Denmark's largest castles not owned by the state, the regal Valdemars Slot has sumptuous, richly decorated rooms and libraries as well as a yachting museum.

MUSEUMS

Brandts Klædefabrik, Odense, Fyn. Inside an impressively refurbished textile factory is a complex of museums covering three main areas: photography, graphic art, and fine art.

Lejre Forsøgscenter, near Roskilde, Sjælland. This living open-air museum has many hands-on activities that convey the character of daily life for the Vikings.

Louisiana, Humlebæk, Sjælland. A half-hour drive north of Copenhagen, this world-class modern-art collection displays the likes of Warhol and Picasso and even has a thoughtfully laid out children's wing.

Ny Carlsberg Glyptotek, Copenhagen. The best collection of Etruscan art outside Italy and Europe's finest gathering of Roman portraits are both here. There's also an impressive collection of rare pre-impressionist works by such masters as Gauguin and Rodin.

Ordrupgaard, Charlottenlund, Sjælland. Housed in a 1918 manor house just north of Copenhagen, this antiques-filled museum showcases one of the largest collections of French impressionism in Europe outside of France, including works by Manet, Monet, Matisse, Renoir, Degas, Gauguin, and Pissarro; also impressive is their extensive collection of Danish Golden Age painters.

Trapholt Museum for Moderne Kunst, Kolding, Jylland. Sprawling along the banks of the Kolding Fjord, the light-filled Trapholt is one of the largest modern-art museums outside Copenhagen.

There's a superb collection of 20th-century Danish art and a massive annex that houses a comprehensive assemblage of Danish-designed chairs.

QUINTESSENTIAL DENMARK

Legoland, Billund, Jylland. This paean to the modular Danish building blocks offers lots of fun for the kids, but the exhibits and general construction of the park provides plenty of interesting aspects for people of all ages.

Setting Foot on Greenland's Ice Cap, Greenland. Whether you get there by foot or skis, dogsled or helicopter, you must stand for a few moments on the massive ice sheet that covers all but the thin rocky crescents of the subcontinent's coast. The scale and grandeur of the frozen landscape is this remote destination's biggest attraction.

Tivoli Gardens, Copenhagen. The magnificent flower beds and wonderful fairy-tale architecture make this park the international icon and tourist attraction it is. There's no need to try the roller coaster; just walking around the meticulously kept grounds is a treat.

SMART TRAVEL TIPS

Addresses
Air Travel
Airports
Bike Travel
Boat & Ferry Travel
Business Hours
Bus Travel
Cameras & Photography
Car Rental
Car Travel
Children in Denmark
Consumer Protection
Customs & Duties
Disabilities & Accessibility
Discounts & Deals
Eating & Drinking
Electricity
Embassies
Emergencies
Gay & Lesbian Travel
Holidays
Insurance
Language
Lodging
Mail & Shipping
Money Matters
Packing
Passports & Visas
Safety
Senior-Citizen Travel
Shopping
Sports & Outdoors
Students in Denmark
Taxes
Telephones
Time
Tipping
Tours & Packages
Train Travel
Travel Agencies
Visitor Information
Web Sites

AIR TRAVEL

BOOKING

When you book, look for nonstop flights and remember that "direct" flights stop at least once. Try to avoid connecting flights, which require a change of plane. Two airlines may operate a connecting flight jointly, so ask whether your airline operates every segment of the trip; you may find that the carrier you prefer flies you only part of the way. To find more booking tips and to check prices and make online flight reservations, log on to www.fodors.com.

CARRIERS

Nearly all international air service to Denmark flies into Copenhagen Airport. SAS, the main carrier, makes nonstop flights to the capital from Chicago, Newark, and Seattle. British Airways offers connecting flights via London from Atlanta, Baltimore, Boston, Charlotte, Chicago, Dallas, Denver, Detroit, Houston, Los Angeles, Miami, New York, Orlando, Philadelphia, Phoenix, Pittsburgh, San Diego, San Francisco, Seattle, Tampa, and Washington, D.C. Icelandair makes connecting flights to Copenhagen via Reykjavík from Baltimore, Fort Lauderdale, New York, and Orlando. Finnair has service through Helsinki from Miami, New York, and— from May to September—San Francisco.

British Airways flies nonstop to Copenhagen from London (Heathrow and Gatwick), Birmingham, and Manchester. SAS Scandinavian Airlines flies nonstop from London, Manchester, and Glasgow, and also from London to Århus. Aer Lingus flies from Dublin, connecting in London; the flights are operated by British Airways. Mærsk Air flies nonstop from Gatwick to Billund and Copenhagen. Easyjet has cheap flights between London's Stansted airport and Copenhagen. Virgin Airlines is also inexpensive and flies between London's Gatwick and Stansted airports via Brussels to Copenhagen. Air France also flies out of Copenhagen.

In Jylland, Billund Airport is Denmark's second-largest airport. Mærsk Air flies to Billund from Amsterdam, Bergen, Brussels, the Faroe Islands, Frankfurt, London, Manchester, Nice, Oslo, Stockholm, and Paris. Sunair serves Århus, Billund, Göteborg, Oslo, and Stockholm. Several domestic airports, including Aalborg, Århus, and Esbjerg, are served by Mærsk and SAS, both of which have good connections to Copenhagen. Cimber Air links Sønderborg, just north of the German border, with Copenhagen.

Cimber Air makes several daily flights to Bornholm from Copenhagen, and flies also from Berlin. Lufthansa flies to Bornholm from Berlin and Hamburg.

For service to the Faroe Islands, *see* The Faroe Islands A to Z *in* Chapter 6.

For carriers and routes to Greenland, *see* Greenland A to Z *in* Chapter 7.

Aer Lingus ☎ 800/474-7424 in North America, 0161/832-5771 in Ireland ⊕ www.aerlingus.com. **Air France** ☎ 800/237-2747 in North America, 82/33-27-01 in Denmark ⊕ www.airfrance.com/dk. **Air Greenland** ☎ 299/34-34-34 in Greenland, 32/31-40-88 in Denmark ⊕ www.airgreenland.gl. **British Airways** ☎ 0207/491-4989 in the U.K., 800/247-9297 in North America, 80/20-80-22 in Denmark ⊕ www.britishairways.com. **Cimber Air** ☎ 74/42-22-77, 56/95-11-11 in Bornholm ⊕ www.cimber.dk. **Finnair** ☎ 800/950-5000 in North America, 32/50-45-10 in Denmark ⊕ www.finnair.fi. **Easyjet** ☎ 0870/6000-000 in the U.K., 70/12-43-21 in Denmark ⊕ www.easyjet.com. **Icelandair** ☎ 354/505-0300 in Iceland, 0207/874-1000 in the U.K., 800/223-5500 in North America, 33/70-22-00 in Denmark ⊕ www.icelandair.com. **Lufthansa** ☎ 33/37-73-33 ⊕ www.lufthansa.com. **Mærsk Air** ☎ 0207/333-0066 in the U.K., 32/31-44-44 or 70/10-74-74 in Denmark ⊕ www.maersk-air.dk. **SAS Scandinavian Airlines** ☎ 0207/706-8832 in the U.K., 800/221-2350 in North America, 32/32-00-00 in Denmark ⊕ www.scandinavian.net. **Sunair** ☎ 75/33-16-11. **Virgin Airlines** ☎ 01293/450-150 in the U.K., 800/862-8621 in North America ⊕ www.virgin-atlantic.com.

CHECK-IN & BOARDING

Always **find out your carrier's check-in policy.** Plan to arrive at the airport about two hours before your scheduled departure time for domestic flights and 2½ to 3 hours before international flights. You may need to arrive earlier if you're flying from one of the busier airports or during peak air-traffic times. To avoid delays at airport-security checkpoints, try not to wear any metal. Jewelry, belt and other buckles, steel-toe shoes, barrettes, and underwire bras are among the items that can set off detectors.

Assuming that not everyone with a ticket will show up, airlines routinely overbook planes. When everyone does, airlines ask for volunteers to give up their seats. In return, these volunteers usually get a several-hundred-dollar flight voucher, which can be used toward the purchase of another ticket, and are rebooked on the next flight out. If there are not enough volunteers, the airline must choose who will be denied boarding. The first to get bumped are passengers who checked in late and those flying on discounted tickets, so get to the gate and check in as early as possible, especially during peak periods.

Always **bring a government-issued photo I.D.** to the airport; even when it's not required, a passport is best.

CUTTING COSTS

Intra-Scandinavian air travel is usually expensive. If you want to economize, look into the **SAS Visit Scandinavia/Europe Air Pass** offered by SAS. One coupon costs about $85; six about $510, but they vary greatly depending on routing and destination—generally, the cost rises the farther north the destination. The coupons are valid for destinations within Denmark, Norway, and Sweden, and also between Sweden and Finland. They are sold only in the United States and only to non-Scandinavians. Coupons can be used year-round for a maximum of three months and must be purchased in conjunction with transatlantic flights. SAS also provides family fares—children between 2 and 17 and a spouse can receive 50% off the full fare of business-class tickets with the purchase of one full-fare business-class ticket. Contact SAS for information.

The least expensive airfares to Scandinavia must usually be purchased in advance and are non-refundable. It's smart to call a number of airlines and check the Internet; when you are quoted a good price, book it on the spot—the same fare may not be available the next day, or even the next hour. Always check different routings and look into using alternate airports. Also, price off-peak flights, which may be significantly less expensive than others. Travel agents, especially low-fare specialists (⇨ Discounts and Deals), are helpful. Consolidators are another good source. They buy tickets for scheduled flights at reduced rates from the airlines, then sell them at prices that beat the best fare available directly from the airlines. Sometimes you can even get your money back if you need to return the ticket. Carefully read the fine print detailing penalties for changes and cancellations, purchase the ticket with a credit card, and confirm your consolidator reservation with the airline.

⌐ Consolidators **AirlineConsolidator.com** ☎ 888/468-5385 ⊕ www.airlineconsolidator.com; for international tickets. **Best Fares** ☎ 800/576-8255 or 800/576-1600 ⊕ www.bestfares.com; $59.90 annual membership. **Cheap Tickets** ☎ 800/377-1000 or 888/922-8849 ⊕ www.cheaptickets.com. **Expedia** ☎ 800/397-3342 or 404/728-8787 ⊕ www.expedia.com. **Hotwire** ☎ 866/468-9473 or 920/330-9418 ⊕ www.hotwire.com. **Now Voyager Travel** ✉ 45 W. 21st St., 5th fl., New York, NY 10010 ☎ 212/459-1616 📠 212/243-2711 ⊕ www.nowvoyagertravel.com. **Onetravel.com** ⊕ www.onetravel.com. **Orbitz** ☎ 888/656-4546 ⊕ www.orbitz.com. **Priceline.com** ⊕ www.priceline.com. **Travelocity** ☎ 888/709-5983, 877/282-2925 in Canada, 0870/111-7060 in the U.K. ⊕ www.travelocity.com.

ENJOYING THE FLIGHT

State your seat preference when purchasing your ticket, and then repeat it when you confirm and when you check in. For more legroom, you can request one of the few emergency-aisle seats at check-in, if you are capable of lifting at least 50 pounds—a Federal Aviation Administration requirement of passengers in these seats. Seats behind a bulkhead also offer more legroom, but they don't have under-seat storage. Don't sit in the row in front of the emergency aisle or in front of a bulkhead, where seats may not recline.

Ask the airline whether a snack or meal is served on the flight. If you have dietary concerns, request special meals when booking. These can be vegetarian, low-cholesterol, or kosher, for example. It's a good idea to pack some healthful snacks and a small (plastic) bottle of water in your carry-on bag. On long flights, try to maintain a normal routine, to help fight jet lag. At night, get some sleep. By day, eat light meals, drink water (not alcohol), and **move around the cabin** to stretch your legs. For additional jet-lag tips consult *Fodor's FYI: Travel Fit & Healthy* (available at bookstores everywhere).

Smoking policies vary from carrier to carrier. Many airlines prohibit smoking on all of their flights; others allow smoking only on certain routes or certain departures. Ask your carrier about its policy.

FLYING TIMES

The flight from London to Copenhagen takes 1 hour, 55 minutes. From New York, flights to Copenhagen take 7 hours, 40 minutes. From Chicago, they take 9 hours, 30 minutes. From Seattle and Los Angeles the flight time is about 10 hours, 55 minutes. Flight times within the country are all less than one hour, except for longer routes from Copenhagen to Greenland (5 hours) and the Faroe Islands (2 hours, 15 minutes).

HOW TO COMPLAIN

If your baggage goes astray or your flight goes awry, complain right away. Most carriers require that you **file a claim immediately.** The Aviation Consumer Protection Division of the Department of Transportation publishes *Fly-Rights,* which discusses airlines and consumer issues and is available on-line. You can also find articles and information on mytravelrights.com, the Web site of the nonprofit Consumer Travel Rights Center.

⌐ Airline Complaints **Aviation Consumer Protection Division** ✉ U.S. Department of Transportation, C-75, Room 4107, 400 7th St. SW, Washington, DC 20590 ☎ 202/366-2220 ⊕ www.airconsumer.ost.dot.gov. **Federal Aviation Administration Consumer Hotline** ✉ for inquiries: FAA, 800 Independence Ave. SW Washington, DC 20591 ☎ 800/322-7873 ⊕ www.faa.gov.

AIRPORTS

Kastrup International Airport (CPH) is the hub of Scandinavian and international air travel in Denmark, 10 km (6 mi) from the center of Copenhagen. Jylland has regional hubs in Aalborg (AAL), Århus (AAR), and Billund (BLL), which handle mainly domestic and some European traffic. Rønne (RNN) is the main airport in Bornholm.

⌐ Kastrup International Airport ☎ 32/31-32-31 ⊕ www.cph.dk.

BIKE TRAVEL

Biking is a way of life in Denmark, with more people biking to work than driving. Biking vacations in Denmark are popular and they are easy for all ages due to the flat landscape. Most towns have rentals, but check with local tourism offices for referrals. For more information, contact the Danish Cyclist Federation. The Danish Tourist Board publishes helpful bicycle maps and brochures.

DSB allows cyclists to check their bikes as luggage on most of their train routes, but only if there is room. S-trains that serve the suburbs of Copenhagen don't permit bikes during rush hour (7 AM–8:30 AM and 3:30 PM–5 PM). Bicycles can also be carried onto most trains and ferries; contact the DSB Travel Office for information; a bicycle ticket usually costs from Dkr 10 to Dkr 60, depending on the distance traveled. Taxis are required to take bikes and are equipped with racks, though they add a modest fee of Dkr 10.

From May to October, you'll also see by-cykler (city bikes) parked at special bike stands placed around the center of Copenhagen and Århus. Deposit Dkr 20 and pedal away. The bikes are often dinged and dented, but they do function. Your deposit will be returned when you return the bike.

🚩 **Danmarks Turistråd** (Danish Tourist Board) ✉ Vesterbrog. 6D, Vesterbro, DK-1620 Copenhagen ☎ 33/11-14-15 🖷 33/93-14-16 ⊕ www. visitdenmark.com. **Dansk Cyklist Forbund** (Danish Cyclist Federation) ✉ Rømersg. 7, Downtown, DK-1362 Copenhagen ☎ 33/32-31-21 🖷 33/ 32-76-83 ⊕ www.dcf.dk. **DSB** ☎ 70/13-14-15 ⊕ www.dsb.dk.

BIKES IN FLIGHT

Most airlines accommodate bikes as luggage, provided they are dismantled and boxed; check with individual airlines about packing requirements. Some airlines sell bike boxes, which are often free at bike shops, for about $15 (bike bags can be considerably more expensive). International travelers often can substitute a bike for a piece of checked luggage at no charge; otherwise, the cost is about $100. U.S. and Canadian airlines charge $40–$80 each way.

BOAT & FERRY TRAVEL

Once upon a time, ferries were an indispensable mode of transport in and around the many islands of Denmark. This is changing as more people drive or take trains over new bridges spanning the waters. However, ferries are still a good way to explore Scandinavia, especially if you have a rail pass.

Scandinavian Seaways Ferries (DFDS) sail from Harwich in the United Kingdom to Esbjerg (20 hours) on Jylland's west coast. Schedules in both summer and winter are highly irregular. DFDS also connects Denmark with the Baltic States, Belgium, Germany, the Netherlands, Norway, Poland, Sweden, and the Faroe Islands. There are many discounts, including 20% for senior citizens and travelers with disabilities, and 50% for children between the ages of 4 and 16.

Molslinien links up Jylland and Sjælland, while Scandlines services the southern islands as well as Germany, Sweden, and the Baltic countries. The island of Bornholm, Denmark's furthest outpost to the East and a popular domestic tourist destination, is reachable with Bornholms Trafikken.

The ScanRail Pass, for travel anywhere within Scandinavia (Denmark, Sweden, Norway, and Finland), and the Interail and EurailPasses are valid on some ferry crossings. Call the DSB Travel Office for information.

CAR FERRIES

Vehicle-bearing hydrofoils operate between Fyn's Ebeltoft or Århus to Odden on Sjælland; the trip takes about one hour. You can also take the slower (2 hours, 40 minutes), but less expensive, car ferry from Århus to Kalundborg on Sjælland. From there, Route 23 leads to Copenhagen. Make reservations for the ferry in advance through Mols-Linien. Scandlines services the southern islands. (*Note:* During the busy summer months, passengers without reservations for their vehicles can wait hours.)

Some well-known international vehicle and passenger ferries run between Helsingør, Denmark, and Helsingborg, Sweden, and between Copenhagen and Göteborg, Sweden. The Helsingør/ Helsingborg ferry (Scandlines) takes only 20 minutes; taking a car costs between SKr 255 and SKr 275 (about $24–$26 or £16–£18.50) one-way. Round-trip fares are cheaper, and on weekends the Øresund Runt pass (for crossing between Copenhagen and Malmö one way and Helsingborg and Helsingør the other way) costs only SKr 475 (about $45 or £31).

FARES & SCHEDULES

Bornholms Trafikken ⊠ Havnen, DK-3700 Rønne ☎ 56/95-18-66 🖶 56/91-07-66 ⊕ www. bornholmstrafikken.dk. **DSB** ☎ 70/13-14-15 ⊕ www.dsb.dk. **Mols-Linien** ☎ 70/10-14-18 🖶 89/52-52-90 ⊕ www.molslinien.dk. **Scandinavian Seaways Ferries** (DFDS) ⊠ Skt. Annæ Pl. 30, DK-1295 Copenhagen ☎ 33/42-33-42 🖶 33/42-33-41 ⊕ www.dfds.com. **Scandlines** ☎ 33/15-15-15 🖶 35/29-02-01 ⊕ www.scandlines.dk.

BUSINESS HOURS

BANKS & OFFICES

Banks in Copenhagen are open weekdays 9:30 to 4 and Thursdays until 6. Several *bureaux de change,* including the ones at Copenhagen's central station and airport, stay open until 10 PM. Outside Copenhagen, banking hours vary.

MUSEUMS & SIGHTS

A number of Copenhagen's museums hold confounding hours, so always call first to confirm. As a rule, however, most museums are open 10 to 3 or 11 to 4 and are closed on Monday. In winter, opening hours are shorter, and some museums close for the season, especially on the smaller islands, including Bornholm, Ærø, and Fanø. Check the local papers or ask at tourist offices for current schedules.

SHOPS

Though many Danish stores are expanding their hours, sometimes even staying open on Sunday, most shops still keep the traditional hours: weekdays 10 to 5:30, until 7 or 8 on Friday, and until 1 or 2 on Saturday—though the larger department stores stay open until 5. Everything except bakeries, kiosks, flower shops, and a handful of grocers are closed on Sunday. The first Saturday of every month is a Long Saturday, when even the smaller shops, especially in large cities, stay open until 4 or 5. Grocery stores stay open until 8 on weekdays, and kiosks until much later.

BUS TRAVEL

Although not particularly comfortable or fast, bus travel is inexpensive. Eurolines departs from London's Victoria Station on Saturday at 2:30 PM, crossing the North Sea on the Dover-Calais ferry, and arrives in Copenhagen about 22 hours later. With its many other routes, Eurolines links the principal Danish cities to a network of service that includes major European cities. Safflebussen is the other main bus company with international routes to Denmark. The company offers regular trips between Copenhagen and Berlin, Göteborg, Karlstad, Stockholm, and Oslo.

To encourage travelers to make full use of Denmark's domestic transportation services, private bus operat ors and Danish State Railways (DSB) have collaborated to create Bus/Tog Samarbejde. This useful resource consolidates schedule and route information for the country's trains and buses.

Domestic bus companies include Thinggaard, which has regular routes between Sjælland and Jutland, and Abildskou, which offers service from Århus to Copenhagen and Ebeltoft, as well as between Roskilde and the Copenhagen airport. Bus tickets are usually sold on board the buses immediately before departure. Ask about discounts for children, senior citizens and groups.

CUTTING COSTS

Eurolines offers 15-, 30-, and 60-day passes for unlimited travel between Stockholm, Copenhagen, and Oslo, and over 20 destinations throughout Europe.

Bus Information Abildskou ⊠ Graham Bellsvej 40, DK-8200 Århus ☎ 70/21-08-88 ⊕ www.abildskou.dk. **Bus/Tog Samarbejde** ⊕ www.rejseplan.dk. **Eurolines** ⊠ 52 Grosvenor Gardens, SW1 London ☎ 0207/730-8235 ⊠ Reventlowsg. 8, DK-1651 Copenhagen ☎ 70/10-00-30 ⊕ www.eurolines.com. **Säfflebussen** ⊠ Halmtorvet 5, DK-1700 Copenhagen ☎ 33/23-54-20 ⊕ www.safflebussen.se. **Thinggaard Ekspres** ⊠ Jyllandsg. 6, DK-9000 Aalborg ☎ 70/10-00-20 ⊕ www.thinggaard-bus.dk.

CAR RENTAL

Rental rates in Copenhagen begin at Dkr 500 a day and Dkr 2,500 a week. This does not include an additional per-km fee and any insurance you choose to purchase; there is also a 25% tax on car rentals.

Major Agencies Alamo ☎ 800/522-9696 ⊕ www.alamo.com. **Avis** ☎ 800/331-1084, 800/879-2847 in Canada, 0870/606-0100 in the U.K., 02/9353-9000 in Australia, 09/526-2847 in New Zealand ⊕ www.avis.com. **Budget** ☎ 800/527-0700, 0870/156-5656 in the U.K. ⊕ www.budget.com. **Dollar** ☎ 800/800-6000, 0124/622-0111 in the U.K., where it's affiliated with Sixt, 02/9223-1444 in Australia ⊕ www.dollar.com. **Hertz** ☎ 800/654-

3001, 800/263-0600 in Canada, 0870/844-8844 in the U.K., 02/9669-2444 in Australia, 09/256-8690 in New Zealand ⊕ www.hertz.com. **National Car Rental** ☎ 800/227-7368, 0870/600-6666 in the U.K. ⊕ www.nationalcar.com.

CUTTING COSTS

For a good deal, book through a travel agent who will shop around. Do look into wholesalers, companies that do not own fleets but rent in bulk from those that do and often offer better rates than traditional car-rental operations. Prices are best during off-peak periods. Rentals booked through wholesalers often must be paid for before you leave home.

⚑ **Wholesalers Auto Europe** ☎ 207/842-2000 or 800/223-5555 📠 207/842-2222 ⊕ www. autoeurope.com. **Europe by Car** ☎ 212/581-3040 or 800/223-1516 📠 212/246-1458 ⊕ www.europebycar. com. **Destination Europe Resources** (DER) ✉ 9501 W. Devon Ave., Rosemont, IL 60018 ☎ 800/782-2424 ⊕ www.der.com. **Kemwel** ☎ 800/678-0678 📠 207/842-2124 ⊕ www.kemwel.com.

INSURANCE

When driving a rented car you are generally responsible for any damage to or loss of the vehicle. Collision policies that car-rental companies sell for European rentals typically do not cover stolen vehicles. Before you rent—and purchase collision or theft coverage—see what coverage you already have under the terms of your personal auto-insurance policy and credit cards.

REQUIREMENTS & RESTRICTIONS

Ask about age requirements. Several countries require drivers to be over 20 years old, but some car-rental companies require that drivers be at least 25.

CAR TRAVEL

The only part of Denmark that is connected to the European continent is Jylland, via the E45 highway from Germany. The E20 highway then leads to Middelfart on Fyn and east to Nyborg. The Storebæltsbro bridge connects Fyn and Sjælland via the E20 highway; the E20 then continues east, over the Lillebæltsbro bridge, to Copenhagen. The bridges have greatly reduced the driving time between the islands. You can reach many of the smaller islands via toll bridges. In some locations, car ferries are still in service; for ferry information, *see* Boat & Ferry Travel.

In Scandinavia your own driver's license is acceptable for a limited time; check with the Danish Tourist Board before you go. International driving permits (IDPs) are available from the American and Canadian automobile associations and, in the United Kingdom, from the Automobile Association and Royal Automobile Club. These international permits, valid only in conjunction with your regular driver's license, are universally recognized; having one may save you a problem with local authorities.

EMERGENCY SERVICES

Members of organizations affiliated with Alliance International de Tourisme (AIT) can get technical and legal advice from the Danish Motoring Organization, open 10–4 weekdays. All highways have emergency phones, and you can call the rental company for help. If you cannot drive your car to a garage for repairs, the rescue corps Falck can help anywhere, anytime. In most cases they do charge for assistance. In the event of an emergency, call 112.

⚑ **Falck** ✉ Polititorvet, DK-1780 Copenhagen ☎ 70/10-20-30 for emergencies, 33/15-83-20 for headquarters 📠 33/91-00-26 ⊕ www.falck.dk.

Forenede Danske Motorejere (Danish Motoring Organization) ✉ Firskovvej 32, DK-2800 Lyngby ☎ 70/13-30-40 📠 45/27-09-93 ⊕ www.fdm.dk.

GASOLINE

Gasoline costs about Dkr 8 per liter (¼ gallon). Stations are mostly self-service and open from 6 or 7 AM to 9 PM or later.

PARKING

You can usually park on the right-hand side of the road, though not on main roads and highways. Signs reading PARKERING/STANDSNING FORBUNDT mean no parking or stopping, though you are allowed a three-minute grace period for loading and unloading. In town, parking disks are used where there are no automated ticket-vending machines. Get disks from gas stations, post offices, police stations, or tourist offices, and set them to show your time of arrival. For most downtown parking, you must buy a ticket from an automatic vending machine and display it on the dash. Parking costs about Dkr 10 or more per hour.

ROAD CONDITIONS

Roads in Denmark are in good condition and largely traffic-free (except for the manageable traffic around Copenhagen).

RULES OF THE ROAD

To drive in Denmark you need a valid adult driver's license, and if you're using your own car, it must have a certificate of registration and national plates. A triangular hazard-warning sign is compulsory in every car and is provided with rentals. No matter where you sit in a car, you must wear a seat belt, and cars must have low beams on at all times. Motorcyclists must wear helmets and use low-beam lights as well. Talking on the phone while operating a car, bicycle, or any other kind of vehicle is illegal.

Bicyclists have equal rights on the road, and a duty to signal moves and observe all traffic regulations. Be especially careful when making turns. Check for bicyclists, who have the right of way if they are going straight and a car is turning.

Drive on the right and give way to traffic—*especially to bicyclists*—on the right. A red-and-white YIELD sign or a line of white triangles across the road means you must yield to traffic on the road you are entering. Do not turn right on red unless there is a green arrow indicating that this is allowed. Speed limits are 50 kph (30 mph) in built-up areas; 100 kph (60 mph) on highways; and 80 kph (50 mph) on other roads. If you are towing a trailer, you must not exceed 70 kph (40 mph). Speeding and, especially, drinking and driving are punished severely, even if no damage is caused. The consumption of one or two beers might lead to a violation, and motorists traveling across the Øresund Bridge must remember that Sweden has an even lower legal limit for blood-alcohol levels. As such, it is possible to drive legally out of Denmark and illegally into Sweden. Americans and other foreign tourists must pay all fines on the spot.

CHILDREN IN DENMARK

In Denmark children are to be seen *and* heard and are genuinely welcome in most public places.

If you are renting a car, don't forget to arrange for a car seat when you reserve. For general advice about traveling with children, consult *Fodor's FYI: Travel with Your Baby* (available in bookstores everywhere).

DISCOUNTS

Children are entitled to discount tickets (often as much as 50% off) on buses, trains, and ferries throughout Denmark, as well as reductions on special City Cards. With the ScanRail Pass (⇨ Train Travel)—good for rail journeys throughout Scandinavia—children under age 4 (on lap) travel free; those ages 4–11 pay half-fare and those ages 12–25 can get a ScanRail Youth Pass, providing a 25% discount off the adult fare.

Youngsters receive a discount at most museums and attractions, but the age limits vary. Check at the gate for information about youth or family discounts.

FLYING

Children under age 12 pay 75% of the adult fare and children under age 2 pay 10% on SAS round-trips. There are no restrictions on children's fares when booked in economy class. "Family fares," only available in business class, are also worth looking into (⇨ Cutting Costs *in* Air Travel).

LODGING

Most hotels in Denmark allow children under a certain age to stay in their parents' room at no extra charge, but others charge for them as extra adults; be sure to find out the cutoff age for children's discounts.

SIGHTS & ATTRACTIONS

Places that are especially appealing to children are indicated by a rubber-duckie icon (☺) in the margin.

CUSTOMS & DUTIES

When shopping abroad, keep receipts for all purchases. Upon reentering the country, **be ready to show customs officials what you've bought.** Pack purchases together in an easily accessible place. If you think a duty is incorrect, appeal the assessment. If you object to the way your clearance was handled, note the inspector's badge number. In either case, first ask to see a supervisor. If the problem isn't resolved, write to the appropriate authorities, beginning with the port director at your point of entry.

IN DENMARK

If you are 16 or older, have purchased goods in a country that is a member of the European Union (EU), and pay that country's value-added tax (V.A.T.) on those goods, you may import duty-free 1½ liters of liquor and 300 cigarettes or 150 cigarillos or 75 cigars or 400 grams of tobacco. If you are entering Denmark from a non-EU country or if you have purchased your goods on a ferryboat or in an airport not taxed in the EU, you must pay Danish taxes on any amount of alcoholic beverages greater than 1 liter of liquor or 2 liters of strong wine, plus 2 liters of table wine. For tobacco, the limit is 200 cigarettes or 100 cigarillos or 50 cigars or 250 grams of tobacco. You are also allowed 50 grams of perfume. Other articles (including beer) are allowed up to a maximum of Dkr 1,350.

Non-EU citizens can save 20% (less a handling fee) off the purchase price if they shop in one of the hundreds of stores throughout Denmark displaying the TAX-FREE SHOPPING sign. The purchased merchandise must value more than Dkr 300 and the taxes will be refunded after submitting the application with customs authorities at their final destination before leaving the EU.

Told og Skat (Toll and Taxes) ✉ Tagensvej 135, DK-2200 Copenhagen ☎ 35/87-73-00 🖷 35/85-90-94 🌐 www.toldskat.dk.

IN AUSTRALIA

Australian residents who are 18 or older may bring home A$400 worth of souvenirs and gifts (including jewelry), 250 cigarettes or 250 grams of cigars or other tobacco products, and 1,125 ml of alcohol (including wine, beer, and spirits). Residents under 18 may bring back A$200 worth of goods. Members of the same family traveling together may pool their allowances. Prohibited items include meat products. Seeds, plants, and fruits need to be declared upon arrival.

Australian Customs Service 🖷 Regional Director, Box 8, Sydney, NSW 2001 ☎ 02/9213-2000 or 1300/363263, 02/9364-7222 or 1800/803-006 quarantine-inquiry line 🖷 02/9213-4043 🌐 www.customs.gov.au.

IN CANADA

Canadian residents who have been out of Canada for at least seven days may bring in C$750 worth of goods duty-free. If you've been away fewer than seven days but more than 48 hours, the duty-free allowance drops to C$200. If your trip lasts 24 to 48 hours, the allowance is C$50. You may not pool allowances with family members. Goods claimed under the C$750 exemption may follow you by mail; those claimed under the lesser exemptions must accompany you. Alcohol and tobacco products may be included in the seven-day and 48-hour exemptions but not in the 24-hour exemption. If you meet the age requirements of the province or territory through which you reenter Canada, you may bring in, duty-free, 1.5 liters of wine or 1.14 liters (40 imperial ounces) of liquor or 24 12-ounce cans or bottles of beer or ale. Also, if you meet the local age requirement for tobacco products, you may bring in, duty-free, 200 cigarettes and 50 cigars. Check ahead of time with the Canada Customs and Revenue Agency or the Department of Agriculture for policies regarding meat products, seeds, plants, and fruits.

You may send an unlimited number of gifts (only one gift per recipient, however) worth up to C$60 each duty-free to Canada. Label the package UNSOLICITED GIFT—VALUE UNDER $60. Alcohol and tobacco are excluded.

Canada Customs and Revenue Agency ✉ 2265 St. Laurent Blvd., Ottawa, Ontario K1G 4K3 ☎ 800/461-9999, 204/983-3500, 506/636-5064 🌐 www.ccra.gc.ca.

IN NEW ZEALAND

All homeward-bound residents may bring back NZ$700 worth of souvenirs and gifts; passengers may not pool their allowances, and children can claim only the concession on goods intended for their own use. For those 17 or older, the duty-free allowance also includes 4.5 liters of wine or beer; one 1,125-ml bottle of spirits; and either 200 cigarettes, 250 grams of tobacco, 50 cigars, or a combination of the three up to 250 grams. Meat products, seeds, plants, and fruits must be declared upon arrival to the Agricultural Services Department.

New Zealand Customs ✉ Head office: The Customhouse, 17–21 Whitmore St., Box 2218, Wellington ☎ 09/300-5399 or 0800/428-786 🌐 www.customs.govt.nz.

IN THE U.K.

If you are a U.K. resident and your journey was wholly within the European Union, you probably won't have to pass through customs when you return to the United Kingdom. If you plan to bring back large quantities of alcohol or tobacco, check EU limits beforehand. In most cases, if you bring back more than 200 cigars, 3,200 cigarettes, 10 liters of spirits, 110 liters of beer, and/or 90 liters of wine, you have to declare the goods upon return.

F HM Customs and Excise ⊠ Portcullis House, 21 Cowbridge Rd. E, Cardiff CF11 9SS ☎ 0845/010–9000 or 0208/929–0152, 0208/929–6731 or 0208/910–3602 complaints ⊕ www.hmce.gov.uk.

IN THE U.S.

U.S. residents who have been out of the country for at least 48 hours may bring home, for personal use, $800 worth of foreign goods duty-free, as long as they haven't used the $800 allowance or any part of it in the past 30 days. This exemption may include 1 liter of alcohol (for travelers 21 and older), 200 cigarettes, and 100 non-Cuban cigars. Family members from the same household who are traveling together may pool their $800 personal exemptions. For fewer than 48 hours, the duty-free allowance drops to $200, which may include 50 cigarettes, 10 non-Cuban cigars, and 150 ml of alcohol (or 150 ml of perfume containing alcohol). The $200 allowance cannot be combined with other individuals' exemptions, and if you exceed it, the full value of all the goods will be taxed. Antiques, which the U.S. Bureau of Customs and Border Protection defines as objects more than 100 years old, enter duty-free, as do original works of art done entirely by hand, including paintings, drawings, and sculptures. This doesn't apply to folk art or handicrafts, which are in general dutiable.

You may also send packages home duty-free, with a limit of one parcel per addressee per day (except alcohol or tobacco products or perfume worth more than $5). You can mail up to $200 worth of goods for personal use; label the package PERSONAL USE and attach a list of its contents and their retail value. If the package contains your used personal belongings, mark it AMERICAN GOODS RETURNED to avoid paying duties. You may send up to $100 worth of goods as a gift; mark the package UNSOLICITED GIFT.

Mailed items do not affect your duty-free allowance on your return.

To avoid paying duty on foreign-made high-ticket items you already own and will take on your trip, register them with Customs before you leave the country. Consider filing a Certificate of Registration for laptops, cameras, watches, and other digital devices identified with serial numbers or other permanent markings; you can keep the certificate for other trips. Otherwise, bring a sales receipt or insurance form to show that you owned the item before you left the United States.

F U.S. Bureau of Customs and Border Protection ⊠ for inquiries and equipment registration, 1300 Pennsylvania Ave. NW, Washington, DC 20229 ⊕ www.customs.gov ☎ 877/287–8667 or 202/354–1000 ⊠ for complaints, Customer Satisfaction Unit, 1300 Pennsylvania Ave. NW, Room 5.5D, Washington, DC 20229.

DISABILITIES & ACCESSIBILITY

Facilities for travelers with disabilities in Denmark are generally good, and most of the major tourist offices offer special booklets and brochures on travel and accommodations. Notify and make all local and public transportation and hotel reservations in advance to ensure a smooth trip.

LODGING

Best Western offers properties with wheelchair-accessible rooms just outside Copenhagen. If wheelchair-accessible rooms on other floors are not available, ground-floor rooms are provided.

F Wheelchair-Friendly Chain **Best Western** ☎ 800/780–7234 (toll-free) in North America, 800/109–88 (toll-free) in Denmark ⊕ www.bestwestern.com.

RESERVATIONS

When discussing accessibility with an operator or reservations agent, ask hard questions. Are there any stairs, inside *or* out? Are there grab bars next to the toilet *and* in the shower/tub? How wide is the doorway to the room? To the bathroom? For the most extensive facilities meeting the latest legal specifications, opt for newer accommodations. If you reserve through a toll-free number, consider also calling the hotel's local number to confirm the information from the central reservations office. Get confirmation in writing when you can.

SIGHTS & ATTRACTIONS

Although most major attractions in Copenhagen present no problems, windy cobblestone streets in the older sections of cities may be challenging for travelers with disabilities.

TRANSPORTATION

With advance notice, most airlines, buses, and trains can arrange assistance for those requiring extra help with boarding. Contact each individual company at least one week in advance, or ideally at the time of booking.

Confirming ahead is especially important when planning travel to less populated regions. The smaller planes and ferries often used in such areas are not all accessible.

TRAVEL AGENCIES

In the United States, the Americans with Disabilities Act requires that travel firms serve the needs of all travelers. Some agencies specialize in working with people with disabilities. ⚑ Travelers with Mobility Problems **Access Adventures/B. Roberts Travel** ⊠ 206 Chestnut Ridge Rd., Scottsville, NY 14624 ☎ 585/889-9096 ⊕ www.brobertstravel.com ⬧ dltravel@prodigy.net, run by a former physical-rehabilitation counselor. **CareVacations** ⊠ No. 5, 5110-50 Ave., Leduc, Alberta, Canada, T9E 6V4 ☎ 780/986-6404 or 877/478-7827 🖶 780/986-8332 ⊕ www.carevacations.com, for group tours and cruise vacations. **Flying Wheels Travel** ⊠ 143 W. Bridge St., Box 382, Owatonna, MN 55060 ☎ 507/451-5005 🖶 507/451-1685 ⊕ www.flyingwheelstravel.com.

DISCOUNTS & DEALS

Be a smart shopper and compare all your options before making decisions. A plane ticket bought with a promotional coupon from travel clubs, coupon books, and direct-mail offers or purchased on the Internet may not be cheaper than the least expensive fare from a discount ticket agency. And always keep in mind that what you get is just as important as what you save.

DISCOUNT RESERVATIONS

To save money, look into discount reservations services with Web sites and toll-free numbers, which use their buying power to get a better price on hotels, airline tickets (⇨ Air Travel), even car rentals. When booking a room, always

call the hotel's local toll-free number (if one is available) rather than the central reservations number—you'll often get a better price. Always ask about special packages or corporate rates.

When shopping for the best deal on hotels and car rentals, look for guaranteed exchange rates, which protect you against a falling dollar. With your rate locked in, you won't pay more, even if the price goes up in the local currency. ⚑ Airline Tickets **Air 4 Less** ☎ 800/AIR4LESS; low-fare specialist. ⚑ Hotel Rooms **Accommodations Express** ☎ 800/444-7666 or 800/277-1064 ⊕ www.accommodationsexpress.com. **Hotels.com** ☎ 800/246-8357 ⊕ www.hotels.com. **Steigenberger Reservation Service** ☎ 800/223-5652 ⊕ www.srsworldhotels.com. **Turbotrip.com** ☎ 800/473-7829 ⊕ www.turbotrip.com.

PACKAGE DEALS

Don't confuse packages and guided tours. When you buy a package, you travel on your own, just as though you had planned the trip yourself. Fly/drive packages, which combine airfare and car rental, are often a good deal. In cities, ask the local visitor's bureau about hotel packages that include tickets to major museum exhibits or other special events. If you **buy a rail/drive pass,** you may save on train tickets and car rentals. All Eurailpass holders get a discount on Eurostar fares through the Channel Tunnel and often receive reduced rates for buses, hotels, ferries, and car rentals. Also check rates for Scanrail Passes (⇨ Train Travel).

EATING & DRINKING

Denmark's major cities have a good selection of restaurants serving both traditional Danish and international cuisines. The restaurants we list are the cream of the crop in each price category. Properties indicated by an ✕▥ are lodging establishments whose restaurant warrants a special trip.

CATEGORY	MAIN CITIES	ELSEWHERE
$$$$	over Dkr 200	over Dkr 180
$$$	Dkr 151–Dkr 200	Dkr 141–Dkr 180
$$	Dkr 121–Dkr 150	Dkr 121–Dkr 140
$	Dkr 90–Dkr 120	Dkr 90–Dkr 120
¢	under Dkr 90	under Dkr 90

Prices are for a main course at dinner and are given in Danish kroner.

CUTTING COSTS

You can reduce the cost of food by planning. Breakfast is often included in your hotel bill; if not, you may wish to buy fruit, sweet rolls, and a beverage for a picnic breakfast. Bakeries abound and offer all the fixings for breakfast, except coffee or tea. In recent years many corner convenience stores have begun to sell hot drinks. Opt for a restaurant lunch instead of dinner, since the latter tends to be significantly more expensive. Instead of beer or wine, drink tap water—liquor can cost four times the price of the same brand in a store—but do specify tap water, as the term "water" can refer to soft drinks and bottled water, which are also expensive.

MEALTIMES

Danes start the workday early, which means they generally eat lunch at noon and consume their evening meal on the early side. Make sure you make your dinner reservations for no later than 9 PM. Bars and cafés stay open later, and most offer at least light fare. Unless otherwise noted, the restaurants listed in this guide are open daily for lunch and dinner.

RESERVATIONS & DRESS

Reservations are always a good idea; we mention them only when they're essential or not accepted. Book as far ahead as you can, and reconfirm as soon as you arrive. (Large parties should always call ahead to check the reservations policy.) We mention dress only when men are required to wear a jacket or a jacket and tie, which is quite unusual; even in the most chic establishments the tone is elegantly casual.

WINE, BEER & SPIRITS

Restaurants' markup on alcoholic beverages is often very high in Denmark: as much as four times that of a standard retail price.

ELECTRICITY

To use electric-powered equipment purchased in the United States or Canada, **bring a converter and adapter.** The electrical current in Denmark is 220 volts, 50 cycles alternating current (AC); wall outlets take Continental-type plugs, with two round prongs.

If your appliances are dual-voltage, you'll need only an adapter. Don't use 110-volt outlets marked FOR SHAVERS ONLY for high-wattage appliances such as blow-dryers. Most laptops operate equally well on 110 and 220 volts and so require only an adapter.

EMBASSIES

New Zealanders should contact the UK embassy for assistance.

▪ Australia ✉ Dampfærgevej 26, 2nd. floor, Østerbro, DK-2100 Copenhagen ☎ 70/26-36-76 🖷 70/26-36-86 ⊕ www.denmark.embassy.gov.au.
▪ Canada ✉ Kristen Bernikows G. 1, Downtown, DK-1105 Copenhagen ☎ 33/48-32-00 🖷 33/48-32-20 ⊕ www.canada.dk.
▪ Ireland ✉ Østbaneg. 21, Østerbro, DK-2100 Copenhagen ☎ 35/42-32-33 🖷 35/43-18-58.
▪ South Africa ✉ Gammel Vartov Vej 8, DK-2900 Hellerup ☎ 39/18-01-55 🖷 39/18-40-06 ⊕ www.southafrica.dk.
▪ United Kingdom ✉ Kastelsvej 36-40, Østerbro, DK-2100 Copenhagen ☎ 35/44-52-00 🖷 35/44-52-93 ⊕ www.britishembassy.dk.
▪ United States ✉ Dag Hammarskjölds Allé 24, Østerbro, DK-2100 Copenhagen ☎ 35/55-31-44 🖷 35/43-02-23 ⊕ www.usembassy.dk.

EMERGENCIES

The general 24-hour emergency number throughout Denmark is 112.

GAY & LESBIAN TRAVEL

Denmark has a liberal and accommodating attitude toward gays and lesbians. The Danish government grants to same-sex couples the same or nearly the same rights as heterosexual married couples. Copenhagen has an active, although not large, gay community.

▪ Gay- & Lesbian-Friendly Travel Agencies **Different Roads Travel** ✉ 8383 Wilshire Blvd., Suite 520, Beverly Hills, CA 90211 ☎ 323/651-5557 or 800/429-8747 (Ext. 14 for both) 🖷 323/651-3678 ✉ lgernert@tzell.com. **Kennedy Travel** ✉ 130 W. 42nd St., Suite 401, New York, NY 10036 ☎ 212/840-8659, 800/237-7433 🖷 212/730-2269 ⊕ www.kennedytravel.com. **Now, Voyager** ✉ 4406 18th St., San Francisco, CA 94114 ☎ 415/626-1169 or 800/255-6951 🖷 415/626-8626 ⊕ www.nowvoyager.com. **Skylink Travel and Tour** ✉ 1455 N. Dutton Ave., Suite A, Santa Rosa, CA 95401 ☎ 707/546-9888 or 800/225-5759 🖷 707/636-0951; serving lesbian travelers.

HOLIDAYS

All Scandinavian countries celebrate New Year's Eve and Day, Good Friday, Easter and Easter Monday, Midsummer Eve and Day (late June), and Christmas (as well as Christmas Eve and Boxing Day, the day after Christmas).

In addition, Denmark has the following holidays: Holy/Maundy Thursday, Common Prayer (May), Ascension (40 days after Easter), Constitution Day (June 5; shops close at noon), and Whitsun/Pentecost (Sunday and Monday 10 days after Ascension).

Schools close for a week in fall, normally the third week in October. The tradition goes back to the days when youngsters were called upon to help with the harvest, so the occasion is sometimes referred to as the "potato holiday." Many lodging and travel-related prices are hiked up significantly during this week.

On major holidays such as Christmas, most shops close or operate on a Sunday schedule. On the eves of such holidays, many shops are also closed all day or are open with reduced hours.

Although May Day (May 1) is not an official holiday, many offices and some merchants close up shop, and the cities are full of celebrations and parades. For Midsummer Day at the end of June, locals flock to the lakes and countryside to celebrate the beginning of long summer days with bonfires and other festivities.

INSURANCE

The most useful travel-insurance plan is a comprehensive policy that includes coverage for trip cancellation and interruption, default, trip delay, and medical expenses (with a waiver for preexisting conditions).

Without insurance you'll lose all or most of your money if you cancel your trip, regardless of the reason. Default insurance covers you if your tour operator, airline, or cruise line goes out of business. Trip-delay covers expenses that arise because of bad weather or mechanical delays. Study the fine print when comparing policies.

If you're traveling internationally, a key component of travel insurance is coverage for medical bills incurred if you get sick on the road. Such expenses aren't generally covered by Medicare or private policies. U.K. residents can buy a travel-insurance policy valid for most vacations taken during the year in which it's purchased (but check preexisting-condition coverage). British and Australian citizens need extra medical coverage when traveling overseas.

Always **buy travel policies directly from the insurance company**; if you buy them from a cruise line, airline, or tour operator that goes out of business you probably won't be covered for the agency or operator's default, a major risk. Before making any purchase, review your existing health and home-owner's policies to find what they cover away from home.

Travel Insurers In the U.S.: **Access America** ✉ 6600 W. Broad St., Richmond, VA 23230 ☎ 800/284-8300 🖷 804/673-1491 or 800/346-9265 🌐 www.accessamerica.com. **Travel Guard International** ✉ 1145 Clark St., Stevens Point, WI 54481 ☎ 715/345-0505 or 800/826-1300 🖷 800/955-8785 🌐 www.travelguard.com.

In the U.K.: **Association of British Insurers** ✉ 51 Gresham St., London EC2V 7HQ ☎ 020/7600-3333 🖷 020/7696-8999 🌐 www.abi.org.uk. In Canada: **RBC Insurance** ✉ 6880 Financial Dr., Mississauga, Ontario L5N 7Y5 ☎ 800/565-3129 🖷 905/813-4704 🌐 www.rbcinsurance.com. In Australia: **Insurance Council of Australia** ✉ Insurance Enquiries and Complaints, Level 3, 56 Pitt St., Sydney, NSW 2000 ☎ 1300/363683 or 02/9251-4456 🖷 02/9251-4453 🌐 www.iecltd.com.au. In New Zealand: **Insurance Council of New Zealand** ✉ Level 7, 111-115 Customhouse Quay, Box 474, Wellington ☎ 04/472-5230 🖷 04/473-3011 🌐 www.icnz.org.nz.

LANGUAGE

Danish is a difficult tongue for foreigners—except those from Norway and Sweden—to understand, let alone speak. Danes are good linguists, however, and almost everyone, except perhaps elderly people in rural areas, speaks English. In Sønderjylland, the southern region of Jylland, most people speak or understand German. If you are planning to visit the countryside or the small islands, it would be a good idea to bring a phrase book.

Difficult-to-pronounce Danish characters include the "ø," pronounced a bit like a very short "er," similar to the French "eu"; "æ," which sounds like the "a" in "ape" but with a glottal stop, or the "a" in "cat," depending on the region; and the "å" (also written "aa"), which sounds like "or". The important thing about these characters isn't that you pronounce them correctly—foreigners usually can't—but that you know to look for them in the phone book at the very end. Mr. Søren Åstrup, for example, will be found after "Z;" Æ and Ø follow.

LODGING

The lodgings we list are the cream of the crop in each price category. We always list the facilities that are available—but we don't specify whether they cost extra: When pricing accommodations, always ask what's included and what costs extra.

In the larger cities, lodging ranges from first-class business hotels run by SAS, Sheraton, and Scandic; to good-quality tourist-class hotels, such as RESO, Best Western, and Scandic Budget; to a wide variety of single-entrepreneur hotels. In the countryside, look for independently run inns and motels called *kroer*.

Before you leave home, **ask your travel agent about discounts,** including summer hotel checks for Best Western and Scandic, and enormous year-round rebates at SAS hotels for travelers over 65. All EuroClass (business class) passengers can get discounts of at least 10% at SAS hotels when they book through SAS.

Two things about hotels usually surprise North Americans: the relatively limited dimensions of Scandinavian beds and the generous size of Scandinavian breakfasts. Scandinavian double beds are often about 60 inches wide or slightly less, close in size to the U.S. queen size. King-size beds (72 inches wide) are difficult to find and, if available, require special reservations.

Older hotels may have some rooms described as "double," which in fact have one double bed plus one foldout sofa big enough for two people. This arrangement is occasionally called a combi-room but is being phased out.

Make reservations whenever possible. Even countryside inns, which usually have space, are sometimes packed with vacationing Europeans.

Assume that hotels operate on the European Plan (EP, with no meals) unless we specify that they use the Continental Plan (CP, with a Continental breakfast) or Breakfast Plan (BP, with a full breakfast).

CATEGORY	MAIN CITIES	ELSEWHERE
$$$$	over Dkr 1,700	over Dkr 1,500
$$$	Dkr 1,400– Dkr 1,700	Dkr 1,200– Dkr 1,500
$$	Dkr 1,000– Dkr 1,400	Dkr 1,000– Dkr 1,200
$	Dkr 700– Dkr 1,000	Dkr 700– Dkr 1,000
¢	under Dkr 700	under Dkr 700

Prices, listed in Danish kroner, are for two people in a standard double room, including service charge and tax.

APARTMENT & VILLA RENTALS

If you want a home base that's roomy enough for a family and comes with cooking facilities, consider a furnished rental. These can save you money, especially if you're traveling with a group. Home-exchange directories sometimes list rentals as well as exchanges.

Each year many Danes choose to rent out their summer homes in the verdant countryside and along the coast. Typically, a simple house accommodating four persons costs from Dkr 1,000 weekly up to ten times that amount during summer. You should book well in advance. A group of Danes who regularly rent out their holiday houses have formed the Association of Danish Holiday House Letters (ADHHL). You can also contact DanCenter and Lejrskolebureauet for information. Homes for You lists fully furnished homes and apartments.

🔲 International Agents Hideaways International ✉ 767 Islington St., Portsmouth, NH 03801 ☎ 603/430-4433 or 800/843-4433 🖷 603/430-4444 ⊕ www.hideaways.com, membership $145. **🔲 Local Agents DanCenter** ✉ Lyngbyvej 20, Østerbro, DK-2100 Copenhagen ☎ 70/13-16-16 🖷 70/13-70-73 ⊕ www.dancenter.com. **Feriehusudlejernes Brancheforeningen (ADHHL)** ✉ Obels Have 32, DK-9000 Aalborg ☎ 96/30-22-44 🖷 96/30-22-45 ⊕ www.fbnet.dk. **Homes for You** ✉ Vimmelskaftet 49, Downtown, DK-1161 Copenhagen ☎ 33/33-08-05 🖷 33/32-08-04 ⊕ www.hay4you.dk. **Lejrskolebureauet (LSB)** ✉ Nordlævej 13, DK-3250 Gilleleje ☎ 48/30-14-88 🖷 48/30-14-66.

B&BS

Contact Dansk Bed & Breakfast to order their B&B catalog for the whole of Denmark. Faaborg Touristbureau maintains its own list for the Fyn and the Central Islands region.

f Reservation Services **Dansk Bed & Breakfast** ✉ Bernstorffsvej 71a, DK-2900 Hellerup ☎ 39/ 61-04-05 🖷 39/61-05-25 ⊕ www.bedandbreakfast. dk. **Faaborg Touristbureau** ✉ Banegaardspl. 2A, DK-5600 Faaborg ☎ 62/61-07-07 🖷 62/61-33-37 ⊕ www.bed-breakfast-fyn.dk.

CAMPING

If you plan to camp in one of Denmark's 500-plus approved campsites, you'll need an International Camping Carnet or Danish Camping Pass (available at any campsite and valid for one year). Call Campingrådet for information.

f **Campingrådet** ✉ Mosedalsvej 15, DK-2500 Valby ☎ 39/27-88-44 🖷 39/27-80-44 ⊕ www. campingraadet.dk.

FARM VACATIONS & HOMESTAYS

A farm vacation is perhaps the best way to experience the Danish countryside, sharing meals with your host family and perhaps helping with the chores. Bed-and-breakfast packages are about Dkr 200, whereas half board—an overnight with breakfast and one hot meal—runs around Dkr 280. Full board, including an overnight with three square meals, can also be arranged. The minimum stay is three nights. Contact Landboferie for details.

If you aren't necessarily looking for a pastoral experience but would still like to get an insider's view of Danish society, you might want to consider a homestay. Meet the Danes helps travelers find accommodation in Danish homes. The informative local hosts can give you invaluable tips regarding sightseeing, shopping, dining, and nightlife.

f **Landboferie** (Holiday in the Country) ✉ Ceresvej 2, DK 8410 Rønde ☎ 86/37-39-00 🖷 86/37-35-50 ⊕ www.bondegaardsferie.dk. **Meet The Danes** ✉ Ravnsborgg. 2, 2nd floor, Nørrebro DK-2200 Copenhagen ☎ 33/46-46-46 🖷 33/ 46-46-47 ⊕ www.meetthedanes.dk.

HOME EXCHANGES

If you would like to exchange your home for someone else's, join a home-exchange organization, which will send you its updated listings of available exchanges for a year and will include your own listing in at least one of them. It's up to you to make specific arrangements.

f Exchange Clubs **HomeLink International** 🕭 Box 47747, Tampa, FL 33647 ☎ 813/975-9825 or 800/638-3841 🖷 813/910-8144 ⊕ www.homelink.

org; $110 yearly for a listing, on-line access, and catalog; $70 without catalog. **Intervac U.S.** ✉ 30 Corte San Fernando, Tiburon, CA 94920 ☎ 800/ 756-4663 🖷 415/435-7440 ⊕ www.intervacus.com; $105 yearly for a listing, on-line access, and a catalog; $50 without catalog.

HOSTELS

No matter what your age, you can save on lodging costs by staying at hostels. In some 4,500 locations in more than 70 countries around the world, Hostelling International (HI), the umbrella group for a number of national youth-hostel associations, offers single-sex, dorm-style beds and, at many hostels, rooms for couples and family accommodations. Membership in any HI national hostel association, open to travelers of all ages, allows you to stay in HI-affiliated hostels at member rates; one-year membership is about $28 for adults (C$35 for a two-year minimum membership in Canada, £13.50 in the U.K., A$52 in Australia, and NZ$40 in New Zealand); hostels charge about $10–$30 per night. Members have priority if the hostel is full; they're also eligible for discounts around the world, even on rail and bus travel in some countries.

Youth hostels in Denmark are open to everyone regardless of age. If you have an International Youth Hostels Association card (it costs Dkr 160 to obtain in Denmark), the rate is roughly Dkr 115 for a single bed, Dkr 150–Dkr 575 for a private room accommodating up to 4 people. Without the card, there's a surcharge of about Dkr 30 per person. Prices don't include breakfast.

The hostels fill up quickly in summer, so make your reservations early. Most hostels are sympathetic to students and will usually find them at least a place on the floor. Bring your own linens or sleep sheet, though these can usually be rented at the hostel. Sleeping bags are not allowed. Contact Danhostel Danmarks Vandrehjem—the organization charges for information, but you can get a free brochure, *Camping/Youth and Family Hostels*, from the Danish Tourist Board.

f Organizations **Danhostel Danmarks Vandrerhjem** ✉ Vesterbrog. 39, Vesterbro, DK-1620, Copenhagen ☎ 33/31-36-12 🖷 33/31-36-26 ⊕ www.danhostel.dk. **Hostelling International– USA** ✉ 8401 Colesville Rd., Suite 600, Silver Spring, MD 20910 ☎ 301/495-1240 🖷 301/495-6697

⊕ www.hiayh.org. **Hostelling International–
Canada** ⊠ 205 Catherine St., Suite 400, Ottawa,
Ontario K2P 1C3 ☎ 613/237-7884 or 800/663-5777
🖷 613/237-7868 ⊕ www.hihostels.ca. **YHA England and Wales** ⊠ Trevelyan House, Dimple Rd.,
Matlock, Derbyshire DE4 3YH, U.K. ☎ 0870/870-
8808, 0870/ 770-8868, 0162/959-2700 🖷 0870/
770-6127 ⊕ www.yha.org.uk. **YHA Australia** ⊠ 422
Kent St., Sydney, NSW 2001 ☎ 02/9261-1111 🖷 02/
9261-1969 ⊕ www.yha.com.au. **YHA New Zealand**
⊠ Level 4, Torrens House, 195 Hereford St., Box 436,
Christchurch ☎ 03/379-9970 or 0800/278-299
🖷 03/365-4476 ⊕ www.yha.org.nz.

HOTELS

All hotels listed have private baths unless
otherwise noted. Many Danes prefer a
shower to a bath, so if you particularly
want a bath, ask for it, but be prepared to
pay more. Taxes are usually included in
prices, but check when making a reservation. As time goes on, it appears that an
increasing number of hotels are eliminat-
ing breakfast from their room rates; even
if it is not included, breakfast is usually
well worth its price. Many of Denmark's
larger hotels, particularly those that cater
to the conference crowd, offer discounted
rates on the weekends, so inquire when
booking. Try www.danishhotels.dk for
listings not included in this book.

The Scandinavian countries offer Inn
Checks, or prepaid hotel vouchers, for accommodations ranging from first-class hotels to country cottages. These vouchers,
which must be purchased from travel
agents or from the Scandinavian Tourist
Board (⇨ Visitor Information) before departure, are sold individually and in pack-
ets for as many nights as needed and offer
savings of up to 50%. Most countries also
offer summer bargains for foreign tourists;
winter bargains can be even greater. For
further information about Scandinavian
hotel vouchers, contact the Scandinavian
Tourist Board.

ProSkandinavia checks can be used in 400
hotels across Scandinavia for savings up to
50%, for reservations made usually no
earlier than 24 hours before arrival, although some hotels allow earlier bookings.
One check costs about $40 U.S. Two
checks will pay for a double room at a
hotel, one check for a room in a cottage.
The checks can be bought at many travel
agencies in Scandinavia or directly from
ProSkandinavia.

The old stagecoach *kroer* (inns) scattered
throughout Denmark can be cheap yet
charming alternatives to standard hotel
rooms. You can cut your costs by contact-
ing Danske Kroer & Hoteller to invest in a
book of Inn Checks, valid at 83 participating inns and hotels throughout the country. Each check costs about Dkr 675 per
couple and entitles you to an overnight
stay in a double room including breakfast.
Family checks for three (Dkr 775) and
four (Dkr 875) are also available. Order a
free catalog from Danske Kroer &
Hoteller, but choose carefully; the organization includes a few chain hotels bereft of
the charm you might be expecting. Some
of the participating establishments tack on
a Dkr 150 surcharge.

🛈 Reservation Services **Danske Kroer & Hoteller**
⊠ Vejlevej 16, DK-8700 Horsens ☎ 75/64-87-00
🖷 75/64-87-20 ⊕ www.krohotel.dk. **ProSkandinavia** ⊠ Akersgt. 11, N-0158 Oslo, Norway ☎ 47/
22-41-13-13 ⊕ www.proskandinavia.com.

RESERVING A ROOM

Make your reservations well in advance,
especially in resort areas near the coasts.
Many places offer summer reductions to
compensate for the slowdown in business
travel and conferences. The very friendly
staff at the hotel booking desk at Wonderful Copenhagen can help find rooms in hotels, hostels, and private homes, or even at
campsites in advance of a trip. If you find
yourself in Copenhagen without a reservation, head for the tourist office's hotel
booking desk, which is open May through
August, Monday to Saturday 9–8 and Sunday 10–8; September through April, weekdays 10–4:30 and Saturday 10–1:30. Note
that hours of the hotel booking desk can
be fickle, and change from year to year depending on staff availability; in the low
season, they are often closed on the weekends. Young travelers looking for a room
should head for Use It, the student and
youth budget travel agency.

Reservations should be made two months
in advance, but last-minute (as in same-day)
hotel rooms booked at the tourist office can
save you 50% off the normal price.
🛈 Local Reservation Services **Hotel booking desk**
⊠ Bernstorffsg. 1, Vesterbro, DK-1577 Copenhagen
☎ 70/22-24-42 ⊕ www.woco.dk. **Use It** ⊠ Rådhusstr. 13, Downtown, DK-1466 Copenhagen ☎ 33/
73-06-20 🖷 33/73-06-49 ⊕ www.useit.dk.
🛈 Toll-Free Numbers **Best Western** ☎ 800/528-
1234 ⊕ www.bestwestern.com. **Choice** ☎ 800/424-

6423 ⊕ www.choicehotels.com. **Clarion** ☎ 800/
424-6423 ⊕ www.choicehotels.com. **Comfort Inn**
☎ 800/424-6423 ⊕ www.choicehotels.com. **Hilton**
☎ 800/445-8667 ⊕ www.hilton.com. **Holiday Inn**
☎ 800/465-4329 ⊕ www.sixcontinentshotels.com.
Inter-Continental ☎ 800/327-0200 ⊕ www.
intercontinental.com. **Marriott** ☎ 800/228-9290
⊕ www.marriott.com. **Le Meridien** ☎ 800/543-
4300 ⊕ www.lemeridien-hotels.com. **Quality Inn**
☎ 800/424-6423 ⊕ www.choicehotels.com. **Radisson** ☎ 800/333-3333 ⊕ www.radisson.com. **Ra-
mada** ☎ 800/228-2828, 800/854-7854
international reservations ⊕ www.ramada.com or
www.ramadahotels.com. **Sheraton** ☎ 800/325-
3535 ⊕ www.starwood.com/sheraton.

MAIL & SHIPPING

POSTAL RATES

Airmail letters and postcards to non-EU
countries cost Dkr 6.50 for 50 grams. Airmail letters and postcards within the EU
cost Dkr 5.50. Length, width, and thickness all influence the postage price. Contact Copenhagen's main post office for
more information. You can buy stamps at
post offices or from shops selling postcards.

RECEIVING MAIL

You can arrange to have your mail sent
general delivery, marked *poste restante,* to
any post office, hotel, or inn. If no post office is specified, the letter or package is automatically sent to the main post office in
Copenhagen.
🚺 **Copenhagen Main Post Office** ✉ Tietgensg. 37,
Vesterbro DK-1566 Copenhagen ☎ 80/20-70-30
⊕ www.postdanmark.dk.

MONEY MATTERS

Denmark's economy is stable, and infla-
tion remains reasonably low. On the other
hand, the Danish cost of living is quite
high, even for Europe. In some areas prices
are comparable to other European capitals, while other goods or services tend to
be higher. As in all of Scandinavia, prices
for alcoholic beverages and tobacco products are steep due to heavy taxation. Prices
are highest in Copenhagen, lower elsewhere in the country. Some sample prices:
cup of coffee, Dkr 15–Dkr 25; bottle of
beer, Dkr 20–Dkr 30; soda, Dkr 20–Dkr
25; ham sandwich, Dkr 20–Dkr 40; 1½-
km (1-mi) taxi ride, about Dkr 50.

Prices throughout this guide are given for
adults. Substantially reduced fees are almost always available for children, students, and senior citizens. For information
on taxes, *see* Taxes.

ATMS

Automatic Teller Machines/ATMs are located around most towns and cities. Look
for the red signs for KONTANTEN/DANKORT
AUTOMAT. You can use Visa, Plus, Master-
card/Eurocard, Eurochequecard, and
sometimes JCB cards to withdraw cash.
Many, but not all, machines are open 24
hours. Check with your bank about daily
withdrawal limits before you go.
🚺 **ATM Locations Mastercard/Cirrus** ☎ 800/424-
7787 ⊕ www.mastercard.com.

CREDIT CARDS

Most major credit cards are accepted in
Denmark, though it's wise to inquire
about American Express and Diners Club
beforehand. Throughout this guide, the
following abbreviations are used: **AE,**
American Express; **DC,** Diners Club; **MC,**
MasterCard; and **V,** Visa.
🚺 Reporting Lost Cards **American Express**
✉ Amagertorv 18, DK-1146 Copenhagen ☎ 33/
11-50-05. **Diners Club** ✉ H. J. Holst Vej 5 DK-2605
Brøndby ☎ 36/73-73-73. **Master Card** ☎ 44/
89-27-50. **Visa** ☎ 44/89-29-29.

CURRENCY

The monetary unit in Denmark is the
krone (Dkr), divided into 100 øre. Even
though Denmark has not adopted the
euro, the Danish krone is firmly bound to
it at about Dkr 7.5 to 1€ with only minimal fluctuations in exchange rates.

At this writing (fall 2003), the krone stood
at 7.43 to the euro, 4.23 to the Australian
dollar, 10.53 to the British pound, 4.67 to
the Canadian dollar, 3.76 to the New
Zealand dollar, 0.89 to the South African
rand, and 6.56 to the U.S. dollar.

CURRENCY EXCHANGE

For the most favorable rates, **change
money through banks.** Although ATM
transaction fees may be higher abroad
than at home, ATM rates are excellent because they are based on wholesale rates offered only by major banks. You won't do
as well at exchange booths in airports or
rail and bus stations, in hotels, in restaurants, or in stores. To avoid lines at airport

exchange booths, **get a bit of local currency before you leave home.**

⚹ Exchange Services International Currency Express ✉ 427 N. Camden Dr., Suite F, Beverly Hills, CA 90210 ☎ 888/278-6628 orders ✆ 310/278-6410 ⊕ www.foreignmoney.com. **Thomas Cook International Money Services** ☎ 800/287-7362 orders and retail locations ⊕ www.us.thomascook.com.

TRAVELER'S CHECKS

Do you need traveler's checks? It depends on where you're headed. If you're going to rural areas and small towns, go with cash; traveler's checks are best used in cities. Lost or stolen checks can usually be replaced within 24 hours. To ensure a speedy refund, buy your own traveler's checks—don't let someone else pay for them: irregularities like this can cause delays. The person who bought the checks should make the call to request a refund. Traveler's checks can be cashed at banks and at many hotels, restaurants, and shops.

PACKING

Bring a folding umbrella and a lightweight raincoat, as it is common for the sky to be clear at 9 AM, rainy at 11 AM, and clear again in time for lunch. Pack casual clothes, as Scandinavians tend to dress more casually than their Continental brethren. Even in summer it's wise to bring a sweater or a jacket, because temperatures can really drop off with an on-shore breeze or a sudden cloudburst. If you have trouble sleeping when it is light or are sensitive to strong sun, bring an eye mask and dark sunglasses; in summer the sun rises as early as 4 AM in some areas, and the far-northern latitude causes it to slant at angles unseen elsewhere on the globe. Bring bug repellent if you plan to venture away from the capital cities; large mosquitoes can be a real nuisance on summer evenings throughout Scandinavia.

In your carry-on luggage, pack an extra pair of eyeglasses or contact lenses and enough of any medication you take to last a few days longer than the entire trip. You may also ask your doctor to write a spare prescription using the drug's generic name, as brand names may vary from country to country. In luggage to be checked, **never pack prescription drugs, valuables, or undeveloped film.** And don't forget to carry with you the addresses of offices that handle refunds of lost traveler's checks. Check

Fodor's How to Pack (available at on-line retailers and bookstores everywhere) for more tips.

To avoid customs and security delays, carry medications in their original packaging. Don't pack any sharp objects in your carry-on luggage, including knives of any size or material, scissors, and corkscrews, or anything else that might arouse suspicion.

To avoid having your checked luggage chosen for hand inspection, don't cram bags full. The U.S. Transportation Security Administration suggests packing shoes on top and placing personal items you don't want touched in clear plastic bags.

CHECKING LUGGAGE

You're allowed to carry aboard one bag and one personal article, such as a purse or a laptop computer. Make sure what you carry on fits under your seat or in the overhead bin. Get to the gate early, so you can board as soon as possible, before the overhead bins fill up.

Baggage allowances vary by carrier, destination, and ticket class. On international flights, you're usually allowed to check two bags weighing up to 70 pounds (32 kilograms) each, although a few airlines allow checked bags of up to 88 pounds (40 kilograms) in first class. Some international carriers don't allow more than 66 pounds (30 kilograms) per bag in business class and 44 pounds (20 kilograms) in economy. On domestic flights, the limit is usually 50 to 70 pounds (23 to 32 kilograms) per bag. In general, carry-on bags shouldn't exceed 40 pounds (18 kilograms). Most airlines won't accept bags that weigh more than 100 pounds (45 kilograms) on domestic or international flights. Check baggage restrictions with your carrier before you pack.

Airline liability for baggage is limited to $2,500 per person on flights within the United States. On international flights it amounts to $9.07 per pound or $20 per kilogram for checked baggage (roughly $640 per 70-pound bag), with a maximum of $634.90 per piece, and $400 per passenger for unchecked baggage. You can buy additional coverage at check-in for about $10 per $1,000 of coverage, but it often excludes a rather extensive list of items, shown on your airline ticket.

Before departure, itemize your bags' contents and their worth, and label the bags with your name, address, and phone number. (If you use your home address, cover it so potential thieves can't see it readily.) Include a label inside each bag and **pack a copy of your itinerary.** At check-in, make sure each bag is correctly tagged with the destination airport's three-letter code. Because some checked bags will be opened for hand inspection, the U.S. Transportation Security Administration recommends that you leave luggage unlocked or use the plastic locks offered at check-in. TSA screeners place an inspection notice inside searched bags, which are re-sealed with a special lock.

If your bag has been searched and contents are missing or damaged, file a claim with the TSA Consumer Response Center as soon as possible. If your bags arrive damaged or fail to arrive at all, file a written report with the airline before leaving the airport.

🛈 Complaints **U.S. Transportation Security Administration Consumer Response Center** ☎ 866/289-9673 ⊕ www.tsa.gov.

PASSPORTS & VISAS

When traveling internationally, carry your passport even if you don't need one (it's always the best form of I.D.) and **make two photocopies of the data page** (one for someone at home and another for you, carried separately from your passport). If you lose your passport, promptly call the nearest embassy or consulate and the local police.

U.S. passport applications for children under age 14 require consent from both parents or legal guardians; both parents must appear together to sign the application. If only one parent appears, he or she must submit a written statement from the other parent authorizing passport issuance for the child. A parent with sole authority must present evidence of it when applying; acceptable documentation includes the child's certified birth certificate listing only the applying parent, a court order specifically permitting this parent's travel with the child, or a death certificate for the nonapplying parent. Application forms and instructions are available on the Web site of the U.S. State Department's Bureau of Consular Affairs (⊕ www.travel.state.gov).

ENTERING DENMARK

U.S., British, Canadian, and Australian citizens need only a valid passport to enter Denmark or any Scandinavian country for stays of up to three months.

PASSPORT OFFICES

The best time to apply for a passport or to renew is in fall and winter. Before any trip, check your passport's expiration date, and, if necessary, renew it as soon as possible.

🛈 Australian Citizens **Passports Australia** ☎ 131-232 ⊕ www.passports.gov.au.
🛈 Canadian Citizens **Passport Office** ✉ to mail in applications: 200 Promenade du Portage, Hull, Québec J8X 4B7 ☎ 819/994-3500 or 800/567-6868 ⊕ www.ppt.gc.ca.
🛈 New Zealand Citizens **New Zealand Passports Office** ☎ 0800/22-5050 or 04/474-8100 ⊕ www.passports.govt.nz.
🛈 U.K. Citizens **U.K. Passport Service** ☎ 0870/521-0410 ⊕ www.passport.gov.uk.
🛈 U.S. Citizens **National Passport Information Center** ☎ 900/225-5674 or 900/225-7778 TTY (calls are 55¢ per minute for automated service or $1.50 per minute for operator service), 888/362-8668 or 888/498-3648 TTY (calls are $5.50 each) ⊕ www.travel.state.gov.

SENIOR-CITIZEN TRAVEL

Seniors over 60 are entitled to discount tickets (often as much as 50% off) on buses, trains, and ferries throughout Scandinavia, as well as reductions on special City Cards. Eurail offers discounts on Scanrail and Eurail train passes (⇨ Train Travel).

To qualify for age-related discounts, mention your senior-citizen status up front when booking hotel reservations (not when checking out) and before you're seated in restaurants (not when paying the bill). Be sure to have identification on hand. When renting a car, ask about promotional car-rental discounts, which can be cheaper than senior-citizen rates.

🛈 Educational Programs **Elderhostel** ✉ 11 Ave. de Lafayette, Boston, MA 02111-1746 ☎ 877/426-8056, 978/323-4141 international callers, 877/426-2167 TTY 🖷 877/426-2166 ⊕ www.elderhostel.org.

SPORTS & OUTDOORS

FISHING

Licenses are required for fishing along the coasts; requirements vary from one area to another for fishing in lakes, streams, and the ocean. Licenses cost about Dkr 100 for a year, Dkr 75 for a week, and Dkr 25 for a day, and you can buy them at any post office. Remember—it is illegal to fish within 1,650 feet of the mouth of a stream. Contact the Danish Tourist Board for more information.

🚹 **Danish Tourist Board** ✉ Vesterbrog. 6D, Vesterbro, DK-1620 Copenhagen ☎ 33/11-14-15 🖷 33/93-14-15 ⊕ www.visitdenmark.dk.

GOLF

Danish golf courses can be a real challenge, with plenty of water, roughs that live up to their name, and wind that is often a factor. Due to environmental controls, chemical fertilization is prohibited, so greens tend to be flatter with fewer breaks. Motorized riding carts are prohibited for general use, though most courses have one on hand for anyone with (documented) ambulatory problems.

Danish golf courses are open to any player who is a members of a certified golf club or has a valid handicap card. When entering a clubhouse to pay a greens fee, you will be asked to present documentation of membership in a club or a card stating your handicap. This can present a problem for Americans, many of whom are unfamiliar with this system and can produce no such evidence. The Danes are generally flexible when a golfer doesn't have a card, but it's wise to have some sort of documentation handy just in case.

🚹 **Dansk Golf Union** ✉ Brøndby Stadium 20, DK-2605 Brøndby ☎ 43/26-27-00 🖷 43/26-27-01 ⊕ www.dgu-golf.dk.

STUDENTS IN DENMARK

🚹 **I.D.s & Services STA Travel** ✉ 10 Downing St., New York, NY 10014 ☎ 212/627-3111, 800/777-0112 24-hr service center 🖷 212/627-3387 ⊕ www.sta.com. **Travel Cuts** ✉ 187 College St., Toronto, Ontario M5T 1P7, Canada ☎ 800/592-2887 in the U.S., 416/979-2406 or 866/246-9762 in Canada 🖷 416/979-8167 ⊕ www.travelcuts.com. **Ungdomsinformationen** (Young Information) ✉ Rådhusstræde 13, DK-1466, Copenhagen ☎ 33/73-06-50 🖷 33/73-06-49 ⊕ www.ui.dk.

TAXES

All hotel, restaurant, and departure taxes and V.A.T. (what the Danes call *moms*) are automatically included in prices.

VALUE-ADDED TAX

V.A.T. is 25%; non-EU citizens can obtain an 18% refund. The more than 1,500 shops that participate in the tax-free scheme have a white TAX FREE sticker on their windows. Purchases must be at least Dkr 300 per store and must be sealed and unused in Denmark. At the shop, you'll be asked to fill out a form and show your passport. The form can then be turned in at any airport or ferry customs desk, where you can choose a cash or charge-card credit. Keep all your receipts and tags; occasionally customs authorities do ask to see purchases, so pack them where they will be accessible.

When making a purchase, **ask for a V.A.T. refund form** and find out whether the merchant gives refunds—not all stores do, nor are they required to. Have the form stamped like any customs form by customs officials when you leave the country or, if you're visiting several European Union countries, when you leave the EU. Be ready to show customs officials what you've bought (pack purchases together, in your carry-on luggage); budget extra time for this. After you're through passport control, take the form to a refund-service counter for an on-the-spot refund, or mail it back to the store or a refund service after you arrive home.

A refund service can save you some hassle, for a fee. Global Refund is a Europe-wide service with 190,000 affiliated stores and more than 700 refund counters—located at every major airport and border crossing. Its refund form is called a Tax Free Check. The service issues refunds in the form of cash, check, or credit-card adjustment, minus a processing fee. If you don't have time to wait at the refund counter, you can mail in the form instead.

🚹 **V.A.T. Refunds Denmark Global Refund** ✉ Alléen 84, 1st floor, DK-2770 Kastrup ☎ 32/52-55-66 🖷 32/52-55-61. **Global Refund** ✉ 99 Main St., Suite 307, Nyack, NY 10960 ☎ 800/566-9828 🖷 845/348-1549 ⊕ www.globalrefund.com.

TELEPHONES

Telephone exchanges throughout Denmark were changed over the past couple of years. If you hear a recorded message or three loud beeps, chances are the number you are trying to reach has been changed.

Contact the main Danish operator, TDC, for current numbers.

Denmark, like most European countries, has a different cellular-phone switching system from the one used in North America. Newer phones can handle both technologies; check with the dealer where you purchased your phone to see if it can work on the European system. If all else fails, several companies rent cellular phones to tourists. Contact local tourist offices for details.

COUNTRY CODE

The country code for Denmark is 45.

DIRECTORY & OPERATOR ASSISTANCE

Most operators speak English. For national directory assistance, dial 118; for an international operator, dial 113; for a directory-assisted international call, dial 115. You can reach U.S. operators by dialing local access codes.

INTERNATIONAL CALLS

Dial 00, then the country code (1 for the United States and Canada, 44 for Great Britain), the area code, and the number. It's very expensive to call or fax from hotels, although the regional phone companies offer a discount after 7:30 PM. You can save a lot on the price of calls by purchasing a country-specific telephone card from any post office or one of the many kiosks and groceries in Copenhagen's Vesterbro and Nørrebro neighborhoods.

LOCAL CALLS

Phones accept 1-, 2-, 5-, 10-, and 20-kroner coins. Pick up the receiver, dial the number, always including the area code, and wait until the party answers; then deposit the coins. You have roughly a minute per krone; on some phones you can make another call on the same payment if your time has not run out. When it does, you will hear a beep and your call will be disconnected unless you deposit another coin. Coin-operated phones are becoming increasingly rare; it is cheaper and less frustrating to buy a local phone card from a kiosk.

Dial the eight-digit number for calls anywhere within the country. For calls to the Faroe Islands (298) and Greenland (299),

dial 00, then the three-digit code, then the five-digit number.

LONG-DISTANCE SERVICES

AT&T, MCI, and Sprint access codes make calling long-distance relatively convenient, but you may find the local access number blocked in many hotel rooms. First ask the hotel operator to connect you. If the hotel operator balks, ask for an international operator, or dial the international operator yourself. One way to improve your odds of getting connected to your long-distance carrier is to travel with more than one company's calling card (a hotel may block Sprint, for example, but not MCI). If all else fails, call from a pay phone.

Access Codes **AT&T USADirect** ☎ 800/10010 ⊕ www.travel.att.com. **World Phone** ☎ 800/10022 ⊕ www.mci.com. **Sprint Global One** ☎ 800/10877 ⊕ www.sprint.com.

TIME

Denmark is one hour ahead of Greenwich Mean Time (GMT) and six hours ahead of Eastern Standard Time (EST). All of Europe goes over to Daylight Savings Time from March to October, and during this time Denmark is two hours ahead of GMT (though still one hour ahead of London).

TIPPING

It has long been held that the egalitarian Danes do not expect to be tipped. This is often the case, but most people do tip and those who receive tips appreciate them. Service is included in hotel bills, but when paying at bars or restaurants a token tip is the general rule of thumb. The same holds true for taxis—if a bill comes to Dkr 58, most people will give the driver Dkr 60. If the driver is extremely friendly or helpful, tip more at your own discretion. Hotel porters expect about Dkr 5 per bag.

TOURS & PACKAGES

Because everything is prearranged on a prepackaged tour or independent vacation, you spend less time planning—and often get it all at a good price. For information on excursions and tours, call the Danish Tourist Board, Copenhagen Excursions, or Auto–Paaske. For organized tours of Greenland, *see* Greenland A to Z *in* Chapter 7.

Auto-Paaske ⊠ Yderlandsvej 2-8, Amager, DK-2300 Copenhagen ☎ 32/66-00-00 ⎙ 32/66-00-25 ⊕ www.auto-paaske.dk. **Copenhagen Excursions** ⊠ Rådhuspl. 57, Downtown, DK-1550 Copenhagen ☎ 32/54-06-06 ⎙ 32/57-49-05 ⊕ www.cex.dk. **Danish Tourist Board** ⊠ Vesterbrog. 6D, Vesterbro, DK-1620 Copenhagen ☎ 33/11-14-15 ⎙ 33/93-14-15 ⊕ www.visitdenmark.dk.

BIKE TOURS

Copenhagen-based BikeDenmark combines the flexibility of individual tours with the security of an organized outing. Choose from seven preplanned 5- to 10-day tours, which include bikes, maps, two fine meals per day, hotel accommodations, and hotel-to-hotel baggage transfers. BikeDenmark tours can be booked directly by fax, via their Web site, or through any travel agency below. Many U.S. tour companies can arrange booking. Try Borton Oversees, Nordique Tours, ScanAm World Tours, or Gerhard's Bicycle Odysseys.

Bike and Sea also leads biking tours through southern Jylland, Fyn, and southern Sjælland.

Bike and Sea ⊠ Svendborgvej 83-85, DK-5260 Odense ☎ 66/13-13-37 ⎙ 66/13-13-38 ⊕ www.bikeandsea-denmark.com. **BikeDenmark** ⊠ Olaf Poulsens Allé 1A, DK-3480 Fredensborg ☎ 48/48-58-00 ⎙ 48/48-59-00 ⊕ www.bikedenmark.com. **Borton Overseas** ⊠ 5412 Lyndale Ave. S, Minneapolis, MN 55419 ☎ 612/822-4640 or 800/843-0602 ⎙ 612/822-4755 ⊕ www.bortonoverseas.com. **Gerhard's Bicycle Odysseys** ⊠ Box 757, Portland, OR, 97207 ☎ 800/966-2402 ⎙ 503/223-5901 ⊕ www.since1974.com. **Nordique Tours Norvista** ☎ 310/645-7527 or 800/995-7997 ⎙ 310/645-1071 ⊕ www.nordiquetours.com. **ScanAm World Tours** ⊠ 108 N. Main St., Cranbury, NJ 08512 ☎ 800/545-2204 (toll free) ⎙ 609/655-1622 ⊕ www.scandinaviantravel.com.

TRAIN TRAVEL

Trains within Europe are well connected to Denmark, with Copenhagen serving as the main hub; however, it's often not much cheaper than flying, especially if you make your arrangements from the United States. Scanrail Passes offer discounts on train, ferry, and car transportation in Denmark, Finland, Sweden, and Norway. EurailPasses, purchased only in the United States, are accepted by the Danish State Railways and on some ferries operated by DSB.

DSB and a few private companies cover the country with a dense network of services, supplemented by buses in remote areas. Hourly intercity trains connect the main towns in Jylland and Fyn with Copenhagen and Sjælland, using high-speed diesels, called IC-3s, on the most important stretches. All these trains make one-hour crossings of the Great Belt Bridge. You can reserve seats (for an extra Dkr 15) on intercity trains, and you *must* have a reservation if you plan to cross the Great Belt. Buy tickets at stations. From London, the transit takes 18 hours, including ferry. Call the British Rail European Travel Center or Wasteels for information.

CUTTING COSTS

The ScanRail pass, which affords unlimited train travel throughout Denmark, Finland, Norway, and Sweden and restricted ferry passage in and beyond Scandinavia, comes in various denominations: five days of travel within 15 days ($249 first class, $187 second class); 10 days within a month ($400 first class, $301 second class); or 21 days unlimited use ($452 first class, $348 second class).

For car and train travel, consider the Scanrail 'n' Drive Pass: over 15 days you can get five days of unlimited train travel and two days of car rental (and a choice of three car categories) with unlimited mileage in Denmark, Norway, and Sweden. You can purchase extra car-rental days and choose from first- or second-class train travel. Individual rates for two adults traveling together (compact car $385 first-class/$308 second-class) are considerably lower (about 25%) than for single adults; the third or fourth person sharing the car only needs to purchase a Scanrail pass.

In the United States, call Rail Europe, Nordic Saga Tours, ScanAm Tours, Passage Tours, or DER Travel Services for rail passes. You can also buy the ScanRail Pass at the train stations in most major cities, including Copenhagen, Odense, and Århus. But no matter where you get it, various discounts are offered to holders of the pass by hotel chains and other organizations; ask DER, Rail Europe, or your travel agent for details. The ScanRail Pass and Interail and Eurail passes are also valid on all DSB trains. Compare prices at www.scanrail.com before you leave home.

Call Arriva for train travel in central and northern Jutland, or the DSB travel office for the rest of the country.

🚂 Train Information **Arriva** ☎ 72/13-96-00 ⊕ www.arriva.dk. **DSB Information** ☎ 70/13-14-15 ⊕ www.dsb.dk.

🚂 Where to Buy Rail Passes **DER Travel Services** ✉ 9501 W. Devon Ave., Rosemont, IL 60018 ☎ 800/782-2424 🖷 888/712-5727 ⊕ www.der.com. **Nordic Saga Tours** ✉ 303 5th Avenue S., Suite 109, Edmonds, WA 98020 ☎ 800/840-6449 or 425/673-4800 🖷 425/673-2600 ⊕ www.nordicsaga.com. **Passage Tours** ✉ 239 Commercial Blvd., Fort Lauderdale, FL 33308 ☎ 954/776-7188 🖷 954/776-7070 ⊕ www.passagetours.com. **Rail Europe** ☎ 800/438-7245 or 877/257-2887 in the U.S., 800/361-7245 in Canada ⊕ www.raileurope.com. **ScanAm World Tours** ✉ 108 N. Main St., Cranbury, NJ 08512 ☎ 800/545-2204 🖷 609/655-1622 ⊕ www.scandinaviantravel.com. **Wasteels** ✉ Skoubog. 6, Downtown, DK-1158 Copenhagen ☎ 33/14-46-33 🖷 33/14-08-65 ⊕ www.wasteels.dk.

TRAVEL AGENCIES

A good travel agent puts your needs first. Look for an agency that has been in business at least five years, emphasizes customer service, and has someone on staff who specializes in your destination. In addition, **make sure the agency belongs to a professional trade organization.** The American Society of Travel Agents (ASTA)—the largest and most influential in the field with more than 20,000 members in some 140 countries—maintains and enforces a strict code of ethics and will step in to help mediate any agent-client disputes involving ASTA members if necessary. ASTA (whose motto is "Without a travel agent, you're on your own") also maintains a Web site that includes a directory of agents. (If a travel agency is also acting as your tour operator, *see* Buyer Beware *in* Tours and Packages.)

🛈 Local Agent Referrals **American Society of Travel Agents (ASTA)** ✉ 1101 King St., Suite 200, Alexandria, VA 22314 ☎ 703/739-2782 or 800/965-2782 24-hr hot line 🖷 703/739-3268 ⊕ www.astanet.com. **Association of British Travel Agents** ✉ 68-71 Newman St., London W1T 3AH ☎ 020/7637-2444 🖷 020/7637-0713 ⊕ www.abta.com. **Association of Canadian Travel Agencies** ✉ 130 Albert St., Suite 1705, Ottawa, Ontario K1P 5G4 ☎ 613/237-3657 🖷 613/237-7052 ⊕ www.acta.ca. **Australian Federation of Travel Agents** ✉ Level 3, 309

Pitt St., Sydney, NSW 2000 ☎ 02/9264-3299 🖷 02/9264-1085 ⊕ www.afta.com.au. **Travel Agents' Association of New Zealand** ✉ Level 5, Tourism and Travel House, 79 Boulcott St., Box 1888, Wellington 6001 ☎ 04/499-0104 🖷 04/499-0786 ⊕ www.taanz.org.nz.

VISITOR INFORMATION

Learn more about foreign destinations by checking government-issued travel advisories and country information. For a broader picture, consider advisory information from more than one country.

🛈 Tourist Information **Danish Tourist Board** ✉ 655 3rd Ave., New York, NY 10017 ☎ 212/885-9700 🖷 212/885-9726 ✉ 55 Sloane St., London SW1X 9SY ☎ 44/20-7259-5959 🖷 44/20-7259-5955 ✉ Level 4, 81 York St. Sydney NSW 2000 ☎ 61/2-9262-5832 🖷 61/2-9290-1981 ⊕ www.visitdenmark.com. **Danmarks Turistråd** (Danish Tourist Board) ✉ Vesterbrog. 6D, Vesterbro, DK-1620 Copenhagen ☎ 33/11-14-15 🖷 33/93-14-16.

🛈 Government Advisories **U.S. Department of State** ✉ Overseas Citizens Services Office, Room 4811, 2201 C St. NW, Washington, DC 20520 ☎ 202/647-5225 interactive hot line or 888/407-4747 ⊕ www.travel.state.gov; enclose a cover letter with your request and a business-size SASE. **Consular Affairs Bureau of Canada** ☎ 800/267-6788 or 613/944-6788 ⊕ www.voyage.gc.ca. **U.K. Foreign and Commonwealth Office** ✉ Travel Advice Unit, Consular Division, Old Admiralty Building, London SW1A 2PA ☎ 020/7008-0232 or 020/7008-0233 ⊕ www.fco.gov.uk/travel. **Australian Department of Foreign Affairs and Trade** ☎ 02/6261-1299 Consular Travel Advice Faxback Service ⊕ www.dfat.gov.au. **New Zealand Ministry of Foreign Affairs and Trade** ☎ 04/439-8000 ⊕ www.mft.govt.nz.

WEB SITES

Do check out the World Wide Web when planning your trip. You'll find everything from weather forecasts to virtual tours of famous cities. Be sure to visit Fodors.com (⊕ www.fodors.com), a complete travel-planning site. You can research prices and book plane tickets, hotel rooms, rental cars, vacation packages, and more. In addition, you can post your pressing questions in the Travel Talk section. Other planning tools include a currency converter and weather reports, and there are loads of links to travel resources.

COPENHAGEN

1

FODOR'S CHOICE

Christiansborg Slot

D'Angleterre, *hotel*

Ida Davidsen, *restaurant*

Kommandanten, *restaurant*

Ny Carlsberg Glyptotek, *museum*

Ordrupgaard, *museum in Charlottenlund*

Radisson SAS Royal, *hotel*

Reinwalds, *restaurant*

Riz Raz, *restaurant*

Rosenborg Slot

Skovshoved, *hotel in Charlottenlund*

Tivoli

Told & Snaps, *restaurant*

HIGHLY RECOMMENDED

Assistens Kirkegård, *cemetery*

Christiania, *commune*

Dragør, *seaside village*

Dyrehaven, *park in Klampenborg*

Nationalmuseet

Nyhavn, *harborfront neighborhood*

Rundetårn, *tower and art gallery*

Strøget, *pedestrian thoroughfare*

Many other great hotels and restaurants enliven this area. For other favorites, look for the black stars as you read this chapter.

Updated by
Eduardo López
de Luzuriaga

COPENHAGEN—KØBENHAVN IN DANISH—has no glittering skylines, few killer views, and only a handful of meager skyscrapers. Bicycles glide alongside manageable traffic at a pace that's utterly human. The early-morning air in the pedestrian streets of the city's core, Strøget, is redolent of freshly baked bread and soap-scrubbed storefronts. If there's such a thing as a cozy city, this is it.

Extremely livable and relatively calm, Copenhagen is not a microcosm of Denmark, but rather a cosmopolitan city with an identity of its own. Denmark's political, cultural, and financial capital is inhabited by 1.5 million Danes, a fifth of the national population, as well as a growing immigrant community. Filled with museums, restaurants, cafés, and lively nightlife, the city has its greatest resource in its spirited inhabitants. The imaginative, unconventional, and affable Copenhageners exude an egalitarian philosophy that embraces nearly all lifestyles and leanings.

The town was a fishing colony until 1157, when Valdemar the Great gave it to Bishop Absalon, who built a castle on what is now Christiansborg. It grew as a center on the Baltic trade route and became known as *købmændenes havn* (merchants' harbor) and eventually København. In the 15th century it became the royal residence and the capital of Norway and Sweden. A hundred years later, Christian IV, a Renaissance king obsessed with fine architecture, began a building boom that crowned the city with towers and castles, many of which still stand. They are almost all that remain of the city's 800-year history; much of Copenhagen was destroyed by two major fires in the 18th century and by British bombing during the Napoleonic Wars.

Despite a tumultuous history, Copenhagen survives as the liveliest Scandinavian capital. With its backdrop of copper towers and crooked rooftops, the venerable city is amused by playful street musicians and performers, soothed by one of the highest standards of living in the world, and spangled by the thousand lights and gardens of Tivoli.

EXPLORING COPENHAGEN

The sites in Copenhagen rarely jump out at you; the city's elegant spires and tangle of cobbled one-way streets are best sought out on foot at an unhurried pace. Excellent bus and train systems can come to the rescue of weary legs. The city is not divided into single-purpose districts; people work, play, shop, and live throughout the central core of this multilayered, densely populated capital.

Be it sea or canal, water surrounds Copenhagen. A network of bridges and drawbridges connects the two main islands—Sjælland and Amager—on which Copenhagen is built. The seafaring atmosphere is indelible, especially around Nyhavn and Christianshavn.

Some Copenhagen sights, especially churches, keep short hours, particularly in the fall and winter. It's a good idea to call directly or check with the tourist offices to confirm opening times.

Rådhus Pladsen, Christiansborg Slot & Strøget

In 1728 and again in 1795, fires broke out in central Copenhagen with devastating effect. Disaster struck again in 1807, when the British fleet, under the command of Admiral Gambier, unleashed a heavy bombardment on the city and destroyed many of its oldest and most beautiful buildings. The attack also inflicted hundreds of civilian casualties. These events still shape modern Copenhagen, which was rebuilt with

When you arrive in the city, get settled in your hotel, turn in for a good night's sleep, and get yourself ready for some serious walking. Copenhagen maps out perfectly for the pedestrian, with nearly all the main attractions less than a half hour's walk from Christiansborg Slot, at the center of downtown. If you're in town for an extended visit or would rather save your legs, the subway, bus, and suburban S-train networks can take you wherever you want to go.

If you have 3 days

Begin your first day at Rådhus Pladsen (City Hall Square) and follow Strøget, a pedestrian-only avenue, toward Nyhavn. Leave Strøget briefly at Amager Torv to visit the parliament building, Christiansborg; then, return to Strøget and make your way to the waterfront, all the while training an occasional glance at the shop windows in case anything catches your eye. Nyhavn is a good place to rest and refuel. You could take this opportunity to sample a classic Danish lunch of smørrebrød washed down with beer and *snaps* (schnapps). After lunch, head up to the royal palace of Amalienborg and take some time to explore the Bredgade area and find your way back to your hotel. If the weather is nice, the evening can be spent in Tivoli, but have your dinner outside the park to avoid the exorbitant prices. Early on the second day, take a boat excursion to see the city and its famed *Den Lille Havfrue* (The Little Mermaid) statue from the harbor. If you would prefer to get off and take pictures at the statue, make sure to take a DFDS sightseeing boat. In the afternoon, cross the inner harbor to the neighborhood of Christianshavn for a stroll along its canals toward Vor Frelsers Kirken (Church of Our Savior), where you can have a great aerial view of Copenhagen from the unique spire. This route leads you past the alternative compound of Christiania—settled by hippies in the '70s—and beyond to the exclusive neighborhood of Holmen. The third day of your stay ought to be spent exploring the outlying Vesterbro neighborhood, with its cafés and shops. For art-lovers, the Ny Carlsberg Glyptotek would make a good several-hour detour on the way down Vesterbrogade.

If you have 7 days

Spend the first three days of your week as outlined above. The fourth and fifth days of your itinerary should be used to visit a few more of Copenhagen's fine museums. Among the best remaining are Rosenborg Slot and the Dansk Design Center, neither of which should be missed. A morning visit to Rosenborg Slot can be followed by an afternoon tour of the botanical gardens and a dinner in Nørrebro. Alternatively, you could head north from the castle and while away the afternoon along the paths and moats of Churchill Park, grabbing your evening meal in Østerbro. The final two days should be spent on day trips outside of the city proper. A day in Charlottenlund should begin with the astounding French impressionism collection at the Ordrupgaard, which can be followed with a snack at the adjacent café and a few hours at the town's pleasant beach, which is considerably less crowded during the week. Use the final day to skip town again for the verdant Deer Park in Klampenborg, or the seaside town of Dragør.

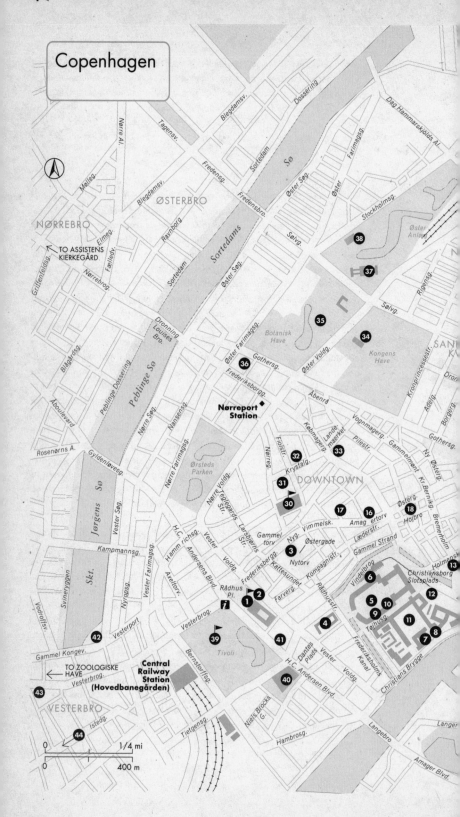

Copenhagen

Rådhus Pladsen, Christiansborg Slot & Strøget ▼

Børsen 12
Christiansborg Slot 5
Dansk Arkitektur Center 15
Dansk Jødisk Museum 8
Det Kongelige Bibliotek 7
Helligaandskirken 17
Holmens Kirke 13
Kongelige Stald 10
Lurblæserne 2
Nationalmuseet 4
Nikolaj Kirken 18
Rådhus 1
Strøget 3
Teatermuseet 9
Thorvaldsen Museum 6
Tøjhusmuseet 11
Vor Frelsers Kirken 14
W. Ø. Larsens Tobakmuseet ...16

Around Amalienborg & Points North ▼

Amalienborg 23
Charlottenborg 21
Den Lille Havfrue 28
Det Kongelige Teater 20
Frihedsmuseet 26
Gefion Springvandet 29
Kastellet 27
Kongelige Teater 20
Kongens Nytorv 19
Kunstindustrimuseet 25
Marmorkirken 24
Nyhavn 22

Northwest toward Nørrebro ▼

Arbejdermuseet 36
Botanisk Have 35
Den Hirschsprungske
Samling 38
Københavns Synagoge 32
Københavns Universitet 31
Rosenborg Slot 34
Rundetårn 33
Statens Museum for Kunst ...37
Vor Frue Kirken 30

In & Around Vesterbrogade ▼

Carlsberg Bryggeri 44
Dansk Design Center 41
Københavns Bymuseum 43
Ny Carlsberg Glyptotek 40
Tivoli 39
Tycho Brahe Planetarium 42

wide, curved-corner streets—making it easier for fire trucks to turn—and large, rectangular apartment buildings centered on courtyards. Arguably the liveliest area of the city, central Copenhagen is packed with shops, restaurants, businesses, and apartment buildings, as well as the crowning architectural achievements of Christian IV—all of it overflowing with Danes and visitors. Copenhagen's central spine consists of the five consecutive pedestrian strands known as Strøget and the surrounding tangle of roads and courtyards—less than a mile square in total. Across the capital's main harbor is the smaller, 17th-century Christianshavn. In the early 1600s, this area was mostly a series of shallows between land, which were eventually dammed. Today Christianshavn's colorful boats and postcard maritime character make it one of the toniest parts of town.

a good walk

The city's heart is the Rådhus Pladsen, home to the baroque-style **Rådhus** ① ▶ and its clock tower. On the east side of the square is the landmark **Lurblæserne** ②. Off the square's northeastern corner is Frederiksberggade, the first of the five pedestrian streets making up **Strøget** ③, Copenhagen's shopping district. Walk northeast past the cafés and trendy boutiques to the double square of Gammeltorv and Nytorv.

Down Rådhusstræde toward Frederiksholms Kanal, the **Nationalmuseet** ④ contains an amazing collection of Viking artifacts. Cross Frederiksholms Kanal to Christiansborg Slotsplads, a small atoll divided by the canal and dominated by the burly **Christiansborg Slot** ⑤. North of the castle is **Thorvaldsens Museum** ⑥, devoted to the works of one of Denmark's most important sculptors, Bertel Thorvaldsen. On the south end of Downtown is the three-story Romanesque **Kongelige Bibliotek** ⑦, edged by carefully tended gardens and tree-lined avenues. To the south, on the harbor side of the royal library, is its glass and granite annex, nicknamed the "Black Diamond." The newest addition to the library complex is the **Dansk Jødisk Museum** ⑧. Back on the south face of Christiansborg are the **Teatermuseet** ⑨ and the **Kongelige Stald** ⑩.

On the street that bears its name is the **Tøjhusmuseet** ⑪, and a few steps away is the architecturally marvelous **Børsen** ⑫ and the **Holmens Kirke** ⑬. To the southeast is **Christianshavn**, connected to downtown by the drawbridge Knippelsbro. Farther north, the former shipyard of Holmen is marked by expansive venues and several departments of the Københavns Universitet.

From nearly anywhere in the area, you can see the green-and-gold spire of **Vor Frelsers Kirken** ⑭. Northwest of the church, the **Dansk Arkitektur Center** ⑮ occupies a hulking old warehouse on Strandgade. Back across the Knippels Torvegade Bridge, about 1½ km (less than a mile) down Børsgade through Højbroplads, is Amagertorv, one of Strøget's five streets. Here stands **W. Ø. Larsens Tobakmuseet** ⑯, and farther west down the street is the 18th-century **Helligaandskirken** ⑰. On Strøget's Østergade, the massive spire of **Nikolaj Kirken** ⑱ looks many sizes too large for the tiny cobble streets below.

TIMING The walk itself takes about two hours. Typically, Christiansborg Slot and its ruins and the Nationalmuseet both take at least 1½ hours to see—even more for Viking fans. The hundreds of shops along Strøget are enticing, so plan extra shopping and café time—at least as much as your wallet can spare. Note that many attractions on this walk are closed Sunday or Monday, and some have odd hours; always call ahead or check with the tourist information office.

What to See

⑫ Børsen (Stock Exchange). This masterpiece of fantasy and architecture is the oldest stock exchange in Europe. The Børsen was built between 1619 and 1640, with the majority of construction in the 1620s. Christian IV commissioned the building in large part because he wanted to make Denmark the economic superpower and crossroads of Europe. Rumor has it that when it was being built, he was the one who twisted the dragons' tails on the spire that tops the building. When it was first opened, it was used as a sort of medieval mall, filled with shopping stalls. Though parts of the Børsen still operate as a stock exchange, the bulk of the building houses the Chamber of Commerce, and therefore it's open only to accredited members and brokers. ⊠ *Christiansborg Slotspl., Downtown.*

> **off the beaten path**
>
> ★ **CHRISTIANIA –** If you are nostalgic for 1960s counterculture, head to this anarchists' commune on Christianshavn. Founded in 1971, when students occupied army barracks, it is now a peaceful community of nonconformists who run a number of businesses, including a bike shop, bakery, rock-music club, and communal bathhouse. Wall cartoons preach drugs and peace, but the inhabitants are less fond of cameras—picture-taking is forbidden. ⊠ *Prinsesseg. and Bådsmandsstr., Christianshavn* ☎ *32/57–96–70 guided tours* ⊕ *www.christiania.org.*

⑤ Christiansborg Slot (Christiansborg Castle). Surrounded by canals on

Fodor's Choice

★ three sides, the massive granite castle is where the queen officially receives guests. From 1441 until the fire of 1795, it was used as the royal residence. Even though the first two castles on the site were burned, Christiansborg remains an impressive baroque compound, even by European standards. Free tours of the **Folketinget** (Parliament House; ☎ 33/37–55–00) are given Monday through Saturday from June to mid-August, as well as Sunday from July to mid-August; tours run Sunday to Friday from mid-August through September, and on weekdays from October through April. English-language groups embark at 2. At the **Kongelige Repræsantationlokaler** (Royal Reception Chambers; ☎ 33/92–64–92), you're asked to don slippers to protect the floors. Admission is Dkr 40; entry is via guided tour only. Tours are given daily May through September, and Tuesday, Thursday, and weekends from October through April; English tours are at 11 and 3. The **Højesteret** (Supreme Court), on the site of the city's first fortress, was built by Bishop Absalon in 1167. The guards at the entrance are knowledgeable and friendly; call them first to double-check the court's complicated opening hours.

While the castle was being rebuilt around 1900, the Nationalmuseet excavated the **ruins** (☎ 33/92–64–92) beneath it. The resulting dark, subterranean maze contains fascinating models and architectural relics. The ruins are open daily 9:30–3:30, May through September; and Tuesday, Thursday, and weekends the rest of the year. Admission is Dkr 20.

Wander around **Højbro Plads** and the delightful row of houses that borders the northern edge of Slotsholmen. The quays here were long ago Copenhagen's fish market, but today most fresh fish is transported directly from boats to the city's fish shops and supermarkets. However, one lone fisherwoman still hawks fresh fish, marinated herring, and eel in the early morning. She is the last fishmonger you'll see carrying on the tradition. ⊠ *Prins Jørgens Gård 1, Downtown* ☎ 33/63–27–50.

Christianshavn. Cobbled avenues, antique street lamps, and Left Bank charm make up one of the oldest neighborhoods in the city. Even the old system of earthworks—the best preserved of Copenhagen's original fortification walls—still exists. In the 17th century, Christian IV offered what were patches of partially flooded land for free, and with additional tax benefits; in return, takers would have to fill them in and construct sturdy buildings for trade, commerce, housing for the shipbuilding workers, and defense against sea attacks. Gentrified today, the area harbors restaurants, cafés, and shops, and its ramparts are edged with green areas and walking paths, making it the perfect neighborhood for an afternoon or evening amble. The central square, Christianshavn Torv, is where all activity emanates from, and Torvegade, a bustling shopping street, is the main thoroughfare. For a pleasant break, relax at one of the cafés along Wilders Canal, which streams through the heart of town.

⑮ Dansk Arkitektur Center. The Danish Architecture Center occupies an old wharfside warehouse built in 1880. The hulking structure fell into a state of disrepair after lying fallow for many years, but was rescued, renovated, and reopened in 1986. The center hosts rotating exhibitions that cover trends and trendsetters in Danish architecture and architectural design. ✉ *Strandg. 27B, Christianshavn* ☎ *32/57–19–30* ⊕ *www.dac. dk* ✉ *Dkr 30; exhibitions vary* ☉ *Mon.–Fri. 10–5.*

❽ Dansk Jødisk Museum (Danish Jewish Museum). At this writing, the museum, in a wing of the Royal Library is nearing completion of the first stage of construction. A date has not been set for the museum's opening. The site was designed by Daniel Libeskind, the architect behind the winning design proposal for the World Trade Center site in New York City. Along with a general overview of Jewish history in Denmark, the museum will give extensive coverage to the Danish resistance movement, whose work during World War II helped bring nearly all of Denmark's 7,000 Jews to safety in Sweden. ✉ *Købmagerg. 5, Downtown* ☎ *33/11–22–18* ⊕ *www.jewmus.dk* ☉ *Hours to be determined.*

❼ Det Kongelige Bibliotek (Royal Library). The Royal Library houses the country's largest collection of books, newspapers, and manuscripts. Among the more than 2 million volumes are accounts of Viking journeys to America and Greenland and original manuscripts by Hans Christian Andersen and Karen Blixen (Isak Dinesen). If you happen to be in the area, ramble around the statue of philosopher Søren Kierkegaard (1813–55), the formal gardens, and tree-lined avenues surrounding the scholarly building. The library's massive glass-and-granite annex, called the Black Diamond, looms between the main building and the waterfront. The Black Diamond hosts temporary historical exhibits that often feature books, manuscripts, and artifacts culled from the library's extensive holdings. The **National Museum of Photography,** also housed in the Black Diamond, contains a far-reaching collection of more than 25,000 Danish and international photographs, from which temporary exhibits display selections. ✉ *Søren Kierkegaards Pl. 1, Downtown* ☎ *33/47–47–47* ⊕ *www.kb.dk* ✉ *Library free, admission varies for temporary exhibits* ☉ *Library Mon.–Fri. 10–7, Sat. 10–2; Black Diamond Mon.–Sat. 10–5.*

⑰ Helligaandskirken (Church of the Holy Ghost). This 18th-century church was founded as an abbey of the Holy Ghost and is still one of the city's oldest places of worship. Its choir contains a font by the sculptor Thorvaldsen, and more-modern art is found in the large exhibition room—once a hospital—that faces Strøget. ✉ *Niels Hemmingseng. 5, Amagertorv section, Downtown* ☎ *33/18–16–45* ⊕ *www.helligaandskirken.dk* ✉ *Free* ☉ *Weekdays 9–1, Sat. 10–noon.*

off the beaten path

HOLMEN – Previously isolated from central Copenhagen, this former navy base just north of Christianshavn produced ships and ammunition until the 1980s. It was formally opened as the site of the 1995 United Nations Summit on Human Development and played an important role as a cultural area during Copenhagen's 1996 reign as the Cultural Capital of Europe. Today, among its several cultural venues is the city's biggest performance space, the Torpedo Hall, where torpedoes were actually assembled. You'll also find the Danish Art Academy's Architecture School, the National Theater School, the Rhythmic Music Conservatory, and the Danish Film School, which all host special activities.

❸ **Holmens Kirke** (Islet's Church). Two of the country's most revered naval heroes are buried here: Niels Juel crushed the Swedish fleet at Køge in 1677, and Peder Tordenskjold defeated Charles XII of Sweden during the Great Northern War in the early 18th century. ⊠ *Holmenskanal, Christianshavn* ☎ *33/11–37–40* ⊕ *www.holmenskirke.dk* ⊠ *Free* ⊙ *Mon.–Fri. 9–2, Sat. 9–noon, Sun. during services.*

need a break?

Øieblikket Espresso Bar m.m. (⊠ Søren Kierkegaards Pl. 1, Downtown ☎ 33/47–49–50) operates out of a prime corner on the ground floor of the Royal Library's Black Diamond. The "m.m" in the name means "and more." It's named after a literary journal to which philosopher Søren Kierkegaard once contributed—and you too may be inspired to wax poetic as you gaze out over the harbor and bask in the sunlight streaming through the soaring glass walls. In summer, the café sets up outdoor tables. When the summer days turn nippy, you can stay snug indoors, while enjoying the illusion of being outside, thanks to the natural light that floods in at all angles. The simple fare includes croissants, brownies, and sandwiches made on fluffy round buns.

❿ **Kongelige Stald** (Royal Stables). Between 9 and noon, time seems to stand still while riders, elegantly clad in breeches and jackets, exercise the horses. The vehicles, including coaches and carriages, and harnesses on display have been used by the Danish monarchy from 1778 to the present. ⊠ *Christiansborg Ridebane 12, Downtown* ☎ *33/40–26–77* ⊠ *Dkr 10* ⊙ *May–Sept., Fri.–Sun. 2–4; Oct.–Apr., weekends 2–4.*

❷ **Lurblæserne** (Lur Blower Column). Topped by two Vikings blowing an ancient trumpet called a *lur,* this column displays a good deal of artistic license—the lur dates from the Bronze Age, 1500 BC, whereas the Vikings lived a mere 1,000 years ago. City tours often start at this important landmark, which was erected in 1914. ⊠ *East side of Rådhus Pl., Downtown.*

★ ☾ ❹ **Nationalmuseet** (National Museum). An 18th-century royal residence, peaked by massive overhead windows, has contained—since the 1930s—what is regarded as one of the best national museums in Europe. Extensive permanent exhibits chronicle Danish cultural history from prehistoric to modern times—included is one of the largest collections of Stone Age tools in the world—and Egyptian, Greek, and Roman antiquities are on display. The children's museum, with replicas of period clothing and all sorts of touchable items, transforms history into something to which children under age 12 can relate. ⊠ *Ny Vesterg. 10, Downtown* ☎ *33/13–44–11* ⊕ *www.natmus.dk* ⊠ *Dkr 50; free Wed.* ⊙ *Tues.–Sun. 10–5.*

⓲ Nikolaj Kirken (Nicholas Church). Though the green spire of the imposing church—named for the patron saint of seafarers—appears as old as the surrounding medieval streets, it is actually relatively young. The current building was finished in 1914; the previous structure, which dated from the 13th century, was destroyed by the 1795 fire. Today the church is a contemporary art gallery and exhibition center that often shows experimental work. ✉ *Nikolaj Pl. 10, Downtown* ☎ *33/93–16–26* ⊕ *www. nikolaj-ccac.dk* ✉ *Dkr 20; free Wed.* ☉ *Daily noon—5.*

need a break? **Café Nikolaj** (✉ Nikolajpl., Downtown ☎ 33/93–16–26), inside Nikolaj Kirken, is a reliable, inexpensive café with good pastries and light meals. It's open noon to 3 for lunch and until 5 for cakes and drinks. From June through August, you can eat on the open terrace.

▶ ❶ Rådhus (City Hall). Completed in 1905, the mock-Renaissance building dominates **Rådhus Pladsen** (City Hall Square), the hub of Copenhagen's commercial district. Architect Martin Nyrop's creation was popular from the start, perhaps because he envisioned that it should give "gaiety to everyday life and spontaneous pleasure to all . . ." A statue of Copenhagen's 12th-century founder, Bishop Absalon, sits atop the main entrance.

Besides being an important ceremonial meeting place for Danish VIPs, the intricately decorated Rådhus contains the first **World Clock.** The multidial, superaccurate astronomical timepiece has a 570,000-year calendar and took inventor Jens Olsen 27 years to complete before it was put into action in 1955. If you're feeling energetic, take a guided tour up the 350-foot bell tower for the panoramic, but not particularly inspiring, view.

The modern glass and gray-steel **bus terminal** flanking the square's northwest side has French granite floors, pear-tree-wood shelving, and underground marble bathrooms. The $2.8 million creation proved so architecturally contentious—more for its placement than for its design—that there was serious discussion of moving it.

Look up to see one of the city's most charming bronze sculptures, created by the Danish artist E. Utzon Frank in 1936. Diagonally across Rådhus Pladsen, atop a corner office building, are a **neon thermometer** and a **gilded barometer.** On sunny days there's a golden sculpture of a girl on a bicycle; come rain, a girl with an umbrella appears. ✉ *Rådhus Pl., Downtown* ☎ *33/66–33–66* ✉ *Tower tours Dkr 20* ☉ *Rådhus Mon.–Fri. 8–5. Tours Oct.–May, Mon.–Sat. at noon; June–Sept., Mon.–Fri. 10, noon, and 2. Sat. at noon.*

need a break? **Vandkunsten** (✉ Rådhusstr. 17, Downtown ☎ 33/13–90–40) is a mom-and-pop joint that makes great Italian-inspired sandwiches and salads, and they offer free coffee while you wait. The shop is tiny, but the efficient service keeps customers moving. There is only one table inside and it's usually surrounded by customers; so long as the weather is nice, get something to go and seek out a sunny spot for munching.

★ ❸ Strøget. Though it is referred to by one name, the city's pedestrian spine, pronounced *Stroy*-et, is actually a series of five streets: Frederiksberggade, Nygade, Vimmelskaftet, Amagertorv, and Østergade. By mid-morning, particularly on Saturday, it is congested with people, baby strollers, and street performers. Past the swank and trendy, and sometimes flashy and trashy, boutiques of **Frederiksberggade** is the double square of **Gammeltorv**

(Old Square) and **Nytorv** (New Square), in summer often crowded with street vendors selling cheap jewelry.

In 1728 and again in 1795, much of Strøget was heavily damaged by fire. When rebuilding, the city fathers straightened and widened the streets. You can still see buildings from this reconstruction period, as well as a few that survived the fires.

In addition to shopping, you can enjoy Strøget for strolling, as hundreds do. Outside the posh fur and porcelain shops and bustling cafés and restaurants, the sidewalks have a festive street-fair atmosphere.

❾ Teatermuseet (Theater Museum). After you brush up on theater and ballet history, wander around the boxes, stage, and dressing rooms of the **Royal Court Theater** of 1767, which King Christian VII had built as the first court theater in Scandinavia. Tours can be arranged. ⊠ *Christiansborg Ridebane 10/18, Downtown* ☎ *33/11–51–76* ⊕ *www.teatermuseet.dk* ☒ *Dkr 30* ☉ *Wed. 2–4, weekends noon–4.*

❻ Thorvaldsens Museum. The 19th-century artist Bertel Thorvaldsen (1770–1844) is buried at the center of this museum in a simple, ivy-covered tomb. Strongly influenced by the statues and reliefs of classical antiquity, he is recognized as one of the world's greatest neoclassical artists, having completed commissions all over Europe. The museum, once a coach house to Christiansborg, now houses Thorvaldsen's interpretations of classical and mythological figures, and an extensive collection of paintings and drawings by other artists that Thorvaldsen assembled while living—for most of his life—in Rome. The outside frieze by Jørgen Sonne depicts the sculptor's triumphant return to Copenhagen after years abroad. ⊠ *Bertel Thorvaldsen Pl. 2, Downtown* ☎ *33/32–15–32* ⊕ *www.thorvaldsensmuseum.dk* ☒ *Dkr 20* ☉ *Tues.–Sun. 10–5.*

⓫ Tøjhusmuseet (Royal Danish Arsenal Museum). This Renaissance structure—built by King Christian IV and one of central Copenhagen's oldest—contains impressive displays of uniforms, weapons, and armor in a 600-foot-long arched hall. ⊠ *Tøjhusg. 3, Downtown* ☎ *33/11–60–37* ⊕ *www.thm.dk* ☒ *Dkr 40* ☉ *Tues.–Sun. noon–4.*

⓮ Vor Frelsers Kirken (Church of Our Savior). The green-and-gold spire of this baroque church has dominated the Christianshavn area since it was completed in 1752. Local legend has it that the staircase encircling it was built curling the wrong way around, and that when its architect, Laurids de Thurah, reached the top and realized what he'd done, he jumped. In this case, however, legend is erroneous: de Thurah died in his own bed in 1759. ⊠ *Skt. Annæg. 29, Christianshavn* ☎ *32/57–27–98* ⊕ *www.vorfrelserskirke.dk* ☉ *Apr.–Aug., daily 11–4:30; Sept.–Mar., daily 11–3:30* ☉ *Tower closed Nov.–Mar. and in inclement weather.*

⓰ W. Ø. Larsens Tobakmuseet (W. Ø. Larsens Tobacco Museum). The Tobacco Museum has a full-fledged collection of pipes made in every conceivable shape from every possible material. Look for the tiny pipe that's no bigger than an embroidery needle. There are also paintings, drawings, and an amazing array of smoking implements. ⊠ *Amagertorv 9, Downtown* ☎ *33/12–20–50* ☒ *Free* ☉ *Mon.–Thurs. 10–6, Fri. 10–7, Sat. 10–5.*

Around Amalienborg & Points North

The Sankt Annæ district of the city was dubbed New Copenhagen when King Christian IV began to expand the city northeastward in the 17th century, building Sankt Annæ Fort (now the Churchillsparken and

Kastellet) in the process. The district takes its name from the Sankt Annæ religious order, which valiantly staffed a 16th-century syphilis ward in the area.

North of Kongens Nytorv, the city becomes a fidgety grid of parks and wider boulevards pointing northwest across the canal toward upscale Østerbro—wreathed by manors commissioned by wealthy merchants and blue bloods. In the mid-1700s, King Frederik V donated parcels of this land to anyone who agreed to build from the work of architect Niels Eigtved, who also designed the Kongelige Theater. The jewel of this crown remains Amalienborg and its rococo mansions.

a good walk

At the end of Strøget, **Kongens Nytorv** ⑲ ▶ is flanked on its south side by the **Kongelige Teater** ⑳, and backed by **Charlottenborg** ㉑, which contains the Danish Academy of Fine Art (call to see if an exhibition has opened the castle to the public). The street leading southeast from Kongens Nytorv is **Nyhavn** ㉒, a onetime sailors' haunt and now a popular waterfront hub. From the south end of the harbor (and the north end of Havnegade) high-speed craft leave for Malmö, Sweden; further north, Kvæsthusbroen—at the end of Skt. Annæ Plads—is the quay for boats to Oslo, Norway, and Bornholm, Denmark; further north still, just before the perch of *The Little Mermaid,* ships depart for Swinoujscie, Poland.

West of the harbor front is the grand square called Skt. Annæ Plads. Perpendicular to the oblong square is Amaliegade, its wooden colonnade bordering the cobbled square of **Amalienborg** ㉓, the royal residence with a pleasant garden on its harbor side. Steps west from the square is Bredgade, where the baroque **Marmorkirken** ㉔ flaunts its Norwegian marble structure. Farther north off Bredgade is the rococo **Kunstindustrimuseet** ㉕. Continuing north on Bredgade (you can also take the more colorful, café-lined Store Kongensgade, just west), turn right onto Esplanaden and you'll see the enormously informative **Frihedsmuseet** ㉖. At the Churchillparken's entrance stands the English church, St. Albans. In the park's center, the **Kastellet** ㉗ serves as a reminder of the city's grim military history. At its eastern perimeter is Langelinie, a waterfront promenade with a view of Denmark's best-known pinup, *Den Lille Havfrue* ㉘. Wending your way back toward Esplanaden and the town center, you'll pass the **Gefion Springvandet** ㉙.

TIMING   This walk amid parks, gardens, canals, and building exteriors should take a full day. If the weather is nice, linger in the parks, especially the Kastellet and Amalienhaven, and plan on a long lunch at Nyhavn. The Kunstindustrimuseet merits about an hour, more if you plan on perusing the design books in the museum's well-stocked library. The Frihedsmuseet may require more time: its evocative portrait of Danish life during World War II intrigues even the most history-weary teens. Avoid taking this tour Monday, when some sites are closed.

What to See

㉓ **Amalienborg** (Amalia's Castle). The four identical rococo buildings occupying this square have housed the royals since 1784. The Christian VIII palace across from the Queen's residence houses the **Amalienborg Museum,** which displays the second part of the Royal Collection (the first is at Rosenborg Slot) and chronicles royal lifestyles between 1863 and 1947. Here you can view the study of King Christian IX (1818–1906) and the drawing room of his wife, Queen Louise. Rooms are packed with family gifts and regal baubles ranging from tacky knickknacks to Fabergé treasures, including a nephrite-and-ruby table clock, and a small costume collection.

THE DANISH ROYALS

THE EQUITABLE DANES may believe that excessive pride is best kept hidden, but ask about their Queen and this philosophy promptly flies out the window. The passion for Queen Margrethe II is infectious, and before long you may find yourself waving the Dannebrog flag along with the rest of them when the Queen passes through. Graceful and gregarious, Queen Margrethe II is the embodiment of the new Danish crown, a monarchy that is steeped in history yet decidedly modern in its outlook.

Denmark's royal lineage has its roots in the 10th-century Kingdom of Gorm the Old. His son, Harald Bluetooth, established the royal headquarters in Sjælland, where it remains to this day. Copenhagen's stately Amalienborg Slot has been the official royal residence since 1784. From here, Queen Margrethe reigns in a true Danish style marked by sociability, not stuffiness. Renowned for her informal charm, the Queen has fostered an open, familial relationship between the royal house and the Danish public. Queen Margrethe's nurturing role has evolved naturally in a country of Denmark's petite size and population. Though she lives in Copenhagen, the Queen is far from Sjælland-bound. She zips around Denmark as if it were the palace backyard, fulfilling her royal function with zeal. She frequently includes the Faroe Islands and Greenland on her meet-and-greet itineraries, no mean feat considering that Greenland is closer to the United States than to Denmark.

Margrethe wasn't always destined to be queen. When she was born in 1940, the law of succession was limited to sons, and it wasn't until 1953 that the law was ratified to include female ascension of the throne. Henceforth, she was groomed to become queen, and on her 18th birthday, the eldest daughter of King Frederik IX and Queen Ingrid, officially stepped into her position as heir apparent to the crown. She studied archaeology and political science both at home and abroad, at the Universities of Copenhagen, Århus, Cambridge, and the Sorbonne. In 1967, Margrethe married the French-born Prince Henrik, born a Count near Cahors, France.

Today's modern monarchy is perhaps best exemplified by what the Queen does when she takes off her crown. An accomplished artist and illustrator, the Queen designed the costumes for an acclaimed television production of Hans Christian Andersen's The Sheperdess and the Chimney Sweep. She also illustrated an edition of J. R. R. Tolkien's The Lord of the Rings. Her paintings have been exhibited in galleries, where they command top prices, all of which she donates to charity.

If there's anyone in the royal circle who has captured the public's hearts like Queen Margrethe once did, it's Hong Kong-born Princess Alexandra, who married Prince Joachim over a decade ago. The Princess not only cuts a gracious figure in her gown and crown, but has also endeared herself forever to the Danes, and to the Queen Mother, by learning to speak flawless Danish and—here's the topper—with hardly a trace of an accent. The birth of two sons, Nikolai and Felix, has not diminished her popularity.

And what of the future King? Crown Prince Frederik, born in 1968, is still Denmark's—if not Northern Europe's—most eligible bachelor, a dashing prince in all respects, with a fondness for yachting and club-hopping. However, his public relationship with Tasmanian-born Mary Donaldson seems to be serious, and the Danes hope that she will soon become the Crown Princess of Denmark, putting to rest Frederik's bachelor days.

In the square's center is a magnificent equestrian statue of King Frederik V by the French sculptor Jacques François Joseph Saly. It reputedly cost as much as all the buildings combined. Every day at noon, the Royal Guard and band march from Rosenborg Slot through the city for the changing of the guard. At noon on Queen Margrethe's birthday, April 16, crowds of Danes gather to cheer their monarch, who stands and waves from her balcony. On Amalienborg's harbor side are the trees, gardens, and fountains of **Amalienhaven.** ⊠ *Christian VIII's Palace–Amalienborg Pl., Sankt Annæ Kvarter* ☎ *33/12–08–08* ⊠ *Dkr 40* ⊙ *May–Oct., daily 11–4; Nov.–Apr., Tues.–Sun. 11–4.*

㉑ **Charlottenborg** (Charlotte's Castle). This Dutch baroque–style castle was built by Frederik III's half brother in 1670. Since 1754 the garden-flanked property has housed the faculty and students of the Danish Academy of Fine Art. It is open only during exhibits, which occur year-round. ⊠ *Nyhavn 2, Downtown* ☎ *33/13–40–22* ⊕ *www. charlottenborg-art.dk* ⊠ *Dkr 40* ⊙ *During exhibitions, daily 10–5 (Wed. until 7).*

㉘ **Den Lille Havfrue** (*The Little Mermaid*). On the Langelinie promenade, this somewhat overhyped 1913 statue commemorates Hans Christian Andersen's lovelorn creation, and is the subject of hundreds of travel posters. Donated to the city by Carl Jacobsen, the son of the founder of Carlsberg Breweries, the innocent waif has also been the subject of some cruel practical jokes, including decapitation and the loss of an arm, but she is currently in one piece. Especially on a sunny Sunday, the Langelinie promenade is thronged with Danes and visitors making their pilgrimage to see the statue. On this occasion, you may want to read the original Hans Christian Andersen tale; it's a heart-wrenching story that's a far cry from the Disney animated movie. ⊠ *Langelinie promenade, Østerbro.*

㉒ **Det Kongelige Teater** (The Royal Danish Theater). The stoic, pillared and gallery-front theater is the country's preeminent venue for music, opera, ballet, and theater. Nearly all theater works performed are in the Danish language, while operas are in their original language with Danish over-titles on a screen above the stage. The Royal Danish Ballet performs on the older stage in the main building; its repertoire ranges from classical to modern works. At this writing, a new opera house was under construction at the harborfront in the former naval base Holmen located in the Christianshavn district. The new facility is scheduled to open in 2005.

㉖ **Frihedsmuseet** (Resistance Museum). Evocative, sometimes moving displays commemorate the heroic Danish resistance movement, which saved 7,000 Jews from the Nazis by hiding and then smuggling them to Sweden. The homemade tank outside was used to spread the news of the Nazi surrender after World War II. ⊠ *Churchillparken, Sankt Annæ Kvarter* ☎ *33/13–77–14* ⊕ *www.natmus.dk* ⊠ *Dkr 40, free Wed.* ⊙ *May–mid-Sept., Tues.–Sat. 10–4, Sun. and holidays 10–5; mid-Sept.–Apr., Tues.–Sat. 11–3, Sun. and holidays 11–4.*

㉙ **Gefion Springvandet** (Gefion Fountain). Not far from *The Little Mermaid* yet another dramatic myth is illustrated. The goddess Gefion was promised as much of Sweden as she could plough in a night. The story goes that she changed her sons to oxen and used them to portion off what is now the island of Sjælland. ⊠ *East of Frihedsmuseet, Sankt Annæ Kvarter.*

㉗ **Kastellet** (Citadel). At Churchill Park's entrance stands the spired English church **St. Albans.** From there, walk north on the main path to reach the Citadel. The structure's smooth, peaceful walking paths, marina, and greenery belie its fierce past as a city fortification. Built in the aftermath of the Swedish siege of the city on February 10, 1659, the double moats were among the improvements made to the city's defense. The Citadel served as the city's main fortress into the 18th century; in a grim reversal during World War II, the Germans used it as headquarters during their occupation. ⊠ *Center of Churchill Park, Sankt Annæ Kvarter* ☎ *Free* ☉ *Daily 6* AM–*sunset.*

The current building was opened in 1874, though the annex, known as **Stærekassen** (Nesting Box) was not inaugurated until 1931. The Nesting Box got its name due to an obscure likeness to a birdhouse. Statues of Danish poet Adam Oehlenschläger and author Ludvig Holberg—whose works remain the core of Danish theater—flank the facade. Born in Bergen, Norway, in 1684, Holberg came to Denmark as a student and stayed. Often compared to Molière, he wrote 32 of his comedies in a "poetic frenzy" between 1722 and 1728, and, legend has it, he complained of interminable headaches the entire time. He published the works himself, made an enormous fortune, and invested in real estate. In the mid-'90s, an annex designed by Norwegian architect Sverre Fehn was planned for construction on the eastern side of the theater. The renovations have been half-finished and half-abandoned in light of the new opera house project. The theater closes for the summer months. ⊠ *Tordenskjoldsg. 3, Downtown* ☎ *33/69–69–33 or 33/69–69–69 for tickets* ⊕ *www.kgl-teater.dk* ☎ *Guided tours 75 Dkr* ☉ *Guided tours Sun. 11; no tours May 27–Aug. 5.*

► ⑲ **Kongens Nytorv** (King's New Square). A mounted statue of Christian V dominates the square. Crafted in 1688 by the French sculptor Lamoureux, the subject is conspicuously depicted as a Roman emperor. Every year, at the end of June, graduating high school students arrive in horse-drawn carriages and dance beneath the furrowed brow of the sober statue. ⊠ *Between Gothersg., Holmenskanal, and Tordenskjoldsg., Downtown.*

need a break? Dozens of restaurants and cafés line Nyhavn. **Cap Horn** (⊠ Nyhavn 21, Downtown ☎ 33/12–85–04) is among the best, with moderately priced and completely organic Danish treats served in a cozy, art-filled dining room that resembles a ship's galley. Try the fried plaice, swimming in a sea of parsley butter with boiled potatoes. In the summertime, try to grab a sidewalk table, the perfect place to enjoy an overstuffed focaccia sandwich and a Carlsberg.

㉕ **Kunstindustrimuseet** (Museum of Decorative Art). Originally built in the 18th century as a royal hospital, the fine rococo museum houses a large selection of European and Asian crafts. Also on display are ceramics, silverware, tapestries, and special exhibitions that often focus on contemporary design. The museum's excellent library is stocked with design books and magazines. A small café also operates here. ⊠ *Bredg. 68, Sankt Annæ Kvarter* ☎ *33/18–56–56* ⊕ *www.kunstindustrimuseet. dk* ☎ *Dkr 40 (additional fee for some special exhibits)* ☉ *Permanent collection Tues.–Fri. 1–4, weekends noon–4; special exhibits Tues.–Fri. 10–4, weekends noon–4.*

㉔ **Marmorkirken** (Marble Church). Officially the Frederikskirke, this ponderous baroque sanctuary of precious Norwegian marble was begun in 1749 and remained unfinished from 1770 to 1874 due to budget constraints. It was finally completed and consecrated in 1894. Around the exterior are 16 statues of various religious leaders from Moses to Luther, and below them stand sculptures of outstanding Danish ministers and bishops. The hardy can scale 273 steps to the outdoor balcony. From here you can walk past the exotic gilded onion domes of the **Russiske Ortodoks Kirke** (Russian Orthodox Church), just to the north of the Marmorkirken. ✉ *Frederiksg. 4, off Bredg., Sankt Annæ Kvarter* ☎ *33/ 15–01–44* ⊕ *www.marmorkirken.dk* ✆ *Free; balcony Dkr 20* ⊙ *Mon., Tues., and Thurs. 10–5; Wed. 10–6; weekends noon–5. Guided tours mid-June–Aug., daily 1–3; Sept.–mid-June, weekends 1–3.*

★ ㉒ **Nyhavn** (New Harbor). This harbor-front neighborhood was built 300 years ago to attract traffic and commerce to the city center. Until 1970, the area was a favorite haunt of sailors. Though restaurants, boutiques, and antiques stores now outnumber tattoo parlors, many old buildings have been well preserved and have retained the harbor's authentic 18th-century maritime character; you can even see a fleet of old-time sailing ships from the quay. Hans Christian Andersen lived at various times in the Nyhavn houses at numbers 18, 20, and 67.

Northwest toward Nørrebro

By the 1880s, many of the buildings that now line Nørrebro were being hastily thrown up as housing for area laborers. Many of these flats—typically decorated with a row of pedimented windows and a portal entrance—have been renovated through a massive urban-renewal program. But to this day, many share hall toilets, have no showers, and are heated only by kerosene heaters. On the Nørrebrogade and Skt. Hans Torv of today, you'll discover a fair number of cafés, restaurants, clubs, and shops.

a good walk

Take the train from Østerport Station, off of Oslo Plads, to Nørreport Station on Nørre Voldg. and walk down Fiolstræde to **Vor Frue Kirken** ㉚ ▷. The church's very tall copper spire and four shorter ones crown the area. Backtrack north on Fiolstræde, to the main building of **Københavns Universitet** ㉛; on the corner of Krystalgade is the **Københavns Synagoge** ㉜.

Fiolstræde ends at the Nørreport train station. Perpendicular to Nørre Voldgade is Frederiksborggade, which leads northwest to the neighborhood of Nørrebro; to the southeast after the Kultorvet, or Coal Square, Frederiksborggade turns into the pedestrian street Købmagergade. From anywhere in the area, you can see the stout **Rundetårn** ㉝: the round tower stands as one of Copenhagen's most beloved landmarks, with an observatory open on autumn and winter evenings. North from the Rundetårn on Landemærket, Gothersgade gives way to **Rosenborg Slot** ㉞, its Dutch Renaissance design standing out against the vivid green of the well-tended Kongens Have. For a heavier dose of plants and living things, head across Øster Voldgade to the 25-acre **Botanisk Have** ㉟. South of the garden is the **Arbejdermuseet** ㊱, which profiles the lives of workers from the late 1800s to the present.

Leave the garden's north exit to reach the **Statens Museum for Kunst** ㊲, notable for exceptional Matisse works. An adjacent building houses **Den Hirschsprungske Samling** ㊳, with 19th-century Danish art on display. Nearby, on the east side of Øster Voldgade, is **Nyboder**, a neighborhood full of tidy homes built by Christian IV for the city's sailors.

TIMING All of the sites on this tour are relatively close together and can be seen in roughly half a day. Note that some sites close Monday or Tuesday; call ahead. The tour can be easily combined with the one that follows—just head back to Nørreport station and catch a train to Hovedbanegården.

What to See

36 Arbejdermuseet (Workers' Museum). The vastly underrated museum chronicles the working class from 1870 to the present, with evocative life-size "day-in-the-life-of" exhibits, including reconstructions of a city street and tram and an original apartment once belonging to a brewery worker, his wife, and eight children. Changing exhibits focusing on Danish and international social issues are often excellent. The museum also has a 19th-century–style restaurant serving old-fashioned Danish specialties and a '50s-style coffee shop. ⊠ *Rømersg. 22, Downtown* ☎ *33/ 93–25–75* ⊕ *www.arbejdermuseet.dk* ⊠ *Dkr 50* ⊙ *July–Oct., daily 10–4; Nov.–June, Tues.–Sun. 10–4.*

> **off the beaten path**

★ **ASSISTENS KIRKEGÅRD** – (Assistens Cemetery) – This peaceful, leafy cemetery in the heart of Nørrebro is the final resting place of numerous great Danes, including Søren Kierkegaard (whose last name means "church garden," or "cemetery"), Hans Christian Andersen, and physicist Niels Bohr. In the summer, the cemetery takes on a cheerful, city-park air as picnicking families, young couples, and sunbathers relax on the sloping lawns amid the dearly departed. ⊠ *Kapelvej 2, Nørrebro* ☎ *35/37–19–17* ⊕ *www. assistens.dk* ⊠ *Free* ⊙ *May–Aug., daily 8–8; Sept.–Oct. and Mar.–Apr., daily 8–6; Nov.–Feb., daily 8–4.*

> **need a break?**

At the bar–café–restaurant combo **Barstarten** (⊠ Kapelvej 1, Nørrebro ☎ 35/24–11–00) you can get three squares, snacks, and a dizzying array of beverages. The kitchen whips up simple French-Italian country cooking and a new menu appears every two weeks. A favorite is *Barstarten's Menu*, a three-course affair with a wine list to accompany the food. DJs liven up the scene late on weekend nights with a soul-and-funk repertoire.

35 Botanisk Have (Botanical Garden). Trees, flowers, ponds, sculptures, and a spectacular 19th-century Palmehuset (Palm House) of tropical and subtropical plants blanket the garden's 25-plus acres. There's also an observatory and a geological museum. Take time to explore the gardens and watch the pensioners feed the birds. Some have been coming here so long that the birds actually alight on their fingers. ⊠ *Gothersg. 128, Sankt Annæ Kvarter* ☎ *35/32–22–40* ⊕ *www.botanic-garden.ku.dk* ⊠ *Free* ⊙ *Grounds May–Sept., daily 8:30–6; Oct.–Apr., Tues.–Sun. 8:30–4. Palm House daily 10–3.*

38 Den Hirschsprungske Samling (The Hirschsprung Collection). This museum showcases paintings from the country's Golden Age—Denmark's mid-19th-century school of naturalism—as well as a collection of paintings by the late-19th-century artists of the Skagen School. Their luminous works capture the play of light and water so characteristic of the Danish countryside. ⊠ *Stockholmsg. 20, Østerbro* ☎ *35/42–03–36* ⊕ *www. hirschsprung.dk* ⊠ *Dkr. 35; free Wed.* ⊙ *Thurs.–Mon. 11–4, Wed. 11–9.*

32 Københavns Synagoge (Copenhagen Synagogue). The contemporary architect Gustav Friedrich Hetsch borrowed from the Doric and Egyptian styles in creating this arklike synagogue. ⊠ *Krystalg. 12, Downtown* ☎ *33/12–88–88* ⊙ *Daily services 4:15.*

31 Københavns Universitet (Copenhagen University). The main building of Denmark's leading institution for higher learning was constructed in the 19th century on the site of a medieval bishops' palace. The university was founded nearby in 1479. ⊠ *Nørreg. 10, Downtown* ☎ *35/32–26–26* ⊕ *www.ku.dk.*

need a
break?
Near Copenhagen University is **Sømods Bolcher** (✉ Nørreg. 24 or 36, Downtown ☎ 33/12–60–46), a Danish confectioner that has been on the scene since the late 19th century. Children and candy-lovers relish seeing the hard candy pulled and cut by hand.

Nyboder. Tour the neat, mustard-color enclave of Nyboder, a perfectly laid-out compound of flat, long, former sailors' homes built by Christian IV. Like Nyhavn, the area was seedy and boisterous at the beginning of the 1970s, but today has become one of Copenhagen's more fashionable neighborhoods. At **Nyboder Mindestuer** (✉ Skt Paulsg. 24 ☎ 33/32–10–05 ✆ Dkr 10), you can view an exhibition of everyday life in Nyboder from its inception in 1631 to the present day. The people at the exhibition center also arrange guided tours of the neighborhood. ✉ *West of Store Kongensg. and east of Rigensg., Sankt Annæ Kvarter.*

㉞
FodorśChoice
★
Rosenborg Slot (Rosenborg Castle). This Dutch Renaissance castle contains ballrooms, halls, and reception chambers, but for all of its grandeur, there's an intimacy that makes you think the king might return any minute. Thousands of objects are displayed, including beer glasses, gilded clocks, golden swords, family portraits, a pearl-studded saddle, and gem-encrusted tables; an adjacent treasury contains the royal jewels. The castle's setting is equally welcoming: it's in the middle of the **Kongens Have** (King's Garden), amid lawns, park benches, and shady walking paths.

King Christian IV built the Rosenborg Castle as a summer residence but loved it so much that he ended up living and dying here. In 1849, when the absolute monarchy was abolished, all the royal castles became state property, except for Rosenborg, which is still passed down from monarch to monarch. Once a year, during the fall holiday, the castle stays open until midnight, and visitors are invited to explore its darkened interior with bicycle lights. ✉ *Øster Voldg. 4A, Sankt Annæ Kvarter* ☎ 33/15–32–86 ✆ *Dkr 50 ☉ Nov.–Apr., Tues.–Sun. 11–2; May and Sept., daily 10–4; June–Aug., daily 10–5; Oct., daily 11–3.*

★ **㉝**
Rundetårn (Round Tower). Instead of climbing the stout Round Tower's stairs, visitors scale a smooth, 600-foot spiral ramp on which—legend has it—Peter the Great of Russia rode a horse alongside his wife, Catherine, who took a carriage. From its top, you enjoy a panoramic view of the twisted streets and crooked roofs of Copenhagen. The unusual building was constructed as an observatory in 1642 by Christian IV and is still maintained as the oldest such structure in Europe.

The art gallery has changing exhibits, and occasional concerts are held within its massive stone walls. An observatory and telescope are open to the public evenings mid-October through March, and an astronomer is on hand to answer questions. ✉ *Købmagerg. 52A, Downtown* ☎ 33/73–03–73 ⊕ *www.rundetaarn.dk ✆ Dkr 20 ☉ Sept.–May, Mon.–Sat. 10–5, Sun. noon–5; June–Aug., Mon.–Sat. 10–8, Sun. noon–8. Observatory mid-Oct.–Mar., Tues. and Wed. 7 PM–10 PM.*

㊲
Statens Museum for Kunst (National Art Gallery). Old Master paintings—including works by Rubens, Rembrandt, Titian, El Greco, and Fragonard—as well as a comprehensive array of antique and 20th-century Danish art make up the gallery collection. Also notable is the modern art, which includes pieces by a very small but select group of artists, including Henri Matisse, Edvard Munch, Henri Laurens, Emil Nolde, and Georges Braque. The space also contains a children's museum, an amphitheater, a documentation center and study room, a bookstore, and a restaurant. A sculpture garden filled with classical, modern, and whim-

sical pieces flanks the building. ✉ *Sølvg. 48–50, Sankt Annæ Kvarter* ☎ *33/74–84–94* ⊕ *www.smk.dk* ✉ *Dkr 50; free Wed.* ☉ *Tues. and Thurs.–Sun. 10–5, Wed. 10–8.*

▶ ③⓪ **Vor Frue Kirken** (Church of Our Lady). The site of this cathedral has drawn worshipers since the 13th century, when Bishop Absalon built a chapel here. Today's church is actually a reconstruction: the original church was destroyed during the Napoleonic Wars. Five towers top the neo-classical structure. Inside you can see Thorvaldsen's marble sculptures depicting Christ and the 12 Apostles, and Moses and David cast in bronze. ✉ *Nørreg., Frue Pl., Downtown* ☎ *33/37–65–40* ⊕ *www. koebenhavnsdomkirke.dk* ✉ *Free* ☉ *Daily 8–5.*

In & Around Vesterbrogade

To the southwest of the city are the vibrant working-class and immigrant neighborhoods of Vesterbro, where you'll find a good selection of inexpensive ethnic restaurants and shops. Like the area around Nørrebro, the buildings date from the late 1800s and were constructed for workers. From Vesterbro, Vesterbrogade leads further west to the neighborhood of Frederiksberg. Originally a farming area that supplied the royal households with fresh produce, Frederiksberg is now lined with residences of the well-heeled and home to the zoo and a vibrant theater district.

a good walk

Begin your tour from Copenhagen's main station, Hovedbanegården. When you exit on Vesterbrogade, take a right and you can see the city's best-known attraction, **Tivoli** ③⑨ ▶. Just southeast of the gardens, on Hans Christian Andersens Boulevard, the neoclassical **Ny Carlsberg Glyptotek** ④⓪ contains one of the most impressive collections of antiquities and sculpture in northern Europe. Just north on Hans Christian Andersens Boulevard, across the street from Tivoli's eastern side, is the sleek **Dansk Design Center** ④① , with innovative temporary exhibits that showcase Danish and international design. To the west of the main station and tucked between Skt. Jørgens Sø (St. Jørgens Lake) and the main arteries of Vestersøgade and Gammel Kongevej is the **Tycho Brahe Planetarium** ④② , with an Omnimax Theater.

Vesterbro, which resembles New York's Lower East Side for its bohemian vibe and ethnically diverse population, is along Vesterbrogade near Tivoli. Running parallel to the south is **Istedgade,** Copenhagen's half-hearted red-light district.

Farther west on Vesterbrogade is **Københavns Bymuseum** ④③ , its entrance flanked by a miniature model of medieval Copenhagen. Beer enthusiasts can head south on Enghavevej and take a right on Ny Carlsbergvej to see the **Carlsberg Bryggeri** ④④ . The visitor center, nearby on Gamle Carslbergvej, has exhibits on the brewing process and Carlsberg's rise to fame.

TIMING   These sights can be seen in half a day, and could be combined easily with a walk around Nørrebo. Tivoli offers charms throughout the day; visit in the late afternoon, and stay until midnight, when colored electrical bulbs and fireworks (on Wednesday and weekend nights) illuminate the park. Be sure to call ahead, since some places may be closed on Monday or Tuesday.

What to See

④④ **Carlsberg Bryggeri** (Carlsberg Brewery). As you approach the world-famous Carlsberg Brewery, the unmistakable smell of fermenting hops greets you, a pungent reminder that this is beer territory. (Indeed, near the Brewery is the appealing little neighborhood of Humleby; "humle" means "hops.") Four giant Bornholm-granite elephants guard the brewery's main entrance on Ny Carlsbergvej. Nearby, on Gamle Carslbergvej, is the visitor center, in an old Carlsberg brewery. Colorful displays take you step by step through the brewing process. You can also walk through the draft horse stalls; at the end of your visit, you're rewarded with a few minutes to quaff a complimentary beer. The free **Carlsberg Museum** (⊠ Valby Langgade 1, Vesterbro ☎ 33/27–12–74), open Monday through Friday 10 to 3, offers a further look into the saga of the Carlsberg family, and how it managed to catapult Carlsberg from a local name into one of the most famous beers in the world. ⊠ *Gamle Carlsbergvej 11, Vesterbro* ☎ *33/27–12–82* ⊕ *www.carlsberg.dk* ✉ *Free* ☉ *Tues.–Sun. 10–4.*

❹ **Dansk Design Center** (Danish Design Center). This sleek, glass-panel structure looms in sharp contrast to the old-world ambience of Tivoli just across the street. More of a design showroom than a museum, the center's highlights are the innovative temporary exhibits on the main floor. Past exhibits have included "75 years of Bang & Olufsen," which covered the famed Danish audio-system company, and "Tooltoy," a playful, interactive exhibit of toys over the last century. One-third of the temporary exhibits showcase Danish design; the rest focus on international design. The semi-permanent collection on the ground floor (renewed every other year) often includes samples from the greats, including chairs by Arne Jacobsen, several artichoke PH lamps (designed by Poul Henningsen), and Bang & Olufsen radios and stereos. Note how the radios they made in the '50s look more modern than many of the radios today. The center's shop carries a wide range of Danish design items and selected pieces from the temporary exhibits. You can enjoy light meals in the atrium café, sitting amid the current exhibits. ⊠ *H. C. Andersens Blvd. 27, Downtown* ☎ *33/69–33–69* ⊕ *www.ddc.dk* ✉ *Dkr 40* ☉ *Mon., Tues., Thurs., and Fri. 10–5, Wed. 10–9, weekends 11–4.*

Istedgade. In what passes for a red-light district in Copenhagen, mom-and-pop kiosks and ethnic restaurants stand side by side with porn shops and shady outfits aiming to satisfy all proclivities. Istedgade, like neighboring Vesterbrogade, has diversified over the past several years, drawing artists and students. Thanks to the city's urban-renewal projects, cafés and businesses are also moving in, mostly on the southwest end of Istedgade, around Enghave Plads (Enghave Square). Mama Lustra, at No. 96–98, is a laid-back café with comfy armchairs and a mixed crowd of students and older artsy types. Though Istedgade is relatively safe, you may want to avoid the area near the Central Station late at night. ⊠ *South of and parallel to Vesterbrogade, running southwest from the Central Station, Vesterbro.*

❸ **Københavns Bymuseum** (Copenhagen City Museum). For a surprisingly evocative collection detailing Copenhagen's history, head to this 17th-century building in the heart of Vesterbro. A meticulously maintained model of 16th-century Copenhagen is kept outdoors from May through September; inside there is also a memorial room for philosopher Søren Kierkegaard, the father of existentialism. ⊠ *Vesterbrog. 59, Vesterbro* ☎ *33/21–07–72* ⊕ *www.kbhbymuseum.dk* ✉ *Dkr 20; free Fri.* ☉ *May–Sept., Wed.–Mon. 10–4; Oct.–Apr., Wed.–Mon. 1–4.*

❹ **Ny Carlsberg Glyptotek** (New Carlsberg Museum). Among Copenhagen's
FodorsChoice most important museums—thanks to its exquisite antiquities and Gau-
★ guins and Rodins—the neoclassical New Carlsberg Museum was donated in 1888 by Carl Jacobsen, son of the founder of the Carlsberg Brewery. Surrounding its lush indoor garden, a series of nooks and

CARLSBERG BREWERIES: ALE & ARTY

ARLSBERG. A BEER BY ANY OTHER NAME *does not bring to mind the sculptures of Giacometti, archaeological undertakings in Rome, or the music of Miles Davis. In Denmark, however, the company behind the world-famous beer supports almost everything that is a part of Danish culture. Call it the ale of art: perhaps the most altruistic beer in the world.*

Carlsberg Breweries, which since 1970 has included the United Breweries/ Tuborg, is owned by the Carlsberg Foundation. The umbrella organization annually pumps about DKr 125 million ($15.6 million) into Danish science, arts, and humanities—programs that touch nearly every aspect of Danish life. Under its own distinct statutes, the New Carlsberg Foundation, a branch of the mother foundation, kicks in DKr 40 million ($4.9 million) to the visual arts every year. While there is a strong tradition of corporate-backed foundations in Denmark, and many companies offer support to the arts and sciences, Carlsberg's scope and commitment to the culture of a single country is unique in the world.

Since its establishment in 1902, the New Carlsberg Foundation has helped build and support the Ny Carlsberg Glyptotek and its collection of antiquities. This Copenhagen museum boasts one of the world's finest collections of Etruscan art, and Europe's finest collection of Roman portraits. Among the other works are Oriental, Egyptian, and Roman masterpieces collected and donated by Carl Jacobsen, the son of Carlsberg founder J. C. Jacobsen—an accomplished brewer in his own right. The museum's permanent collection also contains French sculpture, including works by Rodin and Degas, impressionist and postimpressionist paintings by Manet, Cézanne, and Gauguin, and a Danish collection. Many Danish curators attribute the nation's grand state of the arts largely to the New Carlsberg Foundation. According to one, losing its sponsorship would "be a disaster." But what kind of beer company pours the bulk of its profits into art? Herein lies what makes Carlsberg so unusual. The brewery does not own the foundation: The foundation owns a 51% majority stake in the brewery.

While the New Carlsberg Foundation technically handles endowments for the visual arts, the larger Carlsberg Foundation, which supports the sciences and humanities, overlaps into the area of fine art. Among the wide range of projects they have funded: major archeological excavations in the Roman Forum, studies of the ancient mosaics of the St. George Rotunda in Thessaloniki, Greece, and the complete and continued support of the Frederiksborg Museum north of Copenhagen. A royal residence that burned in 1859 was rebuilt and established as a museum of Danish history by J. C. Jacobsen; it now serves as the nation's portrait museum.

Between the larger foundation and the brewery itself are several smaller foundations, which further support music, industry, and society in general. The Carlsberg Brewery is also the owner of many businesses that deal in the decorative arts, including Holmegaard glass, Royal Copenhagen, and Georg Jensen, all of which exist under the umbrella company Royal Scandinavia. Of course, Carlsberg's associate concern, Tivoli Gardens, is considered by many a work of art in and of itself. Carlsberg also helps to fund annual events such as the Copenhagen Jazz Festival and the Roskilde rock festival, as well as concerts and performances by international artists. Clearly, there is more to these noble suds than meets the lips.

chambers houses works by Degas and other impressionists, plus an extensive assemblage of Egyptian, Greek, Roman, and French sculpture, not to mention Europe's finest collection of Roman portraits and the best collection of Etruscan art outside Italy. A modern wing, designed as a three-story treasure chest by the acclaimed Danish architect Henning Larsen, houses an impressive pre-impressionist collection that includes works from the Barbizon school; impressionist paintings, including works by Monet, Alfred Sisley, and Pissarro; and a postimpressionist section, with 50 Gauguin paintings plus 12 of his very rare sculptures. ⊠ *Dantes Pl. 7, Vesterbro* ☎ *33/41–81–41* ⊕ *www.glyptoteket.dk* ▤ *Dkr 40; free Wed. and Sun.* ⊘ *Tues.–Sun. 10–4.*

Tivoli. Copenhagen's best-known attraction, conveniently next to its main train station, attracts an astounding number of visitors: 4 million people from mid-April to mid-September. Tivoli is more sophisticated than a mere funfair: among its attractions are a pantomime theater, an open-air stage, 24 restaurants (some of them quite elegant), and frequent concerts, which cover the spectrum from classical to rock to jazz. Fantastic flower exhibits color the lush gardens and float on the swan-filled ponds.

The park was established in the 1840s, when Danish architect George Carstensen persuaded a worried King Christian VIII to let him build an amusement park on the edge of the city's fortifications, rationalizing that "when people amuse themselves, they forget politics." On Wednesday and weekend nights, elaborate fireworks are set off, and every day the Tivoli Guard, a youth version of the Queen's Royal Guard, performs. Try to see Tivoli at least once by night, when 100,000 colored lanterns illuminate the Chinese pagoda and the main fountain. Call to double-check prices, which vary throughout the year and often include family discounts at various times during the day. Tivoli is also open from late November to Christmas. ⊠ *Vesterbrog. 3, Vesterbro* ☎ *33/15–10–01* ⊕ *www.tivoli.dk* ▤ *Dkr 45, plus Dkr 10 per attraction-ticket (each attraction requires 1–5 tickets)* ⊘ *Mid-Apr.–mid-Sept., Sun.–Tues. 11–11, Wed. and Thurs. 11 AM–midnight, Fri. and Sat. 11 AM–1 AM; late Nov.–Dec. 23, Sun.–Wed. 11–9, Fri. and Sat. 11–10.*

㊷ Tycho Brahe Planetarium. This modern, cylindrical planetarium, which appears to be sliced at an angle, features astronomy exhibits. The **Omnimax Theater** takes you on visual odysseys as varied as journeys through space and sea, the stages of the Rolling Stones, or Kuwaiti fires from the first Persian Gulf War. These films are not recommended for children under age 7. ⊠ *Gammel Kongevej 10, Vesterbro* ☎ *33/12–12–24* ⊕ *www.planetarium.dk* ▤ *Dkr 85* ⊘ *Mon., Tues., Fri., and Sat. 10:30–9; Wed. 9:45–9; Thurs. 9:30–9; Sun. 10:45–9.*

Vesterbro. Students, union workers, and immigrants (who account for 15% of Vesterbro's population) populate this area. It's a great place to find ethnic groceries, discount shops, and cheap international restaurants. The face of Vesterbro, however, slowly has been gentrifying. Due to the city's ongoing urban-renewal and clean-up efforts, the spruced-up Vesterbro is starting to attract chic cafés and eateries, along with their arty customers. The minimalist fusion restaurant-bar Delicatessen, on Vesterbrogade, has drawn a steady stream of Copenhageners since it joined the neighborhood. The shiny First Hotel Vesterbro is only a five-minute walk from Tivoli on Vesterbrogade. ⊠ *At the southwestern end of Vesterbrogade.*

<table>
<tr><td>off the beaten path</td><td>**ZOOLOGISK HAVE** – Children love the Zoological Gardens, which are home to more than 2,000 animals. The small petting zoo and playground includes cows, horses, rabbits, goats, and hens. The indoor rain forest has butterflies, sloths, alligators, and other tropical creatures. Sea lions, lions, and elephants are fed in the early afternoon. Be warned: on sunny weekends, the line to enter runs far down Roskildevej; get here early. ⊠ *Roskildevej 32, Frederiksberg* ☎ *70/20–02–00* ⊕ *www.zoo.dk* ☒ *Dkr 90* ☉ *June–Aug., daily 9–6; Sept.–Oct., daily 9–5; Apr.–May, weekdays 9–5, weekends 9–6; Nov.–Feb., daily 9–4; Mar. weekdays 9–4, weekends 9–5.*</td></tr>
</table>

WHERE TO EAT

In Copenhagen, with its more than 2,000 restaurants, traditional Danish fare spans all price categories: you can order a light lunch of traditional smørrebrød, munch alfresco from a street-side *pølser* (sausage) cart, or dine out on Limfjord oysters and local plaice. Even the most upscale restaurants have moderate-price fixed menus. Though few Danish restaurants require reservations, it's best to call ahead to avoid a wait. The city's more affordable ethnic restaurants are concentrated in Vesterbro, Nørrebro, and the side streets off Strøget. And for less-expensive, savory noshes in stylish surroundings, consider lingering at a café.

WHAT IT COSTS In kroner					
	$$$$	$$$	$$	$	¢
AT DINNER	over 200	151–200	121–150	90–120	under 90

Prices are for a main course at dinner.

Christianhavn, Holmen & Amager

★ $$$$ ✕ **Era Ora.** This has long been the premier Italian restaurant in the city, if not the country. Era Ora is outfitted perfectly—cozy and warm—for a slow, Italian-style feast of many courses from the dazzling menu. The wine list is quite long and distinguished and the menu is composed of the best of fresh ingredients available in every season. ⊠ *Overgaden neden Vandet 33-B, Christianshavn* ☎ *32/54–06–93* ♨ *Reservations essential* ▤ *AE, DC, MC, V* ☉ *Closed Sun.*

$$–$$$ ✕ **Spiseloppen.** Round out your visit to the Free State of Christiania with a meal at Spiseloppen, a 160-seat warehouse restaurant that was a military storage facility and an army canteen in its former life. Upon entering Christiania, wind your way past shaggy dogs, their shaggy owners, graffiti murals, and wafts of patchouli. (There are few street signs, so just ask; Spiseloppen is the neighborhood's best-known restaurant.) From the outside, this run-down warehouse with splintered windows may seem a bit foreboding, but inside it's a different story. Climb up rickety stairs to the second floor and you're rewarded with a loft-size dining room with low, wood-beam ceilings and candles flickering on the tables. The menu highlights are fresh and inventive vegetarian and fish dishes, which might include artichokes stuffed with eggplant or Portobello mushrooms served with squash, mango, and papaya. One floor down is Loppen, a club that hosts midweek jazz sessions and DJ dance nights on the weekends. ⊠ *Bådmandsstr. 43, Christianshavn* ☎ *32/57–95–58* ▤ *MC, V* ☉ *Closed Mon. No lunch.*

Where to Eat in Copenhagen

ØSTERBRO

NØRREBRO

TO ASSISTENS KIERKEGÅRD

Nørre Al.

Bleġdamsv.

Tagensv.

Fredensg.

Mølleg.

Elmeg.

Skt. Hans Torv

Fælledv.

Nørrebrog.

Griffenfeldsg.

Blågårdsg.

Aboulevard

Rosenørns A.

Gyldenløvesg.

Dronning Louises Bro

Peblinge Dossering

Peblinge Sø

Jørgens Sø

Skt.

Vester Søg.

Nørre Søg.

Vester Farimagsg.

Nørre Farimagsg.

Nansensg.

Kampmannsg.

Svineryggen

Vodroffsv.

Gammel Kongev.

Vesterbrog.

Vesterport

Nyropsg.

Axeltorv

Bernstorffsg.

Central Railway Station (Hovedbanegården)

VESTERBRO

Istedg.

Tietgensg.

Niels Brocks G.

H.C. Andersen Blvd.

Dantes Plads

Tivoli

Rådhus Pl.

Sø

Dosseringl

Bleġdamsv.

Fredensg.

Fredensbro

Ravnborg

Sortedam

Sortedams Sø

Øster Søg.

Sortedam

Øster Farimagsg.

Frederiksborgg.

Nørreport Station

Ørsteds Parken

Nørre Voldg.

Nørreg.

Fiolstr.

Krystalg.

DOWNTOWN

Reġnegårds Str.

Larslejsstr.

H.C.

Andersens Blvd.

Hammerichsg.

Vester Voldg.

Gammel torv

Nytorv

Frederiksbergg.

Kattesundet

Farverg.

Nyg.

Vimmelsk.

Amagertorv

Læderstr.

Kompagnistr.

Rådhusstr.

Dosseringl

Øster Søg.

Øster

Sølvg.

Stockholmsg.

Øster Anlæg

Sølvg.

Botanisk Have

Øster Voldg.

Gothersg.

Åbenrå

Kongens Have

Sølvg.

Rigensg.

Kronprincessestr.

SANKT KV

Adelg.

Borgerg.

Gothersg.

N

Øster Farimagsg.

Vognmagerg.

Gammelmønt

Nr. Bernikg.

Østerg.

Bremerholm

Vester Voldg.

Købmagerg. landemærket

Pilestr.

Ni. Østerg.

Højbro

Gammel Strand

Vester Voldg.

Vindebrog.

Farimagsg.

Øster Søg.

Christiansborg Slotsplads

Holmens

Tøjhusgade

Frederiksholms Kanal

Christians Brygge

Langebro

Lange

Amager Blvd.

Hambrosg.

Vester Voldg.

Dag Hammarskjölds Al.

- ② Skt. Hans Torv
- ①
- ④ ③
- ⑤
- ⑥
- ⑦
- ⑧
- ⑨
- ⑩ ⑪ ⑫ ⑬
- ⑭
- ⑮
- ⑯
- ⑰ ⑱
- ⑲ ⑳
- ㉑
- ㉒
- ㉓
- ㉔
- ㉕
- ㉖
- ㉚
- ㉛ ㉜
- ㉝ ㉞
- ㉟
- ㊹
- ℹ

0   1/4 mi
0   400 m

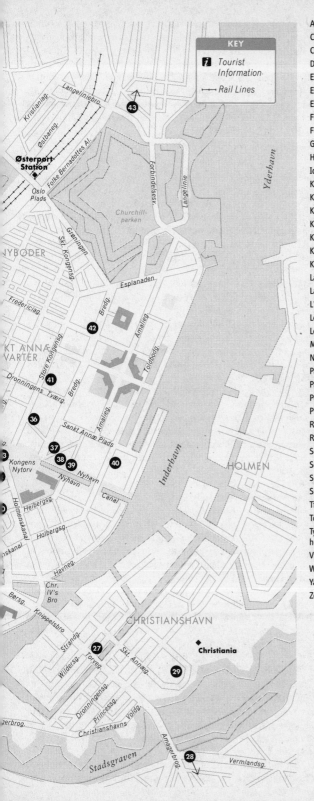

Atlas Bar **12**
Café Ketchup **23**
Copenhagen Corner **14**
Delicatessen **7**
El Mesón **44**
Els **37**
Era Ora **27**
Flyvefisken **11**
Formel B. **8**
Godt **35**
Husmanns Vinstue **13**
Ida Davidson **41**
Kashmir **3**
Københavner Caféen **18**
Kommandanten **34**
Kong Hans Kælder **30**
Konrad **24**
Krogs **25**
Krunch **28**
La Galette **10**
Lai Hoo **36**
L'Alsace **31**
Le Saint Jacques **43**
Le Sommelier **42**
Molevitten **5**
Nyhavns Færgekro **39**
Passagens Spisehus **9**
Pasta Basta **19**
Peder Oxe **20**
Pussy Galore's Flying Circus . . .**2**
Reinwalds **15**
Riz Raz **17, 21**
Sebastopol **1**
Søren K. **26**
Spiseloppen **29**
Sult **22**
Tibet **4**
Told & Snaps **40**
Tyvenkokkenhanskoneog-
hendeselsker **16**
Victor **33**
Wiinblad **32**
Yan's Wok **6**
Zeleste **38**

$–$$$ ✕ **Krunch.** The motto here is "gastronomy within ecology." Krunch serves natural, organic foods from reliable sources and attempts to integrate an environmentally friendly spirit into every facet of the experience. Within these guiding principles, the objective of the owners is to create authentic French-bistro atmosphere and cuisine. The four-course menu changes seasonally; it typically consists of a choice of a fish, meat, or vegetarian main course and an assortment of side dishes. Krunch is also a fine spot for kids. ⊠ *Øresundsvej 14, Amager* ☎ *32/84–50–50* ▭ *MC, V* ⊗ *No lunch. Closed Mon.*

Downtown

$$$$ ✕ **Kommandanten.** Fancifully decorated by master florist Tage Andersen with brushed iron-and-copper furniture, down pillows, and foliage-flanked lights, this is among the city's most exclusive dinner spots, attracting well-heeled businesspeople and local celebrities. The adventuresome international fare might include dishes such as rabbit with bouillon-cooked lentils, herbs, and bacon, and marinated salmon with oysters and parsley. Jackets are recommended. ⊠ *Ny Adelg. 7, Downtown* ☎ *33/12–09–90* ▭ *AE, DC, MC, V* ⊗ *Closed Sun.*

FodorśChoice
★

★ **$$$$** ✕ **Kong Hans Kælder.** Five centuries ago this was a Nordic vineyard—now it's one of Scandinavia's finest restaurants. Chef Thomas Rode Andersen's French-Danish-Asian–inspired dishes employ the freshest local ingredients and are served in a mysterious subterranean space with whitewashed walls and vaulted ceilings. Try the foie gras with raspberry-vinegar sauce or the warm oysters in vichyssoise with smoked cheese and lemon. ⊠ *Vingårdstr. 6, Downtown* ☎ *33/11–68–68* ▭ *AE, DC, MC, V* ⊗ *Closed Sun. No lunch.*

$$$$ ✕ **Krogs.** This elegant canal-front restaurant has developed a loyal clientele—both foreign and local—for its old-fashioned atmosphere and its innovative fish dishes. Pale-green walls are simply adorned with paintings of old Copenhagen. The menu includes such specialties as pan-grilled lobster flavored with vanilla oil and monkfish fillets in a beurre-blanc sauce flavored with arugula and tomato. Jackets are recommended. ⊠ *Gammel Strand 38, Downtown* ☎ *33/15–89–15* ⌲ *Reservations essential* ▭ *AE, DC, MC, V* ⊗ *Closed Sun.*

★ **$$$$** ✕ **Tyvenkokkenhanskoneoghendeselsker.** If you've seen Peter Greenaway's dark and brilliant film *The Cook, the Thief, His Wife, and Her Lover* (with its macabre feast scenes), you may wonder what lies in store at this half-timber town-house restaurant with the same name. It's worth finding out. The same daring humor that inspired the unusual name is exhibited in the innovative seven-course menu, which changes every few weeks. You might be served baked cod in an aromatic coffee sauce or warm rooster simmered in spices and served with horseradish sauce. Desserts include pineapple with mint tortellini. Sit upstairs for a view of the cheery, orange- and yellow-walled old houses that lean against each other just across the narrow street. ⊠ *Magstr. 16, Downtown* ☎ *33/16–12–92* ⌲ *Reservations essential* ▭ *DC, MC, V* ⊗ *Closed Sun. No lunch.*

★ **$$$–$$$$** ✕ **Konrad.** Elegant and minimalist, this restaurant attracts young people and stars, many of whom look like they just walked off a fashion runway. Considering its linear, beige decor, the restaurant seems as geared for people-watching as dining. The French-international menu is inventive without being off-the-wall, with offerings such as potato tortellini filled with oysters and white cream sauce. ⊠ *Pilestr. 12–14, Downtown* ☎ *33/93–29–29* ⌲ *Reservations essential* ▭ *AE, DC, MC, V* ⊗ *Closed Sun.*

$$$–$$$$ ✕ **L'Alsace.** Set in the cobbled courtyard of Pistolstræde and hung with paintings by Danish surrealist Wilhelm Freddie, this restaurant is peaceful and quiet, and has attracted such diverse diners as Queen Margrethe, Elton John, and Pope John Paul II. The hand-drawn menu lists oysters from Brittany, terrine de foie gras, and *choucroûte à la Strasbourgeoise* (a hearty mélange of cold cabbage, homemade sausage, and pork). Try the superb fresh-fruit tarts and cakes for dessert, and ask to sit in the patio overlooking the courtyard. ⊠ *Ny Østerg. 9, Downtown* ☎ *33/14–57–43* ☰ *AE, DC, MC, V* ⊘ *Closed Sun.*

$–$$$$ ✕ **Café Ketchup.** You have a choice at this informal, upbeat eatery: for light meals (at light prices), try the lively front café, where you can settle into a red-and-white wicker chair next to the large picture windows and watch the world go by on chic Pilestræde. Try the spring rolls with smoked salmon and cod, flavored with ginger and coriander. The café also serves a tasty brunch (yogurt with muesli, toast with turkey, mozzarella, and bacon, and black currant–fig marmalade) from 10–1. For more-substantial fare, venture into the restaurant decorated with old French Perrier ads and lit with white candles. Starters include a potato-and-wasabi soup served with a spicy crab cake, and bruschetta topped with a mango salsa. Main dishes range from halibut stuffed with crabmeat and herbs to marinated duck breast served with sun-dried tomatoes and fennel salad sprinkled with pine nuts. By night, the place turns into a lively bar and club. There is also a Café Ketchup in Tivoli, with a large terrace and a similar menu. ⊠ *Pilestr. 19, Downtown* ☎ *33/32–30–30* ☰ *DC, MC, V* ⊘ *Closed Sun.*

$$$ ✕ **El Mesón.** Smoothly worn wooden tables, earthen crockery, and dim lighting characterize the dining room of this Spanish restaurant. The knowledgeable waitstaff serves generous portions of beef spiced with spearmint, lamb with honey sauce, and paella Valenciano—a mixture of rice, chicken, ham, shrimp, lobster, squid, green beans, and peas—for two. ⊠ *Hauser Pl. 12 (behind Kultorvet), Downtown* ☎ *33/11–91–31* ☰ *AE, DC, MC, V* ⊘ *Closed Sun. No lunch.*

$$$ ✕ **Reinwalds.** The comfortable black teak chairs with blue upholstery
FodorśChoice signal the beginning of a series of delightful encounters with comfort
★ and fine food in a pleasant, modern setting. The tables spread out at sufficient intervals to prevent intrusions of privacy or overlap of conversations with neighboring diners. The informative waitstaff ensure that service is far above the norm and is adept at complementing selected dishes with a fine wine. The three- to five-course menus change monthly, according to the season's harvest. You might find offerings like creamy curry soup with rooster and quail eggs or baked sea bream with almond pesto. ⊠ *Farveg. 15, Downtown* ☎ *33/91–82–80* ☰ *AE, DC, MC, V* ⊘ *Closed Sun.*

$$$ ✕ **Søren K.** Occupying a bright corner of the Royal Library's modern Black Diamond extension, this cool-tone restaurant, with clean lines, blond-wood furnishings, and recessed ceiling lights, serves bold French-Scandinavian concoctions using no cream, butter, or stock. The result is a menu of flavorful dishes that please the palate without weighing you down. A popular selection is the five-course menu entitled "a couple of hours in the company of fish," which has featured items such as tuna in soy and sesame sauce or mussels drizzled with lemon and thyme. Vegetarian dishes include tofu marinated with red wine and topped with roasted sesame seeds, radishes, and passion fruit. For waterfront views, choose one of the many tables that sit flush up against the Black Diamond's looming glass walls. In the summer, you can enjoy your meal on the outside terrace. ⊠ *Søren Kierkegaards Pl. 1 (inside the Black Diamond), Downtown* ☎ *33/47–49–50* ☰ *DC, MC, V* ⊘ *Closed Sun.*

$$$ ✕ **Sult.** Norwegian author Knut Hamsun's novel *Sult* now shares its moniker with this restaurant on the premises of the Danish Film Institute. The cuisine is Mediterranean, with strong North African and Asian influences. Try the mussels with carrots in a cream sauce or roast Guinea fowl with sweet potatoes. The wine list is impressive. ⊠ *Vognmagerg. 8B, Downtown* ☎ *33/74–34–17* ▤ *MC, V* ☺ *Closed Mon.*

$$$ ✕ **Wiinblad.** This restaurant in the D'Angleterre hotel doubles as a gallery for the work of contemporary Danish artist Bjørn Wiinblad. Almost everything—tiles, wall partitions, plaques, candlesticks, vases, and even some tables—has been made by the great Dane, and the effect is bright, cheerful, and very elegant. The eatery offers an ample breakfast buffet, lunch, a fabulous and surprisingly affordable tea, and grilled specialties for dinner. Try the pickled herring with new potatoes topped with sour cream, or the breast of duck in cranberry cream sauce. ⊠ *D'Angleterre, Kongens Nytorv 34, Downtown* ☎ *33/37–06–19* ▤ *AE, DC, MC, V.*

$–$$$ ✕ **Peder Oxe.** On a 17th-century square, this lively, countrified bistro has rustic tables and 15th-century Portuguese tiles. All entrées—among them grilled steaks, fish, and the best fancy burgers in town—come with an excellent self-service salad bar. Damask-covered tables are set with heavy cutlery and opened bottles of hearty Pyrénées wine. A clever call-light for the waitress is above each table. In spring, when the high northern sun is shining but the warmth still has not kicked in, you won't do badly sitting outside in the Gråbrødretorv (Gray Friars' Square) sipping drinks while wrapped in blankets left thoughtfully for patrons in wicker chairs. ⊠ *Gråbrødretorv 11, Downtown* ☎ *33/11–00–77* ▤ *DC, MC, V.*

$–$$ ✕ **Flyvefisken.** Silvery stenciled fish swim along blue-and-yellow walls in this Thai eatery. Spicy dishes include chicken with cashew nuts and herring shark in basil sauce. ⊠ *Larsbjørnsstr. 18, Downtown* ☎ *33/14–95–15* ▤ *DC, MC, V* ☺ *Closed Sun. No lunch.*

$–$$ ✕ **Københavner Caféen.** You know you're in for a real Danish meal when you can smell the vinegary *rød kål* (red cabbage, a Danish staple) upon entering. Dimly lit and warm, with a dark wood and burgundy color scheme, this local favorite just oozes with *hygge* (cosiness). Old photographs of Danish royalty line the walls, and a 1798 street lamp stands alongside the inviting bar. Choose from a wide range of smørrebrød selections and also a formidable lineup of down-home Danish dishes such as *frikkedeller* (pork meatballs) and butter-fried salmon with boiled potatoes. In the summer the kitchen offers a traditional Danish Christmas meal "so that everyone can experience Denmark's Christmas traditions." The meal includes roast pork with red cabbage and the much-loved *ris à l'amande* (rice pudding) for dessert. Hidden inside is an almond, and whoever finds it receives a small present. These summer Christmas meals have become so popular that they are generally offered only to tour groups, but it's worth asking when you reserve. ⊠ *Badstuestr. 10, Downtown* ☎ *33/32–80–81* ⌖ *Reservations essential* ▤ *MC, V.*

$–$$ ✕ **Riz Raz.** This Middle Eastern restaurant hops with young locals, families, couples, and anyone who appreciates good value and spicy fare. The inexpensive all-you-can-eat buffet is heaped with lentils, tomatoes, potatoes, olives, hummus, warm pita bread, yogurt and cucumbers, pickled vegetables, and bean salads. Don't be put off by the hordes—just join them, either in the restaurant's endless labyrinth of dining rooms or in the jam-packed summertime patio. The main location is on Kompagnistræde, between Christiansborg Slot and Strøget; there's a second branch behind Vor Frue Kirken. ⊠ *Kompagnistr. 20, Downtown* ☎ *33/15–05–75* ⊠ *Store Kannikestr. 19* ☎ *33/32–33–45* ⌖ *Reservations essential* ▤ *DC, MC, V.*

FodorśChoice
★

$–$$ ✕ **Victor.** Excellent people-watching and good bistro fare are the calling cards at this French-style corner café. It's best during weekend lunches, when young and old gather for such specialties as rib roast, homemade pâté, and smoked salmon and cheese platters. Come here for one of the best brunches in town. Be warned however that the formal restaurant in the back of the space is quite expensive—order from the front café side for a less expensive meal. ⊠ Ny Østerg. 8, Downtown ☎ 33/13–36–13 ▤ AE, DC, MC, V.

¢–$$ ✕ **Husmanns Vinstue.** Founded in 1888, this warmly lit basement restaurant is housed in a former stable dating from 1727, which accounts for the low ceilings. If you're looking for old-world Denmark, this is it. Beer mugs dangle above the bar, dark-green lamps shed light onto the heavy wooden tables, and black-and-white photographs of Copenhagen hang on the walls. Until 1981, women were allowed to enter only if accompanied by a male, a rule established by one of the restaurant's female owners. For more than 100 years, Husmanns has proudly served hearty Danish smørrebrød to everyone from Walt Disney to the Danish royal family. While other Danish lunch spots may serve salads and lighter cuisine, at Husmanns Vinstue you can feast on all types of herring (fried, curried, marinated, and spiced), smoked eel with scrambled eggs, beef tartare with egg yolk, homemade sausage, and roast beef with potato salad, all served on your choice of rye or white bread. ⊠ Larsbjørnsstr. 2, Downtown ☎ 33/11–58–86 ⚓ Reservations essential ▤ AE, DC, MC, V ⊗ No dinner.

¢–$$ ✕ **Pasta Basta.** This bright, casual eatery just off the Strøget is always crammed with happy diners. Pasta Basta has all the ingredients for its well-deserved success: an all-you-can-eat fresh pasta and salad bar for a refreshingly low price (Dkr 79). The cheerful staff navigates a dining area marked by orange walls, an innovative mural, and glass-top tables painted in green and blue swirls. Main courses on the changing menu may include pasta with prawns, spinach, and chili peppers, or smoked salmon served with pasta in a creamy sauce of scallops, spinach, and herbs. Pasta Basta is one of the city's only restaurants (barring fast-food and shawarma joints) that serves food until 3 AM (and until 5 AM on Friday and Saturday). During these early morning hours, the restaurant is popular with dancers and musicians from the Royal Theater and other venues, who come in to relax and dine after their evening performances. ⊠ Valkendorfsg. 22, Downtown ☎ 33/11–21–31 ▤ DC, MC, V.

$ ✕ **Atlas Bar.** The health-food café Atlas Bar in the basement of restaurant Flyvefisken serves excellent food to a steady stream of students and hipsters. The snug eatery serves Oriental-inspired and fusion dishes, such as Manila chicken (chicken breasts in a tomato sauce with garlic, ginger, and chili) and medallions of venison. Atlas is also a favorite of vegetarians for its tempting menu of healthful, tasty dishes. ⊠ Larsbjørnsstr. 18, Downtown ☎ 33/15–03–52 ▤ DC, MC, V ⊗ Closed Sun.

¢ ✕ **La Galette.** Tucked into a bright little courtyard, this cheery creperie serves an array of savory crepes, including the Asterix, stuffed with ratatouille, egg, and chives, and the Quimper, with spinach, egg, bacon, and cheese. The luscious lineup of sweet crepes includes everything from banana and chocolate to flambéed caramel apples. ⊠ Larbjørnsstr. 9, Downtown ☎ 33/32–37–90 ▤ MC, V ⊗ No lunch Sun.

Nørrebro

$–$$ ✕ **Molevitten.** This spacious café–restaurant–club combination serves Asian-inspired dishes. A house favorite is *laksasuppe*, a Malaysian-style salmon soup. Brunch, lunch, and dinner crowds pack the three-level restaurant, and on weekend evenings the music cranks up and the dance-club revelers arrive. ⊠ *Nørrebrog. 13, Nørrebro* ☎ *35/39–49–00* ▤ *MC, V.*

$ ✕ **Pussy Galore's Flying Circus.** Done up with a few Arne Jacobsen swan chairs, naive wall paintings, and tables smashed up against each other, this trendy gathering place is supposed to be as kitsch as its name. While the mix of decor is retro and does a good job of setting a '60s stage, the regulars who come here make it feel more like a low-key neighborhood bar. Frequented by both young families and black-clad poseurs, this place serves surprisingly down-to-earth and affordable fare, with eggs and bacon and other brunch items along with hefty burgers and wok-fried delectables. ⊠ *Skt. Hans Torv 30, Nørrebro* ☎ *35/24–53–00* ▤ *DC, MC, V.*

$ ✕ **Sebastopol.** Students and locals crowd this laid-back eatery for brunch and on weekend evenings, but it's a good choice if you want to get off the beaten tourist path. The menu is varied with lots of salads, warm sandwiches, and burgers—and just about the most American-style brunch in the city. When it's warm, tables are set outside on the square, where there's great people-watching. ⊠ *Skt. Hans Torv 32, Nørrebro* ☎ *35/36–30–02* ☖ *Reservations not accepted* ▤ *AE, DC, MC, V.*

¢–$ ✕ **Kashmir.** The quiet, carpet-shrouded Indian restaurant is a favorite with locals, who come for the unusual vegetarian and fish menu. Specialties include tandoori-fried salmon, a hearty lentil soup, and the basic side dishes—such as *bhajis* (fried vegetables patties); *raita* (yogurt and cucumbers); and naan, Indian flat bread cooked in the tandoori oven. ⊠ *Nørrebrog. 35, Nørrebro* ☎ *35/37–54–71* ▤ *DC, MC, V.*

¢ ✕ **Tibet.** Here is a place that comes close to making authentic Tibetan fare, although they have replaced traditional yak meat and milk dishes with beef and organic cows' milk. National favorites *momo* (steamed dumplings with vegetable or meat filling) and *thentuk* (rice noodles with lamb or beef) share the menu with a selection of dishes from the Szechuan province of China. ⊠ *Blågårds Plads 10, Nørrebro* ☎ *35/36–85–05* ▤ *No credit cards* ☉ *Closed Mon.*

Sankt Annæ Kvarter & Østerbro

★ $$$$ ✕ **Godt.** The name says it all: this elegant little two-story restaurant with cool gray walls, silvery curtain partitions, and tulips in clear-glass bottles is *godt* (good). Actually, it's very, very good—so good that Godt has become the buzz of the town. The superb French-Danish menu showcases Chef Colin Rice's commitment to fresh ingredients and seasonal produce, which he buys every morning. Rice prepares a set daily menu, and you can choose to have three, four, or five courses. Dishes may include a black-bean and crab soup or a fillet of venison drizzled with truffle sauce. ⊠ *Gothersg. 38, Sankt Annæ Kvarter* ☎ *33/15–21–22* ☖ *Reservations essential* ▤ *DC, MC, V* ☉ *Closed Sun. and Mon. No lunch.*

$$$ ✕ **Els.** When it opened in 1853, the intimate Els was the place to be seen before the theater, and the painted Muses on the walls still watch diners rush to make an eight o'clock curtain. Antique wooden columns complement the period furniture, including tables inlaid with Royal Copenhagen tile work. The nouvelle French four-course menu changes every two weeks, always incorporating game, fish, and market produce. Jackets are recommended. ⊠ *Store Strandstr. 3, Sankt Annæ Kvarter* ☎ *33/14–13–41* ☖ *Reservations essential* ▤ *AE, DC, MC, V* ☉ *No lunch Sun.*

★ $$$ ✕ **Le Sommelier.** The grande dame of Copenhagen's French restaurants is appropriately named. The cellar boasts more than 800 varieties of wine, and you can order many of them by the glass. Exquisite French dishes are complemented by an elegant interior of pale yellow walls, rough-hewn wooden floors, brass chandeliers, and hanging copper pots. Dishes include guinea fowl in a foie gras sauce or lamb shank and crispy sweetbreads with parsley and garlic. While waiting for your table, you can sidle up to the burnished dark-wood and brass bar and begin sampling the wine. ⊠ *Bredg. 63–65, Sankt Annæ Kvarter* ☎ *33/11–45–15* ▤ *AE, DC, MC, V.*

$$$ ✕ **Zeleste.** This restaurant specializes in an inventive and refreshing strain of fusion cuisine. Outfitted with a short but well-worn bar, a covered and heated atrium, and—upstairs—a U-shape dining room, it serves as a soothing respite to Nyhavn's canal-front party. Although the food is usually excellent, if you're ravenous, ask specifically about portions—otherwise, you could end up with some tiny slivers of fried foie gras or a few tortellini. For lunch, the famished will do well with either the focaccia sandwich or the lobster salad served with toast and an excellent roux dressing; if the latter is not at your table within five minutes, you get a free glass of champagne. ⊠ *Store Strandstr. 6, Sankt Annæ Kvarter* ☎ *33/16–06–06* ⌃ *Reservations essential* ▤ *DC, MC, V.*

$$–$$$ ✕ **Le Saint Jacques.** The tiny dining room here barely accommodates a dozen tables, but whenever the sun shines, diners spill out from its icon-filled spaces to occupy tables facing busy Østerbrogade. The chef and owners come from some of the finest restaurants in town, but claim they started this place to slow down the pace and enjoy the company of their customers. The fare changes according to what is available at the market, but expect fabulous culinary combinations—smoked salmon with crushed eggplant, Canadian scallops with leeks and salmon roe in a beurre blanc sauce, sole with basil sauce and reduced balsamic glaze, and a savory *poussin* (young, small chicken) with sweetbreads scooped into phyllo pastry atop a bed of polenta and lentils. ⊠ *Skt. Jakobs Pl. 1, Østerbro* ☎ *35/42–77–07* ⌃ *Reservations essential* ▤ *DC, MC, V.*

$$–$$$ ✕ **Nyhavns Færgekro.** Locals pack into this waterfront café every day at lunchtime, when the staff unveils a buffet with 10 kinds of herring. An unsavory sailors' bar when Nyhavn was the city's port, the butter-yellow building retains a rustic charm. Waiters duck under rough wood beams when they deliver your choice of the delicious dinner specials, which might be salmon with dill sauce or steak with shaved truffles. In summer, sit outside and order an aquavit, the local spirit that tastes like caraway seeds. ⊠ *Nyhavn 5, Sankt Annæ Kvarter* ☎ *33/15–15–88* ▤ *DC, MC, V.*

$$
Fodor's Choice
★
✕ **Ida Davidsen.** Five generations old, this world-renowned lunch spot is synonymous with smørrebrød, and the reputation has brought crowds. The often-packed dining area is dimly lit, with worn wooden tables and news clippings of famous visitors on the walls. Creative sandwiches include the H. C. Andersen, with liver pâté, bacon, and tomatoes. The terrific smoked duck is smoked by Ida's husband, Adam, and served alongside a horseradish-spiked cabbage salad. ⊠ *Store Kongensg. 70, Sankt Annæ Kvarter* ☎ *33/91–36–55* ⌃ *Reservations essential* ▤ *AE, DC, MC, V* ☾ *Closed weekends and July. No dinner.*

$$
Fodor's Choice
★
✕ **Told & Snaps.** This authentic Danish smørrebrød restaurant adheres to tradition by offering a long list of Danish delights, and the fare is somewhat cheaper than the city's benchmark smørrebrød restaurant Ida Davidsen. The butter-fried sole with remoulade is a treat, as is the steak tartare. Wine is of course an option, but as this is true Danish cuisine, why not beer and *snaps* (Danish grain alcohol)? ⊠ *Toldbodg. 2, Sankt Annæ Kvarter* ☎ *33/93–83–85* ▤ *No credit cards* ☾ *Closed Sun. No dinner.*

$ ✕ **Lai Hoo.** Denmark's Princess Alexandra, a native of Hong Kong, was a fan of this Chinese restaurant near the city's main square when she lived in Copenhagen. The lunch specialty is an inspired variety of steamed dumplings (dim sum), and the best bet at dinner is the fixed menu—try the salt-baked prawns in pepper or the luscious lemon duck. ⊠ *Store Kongensg. 18, Sankt Annæ Kvarter* ☎ *33/93–93–19* ☰ *MC, V* ⊘ *No lunch Mon.–Wed.*

Vesterbro & Frederiksberg

$$$$ ✕ **Formel B.** The name stands for "basic formula," but this French-Danish fusion restaurant is anything but basic. Kirk, a third-generation chef, is fanatical about freshness, and this comes through in every dish. Dishes might include mussel soup flavored with wood sorrel; smoked salmon with dill seeds, spinach, and bacon; or panfried chicken with parsley root and horseradish, accompanied by all its parts—the liver, the heart, the craw, and the red comb—served on an array of small plates. Dessert is a work of art: a collection of individual delicacies are arranged on a large white eye-shape platter, and drizzled with a passion-fruit glaze and pine nuts. Kirk prepares a six-course menu (Dkr 550) daily, depending on what seasonal ingredients are available. There is no à la carte menu. ⊠ *Vesterbrog. 182, Frederiksberg* ☎ *33/25–10–66* ☰ *AE, DC, MC, V* ♙ *Reservations essential* ⊘ *Closed Sun. No lunch.*

$$$–$$$$ ✕ **Passagens Spisehus.** Tucked into a *passagens* (passageway) just steps from the Det Ny Teater (New Theater), this restaurant is leading the rediscovery of Scandinavia's culinary roots. Starters include smoked heart of reindeer, thinly sliced, served on a bed of marinated onions and beans, and a cream soup with potatoes, carrots, dill, and Baltic salmon. For your main dish, you can carve into bear from the Swedish woods with stuffed cabbage, potatoes, and sweetened beets or fillet of Lapland reindeer with seasonal vegetables. The elegant interior has dark-wood walls, black leather chairs, and soft white globes of light hanging over every table. It's popular with theatergoers who come for the fixed-price theater menu, which includes two or three courses and changes daily. ⊠ *Vesterbrog. 42, Vesterbro* ☎ *33/22–47–57* ☰ *MC, V* ⊘ *No lunch. Closed Sun.*

$–$$$ ✕ **Copenhagen Corner.** Diners here feast on superb views of the Rådhus Pladsen and terrific smørrebrød, which compensate for the uneven pace of the harried but hard-working staff and some of the less appealing dishes on the menu. Specialties include fried veal with bouillon gravy and fried potatoes; entrecôte in garlic and bordelaise sauce with creamed potatoes; and a herring plate with three types of spiced, marinated herring and boiled potatoes. ⊠ *Vesterbrog. 1, Vesterbro* ☎ *33/91–45–45* ☰ *AE, DC, MC, V.*

$–$$ ✕ **Delicatessen.** Happily defying labels, this casual diner–café–bar is done up in Dansk design—silver-gray bucket seats and a stainless steel-top bar—and serves hearty brunches and global cuisine by day, and cocktails and DJ-spun dance tunes by night. Linger over scrambled eggs with bacon and a steaming cup of coffee (served from 11 AM), or tuck into the international cuisine of the month, which runs from North African to Thai to Italian. The menu might include pad thai; lamb curry with basmati rice, mint, and yogurt; or roast pork with thyme and zucchini. A trip to the bathroom is good for grins: On your way you pass by two fun-house mirrors; look to one side, and you're squat and fat. Look to the other, and you're slender and tall. ⊠ *Vesterbrog. 120, Vesterbro* ☎ *33/22–16–33* ☰ *V.*

¢–$$ ✕ **Yan's Wok.** The former chef of Lai Hoo mans the wok here, serving Hong Kong–style cuisine, as well as peppery dishes from the Szechuan province.

The theater menu is a great deal and runs from 4 to 6, while a slightly higher-priced card is offered during dinner hours. Regardless of the hour, you can be sure of getting tasty meals at bargain prices. ⊠ *Bagerstr. 9, Vesterbro* ☎ *33/23–73–33* ▤ *DC, MC, V* ⊙ *Closed Mon. No lunch.*

WHERE TO STAY

Copenhagen is well served by a wide range of hotels, overall among Europe's most expensive. The hotels around the somewhat run-down red-light district of Istedgade—which looks more dangerous than it is—are the least expensive. Copenhagen is a compact, eminently walkable city, and most of the hotels are in or near the city center, usually within walking distance of most of the major sights and thoroughfares.

Breakfast is almost always included in the room rate. Rooms have bath or shower at the following hotels unless otherwise noted. Note that in Copenhagen, as in the rest of Denmark, half (to three-fourths) of the rooms usually have showers only (while the rest have showers and bathtubs) so make sure to state your preference when booking.

WHAT IT COSTS In kroner				
$$$$	$$$	$$	$	¢
FOR 2 PEOPLE over 1,700	1,400–1,700	1,000–1,400	700–1,000	under 700

Prices are for two people in a standard double room, including service charge and tax.

Amager & Kastrup

$$$$ ▥ **Hilton Copenhagen Airport.** Half the rooms at this modern business hotel have views of the city's skyline; the other half look out onto the airport. Rooms are done in a modern Scandinavian style with wooden furniture, light colors, and broad windows. The Copenhagen airport's main terminal is just across the street. ⊠ *Ellehammersvej 20, Copenhagen Airport, DK–2770 Kastrup* ☎ *32/50–15–01* ▤ *32/52–85–28* ⊕ *www.hilton.dk* ⟿ *382 rooms, 8 suites* ♻ *3 restaurants, indoor pool, gym, sauna, bar, meeting rooms, some pets allowed, no-smoking rooms* ▤ *AE, DC, MC, V.*

$$$$ ▥ **Radisson SAS Scandinavia.** South across the Stadsgraven from Christianshavn, this is one of northern Europe's largest hotels, and Copenhagen's token skyscraper. An immense lobby, with cool, recessed lighting and streamlined furniture, gives access to the city's first (and only) casino. Guest rooms are large and somewhat institutional but offer every modern convenience, making this a good choice if you prefer familiar comforts over character. The hotel's Dining Room restaurant, overlooking Copenhagen's copper towers and skyline, is a fine site for a leisurely lunch, while the dinner menu tempts guests with a changing list of six main courses concocted from fresh seasonal ingredients. The restaurant is closed on Sunday. ⊠ *Amager Blvd. 70, Amager DK–2300* ☎ *33/96–50–00* ▤ *33/96–55–00* ⊕ *www.radissonsas.com* ⟿ *542 rooms, 43 suites* ♻ *4 restaurants, cable TV, indoor pool, Internet, meeting rooms* ▤ *AE, DC, MC, V.*

¢ ▥ **Amager Danhostel.** This simple lodging is 4½ km (3 mi) outside town, close to the airport. The hostel is spread over nine interconnecting buildings, all laid out on one story. The student backpackers and families who stay here have access to the communal kitchen or can buy break-

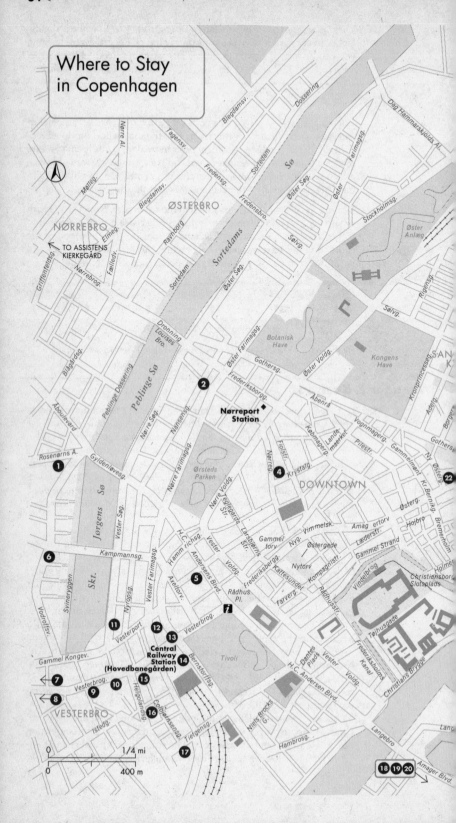

Where to Stay in Copenhagen

Admiral **24**

Amager Danhostel **18**

Ascot **5**

Cab–Inn Scandinavia **1**

Clarion Neptun **25**

Crown **9**

D'Angleterre **22**

DGI Byen **17**

Euroglobe **6**

First Hotel Vesterbro **10**

Grand Hotel **13**

Guldsmeden **7**

Hilton Copenhagen Airport . . .**20**

Ibsens Hotel **2**

Nyhavn 71 . . . .**23**

Phoenix **26**

Plaza Sofitel **14**

Radisson SAS Royal **12**

Radisson SAS Scandinavia . . .**19**

Saga **16**

Sct. Thomas **8**

Skt. Petri **4**

Scandic Copenhagen **11**

Skovshoved **3**

Strand **21**

Triton **15**

fast and dinner from the restaurant. The hostel is also wheelchair-accessible. Before 5 PM on weekdays, take Bus 46 from the main station directly to the hostel. After 5, from Rådhus Pladsen or the main station, take Bus 250 to Sundbyvesterplads, and change to Bus 100. Ask the driver to signal your stop. ⊠ *Vejlands Allé 200, Amager DK–2300* ☎ *32/52–29–08* 🖷 *32/52–27–08* ⊕ *www.copenhagenyouthhostel.dk* ⬐ *64 rooms with 2 beds, 80 family rooms with 5 beds, 4 large communal bathrooms* ♿ *Restaurant, laundry facilities, Internet* ▭ *MC, V.*

Downtown

$$$$ ▦ **D'Angleterre.** The grande dame of Copenhagen welcomes royalty, politi-
FodorśChoice cians, and rock stars—from Margaret Thatcher to Madonna—in pala-
★ tial surroundings: an imposing New Georgian facade leads into an English-style sitting room. Standard guest rooms are furnished in pastels, with overstuffed chairs and a mix of modern and antique furniture. The spit-and-polish staff accommodates every wish. The elegant Wiinblad restaurant serves excellent French-Danish dishes. In winter the square in front of the hotel is converted into a skating rink. ⊠ *Kongens Nytorv 34, Downtown DK–1021* ☎ *33/12–00–95* 🖷 *33/12–11–18* ⊕ *www.remmen.dk* ⬐ *118 rooms, 19 suites* ♿ *Restaurant, indoor pool, bar, Internet, meeting rooms* ▭ *AE, DC, MC, V.*

$$$$ ▦ **Skt. Petri.** For the better part of a century, a beloved department store nicknamed Dalle Valle occupied this site. It has been supplanted by this luxury hotel cast in a modern style. The individual rooms, designed and decorated by Per Arnoldi, are functional, decorated in a spare, modern aesthetic with bright and cheery colors. Most units have a terrace or balcony. The hotel envelops an atrium garden and terrace. ⊠ *Krystalg. 22, Downtown DK–1172* ☎ *33/45–91–00* 🖷 *33/45–91–10* ⊕ *www.hotelsktpetri.com* ⬐ *270 rooms, 27 suites* ♿ *Restaurant, café, free parking* ▭ *AE, DC, MC, V.*

$$$–$$$$ ▦ **Strand.** You can't stay closer to the harbor than here: just a five-minute walk from Nyhavn, this pleasant hotel is housed in a waterfront warehouse dating from 1869. The cozy lobby has brown leather couches and old maritime pictures on the walls. The rooms are small but comfortable, with blue-and-yellow bedspreads and sparkling bathrooms. ⊠ *Havneg. 37, Downtown DK–1058* ☎ *33/48–99–00* 🖷 *33/48–99–01* ⊕ *www.copenhagenstrand.dk* ⬐ *174 rooms, 2 suites* ♿ *Restaurant, bar, meeting rooms, some pets allowed, no-smoking rooms* ▭ *AE, DC, MC, V.*

$$$ ▦ **Ascot.** This charming downtown hotel's two outstanding features are a wrought-iron staircase and an excellent breakfast buffet. The lobby is classic, with marble and columns, and the guest rooms and apartments are comfy, with modern furniture and bright colors; some have kitchenettes. ⊠ *Studiestr. 61, Downtown DK–1554* ☎ *33/12–60–00* 🖷 *33/14–60–40* ⊕ *www.ascothotel.dk* ⬐ *161 rooms, 4 suites* ♿ *Cable TV, bar, meeting room, free parking, some pets allowed* ▭ *AE, DC, V.*

$$ ▦ **Ibsens Hotel.** This winsome, family-owned hotel near the Nørreport station has cozy, immaculate rooms and a lovely courtyard. The friendly staff is particularly attentive and goes out of its way to help. The attention to detail is evident in the hotel's decor, as well. Each floor has its own theme. The Scandinavian floor showcases cool and modern local designs while the Bohemian floor is filled with antique furnishings. The breakfast room is a lovely place to start your morning. ⊠ *Vendersg. 23, Downtown DK–1363* ☎ *33/13–19–13* 🖷 *33/13–19–16* ⊕ *www.ibsenshotel.dk* ⬐ *118 rooms, 3 suites* ♿ *Restaurant, bar, some pets allowed, no-smoking rooms* ▭ *AE, DC, MC, V.*

Sankt Annæ & North

$$$$ ⊞ **Clarion Neptun.** This elegant, central hotel was bought years ago with the intention of making it the bohemian gathering place of Copenhagen, but these days it is more practical than artsy and welcomes business guests, tourists, and even large tour groups. The lobby and lounge are light, with classical furnishings and pale tones, and guest rooms have a tasteful modern decor. Many rooms face an interior covered courtyard. Next door is the Restaurant Gendarmen, run by a group of young restaurateurs who have created a dinner menu on the concept of old-meets-new, marrying traditional Danish dishes (roast pork or cod) with nouveau touches, such as a light truffle or blueberry sauce. The traditional lunch menu consists of good old Danish fare, smørrebrød and the like. ⊠ *Skt. Annæ Pl. 18–20, Sankt Annæ Kvarter DK–1250* 🕿 *33/96–20–00* 🖷 *33/96–20–66* 🌐 *www.clarionhotel.com* 🛏 *133 rooms* ⚘ *Restaurant, bar, baby-sitting, meeting rooms, free parking* ☰ *AE, DC, MC, V.*

★ $$$$ ⊞ **Nyhavn 71.** In a 200-year-old warehouse, this quiet, soothing hotel is a good choice for privacy-seekers. It overlooks the old ships of Nyhavn, and its nautical interiors have been preserved with their original thick plaster walls and exposed brick. The rooms are tiny but cozy, with warm woolen spreads, dark woods, soft leather furniture, and crisscrossing timbers. ⊠ *Nyhavn 71, Sankt Annæ Kvarter DK–1051* 🕿 *33/43–62–00* 🖷 *33/43–62–01* 🌐 *www.71nyhavnhotelcopenhagen.dk* 🛏 *150 rooms, 3 suites* ⚘ *Restaurant, bar, meeting rooms, free parking, some pets allowed, no-smoking rooms* ☰ *AE, DC, MC, V.*

$$$$ ⊞ **Phoenix.** This luxury hotel has automatic glass doors, crystal chandeliers, and gilt touches everywhere. Originally built in the 1680s, the hotel was then torn down and rebuilt into a plush, Victorian-style hotel in 1847, rising from its rubble just like the mythical Phoenix rose from its ashes, and thus its name. The suites and business-class rooms are adorned with faux antiques and 18-carat gold–plated bathroom fixtures; the standard rooms are very small, measuring barely 9 feet by 15 feet. It's so convenient to city-center attractions that the hotel gets a fair amount of street noise; light sleepers should ask for rooms above the second floor. Downstairs is Murdoch's Books & Ale, a snug pub done up in mahogany and brass, with antique Danish tomes lining its bookshelves. The pub serves smørrebrød and light meals, including a green salad topped with chicken marinated in balsamic vinegar and a ham-and-onion quiche. It's closed on Sunday. ⊠ *Bredg. 37, Sankt Annæ Kvarter DK–1260* 🕿 *33/95–95–00* 🖷 *33/33–98–33* 🌐 *www.phoenixcopenhagen.dk* 🛏 *206 rooms, 7 suites* ⚘ *Restaurant, bar, parking (fee), some pets allowed, no-smoking rooms* ☰ *AE, DC, MC, V.*

★ $$$ ⊞ **Admiral.** A five-minute stroll from Nyhavn, overlooking old Copenhagen and Amalienborg, the monolithic Admiral was once a grain warehouse but now affords travelers no-nonsense accommodations. With massive stone walls—broken by rows of tiny windows—it's one of the less-expensive top hotels, cutting frills and prices. Its guest rooms are spare, with jutting beams and modern prints. ⊠ *Toldbodg. 24–28, Sankt Annæ Kvarter DK–1253* 🕿 *33/74–14–14* 🖷 *33/74–14–16* 🌐 *www.admiralhotel.dk* 🛏 *314 rooms, 52 suites* ⚘ *Restaurant, bar, nightclub, meeting room, free parking, some pets allowed, no-smoking rooms* ☰ *AE, DC, V.*

$$ ⊞ **Skovshoved.** This delightful, art-filled inn is 8 km (5 mi) north of town, near a few old fishing cottages beside the yacht harbor. Licensed since 1660, it has retained its provincial charm. Larger rooms overlook the sea, smaller ones rim the courtyard; all have both modern and antique furnishings. The best way to get here is to take Bus 6 from Rådhus Plad-

FodorsChoice
★

sen or the S-train to Charlottenlund and walk 10 minutes from the station. ✉ *Strandvejen 267, DK–2920 Charlottenlund* ☎ *39/64–00–28* 🖷 *39/64–06–72* ☏ *23 rooms, 3 suites* ♨ *Restaurant, billiards, bar, meeting rooms* ▭ *AE, DC, MC, V.*

Vesterbro & Frederiksberg

$$$$ 🏨 **Plaza Sofitel.** With its convenient location and plush homey atmosphere, this hotel has attracted the likes of Tina Turner and Keith Richards. Close to Tivoli and the main station, the building puts its best foot forward with a stately lobby and the adjacent Plaza Restaurant, which serves haute French-Italian cuisine. The older rooms are scattered with antiques; newer ones are furnished in a more modern style. The Library Bar is an elegantly cozy and atmospheric place for a drink, but the prices can be staggeringly high. ✉ *Bernstorffsg. 4, Vesterbro DK–1577* ☎ *33/14–92–62* 🖷 *33/93–93–62* ⊕ *www.sofitel.com* ☏ *93 rooms, 6 suites* ♨ *Restaurant, room service, bar, concierge, meeting rooms, parking (fee), some pets allowed, no-smoking rooms* ▭ *AE, DC, MC, V.*

$$$$ 🏨 **Radisson SAS Royal.** Towering over the heart of town, this high-rise
FodorsChoice   hotel was originally designed by Arne Jacobsen in 1960. Recently the own-
★   ers spent several years—and plenty of kroner—in reembracing its Jacobsen look, and the result is a veritable paean to the legendary designer. The graceful lobby has blue and white Jacobsen swan and egg chairs that are arranged in circles and illuminated by the ceiling's recessed lights. The soothing hotel rooms are paneled in light maple and outfitted with Jacobsen chairs and lamps. Even the heavy door handles, functionally designed to fill the palm, were created by Jacobsen. The headboards are inlaid with pale green and lavender kidney shapes. The most famous room is 606, which looks just like it did in 1960, with all the original furnishings, including a nifty desktop that opens to reveal a lighted makeup mirror. Many of the rooms boast views over Tivoli and the city center's copper-top buildings. The top-floor restaurant, Alberto K, serves top-notch Scandinavian-Italian cuisine. You don't have to be a hotel guest to bask in Jacobsen's aura. For the price of a cocktail, you can hang out in the elegant hotel bar, sitting on—and amid—Jacobsen designs. ✉ *Hammerichsg. 1, Vesterbro DK–1611* ☎ *33/42–60–00* 🖷 *33/42–61–00* ⊕ *www.radissonsas.com* ☏ *260 rooms, 6 suites* ♨ *Restaurant, room service, gym, bar, Internet, meeting rooms, parking (fee), some pets allowed, no-smoking rooms* ▭ *AE, DC, MC, V.*

$$$$ 🏨 **Scandic Copenhagen.** Rising over Copenhagen's lakes, alongside the cylindrical Tycho Brahe Planetarium, is this modern high-rise hotel. The comfortable rooms, done up in cool tones and blond-wood furnishings, have splendid views. One side of the hotel overlooks the peaceful lakes, and the other side the bustling heart of Copenhagen, including Tivoli. The higher up you go, the better the view, so inquire about a room on the 17th floor, which is the highest floor that still has standard doubles; it's suites-only on the 18th. ✉ *Vester Søg. 6, Vesterbro DK–1601* ☎ *33/14–35–35* 🖷 *33/32–12–23* ⊕ *www.scandic-hotels.com* ☏ *472 rooms, 6 suites* ♨ *Restaurant, room service, gym, sauna, bar, concierge, meeting rooms, parking (fee), some pets allowed, no-smoking rooms* ▭ *AE, DC, MC, V.*

$$$–$$$$ 🏨 **First Hotel Vesterbro.** Looming over Vesterbrogade—and just a five-minute walk from Tivoli—this four-star deluxe hotel is Denmark's third largest. The sun-drenched lobby, with floor-to-ceiling windows, has white pillars, blond-wood tables, and gray Dansk design armchairs. It's the first hotel to be newly built in Copenhagen in the past 15 years and, not surprisingly, the rooms are equipped with all the latest gizmos, including Web TV. The rooms have pale yellow walls, cherry-wood furnishings, and contemporary lithographs. Female travelers may want try out the "First Lady" rooms, which include adjustable mirrors and makeup remover in the bathrooms, fluffy bathrobes, an electric kettle, and women's magazines. The hotel's highlight is its magnificent brick-wall atrium awash in sunlight and hanging plants, and outfitted with marble tables and rounded wicker chairs; the ample complimentary breakfast buffet is served here. Later in the day the handsome Alex Vinbar & Kokken restaurant, presided over by an up-and-coming Swedish chef, serves contemporary Scandinavian cuisine and offers more than 250 wines, any of which can be ordered by the glass. ⊠ *Vesterbrog. 23–29, Vesterbro DK–1620* ☎ *33/78–80–00* 🖷 *33/78–80–80* ⊕ *www.firsthotels. com* ➳ *403 rooms, 1 suite* ⚒ *Restaurant, gym, bar, meeting rooms, parking (fee), some pets allowed, no-smoking rooms* ⊟ *AE, DC, MC, V.*

$$$–$$$$ 🏨 **Grand Hotel.** In operation since the turn of the 20th century, the Grand Hotel has a faded elegance that can be comforting. From its old-style lobby, presided over by a crystal chandelier, to its narrow stairs and uneven hallways, this hotel stands as the proud antithesis to all that's sleek and shiny. The rooms are a blend of old and new, with blue-and-gold curtains, traditional cherry-wood furnishings, and all the modern conveniences, such as satellite TV and minibars. The drawback is that some of the rooms have tiny bathrooms, so inquire about this when booking. ⊠ *Vesterbrog. 9, Vesterbro DK–1620* ☎ *33/27–69–00* 🖷 *33/ 27–69–01* ⊕ *www.grandhotelcopenhagen.dk* ➳ *161 rooms, 2 suites* ⚒ *Restaurant, room service, bar, concierge, meeting rooms, parking (fee), no-smoking rooms* ⊟ *AE, DC, MC, V.*

$$$ 🏨 **DGI Byen.** "An unusual meeting place" is how the DGI Byen presents itself, and it's a thoroughly apt description. This state-of-the-art recreation and sports center, just behind the Central train station, boasts a bowling alley, climbing wall, shooting range, swimming pool, spa, and 104-room hotel. The hotel rooms are an exquisite blend of Danish design. Dark blue furnishings and blond-wood floors are softly illuminated by cylindrical lamps. Short poems by the much-loved Danish philosopher Piet Hein grace the cool gray walls. Though most rooms have doubly insulated windows, you can sometimes hear the distant rumble of trains entering the station. The last train passes by at around 12:30 AM, so ask for a quiet room if you're a light sleeper. The pool is free to hotel guests; nonguests pay Dkr 46. You can pamper yourself with a range of soothing treatments at the full-service spa, but it costs extra. Ask about the substantially lower weekend rates. ⊠ *Tietgensg. 65, Vesterbro DK–1704* ☎ *33/29–80–00* 🖷 *33/29–80–80* ⊕ *www.dgi-byen.dk* ➳ *104 rooms* ⚒ *Restaurant, café, pool, sauna, spa, bowling, meeting rooms, parking (fee), no-smoking rooms* ⊟ *AE, DC, MC, V.*

$$ 🏨 **Guldsmeden.** This family hotel, in a 19th-century Vesterbro building, has rooms decorated and restored in French-colonial style with wood paneling, stucco, and high ceilings. The amenities of the rooms differ; they may have four-poster beds, bathtubs, fireplaces, or furnished balconies. Every room has original art on the walls and hand-picked teak furniture. ⊠ *Vesterbrog. 66, Vesterbro DK–1620* ☎ *33/22–15–00* 🖷 *33/22–15–55* ⊕ *www.hotelguldsmeden.dk* ➳ *64 rooms, some with bath, 4 suites* ⚒ *Café, some pets allowed* ⊟ *AE, D, MC, V.*

$ 🏨 **Crown.** Tucked into a small brick courtyard just off busy Vesterbrogade, this simple hotel has small but comfortable rooms with pale-yellow walls and light-green curtains. Some rooms overlook Vesterbrogade and the rest face the interior courtyard. The rooftop breakfast room floods with sunlight during the summer and offers pleasant bird's-eye views of the Vesterbro neighborhood. ⊠ *Vesterbrog. 41, Vesterbro DK–1620* ☎ *33/21–21–66* 🖷 *33/21–00–66* ⊕ *www.ibishotel.dk* ➳ *80 rooms* *with shower ⅃ Meeting rooms, some pets allowed, no-smoking rooms ⊟ AE, DC, MC, V.*

$ 🎴 **Saga.** This is one of the newer, refurbished hotels in the vicinity of the central train station. Some rooms have just a sink, while others have full bathrooms. Breakfast is included in the price, and the hotel is good for families. ⊠ *Colbjørnsensg. 18–20, Vesterbro DK–1652* 🕾 *33/ 24–49–44* 🖷 *33/24–60–33* ⊕ *www.sagahotel.dk* 💺 *79 rooms, 31 with shower ⅃ Some pets allowed ⊟ AE, DC, MC, V.*

$ 🎴 **Triton.** Despite seedy surroundings, this streamlined hotel attracts a cosmopolitan clientele thanks to a central location in Vesterbro. The large rooms, in blond-wood and warm tones, all include modern bathroom fixtures. The buffet breakfast is exceptionally generous and the staff friendly. There are also family suites with a bedroom and a sitting area with a sofabed. ⊠ *Helgolandsg. 7–11, Vesterbro DK–1653* 🕾 *33/ 31–32–66* 🖷 *33/31–69–70* ⊕ *www.ibishotel.dk* 💺 *123 rooms ⅃ Bar, some pets allowed ⊟ AE, DC, MC, V.*

¢ 🎴 **Cab–Inn Scandinavia.** This bright hotel is just west of the lakes and Vesterport Station. Its impeccably maintained rooms are distinctly small, but designed with super efficiency to include ample showers; fold-away and bunk beds; and even electric water kettles. The hotel is popular with business travelers in winter and kroner-pinching backpackers and families in summer. Its sister hotel, the **Cab–Inn Copenhagen,** is just around the corner, at Danasvej 32–34, but it's open only from April through September. ⊠ *Vodroffsvej 55, Frederiksberg DK–1900* 🕾 *35/36–11–11, Cab–Inn Copenhagen 33/21–04–00* 🖷 *35/36–11–14, Cab–Inn Copenhagen 33/21–74–09* ⊕ *www.cabinn.dk* 💺 *201 rooms with shower ⅃ Bar, meeting rooms, parking (fee) ⊟ AE, DC, MC, V.*

¢ 🎴 **Euroglobe.** A no-frills spot for the traveler who's looking for a comfortable bed with a roof overhead. Rooms are minimal, and guests share two common bathrooms on each floor. There's a little kitchen area on each floor where coffee, tea or soups can be prepared. With breakfast included, this spot is a fine choice for the frugal. ⊠ *Niels Ebbesensvej 20, Frederiksberg DK–1911* 🕾 *33/79–79–54* ⊕ *www.euroglobe.dk* 💺 *47 rooms without bath ⅃ Some pets allowed ⊟ No credit cards.*

¢ 🎴 **Sct. Thomas.** A short walk from the center of town in Fredericksberg's theater district, this hotel is a true bargain and just off the beaten path. In a sitting room area for guests, the hotel provides free Internet access. There is free parking in an adjacent garage. ⊠ *Frederiksberg Allé, Vesterbro DK–1621* 🕾 *33/21–64–64* 🖷 *33/25–64–60* ⊕ *www. hotelsctthomas.dk* 💺 *34 rooms, 26 with bath ⅃ Internet, free parking, no-smoking rooms ⊟ V.*

NIGHTLIFE & THE ARTS

Nightlife

Most nightlife is concentrated in the area in and around Strøget, though there are student and "leftist" cafés and bars in Nørrebro and more upscale spots in Østerbro. Vesterbro, whose main drags are Vesterbrogade and Istedgade, is a budding nighttime neighborhood, with a clutch of hip bars and cafés. Many restaurants, cafés, bars, and clubs stay open after midnight, a few until 5 AM. Copenhagen used to be famous for jazz, but unfortunately that has changed, with many of the best clubs closing down. However, you can find nightspots catering to almost all musical tastes, from bop to ballroom music to house, rap, and techno, in trendy clubs soundtracked by local DJs. The area around Nikolaj Kirken has the highest concentration of trendy discos and dance spots. Copenhagen's clubs can be a fickle bunch; new nighttime venues crop up regularly, often replacing last year's red-hot favorites. Call ahead or check out *Copenhagen This Week* (⊕ www.ctw.dk) for current listings. The stylish, biannual magazine *Scandinavian Living* (⊕ www.cphliving.dk) includes informative listings on the latest bars, restaurants, and shops. It also features articles on Danish culture, food, and architecture and is available at stores, hotels, and the tourist office.

Bars & Lounges

Copenhagen is peppered with hip restaurants that get even hipper in the evening, when they morph into lively nightspots. **Bang & Jensen** (⊠ Istedg. 130, Vesterbro ☎ 33/25–53–18), in the spotty-but-becoming-gentrified Vesterbro neighborhood, is a regular café during the day. From 9 PM until 2 AM, however, it turns into a cocktail bar jamming with loud music and a disco ambience. The **D'Angleterre Hotel** (⊠ Kongens Nytorv 34, Downtown ☎ 33/37–06–64) is home to a tiny English-style bar that's just the place to soak up the posh hotel's ambience without forking over the kroner to stay here. When the hotel restaurant closes at 10 PM, bar guests can sit at tables by windows looking out on Copenhagen's most beautiful square, Kongens Nytorv. Moreover, after a peaceful drink or two, you will be within walking distance of a slew of other, more raucous nighttime spots. **Delicatessen** (⊠ Vesterbrog. 120, Vesterbro ☎ 33/22–16–33) serves international cuisine by day, but after 11 PM Thursday through Saturday, it's time for cocktails and dancing to DJ-spun house, hip-hop, and rock. **Café Ketchup** (⊠ Pilestr. 19, Downtown ☎ 33/32–30–30), just off the Strøget, draws an informal—though not unsavvy—crowd that gabs and grooves to the sounds of funk, house, hip-hop, and African music. It gets cooking after 11 PM on the weekends, once cocktails start replacing coffee. **Charlie's Bar** (⊠ Pilestr. 33, Downtown ☎ 33/32–22–89) insists that there are other beers in Copenhagen besides the omnipresent Carlsberg and Tuborg, and serves more than 46 draft and bottled beers to prove it. You can sample a handful of Danish microbreweries or Hoegaarden beer from Belgium. Indeed, there's no better place to enjoy such diversity than at this bar, which calls itself "proudly independent, independently proud" because it doesn't kowtow to the two big Danish brands. The dark room with low ceilings, owned by a transplanted Scotsman, is refreshingly unpretentious, with a laid-back crowd of regulars, both locals and expats.

Hviids Vinstue (⊠ Kongens Nytorv 19, Downtown ☎ 33/15–10–64) dates from the 1730s and attracts all kinds, young and old, singles and couples, for a glass of wine or cognac. **Konrad** (⊠ Pilestr. 12–14, Downtown ☎ 33/93–29–29) attracts a chic crowd that gathers around the classy see-and-be-seen bar. The **Library** (⊠ Bernstorffsg. 4, Vesterbro ☎ 33/14–92–62), in the Plaza, is an elegant spot for a quiet but pricey drink. **"90"** ("halvfems" in Danish; ⊠ Gammel Kongevej 90, Frederiksberg ☎ 33/31–84–90), which goes only by its street number, is the only watering hole that many Copenhagen old-timers trust for a "real beer." Unfortunately, it can take up to 15 minutes for the harried bartender to pull your draft pint. The small, atmospheric bar with dark orange walls and heavy wooden tables is the second home to a cast of crusty Copenhagen characters and outspoken barflies. At lunch, do as the locals do and buy smørrebrød from around the corner, and then bring it into the bar where you can settle in at one of the tables and enjoy your meal with one of the famous drafts. (There's a Dkr 5 charge just to sit at the table.) **Peder Oxe's basement** (⊠ Gråbrødretorv 11, Downtown ☎ 33/11–11–93) is casual and young, though nearly impossible to squeeze into on weekends.

Cafés

Café life appeared in Copenhagen in the '70s and quickly became a compulsory part of its urban existence. The cheapest sit-down eateries in town, where a cappuccino and sandwich often cost less than Dkr 60, cafés are lively and relaxed at night, the crowd usually an interesting mix. Once run-down and neglected, the up-and-coming Istedgade strip is beginning to sprout cheery cafés and restaurants.

Amokka Kaffehus (⊠ Dag Hammarskjölds Allé 36-40, Østerbro ☎ 35/25-35-35), a 10-minute walk from the Østerport train station, is a coffee-lover's dream. Specialty java is served alongside inventive sandwiches and salads. **Bjørg's** (⊠ Vester Voldg. 19, Downtown ☎ 33/14-53-20) has a zinc bar, red seating, and lots of large windows. Guests slouch over huge burgers, club sandwiches, and excellent coffees. **Dan Turrell** (⊠ Store Regneg. 3-5, Downtown ☎ 33/14-10-47), an old café, has become terribly chic of late, partly due to its good food and candlelight. At the fashionable **Europa** (⊠ Amagertorv 1, Downtown ☎ 33/14-28-89), people-watching and coffee naturally go together. **Krasnapolsky** (⊠ Vesterg. 10, Downtown ☎ 33/32-88-00) packs a young, hip, and painfully well-dressed audience at night, while a more mixed group populates its confines on placid afternoons.

Mama Lustra (⊠ Istedg. 96, Vesterbro ☎ 33/25-26-11) looks like it could be a corner of your grandma's attic, with mismatched chairs, old wooden tables, and brass candle holders. Sink into a stuffed chair and sip a coffee or glass of Spanish wine while gazing out over busy Istedgade. The place also serves a simple but tasty brunch with cured ham, Italian sausages, and scrambled eggs, and an assortment of sandwiches including a vegetarian favorite—sun-dried tomatoes, pesto, and arugula. On Sunday, it hosts storytelling and spoken-word sessions. **Norden** (⊠ Østerg. 61, Downtown ☎ 33/11-77-91) resides at the intersection of Købmagergade and Strøget. Substantial portions make up for minimal table space at this art nouveau–style café. **Rust** (⊠ Guldbergsg. 8, Nørrebro ☎ 35/24-52-00) is a constantly crowded all-in-one rock club–restaurant–café on Nørrebro's main square, Skt. Hans Torv. Hearty, fresh dishes are served inside, while grill food is served on the terrace. **Sebastopol** (⊠ Skt. Hans Torv 32, Nørrebro ☎ 35/36-30-02) teems with gussied-up locals in the evening and serves an ample weekend brunch. **Sommersko** (⊠ Kronprinsensg. 6, Downtown ☎ 33/14-81-89) is the granddaddy of Copenhagen cafés, with a surprisingly varied menu (try the delicious french fries with pesto or the wok specialties) and an eclectic crowd. **Victor** (⊠ Ny Østerg. 8, Downtown ☎ 33/13-36-13) is all brass and dark wood, lovely for a light lunch.

Casino

The **Casino Copenhagen** (⊠ Amager Blvd. 70, Amager ☎ 33/96-59-65), at the SAS Scandinavia Hotel, has American and French roulette, blackjack, baccarat, and slot machines. Admission is Dkr 80 (you must be 18 years old and show a photo ID), and a dress code (jackets required; no athletic clothing or jeans) is enforced. Outerwear must be left at the wardrobe, for a fee. The dealers and croupiers are not shy about reminding winners that a tip of a certain percentage is customary, even after hitting just one number on the roulette wheel. The casino is open 2 PM to 4 AM.

Discos, Dancing & Live Music

Most discos open at 11 PM, charging covers of about Dkr 50–Dkr 100 and selling drinks at steep prices. **Absalon** (⊠ Frederiksbergg. 38, Downtown ☎ 33/16-16-98), popular with nearly everyone, has lively live music on the ground floor and a disco above. **Baron & Baroness** (⊠ Vesterbrog.

2E, Vesterbro ☎ 33/16–01–01) has medieval interiors and draws loads of young people almost every night with retro '80s music. The dance floor is one flight up from ground level. **Columbus** (✉ Nørrebrog. 22, Nørrebro ☎ 35/37–00–51) is a lively salsa club where the activity gets hot as a chili pepper on a good night. Excellent salsa lessons are available to the uninitiated and out-of-practice. **Level CPH** (✉ Skinderg. 45, Downtown ☎ 33/13–26–25) pulsates to '80s dance tunes and features a roomy dance floor and a reconstructed airport lounge–like area, outfitted with real airplane seats. **Luft Kastellet** (✉ Strandg. 100-B, Christianshavn ☎ 70/26–26–24) fosters a beach-like atmosphere with its indoor-outdoor layout and harborside location. Guests often dance barefoot on the sand-covered floors to modern jazz, funk or lounge-inspired chill-out tunes. **Nasa** (✉ Gothersg. 8F, Boltens Gård, Sankt Annæ Kvarter ☎ 33/93–74–15) has an exclusive "members only" policy, which has earned it legendary status among Copenhagen's nightclubs. The choosy doorman screens the throngs outside based on his impression of their looks, clothes, and attitude. Luckily, rumor has it that Nasa is relaxing its door policy. Once inside, you get to hobnob in cool, white interiors with the city's chic and moneyed set and local celebrities (Prince Frederik occasionally drops by). Underneath Nasa are two other clubs, Club Bahia and Blue Buddha, with a more casual vibe and much more lax door policies.

Park Café (✉ Østerbrog. 79, Østerbro ☎ 35/42–62–48) offers an old-world café with live music downstairs, a disco upstairs, and a movie theater just next door. **Den Røde Pimpernel** (✉ Bernstorffsg. 3, Vesterbro ☎ 33/75–07–60) draws an adult audience for dancing to live orchestras, trios, and old-time music. The very popular English-style **Rosie McGees** (✉ Vesterbrog. 2A, Vesterbro ☎ 33/32–19–23) pub serves American and Mexican eats and encourages dancing. **Sabor Latino** (✉ Vester Voldg. 85, Downtown ☎ 33/11–97–66) is the United Nations of discos, with an international crowd dancing to salsa and other Latin rhythms. **Sofie Kælder** (✉ Overgaden oven Vandet 32, Christianshavn ☎ 32/57–27–87) is a veteran of the Copenhagen night scene and serves as a frequent hangout for local musicians. Live music plays on Thursday, a DJ spins on Friday, and live jazz on Saturday afternoons gives way to piano-bar tunes in the evening. The kitchen serves simple fare to accompany cocktails. **Stereo Bar** (✉ Linnésg. 16A, Downtown ☎ 33/13–61–13) has lava lamps and '70s furnishings; plays house, soul, and funk music; and draws an eclectic crowd, from design students to writers, providing your best chance for an interesting conversation in Copenhagen's club scene. The **Søpavillionen** (✉ Gyldenløvsg. 24, Vesterbro ☎ 33/15–12–24) invariably inspires first-time visitors to ask, "what *is* that building?" The ornate white wooden structure next to Copenhagen's lakes was built in 1894. The pavilion hosts seminars and private events on weekdays and functions as a dance club until 5 AM on weekends, featuring live music and DJs. **Woodstock** (✉ Vesterg. 12, Downtown ☎ 33/11–20–71) is among the city's most enduring clubs. A mixed audience grooves to music from the '50s to the '80s.

Gay Bars & Establishments

Given Denmark's long-time liberal attitudes toward homosexuality, it's not surprising that Copenhagen has a thriving and varied gay nightlife scene. In August, Copenhagen celebrates "Mermaid Pride," its boisterous annual gay-pride parade.

Amigo Bar (✉ Schønbergsg. 4, Downtown ☎ 33/21–49–15) is popular with men of all ages. For a show-tune showdown, head for the piano bar at **Café Intime** (✉ Allég. 25, Frederiksberg ☎ 38/34–19–58), where you can sip cocktails to Miss Monica's spirited renditions of standards. It's easy to meet mostly men at **Can Can** (✉ Mikkel Bryggesg. 11, Downtown ☎ 33/11–50–10), a small place with a friendly bartender.

The small **Central Hjørnet** (✉ Kattesundet 18, Downtown ☎33/11–85–49) has been around for about 60 years. The dark, casual **Cosy Bar** (✉ Studiestr. 24, Downtown ☎ 33/12–74–27) is the place to go in the wee hours (it usually stays open until 8 AM). **Heaven Café** (✉Kompagnistr. 18, Downtown ☎ 33/15–19–00) is the latest addition to the gay café scene, serving light meals to a casual crowd of locals and foreigners. **Jeppes Club** (✉ Allég. 25, Frederiksberg ☎ 38/87–32–48) is patronized mainly by gay women and opens on the first and last Fridays of every month. **Masken Bar & Café** (✉ Studiestr. 33, Downtown ☎ 33/91–09–37) is a relaxed bar welcoming both men and women. **Men's Bar** (✉ Teglgårdstr. 3, Downtown ☎ 33/12–73–03) is men-only with a leather-and-rubber dress code; the decor is dark and casual. **Never Mind** (✉ Nørre Voldg. 2, Downtown ☎ 33/11–88–86), across the street from a park where gay men cruise, is popular among gay persons of all ages and both genders. **Oscar Café & Bar** (✉ Rådhus Pl. 77, Downtown ☎ 33/12–09–99) is a relaxed spot for a drink or a cup of coffee. **Pan Caféen** (✉ Knabrostr. 3, off Strøget, Downtown ☎ 33/11–37–84) packs men and women into its three floors of coffee and cocktail bars; the disco is open Wednesday through Saturday.

For more information, call or visit the **Landsforeningen for Bøsser og Lesbiske** (Gay and Lesbian Association; ✉ Teglgårdstr. 13, Boks 1023, Downtown DK–1007 ☎ 33/13–19–48 ⊕ www.lbl.dk), which has a library and more than 45 years of experience. Check out the free paper *Panbladet* (⊕ www.panbladet.dk), or the gay guides *Gayguide* (⊕ www.gayguide.dk) and *Copenhagen Gay Life* (⊕ www.copenhagen-gay-life.dk) for listings of nightlife events and clubs, and other topical information of special interest to the gay individual.

Jazz Clubs

Hard times have thinned Copenhagen's once-thriving jazz scene. Most of the clubs still open headline local talents, but European and international artists also perform, especially in July, when the Copenhagen Jazz Festival spills over into the clubs. Many jazz clubs host Sunday afternoon sessions that draw spirited crowds of Danes. **Copenhagen Jazzhouse** (✉ Niels Hemmingsensg. 10, Downtown ☎ 33/15–26–00) attracts European and some international names to its chic, modern, barlike interior. **Drop Inn** (✉ Kompagnistr. 34, Downtown ☎33/11–24–04) draws a capacity crowd for its popular Sunday afternoon jazz sessions. The bar was designed with the audience in mind. The stage faces an informal semicircle of chairs and booths so there isn't a bad seat in the house. The eclectic decor includes wrought-iron, wreath-shape candelabras, iron statues of winged bacchanalian figures, and an M. C. Escher–style ceiling fresco. **Jazzhuset** (✉ Rådhusstr. 13, Downtown ☎ 33/15–63–53), with exposed concrete walls decorated with local art, showcases traditional New Orleans–style jazz acts on Friday and Saturday. (It's closed on Sunday.) During the day, it functions as a café, in whose sunlit back room you can enjoy coffee, beer, and light sandwiches. An adjoining theater features everything from Shakespeare to experimental plays. **La Fontaine** (✉ Kompagnistr. 11, Downtown ☎ 33/11–60–98) is Copenhagen's quintessential jazz dive, with sagging curtains, impenetrable smoke, and hep cats. This is a must for jazz lovers.

Rock Clubs

Copenhagen has a good selection of rock clubs, most of which cost less than Dkr 50. Almost all are filled with young, fashionable crowds.

DENMARK'S CINEMA VERITÉ

CAUTION: WATCHING contemporary Danish films may induce dizziness and nausea and provoke a mild depression (or, if you prefer, a newfound understanding of the human capacity for evil). Whatever your take, it's the type of cinema that's hard to take sitting down, even with a tub of buttered popcorn in your lap. Denmark's bad boy of film is Lars von Trier, who has been called "bold, angry, and defiant" by one critic, and "ineptitude coupled with arrogance" by another. His best-known films include Dancer in the Dark (2000) starring the Icelandic singer Bjork, Breaking the Waves (1996) with actress Emily Watson, and Europa (1991) for which von Trier won the Palm d'Or prize at Cannes. His latest movie, Dogville (2003), stars Nicole Kidman, Lauren Bacall, and James Caan, and also stole a lot of attention at Cannes.

Von Trier is also the founder of Dogma 95, a union of Danish filmmakers who took a collective "Vow of Chastity" in 1995 to eschew modern (read: Hollywood) filmmaking methods and get back to the basics—handheld cameras instead of tripods, and no artificial lighting, special effects, or dubbed-in musical scores. The result, both in content and in camera angles, has been moving—some would say stomach-churning—to say the least. A hyggelig evening turns to hell in the 1998 film The Celebration directed by Dogma 95 cofounder Thomas Vinterberg. Something in this disturbing tale clicked with worldwide audiences, because the film won the Special Jury prize at Cannes and screened in both the mainstream and art house circuit to great acclaim. The tagline could well have been lifted straight from Shakespeare's Hamlet, that "something is rotten in the state of Denmark." What starts out as a refined, candle-lit celebration for the father's 60th birthday soon degenerates into accusations and innuendo. A speech by the eldest son guts wide open the family's festering emotional wounds, brought on by years of mental and physical abuse from the aging patriarch himself. Rigidly upholding the Dogma 95 credo, Vinterberg shot the entire film with handheld cameras and used minimal extra lighting. The effect for the moviegoer is one of sitting right there at the dinner table, amid the tearful allegations and finger-pointing. That the audience is both participant and voyeur is, of course, exactly what Vinterberg intended. The Dogma 95 philosophy is that the camera should be used merely to record, following the action like an observing eye, so that the moviegoer can experience the characters' emotions as directly and purely as possible. The other Dogma 95 splash of 1998 was Von Trier's satirical The Idiots, about a group of young people who seek to undo the fabric of a small town by pretending to be mentally retarded.

Von Trier, Vinterberg, and their cronies hark from a rich cinematic tradition. Danish film blossomed in the 1930s with a spate of successful comedies and probing documentaries. The German occupation of Denmark from 1940 to 1945 proved to be a blessing in disguise for Danish cinema. All films from Allied countries were banned, giving rise to a proliferation of homegrown films. It was during the Occupation that Carl Theodor Dreyer, considered to be one of Denmark's most daring and brilliant filmmakers, solidified his already acclaimed filmic reputation with the making of Day of Wrath, an allegorical protest against the German invasion. Denmark's best-known contribution to the contemporary international film scene is director Bille August, who made a name for himself in the 1980s with a series of acclaimed films including, in 1987, Pelle the Conqueror, based on the novel by Danish author Martin Andersen Nexø.

Like any well-paced thriller, a surprise finale awaits: Von Trier is working on what he calls a "filmic monument"—tentatively titled Dimension—which he films a tiny part of each year. It's due for release in 2025 and, judging from his previous films, you won't want to miss it when it comes to a theater near you.

Clubs tend to open and go out of business with some frequency, but you can get free entertainment newspapers and flyers advertising gigs at almost any café.

Lades Kælder (✉ Kattesundet 6, Downtown ☎ 33/14–00–67), a local hangout just off Strøget, hosts bands that play good old-fashioned rock and roll. **Loppen** (✉ Bådsmandsstr. 43, Christianshavn ☎ 32/57–84–22), in Christiania, is a medium-sized concert venue featuring some of the bigger names in Danish music (pop, rock, urban, and jazz) and budding artists from abroad. The **Pumpehuset** (✉ Studiestr. 52, Downtown ☎ 33/93–19–60) is the place for soul and rock. **Rust** (✉ Guldbergsg. 8, Nørrebro ☎ 35/24–52–00) is a smaller club, mainly featuring rock, pop, and urban acts. **Stengade 30** (✉ Steng. 18, Nørrebro ☎ 35/36–09–38), named for an address right down the street from the actual club, is a smallish rock venue doubling as a bar that remains open through the night. **Vega** (✉ Enghavevej 40, Vesterbro ☎ 32/25–70–11) has evening rock bands, after which the dance club plays house and techno, dragging action into the wee hours.

The Arts

The most complete English calendar of events is listed in the tourist magazine *Copenhagen This Week* (www.ctw.dk), and includes musical and theatrical events as well as films and exhibitions. Copenhagen's main theater and concert season runs from September through May, and tickets can be obtained either directly from theaters and concert halls, or from ticket agencies. **Billetnet** (☎ 70/15–65–65 ⊕ www.billetnet.dk), a box-office service available at all post offices, has tickets for most major events. The main phone line is often busy; for information go in person to any post office. There's one on Købmagergade, just off Strøget. Same-day purchases at the box office at **Tivoli** (✉ Vesterbrog. 3, Downtown ☎ 33/15–10–12) are half price if you pick them up after noon; the half-price tickets are for shows all over town, but the ticket center also has full-price tickets for the park's own performances. The box office is open Monday through Friday, 11 to 5.

Film

Films open in Copenhagen a few months to a year after their U.S. premieres. The Danes are avid viewers, willing to pay Dkr 70 per ticket, wait in lines for premieres, and read subtitles. Call the theater for reservations, and pick up tickets (with assigned seat numbers) an hour before the movie. Most theaters have a café. **Cinemateket** (✉ Gothersg. 55, Downtown ☎ 33/74–34–00), in the Danish Film Institute building, runs art films—often a series with a theme—and houses an excellent gift shop and café. **Gloria** (✉ Rådhus Pl. 59, Downtown ☎ 33/12–42–92) plays recent independent releases and art-house favorites. **Grand Teatret** (✉ Mikkel Bryggersg. 8, Downtown ☎ 33/15–16–11) shows new foreign and art films, and is next door to its sister café. **Vester Vov Vov** (✉ Absalonsg. 5, Vesterbro ☎ 33/24–42–00) is an alternative venue for art-house and second-run films.

Opera, Ballet, Theater & Music

Concert and festival information is available from the **Dansk Musik Information Center** (DMIC; ✉ Gråbrødre Torv 16, Downtown ☎ 33/11–20–66 ⊕ www.mic.dk).

Det Kongelige Teater (The Royal Theater) (✉ Kongens Nytorv, Downtown ⌂ Box 2185, 1017 Kobenhavn K ☎ 33/69–69–33 ⊕ www.kglteater.dk), where the season runs October to May, is home to the Royal Danish Ballet, one of the premier companies in the world. Not as famous, but also accomplished, are the Royal Danish Opera and the Royal Danish Orchestra, the latter of which performs in all productions. Plays are exclusively in Danish. For information and reservations, call the theater. Beginning at the end of July, you can order tickets for the next season by writing to the theater.

If you are in search of experimental opera then **Den Anden Opera** (⊠ Kronprinsensg. 7, Downtown ☎ 33/32–38–30 ⊕ www.denandenopera.dk) is worth a visit. **Dansescenen** (⊠ Øster Fælled Torv 34, Østerbro ☎ 34/35–83–00 ⊕ www.dansescenen.dk) hosts various modern and experimental dance performances, some of which are put together by their choreographer-in-residence. **Kanonhallen** (⊠ Øster Fælled Torv 37 Østerbro ☎ 70/15–65–65 ⊕ www.kanonhallen.net) runs a modern dance troupe in the city. **Nyt Dansk Danseteater** (⊠ Guldbergsg. 29A, Nørrebro ☎ 35/39–87–87 ⊕ www.nddt.dk) has a modern dance company but not a performance space; Copenhagen performances are held at other venues.

Tivoli Concert Hall (⊠ Tietensg. 20, Downtown ☎ 33/15–10–12) offers more than 150 concerts each summer, presenting a host of Danish and foreign soloists, conductors, and orchestras.

London Toast Theatre (⊠ Kochsvej 18, Frederiksberg ☎ 33/22–86–86 ⊕ www.londontoast.dk) hosts English-language theater productions. **Københavns Internationale Teater (KIT)** (Copenhagen International Theatre) (⊠ Vesterg. 5, 3rd floor, Downtown ☎ 33/15–15–64 ⊕ www.kit.dk) offers an interesting lineup of entertainment for all ages between June and August. Under the title "Summerscene," KIT presents international contemporary theater, dance, inventive circus-style shows, and myriad other performances.

SPORTS & THE OUTDOORS

Beaches

North of Copenhagen along the old beach road, **Strandvejen** is a string of lovely old seaside towns and beaches. **Bellevue Beach** (⊠ across the street from Klampenborg Station, Klampenborg) is packed with locals and has cafés, kiosks, and surfboard rentals. **Charlottenlund Fort** (Bus 6 from Rådhus Pl.) is a bit more private, but you have to pay (about Dkr 20) to swim off the pier. The beaches along the tony town of **Vedbæk**, 18 km (11 mi) north of Copenhagen, are not very crowded as they are not as close to Copenhagen nor as easily accessible by public transportation.

Closest to the city, the route along **Amager Strandvej** to and from the airport is a 12-km (7½-mi) stretch of beaches and wooded areas. Helgoland beach, on the north end of this strand, has bathhouses and a long dock and requires a token entrance fee.

Biking

Bike rentals are available throughout the city, and most roads have bike lanes. You might also be lucky and find an advertisement-flanked "city bike," parked at busy points around the city including Kongens Nytorv and the Nørreport train station. Deposit Dkr 20 and pedal away; your money is returned when you return the bike. The city bikes are out and about from May to September. The Wonderful Copenhagen tourist information office has city bike maps with suggested bike routes including a route of the city's ramparts or of the Copenhagen harbor. Follow all traffic signs and signals; bicycle lights and reflectors must be used at night. The **Danish Cyclist Federation** (✉ Rømersg. 7, Downtown ☎ 33/ 32–31–21 ⊕ www.dcf.dk) has information about biking in the city. **Wonderful Copenhagen** (✉ Gammel Kongevej 1, Downtown ☎ 33/25–74–00 ⊕ www.woco.dk) can provide information about bike rental companies and routes throughout the city.

Canoeing

About 15 km (10 mi) north of Copenhagen, especially in the Lyngby area, several calm lakes and rivers are perfect for canoeing: the Mølleå (Mølle River) and the Bagsværd, Lyngby, and Furesø (Bagsværd, Lyngby, and Fur lakes). Hourly and daily rentals and package canoe tours are available throughout the region.

Golf

Although almost all courses in Denmark are run by private clubs, anybody who is a member of a club approved by a recognized authority—such as USPGA or R & A—can play. You will generally be asked to present a handicap card, something many American golfers do not carry around with them. It might be a good idea to have some proof of membership with you when you go to sign in. Otherwise, you will need to convince the staff you are indeed a golfer. It would be wise to call beforehand to find out if and when it is possible to play. Most golf course staffs are accommodating, especially for visitors. At this writing, there were only three pay-and-play courses within a 20-mi (30 km) radius of Copenhagen, and they tend to be crowded. They also follow varying restrictions that tend to be as strict as those of private clubs. Most courses have handicap limits, normally around 28, for prospective players. Clubs, bags, and handcarts can be rented at virtually all courses, but carts are a rarity. With few exceptions, carts may not be used without a letter from a doctor stating it is necessary. Some clubs do not accept reservations; call for details. **Copenhagen Golf Center** (✉ Golfsvinget 16–20, Vallenbæk ☎ 43/64–92–93) is one of the publicly accessible courses close to the city center. The 18-hole course is rather flat but challenging; there is a variety of practice facilities, including a driving range. **Copenhagen Indoor Golf Center** (✉ Refshalevej 177-B, Holmen ☎ 32/66–11–00) is a newly expanded indoor practice center in what was once the huge B & W shipbuilding plant. Pros are on hand to give lessons at the driving and chipping ranges, or the practice green. The 18-hole course at **Københavns Golf Klub** (✉ Dyrehaven 2, Lyngby ☎ 39/ 63–04–83) is said to be Scandinavia's oldest. It is located on the former royal hunting grounds, which is now a public park, so golfers must yield to people out strolling and to the herds of wild deer who live in the park. Greens fees cost about Dkr 280; check local rules about obstructions. One of Denmark's best courses, a frequent host of international tournaments, is the 18-hole **Rungsted Golf Klub** (✉ Vestre Stationsvej 16, Rungsted Kyst ☎ 45/86–34–44). A 30 handicap for all players is required on weekdays; on weekends and holidays the required handicap is 24 for men and a 29 for women. In 2003 **Simons Golf Club** (✉ Nybovej 5, Kvistgård ☎ 49/19–14–78) became the first course in Denmark to host European Tour competition. One of the finest in the country, the course was made even more challenging for the professionals who played there. There are fine practice facilities; call to check about the handicap requirement.

Horseback Riding

You can ride at the Dyrehavebakken (Deer Forest Hills) at **Fortunens Ponyudlejning** (✉ Ved Fortunen 33, Lyngby ☎ 45/87–60–58). A one-hour session (English saddle), in which both experienced and inexperienced riders go out with a guide, costs about Dkr 100.

Running

The 6-km (4-mi) loop around the three lakes just west of city center—Skt. Jørgens, Peblinge, and Sortedams—is a runner's nirvana. There are also paths at the Rosenborg Have; the Frederiksberg Garden (near Frederiksberg Station, corner of Frederiksberg Allé and Pile Allé); and the Dyrehaven, north of the city near Klampenborg.

Soccer

Danish soccer fans call themselves Rooligans, which loosely translates as well-behaved fans, as opposed to hooligans. These Rooligans idolize the national team's soccer players as superstars. When the rivalry is most intense (especially against Sweden and Norway), fans don face paint, wear head-to-toe red and white, incessantly wave the Dannebrog (Danish flag), and have a good time whether or not they win. The biggest stadium in town for national and international games is **Parken** (✉ Øster Allé 50, Østerbro ☎ 35/43–31–31). **Billetnet** (☎ 70/15–65–65) sells tickets for all matches. Prices are about Dkr 140 for slightly obstructed views at local matches, Dkr 220–Dkr 320 for unobstructed; international matches are more expensive.

Swimming

Swimming is very popular here, and the pools (all of which are indoor) are crowded but well maintained. Separate bath tickets can also be purchased. Admission to local pools (Dkr 20–Dkr 50) includes a locker key, but you have to bring your own towel. Most pools are 25 meters long. The **DGI Byen Swim Center** (✉ Tietgensg. 65, Vesterbro ☎ 33/29–80–00) contains a massive oval pool with 100-meter lanes and a nifty platform in the middle that can be raised for parties and conferences. The swim center also has a children's pool and a "mountain pool," with a climbing wall, wet trampoline, and several diving boards. Admission to the swim center is Dkr 50. During the popular monthly "spa night," candles are placed around the pool; dinner and wine are served on the raised pool platform; and massages and other spa services are offered. The beautiful **Frederiksberg Svømmehal** (✉ Helgesvej 29, Frederiksberg ☎ 38/14–04–00) maintains its old art-deco decor of sculptures and decorative tiles. The 50-meter **Lyngby Svømmehal** (✉ Lundtoftevej 53, Lyngby ☎ 45/97–39–60) has a separate diving pool. In the modern concrete **Vesterbro Svømmehal** (✉ Angelg. 4, Vesterbro ☎ 33/22–05–00), many enjoy swimming next to the large glass windows.

SHOPPING

A showcase for world-famous Danish design and craftsmanship, Copenhagen seems to have been designed with shoppers in mind. The best buys are such luxury items as crystal, porcelain, silver, and furs. Look for offers and sales (*tilbud* or *udsalg* in Danish) and check antiques and secondhand shops for classics at cut-rate prices. Although prices are inflated by a hefty 25% Value-Added Tax (Danes call it MOMS), non–European Union citizens can receive about an 18% refund. For more details and a list of all tax-free shops, ask at the tourist office for a copy of the *Tax-Free Shopping Guide*.

The **Information Center for Danish Crafts and Design** (✉ Amagertorv 1, Downtown ☎ 33/12–61–62 ⊕ www.danishcrafts.dk) provides helpful information on the city's galleries, shops, and workshops specializing in Danish crafts and design, from jewelry to ceramics to wooden toys to furniture. Its Web site has listings and reviews of the city's best crafts shops.

Shopping Districts & Malls

The pedestrian-only **Strøget** and adjacent Købmagergade are *the* shopping streets, but wander down the smaller streets for lower-priced, offbeat stores. The most exclusive shops are at the end of Strøget, around Kongens Nytorv, and on Ny Adelgade, Grønnegade, and Pistolstræde. **Kronprinsensgade** has become the in-vogue fashion strip, where a number of young Danish clothing designers have opened boutiques. **Bredgade**, just off Kongens Nytorv, is lined with elegant antique and silver shops, furniture stores, and auction houses. **Scala**, a city-center mall across the street from Tivoli, has several clothing stores, a couple of boisterous pubs, and a main-floor food court for the famished. Copenhagen's latest mall is the gleaming **Fisketorvet Shopping Center**, built in what was Copenhagen's old fish market. It's near the canal, south of the city center, within walking distance to the Dybbølsbro station. It includes all the usual mall shops, from chain clothing stores (Mango, Hennes & Mauritz) and shoe shops (including the ubiquitous Ecco) to a smattering of jewelry, watch, and stereo retailers, such as Swatch and Bang & Olufsen. Fast-food outlets abound. In the south part of the city, on **Vesterbrogade**, you can find discount stores—especially leather and clothing shops.

Department Stores

Hennes & Mauritz (✉ Amagertorv 21–24, Downtown ☎ 33/73–70–90), H & M for short, has stores all over town. They offer reasonably priced clothing and accessories for men, women, and children; best of all are the to-die-for baby clothes. **Illum** (✉ Østerg. 52, Downtown ☎ 33/14–40–02), not to be confused with Illums Bolighus, is well stocked, with a lovely rooftop café and excellent basement grocery. **Magasin** (✉ Kongens Nytorv 13, Downtown ☎ 33/11–44–33), Scandinavia's largest department store, also has a top-quality basement marketplace.

Specialty Stores

Antiques

For silver, porcelain, and crystal, the well-stocked shops on **Bredgade** are upscale and expensive. **Danborg Gold and Silver** (✉ Holbergsg. 17, Downtown ☎ 33/32–93–94) is one of the best places for estate jewelry and silver flatware. **Dansk Møbelkunst** (✉ Bredg. 32, Sankt Annæ Kvarter ☎ 33/32–38–37) is spacious and elegant, and home to one of the city's largest collections of vintage Danish furniture. Some of the pieces are by Arne Jacobsen, Kaare Klimt, and Finn Juhl, whose lustrous, rosewood furnishings are some of the finest examples of Danish design. **H. Danielsens** (✉ Læderstr. 11, Downtown ☎ 33/13–02–74) is a good bet for silver, Christmas plates, and porcelain. **Kaabers Antikvariat** (✉ Skinderg. 34, Downtown ☎ 33/15–41–77) is an emporium for old and rare books, prints, and maps. The dozens of **Ravnsborggade** (✉ Nørrebro) stores carry traditional pine, oak, and mahogany furniture, and smaller items such as lamps and tableware. Some of them sell tax-free items and can arrange shipping. **Royal Copenhagen** (✉ Amagertorv 6, Downtown ☎ 33/13–71–81), along Strøget, carries old and new china, porcelain patterns, and figurines, as well as seconds.

Audio Equipment

For high-tech design and acoustics, **Bang & Olufsen** (✉ Østerg. 3, Downtown ☎ 33/15–04–22) is so renowned that its products are in the permanent design collection of New York's Museum of Modern Art. (Check prices at home first to make sure you are getting a deal.)

Clothing

It used to be that Danish clothing design took a back seat to the famous Dansk-designed furniture and silver, but increasingly that's no longer the case. If you're on the prowl for the newest Danish threads, you'll find a burgeoning number of cooperatives and designer-owned stores around town, particularly along Kronprinsensgade, near the Strøget.

Artium (✉ Vesterbrog. 1, Vesterbro ☎ 33/12–34–88) offers an array of colorful, Scandinavian-designed sweaters and clothes alongside useful and artful household gifts. **Bruuns Bazaar** (✉ Kronprinsensg. 8, Downtown ☎ 33/32–19–99) has its items hanging in the closet of almost every stylish Dane. Here you can buy the Bruuns label—inspired designs with a classic, clean-cut Danish look—and other high-end names, including Gucci. **Companys** (✉ Frederiksbergg. 24, Downtown ☎ 33/11–35–55) carries a trendy, youthful style, typified by the Danish Matinique label. **Mett–Mari** (✉ Vesterg. 11, Downtown ☎ 33/15–87–25) is among the most inventive handmade women's clothing shops. **Munthe plus Simonsen** (✉ Kronprinsensg. 11, Downtown ☎ 33/32–03–12) sells innovative and playful—and pricey—Danish designs. **Petitgas Herrehatte** (✉ Købmagerg. 5, Downtown ☎ 33/13–62–70) is a venerable shop for old-fashioned men's hats. The **Sweater Market** (✉ Frederiksbergg. 15, Downtown ☎ 33/15–27–73) specializes in thick, traditional, patterned, and solid Scandinavian sweaters.

Crystal & Porcelain

Minus the VAT, such Danish classics as Holmegaards crystal and Royal Copenhagen porcelain usually are less expensive than they are back home. Signed art glass is always more expensive, but be on the lookout for seconds as well as secondhand and unsigned pieces. **Bodum Hus** (✉ Østerg. 10, on Strøget, Downtown ☎ 33/36–40–80) shows off a wide variety of reasonably priced Danish-designed functional, and especially kitchen-oriented, accoutrements; the milk foamers are indispensable for cappuccino lovers. **Royal Copenhagen** (✉ Amagertorv 6, Downtown ☎ 33/13–71–81) has firsts and seconds of its famous porcelain ware. The **Royal Copenhagen Factory** (✉ Smalleg. 47, Frederiksberg ☎ 38/14–92–97) offers a look at the goods at their source. The factory runs tours through its facilities on weekdays 9, 10, and 11 from mid-September through April, and weekdays at 9, 10, 11, 1, and 2 from May to mid-September. Holmegaards Glass can be purchased at either the Royal Copenhagen store on Amagertorv or at the factory on Smallegade (for seconds). Alternatively, you can travel to their dedicated factory **Holmegaards Glasværker** (✉ Glasværkvej 45, Holme-Olstrup ☎ 55/54–50–00), 97 km (60 mi) south of Copenhagen near the town of Næstved. **Rosenthal Studio-Haus** (✉ Frederiksberg. 21, on Strøget, Downtown ☎ 33/14–21–01) offers the lead-crystal wildlife reliefs of Mats Johansson as well as the very modern functional and decorative works of many other Italian and Scandinavian artisans. **Skandinavisk Glas** (✉ Ny Østerg. 4, Downtown ☎ 33/13–80–95) has a large selection of Danish and international glass and a helpful, informative staff.

Fur

Denmark, the world's biggest producer of ranched minks, is the place to go for quality furs. Furs are ranked into four grades: Saga Royal (the best), Saga, Quality 1, and Quality 2. **Birger Christensen** (⊠ Østerg. 38, Downtown ☎ 33/11–55–55), purveyor to the royal family and Copenhagen's finest furrier, deals only in Saga Royal quality. The store presents a new collection yearly from its in-house design team. Expect to spend about 20% less than in the United States for same-quality furs ($5,000–$10,000 for mink, $3,000 for a fur-lined coat) but as always, it pays to do your homework before you leave home. Birger Christensen is also among the preeminent fashion houses in town, carrying labels like Donna Karan, Chanel, Prada, Kenzo, Jil Sander, and Yves Saint Laurent. **A. C. Bang** (⊠ Lyngby Hovedg. 55, Lyngby ☎ 45/88–00–54) carries less expensive furs than Birger Christensen, but has an old-world, old-money aura and very high quality.

Furniture & Design

Gubi Design (⊠ Grønnegade 10, Downtown ☎ 33/32–63–68) is where to go for the super-clean *Wallpaper* look. The chic kitchens are amazing and amazingly priced, but if you can't afford to move one back home, you can at least gain inspiration before you remodel your own kitchen. **Illums Bolighus** (⊠ Amagertorv 10, Downtown ☎ 33/14–19–41) is part gallery, part department store, showing off cutting-edge Danish and international design—art glass, porcelain, silverware, carpets, and loads of grown-up toys. **Lysberg, Hansen & Therp** (⊠ Bredg. 75, Sankt Annæ Kvarter ☎ 33/14–47–87), one of the most prestigious interior-design firms in Denmark, has sumptuous showrooms done up in traditional and modern styles. **Paustian** (⊠ Kalkbrænderiløbskaj 2, Østerbro ☎ 39/16–65–65) offers you the chance to peruse elegant contemporary furniture and accessories in a building designed by Dane Jørn Utzon, the architect of the Sydney Opera House. You can also have a gourmet lunch at the Restaurant Paustian (it's open only for lunch). **Tage Andersen** (⊠ Ny Adelg. 12, Downtown ☎ 33/93–09–13) has a fantasy-infused floral gallery-like shop filled with one-of-a-kind gifts and arrangements; browsers (who generally don't purchase the expensive items) are charged a Dkr 45 admission.

Silver

Check the silver standard of a piece by its stamp. Three towers and "925S" (which means 925 parts out of 1,000) mark sterling. Two towers are used for silver plate. The "826S" stamp (also denoting sterling, but less pure) was used until the 1920s. Even with shipping charges, you can expect to save 50% versus American prices when buying Danish silver (especially used) at the source. **Georg Jensen** (⊠ Amagertorv 4, Downtown ☎ 33/11–40–80) is one of the most recognized names in international silver and his elegant, austere shop is aglitter with sterling. Jensen has its own museum next door. **Danish Silver** (⊠ Bredg. 22, Sankt Annæ Kvarter ☎ 33/11–52–52), owned by long-time Jensen collector Gregory Pepin, houses a remarkable collection of classic Jensen designs from holloware and place settings to art deco jewelry. Pepin, an American who has lived in Denmark for over a decade, is a font of information on Danish silver design, so if you're in the market, it's well worth a visit. The **English Silver House** (⊠ Pilestr. 4, Downtown ☎ 33/14–83–81) is an emporium of used estate silver. **Ira Hartogsohn** (⊠ Palæg. 8, Sankt Annæ Kvarter ☎ 33/15–53–98) carries all sorts of silver knickknacks and settings. **Sølvkælderen** (⊠ Kompagnistr. 1, Downtown ☎ 33/13–36–34) is the city's largest (and brightest) silver store, carrying an endless selection of tea services, place settings, and jewelry.

THE RISE OF DANISH DESIGN

WHAT DO THE SWAN, the Egg, and the Ant have in common? All are chairs · designed by the legendary Danish designer Arne Jacobsen. His furniture designs, along with those of numerous other Danes from Hans J. Wegner to Finn Juhl, have made their way into living rooms, offices, and museums around the world. Indeed, Danish furniture has become synonymous with superb craftsmanship and quality, and its popularity shows no signs of slowing down.

The timeless allure of Danish design, which had its heyday in the 1950s, has ensured its enduring success. Lego is as popular now—even amid the modern mania that all toys should have computer chips embedded in them—as when it was first designed back in the '50s. Bang & Olufsen radios from the late 1940s look positively futuristic alongside their blocky counterparts from the same era. And Danish furniture, from Jacobsen's stylishly simple chairs to Wegner's rounded, organic furniture are still displayed in design showrooms across the globe as the picture of modernity. Even Hollywood has come calling: in the sci-fi film "Men in Black," there's a scene where actor Will Smith spins around in a Jacobsen-designed Swan chair.

Whereas plenty of '50s designs have made a comeback for their kitsch value, Danish furniture never went out of style. The reason lies in its roots. Danish furniture designs are grounded in early 19th-century classicism, characterized by simple lines and a deliberate lack of decoration. This led many Danish designers to later embrace functionalism, which became the cornerstone of Danish design. Faced with this rapidly growing design movement, socialist Denmark did what it does best, and initiated various government aid programs to support new designers. In 1924, the Royal Academy of Fine Arts founded its furniture design school, appointing renowned designer and architect Kaare Klint as one of its first lecturers.

The rallying cry behind Danish designs in the 1940s and '50s continued to be "form follows function." Danish designers elevated the concept of functionalism to a new level, basing their designs wholly on the human body, and all its infinite needs and variations. "A chair is only finished when someone sits in it," said Wegner, summing up the era's design ethic with his signature simplicity. A cabinet maker by trade, Wegner is credited with creating the chair (called, appropriately enough, "The Chair") that first introduced Danish design to an international audience. In 1950, the American magazine Interiors featured on its cover Wegner's Round Chair (as it was originally titled), naming it the world's most beautiful chair. Kennedy and Nixon each sat in one of these Wegner chairs during their televised presidential debates, resulting in more American commissions than Wegner and his round-the-clock factory workers could handle. Denmark became the darling of the international design world, a position that it's held onto ever since.

The use of organic materials is a natural offshoot of functionalism, and Danish designers were early masters in employing wood—from rich mahogany to pale beech—in their designs. "The feeling for materials is universal," says Wegner. "Love of wood is something that all of mankind has in common. Regardless of where people come from, they cannot stop themselves from letting their hands stroke a piece of wood, hold it, sniff it, and experience the material."

For all the international success of Danish furniture, it's the Danes themselves who are its greatest fans. Settle into the well-appointed living room of many a Dane, and chances are that you're sitting on a Wegner chair at a table designed by Finn Juhl; a Poul Henningsen lamp might be lighting up the room, and you will likely be slicing your Danish meatballs with Jacobsen-designed cutlery.

Street Markets

Check with the tourist office or the tourist magazine *Copenhagen This Week* (www.ctw.dk) for flea markets. Bargaining is expected. When the weather gets warm it's time for outdoor flea markets in Denmark and the adventure of finding treasure among a vast amount of goods. Throughout the summer and into the autumn, there are six major flea markets every weekend. Two of the sites are right downtown. Along the walls of the cemetery **Assistens Kirkegård** (⊠ Nørrebro), where Hans Christian Andersen and Søren Kierkegaard are buried, there is a flea market on Saturdays with vendors who carry cutlery, dishes, clothes, books, and various other wares. At **Gammel Strand** on Fridays and Saturdays, the "market" is more of an outdoor antique shop; you might find porcelain and crystal figurines, silver, or even, on occasion, furniture. **Kongens Nytorv** hosts a Saturday flea market in the shadow of the Royal Theater; the pickings are not so regal, but if you arrive early enough, you might nab a piece of jewelry or some Danish porcelain. **Israel Plads** (⊠ near Nørreport Station) has a Saturday flea market from May through October, open 8–2. More than 100 professional dealers vend classic Danish porcelain, silver, jewelry, and crystal, plus books, prints, postcards, and more. The side street **Ravnsborggade** (⊠ Nørrebro) is dotted with antiques shops that move their wares outdoors on Sundays.

SIDE TRIPS FROM COPENHAGEN

Experimentarium

8 km (5 mi) north of Copenhagen.

In the beachside town of Hellerup is the user-friendly **Experimentarium**, where more than 300 exhibitions are clustered in various "Discovery Islands," each exploring a different facet of science, technology, and natural phenomena. A dozen body- and hands-on exhibits allow you to take skeleton-revealing bike rides, measure your lung capacity, stir up magnetic goop, play ball on a jet stream, and gyrate to gyroscopes. Once a bottling plant for the Tuborg Brewery, this center organizes one or two special exhibits a year; past installations have included interactive exhibits of the brain and tongue-wagging, life-size dinosaurs. Take Bus 6 or 650S from Rådhus Pladsen or the S-train to Hellerup; transfer to Bus 21 or 650S. Alternatively, take the S-train to Svanemøllen station, then walk north for 10 minutes. ⊠ *Tuborg Havnevej 7, Hellerup* ☎ *39/27-33-33* ⊕ *www.experimentarium.dk* ✆ *Dkr 95* ⊙ *Mon. and Wed.–Fri. 9–5, Tues. 9–9, weekends and holidays 11–5.*

Charlottenlund

10 km (6 mi) north of Copenhagen (take Bus 6 from Rådhus Pladsen or S-train to Charlottenlund station).

Just north of Copenhagen is the leafy, affluent coastal suburb of Charlottenlund, with a small, appealing beach that gets predictably crowded on sunny weekends. A little farther north is Charlottenlund Slot (Charlottenlund Palace), a graceful mansion that has housed various Danish royals since the 17th century. Today, it houses only offices and is not open to the public. The surrounding peaceful palace gardens, however, are open to all, and Copenhageners enjoy coming up here for weekend ambles and picnics.

A favorite with families is the nearby **Danmarks Akvarium** (Danmarks Aquarium), a sizeable, well-designed aquarium near the palace with all the usual aquatic suspects, from gliding sharks to brightly colored tropical fish to snapping crocodiles. ⊠ *Kavalergården 1, Charlottenlund* ☎ *39/ 62–32–83* ⊕ *www.akvarium.dk* ✉ *Dkr 70* ☉ *Nov.–Jan., daily 10–4; Feb.–Apr., daily 10–5; May–Aug., daily 10–6; Sept. and Oct., daily 10–5.*

Fodor'sChoice
★
While in Charlottenlund, don't miss the remarkable **Ordrupgaard,** one of the largest museum collections of French impressionism in Europe outside of France. Most of the great 19th-century French artists are represented, including Manet, Monet, Matisse, Cezanne, Renoir, Degas, Gauguin, Alfred Sisley, Delacroix, and Pissarro. Particularly noteworthy is Delacroix's 1838 painting of George Sand. The original painting depicted Sand listening to her lover Chopin play the piano. For unknown reasons, the painting was divided, and the half portraying Chopin now hangs in the Louvre. The Ordrupgaard also has a superb collection of Danish Golden Age painters, from Christen Købke to Vilhelm Hammershøj, who has been called "the Danish Edward Hopper" because of the deft use of light and space in his haunting, solitary paintings. Perhaps best of all is that much of the magnificent collection is displayed, refreshingly, in a non-museumlike setting. The paintings hang on the walls of what was once the home of museum founder and art collector Wilhelm Hansen. The lovely interior of this graceful manor house dating from 1918 has been left just as it was when Hansen and his wife Henny lived here. The white-and-gold ceiling has intricate flower moldings, and the gleaming dark-wood tables are set with Royal Copenhagen Flora Danica porcelain. Interspersed among the paintings are windows that provide glimpses of the surrounding lush, park-size grounds of beech trees, sloping lawns, a rose garden, and an orchard. Note that the museum may be closed for renovations, so call ahead. ⊠ *Vilvordevej 110, Charlottenlund* ☎ *39/64–11–83* ⊕ *www.ordrupgaard.dk* ✉ *Dkr 35; Dkr 55 for special exhibits* ☉ *Tues.–Sun. 1–4.*

need a
break?
Before or after your visit to the Ordrupgaard museum, wind down next door at the soothing **Ordrupgaard Café** (⊠ Vilvordevej 110, Charlottenlund ☎ 39/63–00–33), housed in the former stable of the manor house–turned–museum. Large picture windows overlook the wooded grounds, and museum posters of French and Danish artists line the café's whitewashed walls. Sink into one of the rustic cane chairs and enjoy the daily changing menu of light Danish-French dishes, such as the smoked salmon drizzled with lime sauce or a fluffy ham quiche served with fresh greens. For an afternoon snack, try a pastry along with a pot of coffee that you can refill as often as you wish. On Sunday from noon to 2, it serves a hearty brunch of eggs, bacon, smoked ham, and rye bread. The café is open Tuesday through Sunday, noon–5. Credit cards are not accepted.

Dragør

★ *22 km (14 mi) southeast of Copenhagen (take Bus 30 or 33 from Rådhus Pladsen).*

On the island of Amager, less than a half hour from Copenhagen, the quaint fishing town of Dragør (pronounced *drah*-wer) feels far away in distance and time. The town is set apart from the rest of the area around Copenhagen because it was settled by Dutch farmers in the 16th century. King Christian II ordered the community to provide fresh produce and flowers for the royal court. Today, neat rows of terra-cotta–roof houses trimmed with wandering ivy, roses, and the occasional waddling goose characterize the still meticulously maintained community. If there's one color that characterizes Dragør, it's the lovely pale yellow (called Dragør gul, or Dragør yellow) of its houses. According to local legend, the former town hall's chimney was built with a twist so that meetings couldn't be overheard.

As you're wandering around Dragør, notice that many of the older houses have an angled mirror contraption attached to their street-level windows. This *gade spejl* (street mirror), unique to Scandinavia, was— and perhaps still is—used by the occupants of the house to "spy" on the street activity. Usually positioned at seat-level, this is where the curious (often the older ladies of town) could pull up a chair and observe all the comings and goings of the neighborhood from the warmth and privacy of their own homes. You can see these street mirrors all across Denmark's small towns and sometimes in the older neighborhoods of the bigger cities.

The **Dragør Museum,** in one of the oldest houses in town, sits near the water on Dragør's colorful little harbor. The collection includes furniture from old skipper houses, costumes, drawings, and model ships. The museum shop has a good range of books on Dragør's history. ⊠ *Havnepl., Dragør* 🕾 *32/53–41–06* ⊕ *www.dragoermuseum.dk* ⊠ *Dkr 30* ⊘ *May–Sept., Tues.–Sun. 2–5, noon–4.*

A ticket to the Dragør Museum also affords entrance to the **Mølsted Museum,** which displays paintings by the famous local artist Christian Mølsted, whose colorful canvases capture the maritime ambience of Dragør and its rich natural surroundings. ⊠ *Dr. Dichs Pl. 1, Dragør* 🕾 *32/53–41–06* ⊕ *www.dragoermuseum.dk* ⊠ *Dkr 30* ⊘ *May–Aug., weekends noon–4.*

You can swing by the **Amagermuseet** in the nearby village of Store Magleby, 2 km (1 mi) west of Dragør. The museum is housed in two thatch-roof, whitewashed vintage farmhouses, which were once the home of the Dutch farmers and their families who settled here in the 16th century. The farmhouses are done up in period interiors, with original furnishings and displays of traditional Dutch costumes. Round out your visit with an outdoor stroll past grazing dairy cows and through well-tended vegetable gardens flourishing with the same vegetables that the settlers grew. ⊠ *Hovedg. 4 and 12, Dragør* 🕾 *32/53–93–07* ⊕ *www.amagermuseet.dk* ⊠ *Dkr 30* ⊘ *May–Sept., Tues.–Sun. noon–4; Oct.–Apr., Wed. and Sun. noon–4.*

Where to Stay & Eat

$$$ ╳ **Restaurant Beghuset.** This handsome restaurant with rustic stone floors and green-and-gold painted doors is named Beghuset (Pitch House), because this is where Dragør's fishermen used to boil the pitch that waterproofed their wooden ships. The creative Danish cuisine includes fried pigeon with mushrooms, grapes, and potatoes drizzled with a thyme-and-balsamic-vinegar dressing. The front-room café was once an old dry-foods store, hence all the old wooden shelves and drawers behind the bar. Here you can order simple (and inexpensive) dishes such as a beef patty with onions and baked potatoes, and wash them down with a cold beer. ⊠ *Strandg. 14, Dragør* 🕾 *32/53–01–36* ⊟ *AE, DC, MC, V* ⊘ *Closed Mon.*

$$-$$$ ╳ **Dragør Strandhotel.** Dragør's harborside centerpiece is this spacious, sunny restaurant and café, its exterior awash in a cool yellow like so many of the buildings in town. The Strandhotel started life as an inn, nearly 700 years ago, making it one of Denmark's oldest inns. Danish

royalty used to stay here in the 1500s, after going swan hunting nearby, and in the 1800s, Søren Kierkegaard was a regular guest. Though it has kept the "hotel" in its name, today it is only a restaurant. Owned and run by the Helgstrand family for the past 25 years, the Strandhotel has retained its former charms—vintage wooden cupboards and colored ceramics—with views of Dragør's small, bustling harbor. The menu is, disappointingly, tourist-driven (with items such as Mexi-burgers and Caesar salads), but the restaurant also serves Danish fare, including *frikadeller* (pork meatballs) with potato salad; fillet of sole with *remoulade* (a creamy sauce); and cod with red beets, mustard sauce, and chopped boiled egg. ⊠ *Strandlinien 9, Dragør* ☎ *32/52–00–75* ▭ *DC, MC, V* ☺ *Closed mid-Oct.–mid-Mar.*

$ 🏨 **Dragør Badehotel.** Built in 1907 as a seaside hotel for vacationing Copenhageners, this plain, comfortable hotel is still geared to the summer crowds, yet manages to maintain its wonderfully low prices (you'd easily pay twice the price in Copenhagen). The basic rooms have dark-green carpets and simple furniture; half the rooms include little terraces that face toward the water, so make sure to ask for one when booking. The bathrooms are small and basic, with a shower only (no bathtubs). Breakfast, which is included in the price, is served on the outside terrace during the summer. ⊠ *Drogdensvej 43, DK–2791 Dragør* ☎ *32/53–05–00* 🖷 *32/53–04–99* ⊕ *www.badehotellet.dk* ⇜ *34 rooms* ♨ *Restaurant, bar, meeting room, some pets allowed* ▭ *AE, DC, MC, V.*

Klampenborg, Bakken & Dyrehaven

15 km (9 mi) north of Copenhagen (take Bus 6 from Rådhus Pladsen or S-train to Klampenborg station).

As you follow the coast north of Copenhagen, you'll come upon the wealthy enclave of Klampenborg, whose residents are lucky enough to have the pleasant **Bellevue Beach** nearby. In summer, this luck may seem double-edged, when scores of city-weary sun-seekers pile out at the Klampenborg S-train station and head for the sand. The Danes have a perfect word for this: they call Bellevue a *fluepapir* (flypaper) beach. Still and all, Bellevue is an appealing seaside spot to soak up some rays, especially considering that it's just a 20-minute train ride from Copenhagen.

Klampenborg is no stranger to crowds. Just a few kilometers inland, within the peaceful Dyrehaven, is **Bakken**, the world's oldest amusement park—and one of Denmark's most popular attractions. If Tivoli is champagne in a fluted glass, then Bakken is a pint of beer. Bakken's crowd is working-class Danes, and lunch is hot dogs and cotton candy. Of course, Tivoli, with its trimmed hedges, dazzling firework displays, and evening concerts is still Copenhagen's reigning queen, but unpretentious Bakken makes no claims to the throne; instead, it is unabashedly about having a good time—being silly in the bumper cars, screaming at the top of your lungs on the rides, and eating food that's bad for you. There's something comfortable and nostalgic about Bakken's vaguely dilapidated state. Bakken has more than 100 rides, from quaint, rickety roller coasters (refreshingly free of that Disney gloss) to newer, faster rides to little-kid favorites such as Kaffekoppen, the Danish version of twirling teacups, where you sit in traditional Royal Copenhagen–style blue-and-white coffee cups. Bakken opens in the last weekend in March, with a festive ride by motorcyclists across Copenhagen to Bakken. It closes in late August, because this is when the Dyrehaven park animals begin to mate, and during their raging hormonal stage, the animals can be dangerous around children. ✉ *Dyrehavevej 62, inside Dyrhaven, Klampenborg, (take S-train to Klampenborg Station)* ☎ *39/63–73–00* ⊕ *www.bakken.dk* ✉ *Free; rides cost Dkr 10–Dkr 25; Dkr 200 for a day pass to all rides* ☉ *Late Mar.–late Aug., 2 PM–midnight.*

★ Bakken sits within the verdant, 2,500-acre **Dyrehaven** (Deer Park), where herds of wild deer roam freely. Once the favored hunting grounds of Danish royals, today Dyrehaven has become a cherished weekend oasis for Copenhageners. Hiking and biking trails traverse the park, and lush fields beckon to nature-seekers and families with picnic hampers. The deer are everywhere; in the less-trafficked regions of the park, you may find yourself surrounded by an entire herd of deer delicately stepping through the fields. The park's centerpiece is the copper-top, 17th-century **Eremitagen**, formerly a royal hunting lodge. It is closed to the public. Today, the Royal Hunting Society gathers here for annual lunches and celebrations, most famously on the first Sunday in November, when the society hosts a popular (and televised) steeplechase event in the park. The wet and muddy finale takes place near the Eremitagen when the riders attempt to make it across a small lake. Dyrehaven is a haven for hikers and bikers, but you can also go in for the royal treatment and enjoy it from the high seat of a horse-drawn carriage. The carriages gather at the park entrance near the Klampenborg S-train station. The cost is around Dkr 40 for 15 minutes, Dkr 60 to Bakken, Dkr 250 to the Eremitagen, and Dkr 400 for an hour. ✉ *Park entrance is near Klampenborg S-train station, Klampenborg* ☎ *39/63–39–00.*

Where to Eat

★ $$$$ ✕ **Strandmøllekroen.** The 200-year-old beachfront inn is filled with antiques and hunting trophies. The best views are of the Øresund from the back dining room. Elegantly served seafood and steaks are the mainstays, and for a bit of everything, try the seafood platter, with lobster, crab claws, and Greenland shrimp. ✉ *Strandvejen 808, Klampenborg* ☎ *39/63–01–04* ▭ *AE, DC, MC, V.*

Frilandsmuseet

16 km (10 mi) northwest of Copenhagen.

North of Copenhagen is Lyngby, its main draw the Frilandsmuseet, an open-air museum. About 50 farmhouses and cottages representing various periods of Danish history have been painstakingly dismantled, moved here, reconstructed, and filled with period furniture and tools. Trees and gardens surround the museum; bring lunch and plan to spend the day. To get here, take the S-train to the Sorgenfri Station, then walk right and follow the signs. ✉ *Kongevejen, Lyngby* ☎ *33/13–44–41* ⊕ *www.frilandsmuseet.dk* ✉ *Dkr 50; free Wed.* ☉ *Easter–Sept., Tues.–Sun. 10–5.*

Museet for Moderne Kunst (Arken)

20 km (12 mi) southwest of Copenhagen (take the S-train in the direction of either Hundige, Solrød Strand, or Køge to Ishøj Station, then pick up Bus 128 to the museum).

Architect Søren Robert Lund was just 25 when awarded the commission for this forward-looking museum, which he designed in metal and white concrete set against the flat coast southwest of Copenhagen. The museum, also known as the *Arken,* opened in March 1996 to great acclaim, both for its architecture and its collection. Unfortunately, for a couple of years following its opening, it was plagued with a string of stranger-than-fiction occurrences, including a director with an allegedly bogus resume. The situation has greatly improved and today the museum's massive sculpture room exhibits both modern Danish and international art, as well as experimental works. Dance, theater, film, and multimedia exhibits are additional attractions. ⊠ *Skovvej 100, Ishøj* ☎ *43/54-02-22* ⊕ *www.arken.dk* ⊠ *Dkr 55* ◷ *Tues.–Sun. 10–5, Wed. 10–9.*

COPENHAGEN A TO Z

ADDRESSES
Copenhagen began as Havnen (the harbor) with the seat of local government being near what is now Gammel Torv, just off the main pedestrian thoroughfare Strøget. Much of what is now the northeastern section of the downtown area was once under water. The harbor was dotted with islands. Through the centuries, various kings filled in the shallow waters and joined the islands to the mainland of Sjælland. During those years, the ramparts of the city were constructed and a system of moats and other water defenses were created. Most maps of the city still reveal the general plan of older defense measures.

Copenhagen grew up within and, eventually, beyond these fortified ramparts. Many of the main neighborhood districts are named after what were once the few points of entry to the city. What can confuse some visitors is the districts are named after points on the compass, but do not lie in that direction in relation to the city center. For instance, Vesterport means "western bridge" (the bridge was the western entry to Copenhagen), while the district lies southwest of downtown.

Nowadays downtown Copenhagen (indicated by a KBH K in mailing addresses) is concentrated around Strøget, in a one-square-km area containing lots of stores, cafés, restaurants, office buildings and galleries, with residential properties on the upper floors. Just ten years ago, the center of town (including its northeastern subdistrict Sankt Annæ Kvarter) was the absolute center of all shopping, dining and nightlife activity. It still is thriving, but some of the action has moved to neighboring districts.

A couple of centuries ago the districts of Vesterbro (KBH V), Nørrebro (KBH N) and Østerbro (KBH Ø) were once the outskirts of Copenhagen, named after the ports for entering the city. In the past decade, nightlife and shops have moved into these districts to make them much sought-after spots to live and play. Halmtorv in Vesterbro was once a haunt for street walkers and other urchins, but has become an "in" and increasingly gentrified neighborhood in recent years. The area of Nørrebro closest to downtown was once the working-class area of the city, but now contains some of the hottest property in town after cafés and shops sprouted in the area. Østerbro was mostly a bourgeois bastion, but has turned into a center for young families with lots of opportunity for shopping and recreation.

The man-made island of Christianshavn (KBH K) was filled and raised between Copenhagen and Amager island by King Christian IV to bolster the city's defense installations. Many of the military fortifications can still be seen, such as the Holmen naval base, which has become a thriving spot for creative offices, nightlife, and new residential growth. To the south Amager Island (KBH S) is a main focus of development and expansion plans for the Copenhagen metropolitan region.

AIR TRAVEL TO & FROM COPENHAGEN
For information, *see* Air Travel *in* Smart Travel Tips A to Z.

AIRPORTS & TRANSFERS
Copenhagen Airport, 10 km (6 mi) southeast of downtown in Kastrup, is the gateway to Scandinavia and the rest of Europe.
🔒 **Kastrup International Airport** ☎ 32/31-32-31 ⊕ www.cph.dk.

TRANSFERS   Although the 10-km (6-mi) drive from the airport to downtown is quick and easy, public transportation is excellent and much cheaper. The airport's sleek subterra nean train system takes less than 12 minutes to zip passengers into Copenhagen's main train station. Buy a ticket (Dkr 22.50) upstairs in the airport train station at terminal three; a free airport bus connects the international terminal with the domestic terminal. Three trains an hour leave for Copenhagen, while a fourth travels to Roskilde. Trains also travel from the airport directly to Malmö, Sweden (Dkr 60), via the Øresund Bridge, leaving every 20 minutes and taking 35 minutes in transit. Trains run on weekdays from 5 AM to midnight, on Saturday from 6 AM to midnight, and on Sunday from 6 AM to 11 PM.

SAS coach buses leave the international arrivals terminal every 15 minutes from 5:45 AM to 9:45 PM, cost Dkr 50, and take 25 minutes to reach Copenhagen's main train station on Vesterbrogade. Another SAS coach from Christiansborg, on Slotsholmsgade, to the airport runs every 15 minutes between 8:30 AM and noon, and every half-hour from noon to 6 PM. HT city buses depart from the international arrivals terminal every 15 minutes from 4:30 AM (Sunday 5:30 AM) to 11:45 PM, but take a long, circuitous route. Take Bus 250S for the Rådhus Pladsen and transfer. One-way tickets cost about Dkr 22.50.

The 20-minute taxi ride downtown costs around Dkr 170, though slightly more after 4 PM and weekends. Lines form at the international arrivals terminal. In the unlikely event there is no taxi available, there are several taxi companies you can call including Københavns Taxa.
🔒 Taxis **Københavns Taxa** ☎ 35/35-35-35.

BIKE TRAVEL
Bikes are delightfully well suited to Copenhagen's flat terrain and are popular among Danes as well as visitors. Bike rental costs Dkr 35–Dkr 70 a day, with a deposit of Dkr 100–Dkr 300. You may also be lucky enough to find a free city bike chained up at bike racks in various spots throughout the city, including Nørreport and Nyhavn. Insert a Dkr 20 coin, which will be returned to you when you return the bike.
🔒 Bike Rentals **Københavns Cykler** ✉ Central Station, Reventlowsg. 11, Vesterbro ☎ 33/33-86-13 ⊕ www.rentabike.dk. **Østerport Cykler** ✉ Oslo Plads 9, Østerbro ☎ 33/33-85-13 ⊕ www.rentabike.dk. **Urania Cykler** ✉ Gammel Kongevej 1, Vesterbro ☎ 33/21-80-88 ⊕ www.urania.dk.

CAR RENTAL
All major international car-rental agencies are represented in Copenhagen; most are at Copenhagen Airport or near the Vesterport Station.
🔒 **Avis** ✉ Copenhagen Airport, Kastrup ☎ 32/51-22-99 or 32/51-20-99 ✉ Kampmannsg. 1, Vesterbro ☎ 33/73-40-99 ⊕ www.avis.dk. **Budget** ✉ Copenhagen Airport, Kastrup ☎ 32/52-39-00 ⊕ www.budget.com. **Europcar-Pitzner Auto** ✉ Copenhagen Airport, Kastrup ☎ 32/50-30-90 or 32/50-66-60 ✉ Gammel Kongevej 13A, Vesterbro ☎ 33/55-99-00 ⊕ www.europcar.com. **Hertz** ✉ Copenhagen Airport, Kastrup ☎ 32/50-93-00 or 32/50-30-40 ✉ Vester Farimagsg. 1, Vesterbro ☎ 33/17-90-00 ⊕ www.hertzdk.dk.

CAR TRAVEL

The E20 highway, via bridges, connects Fredericia (on Jylland) with Middelfart (on Fyn), a distance of 16 km (10 mi), and goes on to Copenhagen, another 180 km (120 mi) east. Farther north, from Århus (in Jylland), you can get direct auto-catamaran service to Kalundborg (on Sjælland). From there, Route 23 leads to Roskilde, about 72 km (45 mi) east. Take Route 21 east and follow the signs to Copenhagen, another 40 km (25 mi). Make reservations for the ferry in advance through the Danish State Railways. Since the inauguration of the Øresund Bridge in 2000, Copenhagen is now linked to Malmö, Sweden. The trip takes about 30 minutes, and the steep bridge toll stands at Dkr 225 per car at this writing, though prices are likely to decrease to encourage more use.

If you are planning on seeing the sites of central Copenhagen, a car is not convenient. Parking spaces are at a premium and, when available, are expensive. A maze of one-way streets, relatively aggressive drivers, and bicycle lanes make it even more complicated. If you are going to drive, choose a small car that's easy to parallel park, bring a lot of small change to feed the meters, and be very aware of the cyclists on your right-hand side: they always have the right-of-way. For emergencies, contact Falck.

🔲 **Auto Rescue/Falck** ☎ 70/10-20-30 ⊕ www.falck.dk. **Danish State Railways** (DSB) ✉ Hovedbanegården (main train station), Vesterbro ☎ 70/13-14-15.

EMERGENCIES

Denmark's general emergency number is ☎ 112. Emergency dentists, near Østerport Station, are available weekdays 8 PM–9:30 PM and weekends and holidays 10–noon. The only acceptable payment method is cash. For emergency doctors, look in the phone book under *læge*. After normal business hours, emergency doctors make house calls in the central city and accept cash only; night fees are approximately Dkr 300–Dkr 400. You can also contact the U.S., Canadian, or British embassies for information on English-speaking doctors.

🔲 Doctors & Dentists **Casualty Wards-Skadestuen** ✉ Italiensvej 1, Amager ☎ 32/34-35-00 ✉ Niels Andersens Vej 65, Hellerup ☎ 39/77-37-64 or 39/77-39-77. **Doctor Emergency Service** ☎ 70/13-00-41 or 44/53-44-00, daily 4 PM–8 AM. **Tandlægevagt** (Dental Emergency Service) ✉ 14 Oslo Pl., Østerbro ☎ No phone.
🔲 Emergency Services **Police, fire, and ambulance** ☎ 112.
🔲 Hospitals **Frederiksberg Hospital** ✉ Nordre Fasanvej 57, Frederiksberg ☎ 38/16-38-16. **Rigshospitalet** ✉ Blegdamsvej 9, Østerbro ☎ 35/45-35-45.
🔲 24-Hour Pharmacies **Steno Apotek** ✉ Vesterbrog. 6C, Vesterbro ☎ 33/14-82-66. **Sønderbro Apotek** ✉ Amangerbrog. 158, Amager ☎ 32/58-01-40.

ENGLISH-LANGUAGE MEDIA

BOOKS Boghallen, the bookstore of the Politiken publishing house, offers a good selection of English-language books. Arnold Busck has an excellent selection, and also textbooks, CDs, and comic books. Gad Boglader runs shops in various parts of the city, including one on Strøget and another in the new Royal Library, and offers a broad assortment of English-language volumes, fiction and non-fiction, along with other items of interest. Most of these stores have a large section devoted to Denmark and Danish literature. Another option for the bookworm would be to browse the many used-book shops that dot many areas of the city.

🔲 **Arnold Busck** ✉ Kobmagerg. 49, Downtown ☎ 33/73-35-00. **Boghallen** ✉ Rådhus Pl. 37, Downtown ☎ 33/47-25-60. **Gad Boglader** ✉ Vimmelskaftet 32, Downtown ☎ 33/15-05-58.

NEWSPAPERS & *The Copenhagen Post* (www.cphpost.dk) is a weekly newspaper that
MAGAZINES covers Danish news events in English. Particularly helpful is its insert, *In & Out,* with reviews and listings of restaurants, bars, nightclubs, con-

certs, theater, temporary exhibits, flea markets, and festivals in Copenhagen. Anyone planning on staying in Copenhagen for a long period should peruse the classified ads listing apartment-rental agencies and jobs for English-speakers. It's available at select bookstores, some hotels, and tourist offices. The biannual magazine *Scandinavian Living* (www.scandinavianliving.com) includes articles on Scandinavian culture, food, and architecture and also lists the latest bars, restaurants, and shops. It's sold at the tourist office, as well as some stores and hotels.

LODGING

LOCAL AGENTS In summer, reservations are recommended, but should you arrive without one, try the hotel booking desk at the Wonderful Copenhagen tourist information office. The desk offers same-day, last-minute prices (if available) for remaining rooms in hotels and private homes. A fee of Dkr 50 is applied to each booking. You can also reserve private-home accommodations at Meet the Danes. The agency Hay4You has a selection of fully furnished apartments for rent to visitors staying in the city for a week or more. Young travelers looking for a room should head for Use It, the student and youth budget travel agency.

🔲 **Hay4You** ✉ Vimmelskaftet 49, Downtown 🕾 33/33-08-05 🖶 33/32-08-04 🌐 www.hay4you.dk. **Hotel booking desk** ✉ Bernstorffsg. 1, Downtown 🕾 70/22-24-42 🌐 www.woco.dk. **Meet the Danes** ✉ Ravnsborgg. 2, 2nd fl., Nørrebro 🕾 33/46-46-46 🖶 33/46-46-47 🌐 www.meetthedanes.dk. **Use It** ✉ Rådhusstr. 13, Downtown 🕾 33/73-06-20 🌐 www.useit.dk.

MONEY MATTERS

ATMS ATMs are located around town. Look for the red logos "Kontanten/Dankort Automat." Here you can use Visa, Plus, Mastercard/Eurocard, Eurochequecard and sometimes JCB cards to withdraw money. Machines are usually open 24 hours but some are closed at night.

CURRENCY EXCHANGE Almost all banks (including the Danske Bank at the airport) exchange money. Most hotels cash traveler's checks and exchange major foreign currencies, but they charge a substantial fee and give a lower rate. The exception to the rule—if you travel with cash—are the several locations of Forex (including the main train station and close to the Nørreport station). For up to $500, Forex charges only Dkr 20 for the entire transaction. Keep your receipt and it will even change any remaining kroner you may still have back to dollars or another currency for free. For traveler's checks, it charges Dkr 10 per check. Den Danske Bank exchange is open during and after normal banking hours at the main railway station, daily June through August 7 AM–10 PM, and daily September through May, 7 AM–9 PM. American Express is open weekdays 9–5 and Saturday 9–noon. The Change Group—open April through October daily 10–8, November through March daily 10–6—has several locations in the city center. Tivoli also exchanges money; it is open May through September, daily noon–11 PM.

🔲 **American Express Corporate Travel** ✉ Nansensg. 19, Downtown 🕾 70/23-04-60. **The Change Group** ✉ Vimmelskaftet 47, Downtown 🕾 33/93-04-18, ✉ Frederiksbergg. 5, Downtown 🕾 33/93-04-15 ✉ Østerg. 61, Østerbro 🕾 33/93-04-55 ✉ Vesterbrog. 9A, Vesterbro 🕾 33/24-04-47. **Den Danske Bank** ✉ Banegårdspl. (main train station), Vesterbro 🕾 33/12-04-11 ✉ Copenhagen Airport, Kastrup 🕾 32/46-02-80. **Forex** ✉ Hovedbanegården 22 (main train station), Vesterbro 🕾 33/11-22-20 ✉ Nørre Voldg. 90, Downtown 🕾 33/32-81-00. **Tivoli** ✉ Vesterbrog. 3, Vesterbro 🕾 33/15-10-01.

TAXIS

The shiny computer-metered Mercedes and Volvo cabs are not cheap. The base charge is Dkr 15, plus Dkr 8–Dkr 10 per km. A cab is available when it displays the sign FRI (free); one can be hailed or picked up in front of the main train station or at taxi stands, or by calling the numbers below. Outside the city center, always call for a cab, as your attempts to hail one will be in vain. Try Kobenhavns Taxaor Amager Øbro Taxi. A 40% surcharge applies if you order a cab at night or on the weekend.

🚌 **AmagerØbro Taxi** ☎ 32/52-31-11. **Kobenhavns Taxa** ☎ 35/35-35-35.

TOURS

The tourist office monitors all tours and has brochures and information. Most tours run through the summer until September.

BIKE TOURS Basic bicycle tours of Copenhagen with City Safari run around 2½ hours and cover the main sights of the city, while there is a more comprehensive trip (4½ hours) with lunch included. The guides not only point out the main attractions of Copenhagen and provide helpful information for travelers, but also give some insight into the daily routines of the Danes. Special theme tours are also available, such as a trip through historical Copenhagen, a tour to and around the Carlsberg brewery, a junket showing modern architecture, a route following the footsteps of Hans Christian Andersen, and an exciting Copenhagen-by-night trip. Prices range from Dkr 150 to Dkr 350 (lunch included).

If you would prefer that someone else do the peddling, an increasingly popular sightseeing method is provided by Quickshaw, one of the city's many cycle-taxi and -tour companies. Quickshaw bicycle chauffeurs can accommodate two passengers and offer two best-of-Copenhagen sightseeing routes or allow you to dictate your own trip; they will even wait out front while you visit museums or other points of interest. The cyclist-drivers are comfortable and adept as tour guides, narrating as they pedal. The cycle-taxis in service are parked at 18 strategic sites in the inner city.

🚌 **City Safari** ✉ Dansk Arkitektur Center (Gammel Dok) Strandg. 27B, Christianshavn ☎ 33/23-94-90 ⊕ www.citysafari.dk. **Quickshaw** ✉ Esplanaden 8D, Downtown ☎ 70/20-13-75 ⊕ www.quickshaw.dk.

BOAT TOURS The Harbor and Canal Tour (one hour) leaves from Gammel Strand and the east side of Kongens Nytorv from May to mid-September. Contact Canal Tours or the tourist office for times and rates. The City and Harbor Tour (2½ hours) includes a short bus trip through town and sails from the Fish Market on Holmens Canal through several more waterways, ending near Strøget. Just south of the embarkation point for the City and Harbor Tour is the equally charming Netto Boats, which also offers hour-long tours for about half the price of its competitors.

🚌 **Canal Tours** ☎ 33/42-33-20 ⊕ www.canal-tours.dk. **Netto Boats** ☎ 32/54-41-02 ⊕ www.havnerundfart.dk.

BUS TOURS The Grand Tour of Copenhagen (2½ hours) includes Tivoli, the New Carlsberg Museum, Christiansborg Castle, the Stock Exchange, the Danish Royal Theater, Nyhavn, Amalienborg Castle, Gefion Fountain, Grundtvig Church, and Rosenborg Castle. The City Tour (1½ hours) is more general, passing the New Carlsberg Museum, Christiansborg Castle, the Thorvaldsen Museum, the National Museum, the Stock Exchange, the Danish Royal Theater, Rosenborg Castle, the National Art Gallery, the Botanical Gardens, Amalienborg Castle, Gefion Fountain, and The Little Mermaid. The Open Top Tours (about 1 hour), which are given on London-style double-decker buses, include stops at Amalienborg, the Stock Exchange, Christiansborg, The Little Mermaid, Louis Tussaud's Wax Museum, the National Museum, the New Carlsberg Museum, Nyhavn, the Thorvaldsen Museum, and Tivoli. This tour gives attendees the option to disembark and embark on a later bus. Only the Grand Tour of Copenhagen, which covers the exteriors of the major sites, and the Open Top Tour, which covers less ground but more quickly, operate year-round. It's always a good idea to call first to confirm availability. Several other sightseeing tours leave from the Lur Blowers Column in Rådhus Pladsen 57, late March through September. For tour information call Copenhagen Excursions or Open Top Tours.

Copenhagen Excursions ☎ 32/54-06-06 ⊕ www.cex.dk. **Open Top Tours** ☎ 32/66-00-00 ⊕ www.sightseeing.dk.

WALKING TOURS Due to its manageable size and meandering avenues, Copenhagen is a great city for pedestrians. A number of companies offer walking tours of parts of the city, some catering to Danes and others offering outings in various languages. One of the best companies is Copenhagen Walking Tours, which schedules 10 different English-language guided tours. In addition to tours related to culture and city history, the service offers a Copenhagen shopping primer and a tour of Jewish Copenhagen. The outings begin at the Wonderful Copenhagen tourist information office on weekends—from June through August there are tours from Thursday through Sunday. In addition, there is also a special tour of Rosenborg Castle beginning in front of the palace at 11:30 on Tuesday.

Two-hour walking tours organized by Copenhagen Walks begin in front of the Wonderful Copenhagen office at 10:30 Monday through Saturday from May to September (call to confirm). There are three different routes: uptown on Monday and Thursday, crosstown on Tuesday and Friday, and downtown on Saturday. Richard Karpen, an American who has been living in Denmark for 14 years, leads the tours, offering information on both the interiors and exteriors of buildings and giving insight into the lifestyles, society, and politics of the Danes. His tour of Rosenborg Castle, including the treasury, meets at the castle at 1:30 Monday through Thursday from May to September.

Copenhagen Walking Tours ☎ 40/81-12-17 ⊕ www.copenhagen-walkingtours.dk. **Copenhagen Walks** ☎ 32/84-74-35 ⊕ www.copenhagenwalks.com. **Wonderful Copenhagen** ✉ Bernstorffsg. 1, Vesterbro ☎ 70/22-24-42 ⊕ www.woco.dk.

TRAIN TRAVEL

Copenhagen's Hovedbanegården (Central Station) is the hub of the DSB network and is connected to most major cities in Europe. Intercity trains leave every hour, usually on the hour, from 6 AM to 10 PM for principal towns in Fyn and Jylland. To find out more, contact the DSB. You can make reservations at the central station, at most other stations, and through travel agents.

DSB Information ☎ 70/13-14-15 ⊕ www.dsb.dk. **Hovedbanegården** ✉ Banegårdspl. 1 ☎ 33/14-17-01 ⊕ www.hovedbanen.dk.

TRANSPORTATION AROUND COPENHAGEN

Copenhagen is small, with most sights within one square mi at its center. Wear comfortable shoes and explore downtown on foot. Or follow the example of the Danes and rent a bike. For those with aching feet, an efficient transit system is available.

The Copenhagen Card offers unlimited travel on buses, metro and suburban trains (S-trains) as well as admission to some 60 museums and sights throughout both metropolitan Copenhagen and Malmö, Sweden. They're valid for a limited time, though, and therefore only worthwhile if you're planning a nonstop, intense sightseeing tour. The card costs

Dkr 225 (24 hours), Dkr 375 (48 hours), or Dkr 500 (72 hours) and is half-price for children ages 5 to 11. It can be purchased at bus and train stations, tourist offices, and hotels, or from travel agents.

Trains and buses operate from 5 AM (Sunday 6 AM) to midnight. After that, night buses run every half hour from 1 AM to 4:30 AM from the main bus station at Rådhus Pladsen to most areas of the city and surroundings. Trains and buses operate on the same ticket system and divide Copenhagen and surrounding areas into three zones. Tickets are validated on a time basis: on the basic ticket, which costs about Dkr 11 per hour, you can travel anywhere in the zone in which you started. A discount *klip kort* (clip card), good for 10 rides, costs Dkr 85 and must be stamped in the automatic ticket machines on buses or at stations. (If you don't stamp your clip card, you can be fined up to Dkr 500.) Get zone details for S-trains on the information line. The buses have a Danish information line with an automatic answering menu that is not very helpful, but try pressing the number 1 on your phone and wait for a human to pick up. The phone information line operates daily 7 AM–9:30 PM. You might do better by asking a bus driver or stopping by the HT Buses main office (open weekdays 9–7, Saturday 9–3) on the Rådhus Pladsen, where the helpful staff is organized and speaks enough English to adequately explain bus routes and schedules to tourists.

The HT harbor buses are ferries that travel up and down the canal, embarking from outside the Royal Library's Black Diamond, with stops at Knippelsbro, Nyhavn, and Holmen, and then back again, with lovely vistas along the way. The harbor buses run 6 times an hour, daily from 6 AM to 6:25 PM, and tickets cost around Dkr 25. If you have a klip kort, you can use it for a trip on the harbor bus.

The metro system runs regularly from 5 AM to 1 AM, and all night on weekends. Until the end of 2007 only two metro lines are in operation linking the northern neighborhood of Vanløse to the beginning of southern Amager through the downtown area.

Bus information ☎ 36/13-14-15 ⊕ www.ht.dk. **Metro information** ☎ 70/15-16-15 ⊕ www.m.dk. **S-train information** ☎ 70/13-14-15 ⊕ www.rejseplan.dk.

TRAVEL AGENCIES
For student and budget travel, try Kilroy Travels Denmark. For charter packages, stick with Spies. Star Tours also handles packages.
American Express Corporate Travel ✉ Nansensg. 19, Downtown ☎ 70/23-04-60 ⊕ www.nymans.dk. **Carlson Wagonlit** ✉ Vester Farimagsg. 7, 2nd fl., Vesterbro ☎ 33/63-78-78 ⊕ www.cwt.dk. **DSB Travel Bureau** ✉ Hovedbanegården (main train station), Vesterbro ☎ 33/13-14-18 ⊕ www.dsb.dk/rejsebureau. **Kilroy Travels Denmark** ✉ Skinderg. 28, Downtown ☎ 70/80-80-15 ⊕ www.kilroytravels.dk. **Spies** ✉ Nyropsg. 41, Vesterbro ☎ 70/10-42-00 ⊕ www.spies.dk. **Star Tour** ✉ H. C. Andersens Blvd. 12, Vesterbro ☎ 70/11-10-50 ⊕ www.startour.dk.

VISITOR INFORMATION
The Wonderful Copenhagen tourist information office is open May through the first two weeks of September, daily 9–8; the rest of September through April, weekdays 9–4:30 and Saturday 9–1:30. Note that the tourist office hours vary slightly from year to year, so you may want to call ahead. Its well-maintained Web site includes extensive listings of sights and events. Youth information in Copenhagen is available from Use It. Listings and reviews of Copenhagen's museums (including temporary exhibits), sights, and shops are included on www.aok.dk. The Danish Tourist Board's Web site has listings on hotels, restaurants, and

sights in Copenhagen and around Denmark; AOK also has an excellent Web site on Copenhagen. For more information on the outlying fishing village of Dragør, visit the office or Web site of Dragør Tourist Information.

AOK ⊕ www.aok.dk. **Danish Tourist Board** ⊕ www.visitdenmark.com. **Dragør Tourist Information** ✉ Havnepladsen 2, Dragør ☎ 32/53-41-06 ⊕ www.dragoer-information. dk. **Use It** ✉ Rådhusstr. 13, Downtown ☎33/73-06-20 ⊕www.useit.dk. **Wonderful Copenhagen** ✉ Bernstorffsg. 1, Vesterbro ☎ 70/22-24-42 ⊕ www.woco.dk.

SJÆLLAND &
ITS ISLANDS

2

FODOR'S CHOICE

Domkirke, *cathedral in Roskilde*

Hotel Vallø Slotskro, *Køge*

Kronborg Slot, *castle in Helsingør*

Lejre Forsøgscenter, *re-created Viking village in Lejre*

Louisiana, *museum in Humlebæk*

Skipperhuset, *hotel in Fredensborg*

HIGHLY RECOMMENDED

RESTAURANTS Club 42, *Roskilde*

Hansen's Café, *Hornbæk*

Nokken, *Rungsted Kyst*

Novo Latino, *Ålsgarde*

HOTELS Hotel Marienlyst, *Helsingør*

Hotel Store Kro, *Fredensborg*

Liselund Ny Slot, *Borre*

SIGHTS Frederiksborg Slot, *castle in Hillerød*

Rudolph Tegners Museum, *Dronningmølle*

Sorø

Updated by
Eduardo López
de Luzuriaga

THE GODDESS GEFION is said to have carved Sjælland (Zealand) from Sweden. If she did, she must have sliced the north deep with a fjord, while she chopped the south to pieces and left the sides bowing west. Though the coasts are deeply serrated, Gefion's myth is more dramatic than the flat, fertile land of rich meadows and beech stands.

Slightly larger than the state of Delaware, Sjælland is the largest of the Danish islands. From Copenhagen, almost any point on it can be reached in an hour and a half, making it the most traveled portion of the country—and it is especially easy to explore thanks to the extensive road network. North of the capital, ritzy beach towns line up between Hellerup and Humlebæk. Helsingør's Kronborg, which Shakespeare immortalized in *Hamlet,* and Hillerød's stronghold of Frederiksborg, considered one of the most magnificent Renaissance castles in Europe, also lie to the north. To the west of Copenhagen is Roskilde, medieval Denmark's most important town, with an eclectic cathedral that served as northern Europe's spiritual center 1,000 years ago.

West and south, rural towns and farms edge up to seaside communities and fine white beaches, often encompassed by forests. Beaches with summer cottages, white dunes, and calm waters surround Gilleleje and the neighboring town of Hornbæk. The beach in Tisvildeleje is quieter and close to woods. Even more unspoiled are the lilliputian islands around southern Sjælland, virtually unchanged over the past century.

WHAT IT COSTS In kroner					
	$$$$	$$$	$$	$	¢
RESTAURANTS	over 180	141–180	121–140	90–120	under 90
HOTELS	over 1,500	1,200–1,500	1,000–1,200	700–1,000	under 700

Restaurant prices are for a main course at dinner. Hotel prices are for two people in a standard double room, including service charge and tax.

Rungsted

❶ *21 km (13 mi) north of Copenhagen.*

Between Copenhagen and Helsingør is **Rungstedlund,** the elegant, airy former manor of Baroness Karen Blixen, who wrote *Out of Africa* and several accounts of aristocratic Danish life under the pen name Isak Dinesen. The manor house, where she lived as a child and to which she returned in 1931, is open as a museum and displays manuscripts, photographs, paintings, and memorabilia documenting her years in Africa and Denmark. Leave time to wander around the gardens. ⊠ *Rungsted Strandvej 111, Rungsted Kyst* ☎ *45/57–10–57, for combined train and admission tickets, 70/13–14–16 international or 70/13–14–15 domestic* 🖷 *45/57–10–58* ⊕ *www.karen-blixen.dk* 🖂 *Dkr 35* ☉ *May–Sept., Tues.–Sun. 10–5; Oct.–Apr., Wed.–Fri. 1–4, weekends 11–4.*

Where to Eat

★ **$$$** ✕ **Nokken.** The terrace, stretching from the base of the harbor to the waters of Øresund, provides a view of the sailboats returning to port as well as a tranquil skyline in the evening. The elegant Italian-style interior pleasantly contradicts the classic French cuisine served. Seafood fresh from the sound is the main attraction but tournedos and other succulent meat dishes are also available. French reserves dominate the wine

Most of Sjælland can be explored on day trips from Copenhagen, which makes a nice hub. The exceptions are the northwestern beaches around the Sejerø Bugt (Sejerø Bay) and those south of Møn, all of which require at least a night's stay and a day's visit. If you have the time to take a more extended tour, the train and bus networks are extensive and can deliver you from point to point quite fluidly without routing you back through Copenhagen.

Numbers in the text correspond to numbers in the margin and on the Sjælland & Its Islands map.

If you have 3 days

Rent a car or catch the train, and head up the east coast of Sjælland towards ⊞ **Helsingør** ❸ ▶, stopping briefly in **Rungsted** ❶ to see Isak Dinesen's home and in **Humlebæk** ❷ to visit the beautiful Louisiana museum. If the weather is nice, have a sandwich on the beach. Make your way to Helsingør by evening and spend your first night there. Get up early the next morning and spend some time exploring Kronborg, Hamlet's castle, and continue up north towards **Hornbæk** ❻, **Gilleleje** ❽, or **Tisvildeleje** ❾ where you can spend the day swimming and lolling around on the beach. In the evening head for ⊞ **Hillerød** ❺ and stroll around the city. The following day visit the beautiful Frederiksborg Slot and its baroque garden. From there, travel on to **Roskilde** ⓭ to visit the impressive cathedral and the Viking Ship Museum. Return to Copenhagen in the evening.

If you have 7 days

Leave Copenhagen early in the morning, heading south toward **Møn** ⓰ ▶. Spend the day climbing the steep cliffs and visiting Liselund Slot. In the evening head for ⊞ **Ringsted** ⓳, where you can bed down after an exhausting day. In the morning take a stroll through Ringsted and then go to the village of Sorø for a beautiful walk. If Denmark's Viking history interests you, you can also spend the day in Trælleborg at the excavated site of a Viking encampment. Return to Ringsted to spend a second night there. On the third day drive northeast to **Lejre** ⓮, where you can visit the open-air museum or Ledreborg Slot. In the afternoon, move on to ⊞ **Roskilde** ⓭ to see the sights and find lodging. On the fourth day leave in the morning for ⊞ **Hillerød** ❺, where you should base yourself for two days. Visit Frederiksborg Castle and continue to Fredensborg Castle for another impression of Danish royal digs. Take the sixth day to relax on one of the many beaches on the northern coast, spending the night in ⊞ **Hornbæk** ❻ or camping on the beach at ⚠ **Dronningmølle** ❼. On the last day of your Sjælland week, travel to **Helsingør** ❸ to visit Kronborg and end the trip with a viewing of modern art at the Louisiana museum in **Humlebæk** ❷. Return to Copenhagen in the evening.

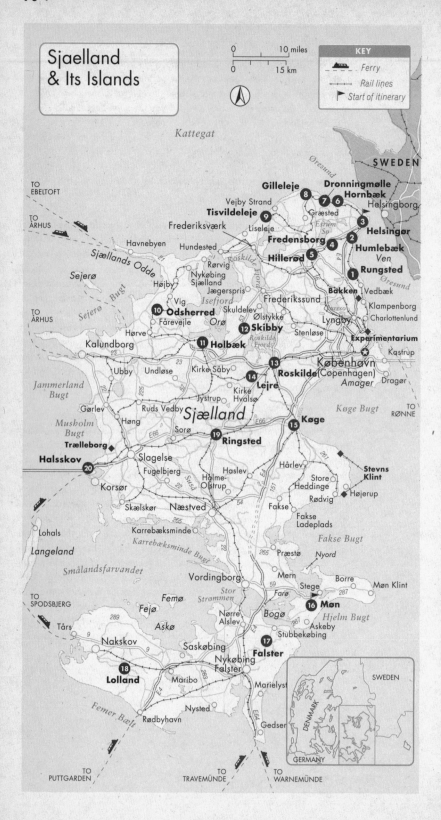

Sjaelland
& Its Islands

0 ___ 10 miles
0 ___ 15 km

KEY

⛴ *Ferry*
⊢⊢⊢ *Rail lines*
▶ *Start of itinerary*

Kattegat

SWEDEN

Øresund

TO
EBELTOFT

TO
ÅRHUS

Sjællands Odde

Havnebyen

Gilleleje 8
Dronningmølle 7 6 **Hornbæk**
Vejby Strand
Græsted
Helsingborg
Tisvildeleje 9
3
Frederiksværk
Liseleje
Esrum Sø
Helsingør
Fredensborg 2
Hundested
4
Humlebæk
Ven
Hillerød 5
1 **Rungsted**
Rørvig
Nykøbing
Sjælland
Jægerspris
Frederikssund
Øresund
Bakken Vedbæk
Sejerø
Højby
Vig
Isefjord
Skuldelev
Sureso
Klampenborg
Sejerø Bugt
10 **Odsherred**
Fåreveile
Ørø
Ølstykke
Lyngby
Charlottenlund
TO
ÅRHUS
Hørve
12 **Skibby**
Stenløse
Experimentarium
Kalundborg
11 **Holbæk**
Roskilde Fjord
Kastrup
Ubby
Undløse
Kirke Såby
13
København
Jammerland Bugt
22
14 **Lejre**
Roskilde (Copenhagen)
Dragør
Gørlev
Jystrup
Kirke
Hvalsø
Amager
TO
RØNNE
Musholm Bugt
Høng
Ruds Vedby
Sjælland
E66
Trælleborg
Sorø
15 **Køge**
Køge Bugt
Halsskov
20
Slagelse
19 **Ringsted**
Fugelbjerg
Hårlev
Stevns Klint
Korsør
Haslev
Store
Heddinge
Lohals
Skælskør
Næstved
Holme-
Olstrup
Rødvig
Højerup
Langeland
Fakse
Karrebæksminde
Fakse
Ladeplads
Karrebæksminde Bugt
Fakse Bugt
265
Præstø
Nyord
Smålandsfarvandet
Vordingborg
Stor Strømmen
Mern
Borre
Møn Klint
TO
SPODSBJERG
Femø
Fejø
Nørre
Alslev
Farø
Stege
287
Tårs
Askø
Bogø
16 **Møn**
Hjelm Bugt
Nakskov
Saskøbing
Askeby
Stubbekøbing
17 **Falster**
Nykøbing
Falster
18 **Lolland**
Maribo
Marielyst
SWEDEN
Femer Bælt
Nysted
DENMARK
Rødbyhavn
Gedser
GERMANY
TO
PUTTGARDEN
TO
TRAVEMÜNDE
TO
WARNEMÜNDE

menu. ⊠ *Rungsted Havn 44, Rungsted Kyst* ☎ *45/57–13–14* ⊟ *AE, DC, MC, V.*

Humlebæk

❷ *10 km (6 mi) north of Rungsted, 31 km (19 mi) north of Copenhagen.*

Historically a fishing village, this elegant seaside town, with a population of about 6,000, has of late become a suburb of both Copenhagen and Helsingør. In summer the town's many cottages fill with vacationers and the gardens come alive with vibrant colors. The town takes its name from the plant *humle* (hops), which is abundant in the area.

Ⓒ Humlebæk is home of the must-see **Louisiana,** a modern-art museum as
Fodor'sChoice famed for its stunning location and architecture as for its collection. Even
★ if you can't tell a Monet from a Duchamp, you should make the 30-minute trip from Copenhagen to see its elegant rambling structure, surrounded by a large park. Housed in a pearly 19th-century villa surrounded by dramatic views of the Øresund waters, the permanent collection includes modern American paintings and Danish paintings from the COBRA (a trend in northern European painting that took its name from its active locations, Copenhagen, Brussels, and Amsterdam) and deconstructionism movements. Be sure to see the haunting collection of Giacomettis backdropped by picture windows overlooking the sound. The children's wing has pyramid-shape chalkboards, child-proof computers, and weekend activities under the guidance of an artist or museum coordinator. To get here from the station, walk north about 10 minutes. ⊠ *Gammel Strandvej 13, Humlebæk* ☎ *49/19–07–19* 🖷 *49/19–35–05* ⊕ *www.louisiana.dk* 🖭 *Dkr 75* ☻ *Thurs.–Tues. 10–5, Wed. 10–10.*

Helsingør

▶ ❸ *14 km (8½ mi) north of Humlebæk, 45 km (28 mi) north of Copenhagen.*

Helsingør dates back to the early 13th century. It wasn't until the 1400s when Erik of Pomerania established a tariff for all ships passing through the sound that the town began to prosper. Perhaps Helsingør is best known as the home of Shakespeare's fictional Hamlet. Today more than 55,000 people populate the city.

At the northeastern tip of the island, Helsingør is the departure point for ferries to the Swedish town of Helsingborg, and it's the site of
Fodor'sChoice **Kronborg Slot** (Kronborg Castle), which was added to UNESCO's World
★ Heritage List in 2000. William Shakespeare based *Hamlet* on Danish mythology's Amleth, and used this castle as the setting even though he had probably never seen it. Built in the late 16th century, it is 600 years younger than the Elsinore we imagine from the tragedy. It was built as a Renaissance tollbooth: from its cannon-studded bastions, forces collected Erik of Pomerania's much-hated Sound Dues, a tariff charged to all ships crossing the sliver of water between Denmark and Sweden. Coming through the entrance arch decorated in Flemish style, you see the castle lawn in front of an octagonal tower, the Trumpeters Tower, whose decoration stands out from the whole.

From the yard there is access to the royal chapel. Still true to its original Renaissance style from 1582, the chapel accommodates the royal throne, which has multicolor carved wood. Among the 27 rooms open to the public are two deserving of more attention: the so-called "lille sal" (small room) and the king's bedroom. In the "small room," on the second floor, hang seven tapestries made of silk and wool and created by the Flemish painter Hans Knieper between 1581 and 1586. What makes these tapestries exceptional is not merely their artistic quality but also their subject matter. They portray several Danish kings against backgrounds of stately buildings and luxuriant scenery with German translations accompanying Danish verses describing their respective achievements. The ceiling of the king's bedroom is worth a couple of extra minutes. If you crane your neck, you can see four scenes of royal life painted by the Dutch artist Gerrit van Honthorst in 1630. Also well worth seeing are the 200-foot-long dining hall and the dungeons, where there is a brooding statue of Holger Danske (Ogier the Dane). According to legend, the Viking chief sleeps, but will awaken to defend Denmark when it is in danger. (The largest Danish resistance group during World War II called itself Holger Danske after its fearless forefather.) ⊠ *At the point on the harborfront* ☎ *49/21–30–78* ⊕ *www.kronborg. dk* ⊠ *Dkr 60* ☉ *May–Sept., daily 10:30–5; Oct. and Apr., Tues.–Sun. 11–4; Nov.–Mar., Tues.–Sun. 11–3.*

Thanks to the hefty tolls collected by Erik of Pomerania, Helsingør prospered. Stroll past the carefully restored medieval merchants' and ferrymen's houses in the middle of town. On the corner of Stengade and Skt. Annæ gade near the harbor is **Skt. Olai Kirke** (St. Olaf's Church), the country's largest parish church and worth a peek for its elaborately carved wooden altar. ⊠ *Skt. Olai G. 51* ☎ *49/21–04–43 (9–noon)* ⊕ *www. helsingordomkirke.dk* ⊠ *Free* ☉ *May–Sept., daily noon–3; Oct.–Apr., daily noon–2.*

Close to Skt. Olai Kirke is Skt. Marie Kirke with the 15th-century **Carmelite Kloster** (Carmelite Convent), one of the best-preserved examples of medieval architecture in Scandinavia. After the Reformation it was used as a hospital, and by 1630 it had become a poorhouse. ⊠ *Skt. Annæ G. 38* ☎ *49/21–17–74* ⊠ *Dkr 15* ☉ *Mid-May–mid-Sept., tour daily at 2; call ahead.*

If you want to know more about Helsingør, head to the modest **By Museum** (Town Museum), which has exhibits of 19th-century handicrafts, dolls, and a model of the town. ⊠ *Skt. Annæ G. 36* ☎ *49/28–18–00* ⊠ *Dkr 15* ☉ *Weekdays noon–4.*

off the beaten path

MARIENLYST SLOT – One kilometer (½ mi) north of Helsingør is the Louis XVI–style Marienlyst Castle. Built in 1587, it provided King Frederik II with a garden, as well as a delicate change of scenery from the militant Kronborg. Today the castle has been renovated and the gardens replanted. Inside are paintings by north Sjælland artists and a gallery with changing arts and crafts exhibitions. ⊠ *Marienlyst Allé* ☎ *49/28–37–91* ☎ *49/21–20–06* ⊠ *Dkr 25* ☉ *Daily noon–4.*

Where to Stay & Eat

$$ ╳⊡ **Hotel Hamlet.** A few minutes from the harbor, this overly renovated hotel has lost some of its charm but makes an attempt at character with raw timbers and deep-green walls. The rooms are furnished in rose schemes and dark wood, and all are comfortable, if nondescript. Downstairs, the Ophelia Restaurant serves traditional Danish seafood, steaks, and openface sandwiches. ⊠ *Bramstr. 5, DK–3000* ☎ *49/21–05–91* ☎ *49/ 26–01–30* ⌐ *36 rooms with bath* ♢ *Restaurant, bar, some pets allowed, no-smoking rooms* ⊟ *AE, DC, MC, V.*

★ $$$$ ⊡ **Hotel Marienlyst.** The rooms in this hotel full of flashy neon lights, bolts of drapery, and glass are all plush and pastel and include plenty of conveniences. Those situated on the sound side present a magnificent view of Kronborg Castle and the Swedish coastline, weather permitting. Of course these rooms with scenic views are more expensive. The hotel offers live music on Friday and Saturday. ⊠ *Nordre Strandvej 2, DK–3000* ☎ *49/21–40–00* 🖷 *49/21–49–00* ⊕ *www.marienlyst. dk* ⇌ *224 rooms, 17 suites.* ⚲ *Restaurant, cafeteria, indoor pool, bar, gym, casino, nightclub, meeting rooms, some pets allowed, no-smoking rooms* ▱ *AE, DC, MC, V.*

¢ 🏠 **Villa Moltke Vandrerhjem.** This youth hostel faces the sound and has a private beach. It is located 2 km (1 mi) from the city center, but is well served by both bus and train. ⊠ *Nordre Strandvej 24, DK–3000* ☎ *49/ 21–16–40* 🖷 *49/21–13–99* ⊕ *www.helsingorhostel.dk* ⇌ *180 beds* ⚲ *Cafeteria, fishing, badminton, Ping-Pong, soccer, library, laundry facilities* ▱ *MC, V.*

Sports & the Outdoors

GOLF The **Helsingør Golf Klub** (⊠ Gamle Hellebækvej 73 ☎ 49/21–29–70) has 18 holes on a lush green course flanked by trees and, on clear days, views across the sound to Sweden. A weekday handicap of 36 for men and women, and a weekend handicap of 24 for men and 36 for women, is expected.

Nightlife & the Arts

In summer, Kronborg Castle is the site of the **Hamlet Festival** (⊠ Havnepl. 1 ☎ 49/28–20–45 ⊕ www.hamletsommer.dk), during which internationally renowned theater companies offer outdoor performances of *Hamlet*. The schedule varies from year to year.

Fredensborg

❹ *15 km (9 mi) southwest of Helsingør, 33 km (20 mi) northwest of Copenhagen.*

Fredensborg means "town of peace," and it was here that the Great Nordic War peace treaty was commemorated in 1722. The excellent Fredensborg Castle is a major draw, but the town also accommodates those who come to enjoy the great outdoors.

Commanding the town is the **Fredensborg Slot** (Castle of Peace), built by Frederik IV to commemorate the 1720 peace treaty with Sweden. The castle, with a towering domed hall in the center, was originally inspired by French and Italian castles, but 18th-century reconstructions, concealing the original design, instead serve as a review of domestic architecture. The castle became a favorite of Frederik V, who lined the gardens with marble sculptures of ordinary people. It is now the summer residence of the royal family, and interiors are closed except in July. Queen Margrethe II resides in the castle some months every year, usually in the spring and autumn. When the Queen is present, the Royal Life Guards perform reveille at 8 AM and sound the tattoo (taps) at 10 PM. At noon there is the changing of the guard.

The stately **Slotshave** (castle garden), inspired by the French gardens of Versailles, is Denmark's largest historical garden and well worth a stroll. The garden is open to the public all year with the exception of *den reserverede have* (the reserved garden), which is used privately by the Danish Royal Family but open to the public in July. The reserved garden includes a flower garden, an herb garden, and the orangerie where Denmark's oldest myrtles, which date back to the 1750s, are preserved. ⊠ *Fredensborg* ☎ *33/40–31–87* ⊕ *www.ses.dk* ▱ *Castle Dkr 35; reserved gardens Dkr 35; common ticket Dkr 55* ☼ *Castle July, daily 1–5; reserved gardens July, daily 9–5.*

off the
beaten
path

GRIBSKOV – On the opposite side of Lake Esrum from Fredensborg is Gribskov, the largest forest in Sjælland (14,079 acres). This former royal hunting ground has kept its natural shape since the times of Valdemar II in the 13th century, except for the clearing works done after the hurricane of 1981. Gribskov is one of the few places in Denmark where visitors can have a sense of natural solitude while being immersed in a wooded cloak of mystery. Black woodpeckers, woodcocks, sandpipers, buzzards, goshawks, and deer can be seen among the oaks and flowering trees.

Where to Stay & Eat

$$–$$$ ✕ **Skipperhuset.** On the grounds of the royal summer residence of Fre-
Fodor'sChoice densborg Slot, this 18th-century former royal boathouse is on the shore
★ of Lake Esrum. When weather permits, an alfresco meal as the sun sets across the lake is pure enchantment. The three-course menu changes every two weeks. Warm-smoked wild Baltic salmon served with spinach flash-fried in soy sauce and balsamic vinegar is a delightful favorite and a fabulous buy for the money. ⊠ *Skipperallé 6* ☎ *48/48–17–17* ▤ *MC, V* ⊗ *Closed mid-Oct.–Easter.*

★ **$$$$** ✕▥ **Hotel Store Kro.** Built by King Frederik IV, this magnificent Renaissance annex to Fredensborg Castle is the archetypal stately inn. Inside are European antiques and paintings; outside, glass gazebos and classical statues overlook a lovely garden. The rooms are equally sumptuous, with delicately patterned wallpapers and antiques. The romantic restaurant, specializing in French fare, has a fireplace and grand piano. ⊠ *Slotsg. 6, DK–3480* ☎ *48/40–01–11* 🖷 *48/48–45–61* ⊕ *www.storekro.dk* ⇆ *49 rooms, 6 suites* ♿ *Restaurant, minibars, sauna, bar, meeting room* ▤ *AE, DC, MC, V.*

¢ ▥ **Fredensborg Vandrerhjem.** This youth and family hostel offers a wide selection of sleeping arrangements. Both shared and private rooms (accommodating up to six people) are available. Breakfast can be ordered for Dkr 45. The restaurant serves lunch and dinner for groups only; however, the kitchen is available to all guests. ⊠ *Østrupvej 3, DK–3480* ☎ *48/ 48–03–15* 🖷 *48/48–16–56* ⊕ *www.fredensborghostel.dk* ⇆ *42 rooms without bath* ♿ *Ping-Pong, playground* ▤ *No credit cards.*

Sports & the Outdoors

Magnificent displays of hawks and eagles in flight can be seen at **Falkonergården.** Located 1 km (½ mi) northeast of Fredensborg, this former farm keeps alive the Danish tradition of hunting with hawks, a method used from the time of the Vikings until early in the 19th century. Falcons swooping at speeds approaching 300 kph (186 mph) can be witnessed in the hour-long shows. ⊠ *Davidsvænge 11* ☎ *48/48–25–83* ⊕ *www.falkonergaarden.dk* ▦ *Dkr 65* ⊗ *Showtimes: Apr. and May, Sun. at 2; June, Sept., and Oct., weekends at 2; July, Wed. at 10 and 5, Thurs. at 10, weekends at 5; Aug., Wed. and weekends at 5.*

The **Fredensborg Golf Club** (⊠ Skovsvinget 25 ☎ 48/47–56–59) has 18 holes surrounded by woodlands. Men are required to have a handicap of 38 on weekdays and 24 on weekends whereas women need a handicap of 43 and 30, respectively.

Hillerød

⑤ *10 km (6 mi) southwest of Fredensborg, 40 km (25 mi) northwest of Copenhagen.*

Hillerød is the main town of Frederiksborg County and appropriately enough is at its center. The town, founded in the 15th century, has developed itself around the Frederiksborg Castle and nowadays is an important industrial area.

★ Hillerød's **Frederiksborg Slot** (Frederiksborg Castle) is probably Denmark's most beautiful royal residence. Acquired in 1560, the castle was rebuilt by King Frederik II, who gave his name to the building. That structure was eventually demolished by his son, king-cum-architect Christian IV, who rebuilt it as one of Scandinavia's most magnificent castles. With three wings and a lower portal entrance, the Dutch Renaissance building is enclosed by a moat, covers three islets, and is peaked with dozens of gables, spires, and turrets. The two-story marble gallery known as the **Great Hall,** with its audacious festooning of drapery, paintings, and reliefs, sits on top of the vaulted chapel where monarchs were crowned for more than 200 years. Devastated by a fire in 1859, the castle was reconstructed with the support of the Carlsberg Foundation and now includes the **Nationalhistoriske Museum** (National History Museum). Frederiksberg Slot has 69 rooms, all of them decorated as they were before the fire. Those works of art that had been destroyed were substituted by other private pieces from the Danish aristocracy. The castle has an admirable Renaissance chapel, **Slotskirke**, with abundant ornamentation. The three-aisle chapel has a wide gallery with large windows. Between them hang Denmark's most important coat of arms, the knights of the Elephant Order, and the Great Cross of Dannebrog. Look for the 17th-century aisle seats as well as the altarpiece and the pulpit made of mahogany with gold and silver panels. The carved organ, made in 1610 and restored in 1988, still proudly carries its original tubes and manual bellows. The lovely **Baroque Gardens,** rebuilt according to J. C. Krieger's layout from 1725, include a series of wide, horizontal waterfalls that make the neatly trimmed park a lovely place for a stroll. ⊠ *Hillerød* ☎ *48/26–04–39* ⊕ *www.frederiksborgmuseet.dk* ✆ *Dkr 60; Baroque Gardens free* ☉ *Castle Apr.–Oct., daily 10–5; Nov.–Mar., daily 11–3. Baroque Gardens May–Aug., daily 10–9; Sept., Oct., Mar., and Apr., daily 10–7; Nov.–Feb., daily 10–4.*

off the beaten path

ESRUM KLOSTER – Fifteen km (10 mi) north of Hillerød is the Cistercian monastery of Esrum. Originally built in the 1140s by the Benedictine monks, the monastery was abandoned by this order and occupied by Cistercian monks in 1151. After the Lutheran reformation, the church was demolished and the building materials were used to erect the Castle of Kronborg in Helsingør. The oldest remains are from the late Middle Ages. ⊠ *Klosterg. 11, Esrum, DK–3230 Græsted* ☎ *48/36–04–00* 🖶 *48/39–80–16* ⊕ *www.esrum. dk/kloster* ✆ *Dkr 40* ☉ *May–mid-June and mid-Aug.–mid-Oct., Tues.–Sun. 10–4; mid-June–mid-Aug., Tues.–Sun. 10–5; mid-Oct.–Apr., Thurs.–Sun. 10–4.*

Where to Stay & Eat

$$$ ✕ **La Perla.** Simple but good Italian food is served in this beautiful old house in the very center of town. The decor is an interesting mix of Italian and Danish styles, a thoroughly modern twist on the Mediterranean. ⊠ *Torvet 1* ☎ *48/24–35–33* ⌁ *Reservations essential* ⊟ *AE, DC, MC, V.*

$$$ ✕ **Slotskroen.** Functioning as an inn since 1795, Slotskroen is one of the oldest buildings of this royal town. The restaurant has been completely renovated, but it maintains its antique flavor and stands out for its veal and ox dishes. ⊠ *Slotsg. 67* ☎ *48/26–01–82* ⊟ *AE, DC, MC, V.*

$–$$ ✕ **Spisestedet Leonora.** In the shadow of Frederiksborg Castle, this family restaurant bustles in what used to be the castle stables. Antique on the outside and bright orange on the inside with hanging prints and paintings of royalty and the castle, it is a popular stopover for castle visitors. The Danish menu ranges from quick open-face sandwiches to savory stews, soups, and steaks. ⊠ *Frederiksborgslot 5* ☎ *48/26–75–16* ☰ *DC, MC, V.*

$$ 🏨 **Hotel Hillerød.** In a typically Scandinavian fashion, this hotel's decor is furnished with sensible Danish designs and luxurious lighting accessories. The hotel's attentiveness extends to providing some rooms specifically for nonsmokers. The hotel is wheelchair accessible. Packages that include greens fees at a local golf course can be arranged. ⊠ *Milnersvej 41, DK–3400* ☎ *48/24–08–00* 🖷 *48/24–08–74* ⊕ *www.hotelhillerod. dk* ⇆ *74 rooms* ♿ *Restaurant, meeting room, some pets allowed, no-smoking rooms* ☰ *AE, DC, MC, V.*

Hornbæk

❻ *27 km (17 mi) northeast of Hillerød, 47 km (29 mi) north of Copenhagen.*

Hornbæk is Denmark's answer to France's Riviera. Danish society's upper echelon maintains palatial summer homes here that line the streets closest to the water and are discreetly tucked away behind protective sand dunes. Regardless of your social standing, the bustling town offers lovely shopping opportunities and exciting nightlife year round. Summer brings the expansive beach alive with parties, volleyball tournaments, and more.

Where to Stay & Eat

$$$$ ✕ **Le Provençal.** On the "Danish Riviera," Le Provençal lives up to its name. The restaurant's south-of-France atmosphere is created with Limoges and Valdrôme porcelain along with gorgeous glass, expensive cutlery, and handmade chairs. The best seating on a warm afternoon is outside on the rustic terrace, where you can sip a glass of Corsican or Rhône wine. Main dishes include *filet de sandre* (a fillet of pike perch with aïoli and tomato confit), and *cailles àux raisins* (oven-roasted quails in grape sauce with roasted potatoes and chanterelles). ⊠ *Havnevej 1* ☎ *49/76–11–77* ☰ *AE, DC, MC, V.*

★ $$$$ ✕ **Novo Latino.** The elegant restaurant is decorated in light, soft tones, but the terrace takes the cake with its outdoor fireplace. Inspired by classic Latin American cooking, Novo Latino modernizes the cuisine by adding its own touches. The chef here travels every autumn to the tropics to collect recipes and inspiration, which determine the menu for each coming year. For about Dkr 500 the restaurant offers a six-course menu that keeps pace with seasonal products. This is the ideal place to try innovative dishes such as fish with chocolate sauce. A wide range of excellent wines from the New and Old Worlds is on hand at prices starting from Dkr 300. ⊠ *Nordre Strandvej 154, 5 km (3 mi) east of Hornbæk, Ålsgårde* ☎ *49/70–90–03* ☰ *AE, DC, MC, V* ☉ *Closed Mon. and Oct.–Mar.*

★ $$ ✕ **Hansen's Café.** This intimate restaurant, in a national trust building constructed in 1783, is just a few steps from the harbor. The Danish art hanging from the timber walls provides a cozy ambience for a casual crowd that often lingers for drinks well after dinner. The daily menu is short but provides a taste of what's fresh—especially seafood. Try the lumpfish roe for a tasty local treat. Business hours vary so it's wise to call in advance. ⊠ *Havnevej 19* ☎ *49/70–04–79* ☰ *DC, MC, V.*

$$$$ 🏨 **Havreholm Slot.** A few miles southwest of Hornbæk beach, this small former castle is surrounded by wooded grounds, which hide a couple of fair-sized ponds in their midst. The guesthouses' rooms and suites are

decorated with Bang & Olufsen televisions and design furniture; most open onto balconies or terraces. Rowboats are available for use on the ponds, as is fishing gear—just remember to get your fishing permit first. There are also tennis courts and a 9-hole par-3 golf course. The restaurant produces elaborate French cuisine at dinner and serves smørrebrød and Danish comfort food at lunch. ⊠ *Klosterrisvej 4, Havreholm, DK–3100* ☎ *49/75–86–00* 🖷 *49/75–80–23* ⊕ *www.havreholm.dk* ↩ *32 rooms, 3 suites* ⚐ *Restaurant, 9-hole golf course, indoor-outdoor pool, sauna, fishing, billiards, Ping-Pong, squash, meeting rooms* 🖃 *AE, DC, MC, V.*

$$$ 🖫 **Hotelpension Ewaldsgaarden.** This seaside pension is just a few blocks from the marina and the beach in a residential neighborhood just off one of the town's main (though quiet) streets. An informal family hotel, it is very casual, extremely well kept and service is provided with commendable pride. Inside the restaurant the Danish food is not fancy, but it's authentic and exceptionally good. Breakfast is included. ⊠ *Johannes Ewaldsvej 5, DK–3100* ☎ *49/70–00–82* 🖷 *49/70–00–82* ⊕ *www. ewaldsgaarden.dk* ↩ *12 rooms* ⚐ *Restaurant* 🖃 *No credit cards.*

¢ 🖫 **Hornbæk Bed & Breakfast.** Owned by an American-Danish couple, this country villa sits at the edge of the woods only 100 meters from the Danish Riviera. On fair days you can see the Swedish coastline out the window. The rooms are a decent size for the reasonable price, and guests are allowed use of the kitchen. ⊠ *Skovvej 15C, DK–3100* ☎ *49/ 76–19–10* 🖷 *49/76–19–11* ⊕ *www.hornbaekbandb.dk* ↩ *7 rooms without bath* ⚐ *Kitchen, no-smoking rooms* 🖃 *No credit cards.*

Dronningmølle

❼ *10 km (6 mi) west of Hornbæk, 57 km (35 mi) north of Copenhagen.*

There's little more than a camping ground flanked by a very clean beach and a sculpture museum in Dronningmølle. The beauty of the area lies in the fact that it is largely undiscovered so it's quite easy to find a spot on the sand away from the crowds.

In 1916 Rudolph Tegner began to buy adjacent parcels of land to realize his dream of a museum and sculpture park dedicated to his own work.
★ The centerpiece of the resultant **Rudolph Tegners Museum** is the 36-foot-high octagonal building in the center of which Rudolph Tegner is buried. On display here are 191 of his sculptures in plaster, marble, and bronze; works in other media are represented including 12 paintings, many drafts, and several pieces of furniture he constructed. Tegner withstood the pressure towards normality in Danish society during his era and his best works are both provocative and disquieting. ⊠ *Museumsvej 19* ☎ *49/ 71–91–77* ⊕ *www.rudolphtegner.dk* 🎟 *Dkr 25* ☉ *Mid-Apr.–May and Sept.–mid-Oct., noon–5; June–Aug., 9:30–5* ☉ *Closed Mon.*

Where to Stay

¢ 🏕 **Dronningmølle Strandcamping.** Camp right on the sand and enjoy the best of the Danish Riviera without the crowds and high prices of other, better known coastal towns in north Sjælland. The surrounding countryside is a nature conservation area and has trails and bicycle paths. Kitchen facilities are available. ⊠ *Strandkrogen 2B, DK–3120* ☎ *49/ 71–92–90* 🖷 *49/71–98–93* ⊕ *www.dronningmolle.dk* ⚐ *Restaurant, cafeteria, sauna, miniature golf, shop, laundry* 🖃 *No credit cards* ☉ *Closed mid-Sept.–mid-Apr.*

Gilleleje

❽ *3 km (2 mi) north of Dronningmølle, 58 km (36 mi) northwest of Copenhagen.*

At the northern tip of Sjælland, Gilleleje was once a small fishing community. These days the population explodes every summer when northern Europeans take to its woods and fine, sandy beaches. It was a favorite getaway of philosopher Søren Kierkegaard, who wrote: "I often stood there and reflected over my past life. The force of the sea and the struggle of the elements made me realize how unimportant I was." The less existential can go for a swim and visit the philosopher's monument on a nearby hill. The old part of town, with its thatch-roof, colorfully painted houses, is good for a walk.

> off the
> beaten
> path

NORDSJÆLLANDS SOMMERPARK – Situated 30 km (18 mi) west of Helsingør, this amusement park mixes water recreation with other attractions such as theater, concerts, and a mini zoo. The Sommerpark bus departs from the Gilleleje or Helsingør train station at 9:30 AM. ⊠ *Kirkevej 33, Græsted* ☎ *48/71–41–41* 🖶 *48/ 71–66–05* ⊕ *www.forlystelsespark.dk* 🗢 *Dkr 50* ⊙ *Mid-June–July, daily 10–9; mid-May–mid-June and Aug., daily noon–8.*

Tisvildeleje

❾ *28 km (17 mi) west of Gilleleje, 65 km (40 mi) northwest of Copenhagen.*

Tisvildeleje is one of the most popular beaches in north Sjælland. There is more than 1 km (½ mi) of sandy beach backed by woods.

Where to Stay & Eat

$ ✕🍴 **Havgården.** The refurbished old manor house offers comfortable lodging within a typical Danish building. Dinner, served from 6 PM, is primarily Danish—John Dory is the house specialty. The site also rents out vacation cottages, fully furnished with all the comforts of home. Payment with credit card is subject to a 6% surcharge. ⊠ *Strandlyvej 1, Vejby Strand, DK–3210* ☎ *48/70–57–30* 🖶 *48/70–57–72* ⊕ *www. havgaarden.dk* 🗢 *13 rooms* 🍴 *Restaurant* ▤ *MC, V* ⊙ *Restaurant closed Sept.–May.*

¢ 🍴 **Skt. Helene Vandrerhjem.** This youth hostel is a 10-minute walk from the beach. The property also houses 28 chalets accommodating four to five people each. The whole complex is ecofriendly, with a farm, and organic food on offer. Guests are welcome to pitch in. There are also 15 apartments with kitchen and bath for rent. ⊠ *Bygmarken 30, DK–3220* ☎ *48/70–98–50* 🖶 *48/70–98–97* ⊕ *www.helene.dk* 🗢 *40 family rooms* 🍴 *Restaurant, cafeteria, miniature golf, tennis court, basketball, soccer, volleyball, laundry facilities.*

Odsherred

❿ *45 km (28 mi) southwest of Gilleleje, 80 km (50 mi) northwest of Copenhagen (via Roskilde).*

With steep cliffs, white-sand dunes, and acres of forests to admire, the Odsherred peninsula is a big draw to people who want to relax in beautiful surroundings. The long beaches have silky sand and offer plenty of opportunities to take a refreshing swim in Sejerø Bugt (Sejerø Bay). This hammer-shape peninsula, which curves around Sejerø Bugt, is dotted with hundreds of burial mounds. You can get here either by driv-

SUN, SAND & WAVES

FROM ANY POINT IN DENMARK you're never more than 50 km away from the ocean and for this reason, the Danish people have developed a special fondness for their beaches. On Sjælland there are plenty of calm sandy strands, which are far gentler than their wilder and more abrasive—though more expansive—counterparts along the west coast of Jylland. The most pristine Sjælland shorelines are on the northern edge of the island, where long stretches of lovely, white sand are massaged by lapping waves. Though this is the preferred sunbathing spot for the Danish in-crowd, it's rarely a problem finding prime real estate on which to throw down your towel. Generally speaking, the vast majority of the island's beaches across the island are of excellent quality and are easily accessible, making them great retreats for families with small children. Sjællands coastal playgrounds are

defined by the people who frequent them from the jet-set beaches of Hornbæk, where the babes and hunks strut thei stuff, to the child-friendly sands of Tisvildeleje, where inner tubes and sandcastles are the rule. During sumn. heat waves, people even swim in Copenhagen's harbor. You should be aware before you go that there are beaches where nudists put it all to the wind, and "nude beaches" are seldom designated as such. Topless sunbathing is also common in Denmark, and one should take care to follow proper etiquette; avoid gawking and leave plenty of room between yourself and the bather in question. If you're fortunate enough to be of the "hot bod" variety, don't show off—the Danish rule is: "good body, low profile." And just so you know, it's not uncommon for beachgoers to change clothes on the beach as a matter of convenience.

ing around the fjords to the south and through the town of Holbæk, or by driving to Hundested and catching the 25-minute ferry ride to Rørvig.

If you are a devotee of ecclesiastical art, make a pilgrimage to explore the frescoes of the Romanesque-Gothic-Renaissance **Højby Kirke** (Højby Church) in the town of Højby, near Nykøbing Sjælland. In the town of Fårevejle is the Gothic **Fårevejle Kirke,** with the Earl of Bothwell's chapel.

Fewer than 5 km (3 mi) south of Nykøbing Sjælland, more than 500 animals of 85 different species can be seen at **Odsherreds Zoo Dyrepark.** Children love the monkey house. Other attractive inhabitants include raccoons, llamas, reptiles, exotic birds, and the unique black swan. On weekends children can ride ponies. ⊠ Esterhøjvej 94–96, Asnæs ☎ 59/65–12–31 🖷 59/65–12–28 ⊕ www.odsherreds-zoo.dk ☜ Dkr 50 ⊙ Apr., Sept.–mid-Oct., daily 10–3:30; May, June, and Aug., daily 10–5; July, daily 10–6.

Sjællands Odde (Zealand's Tongue), the tiny strip of land north of the Sejerø Bay, offers slightly marshy but secluded beach strands. Inside the bay, the beaches are once again smooth and blond. From here there is access to Århus and Ebeltoft in Jylland by ferry.

Sommerland Sjælland, Zealand's amusement park, caters to visitors of all ages. The dozens of activities include a roller coaster, an aquapark, and a small zoo with pony rides. Children under 10 especially enjoy Miniland. ⊠ Gammel Nykøbingvej 169, Nykøbing Sjælland ☎ 59/31–21–00 ⊕ www.sommerlandsj.dk ☜ Dkr 130 ⊙ Mid-May–mid-June and mid-Aug.–Sept., weekends 10–6; mid-June–mid-Aug., daily 10–7.

Where to Stay & Eat

¢ ✕ **Den Gyldne Hane.** Built at the beginning of the 19th century by a community of fishermen, Den Gyldne Hane is a family hotel best known for the fish dishes served in its restaurant. The view of the harbor overlooking the fishing boats makes for an enjoyable meal. ⊠ *Vestre Havnevej 34, DK–4583 Sjællands Odde* ☎ *59/32–63–86* 🖷 *59/32–65–52* ⊕*www.dengyldnehane.dk* ▤*DC, MC, V* ⊘*No lunch. Closed Dec.–Mar.*

$$$ 🍽 **Dragsholm Slot.** Ideally located at Nekselø Bay, close to the forest and the beach, Dragsholm Castle, originally built in the 12th century, has been a home since the 18th century. Today the owners cultivate the land and raise their own livestock to provide wholesome ingredients for the restaurant on the premises. ⊠ *Dragsholm Allé 1, DK–4534 Hørve* ☎ *59/65–33–00* 🖷 *59/65–30–33* ⊕ *www.dragsholm-slot.dk* ⇗ *30 rooms with bath, 2 suites* ♢ *Restaurant* ▤ *AE, DC, MC, V.*

Holbæk

⑪ *83 km (51½ mi) southwest of Tisvildeleje (via Odsherred), 67 km (41½ mi) west of Copenhagen.*

Expanding out from the old fortress built in the 13th century by Valdemar II to defend Denmark against its attacking enemies, Holbæk is today an industrial and commercial town.

Situated close to the neo-Gothic Skt. Nicolaj Kirke, the **Holbæk Museum** consists of three wooden buildings from the 17th century and another two from the 19th century. The museum collection showcases handicrafts, archaeological artifacts, and objects from the town's contemporary history, such as household equipment from typical urban and rural houses of the 17th and 18th centuries. ⊠ *Klosterstr. 18* ☎ *59/43–23–53* 🖷*59/43–24–52* ⊕*www.holbmus.dk* ▤*Dkr 30* ⊘*Tues.–Fri. 10–4, weekends noon–4.*

> **off the beaten path**

CHURCHES OF HOLBÆK FJORD – A 2 km (1 mi) drive south of Holbæk down the A57 delivers you to **Tveje Merløse**, built in the 13th century and restored at the end of the 19th century. Luckily, you can still see the 13th-century frescoes here. Just 4 km (2½ mi) to the southwest stands the 12th-century **Søstrup Kirke**, with Byzantine-style frescoes. West along road 155 another 4 km (2½ mi) stands **Tuse Kirke**, a typical example of a rural church from the 13th century. Inside the church are Gothic frescoes from the 15th century. North on road A21 is the 12th-century **Hagested Kirke**, which has 13th-century frescoes.

Where to Stay & Eat

¢ ✕🍽 **Hotel Orø Kro.** On the tiny island of Orø, this hotel radiates tranquility with the blue of Isefjord on one side and green fields on the other. The restaurant stands out for its simple and tasty fish specialties. On a warm summer evening, the inn's terrace is a delightful place to sit. The restaurant is closed on Monday. ⊠ *Byg. 57, Orø, DK–4300* ☎ *59/47–00–06* 🖷*59/47–01–99* ⊕*www.oroe.dk/kro* ⇗*21 rooms* ♢ *Restaurant, some pets allowed* ▤ *AE, MC, V.*

$$ 🍽 **Hotel Strandparken.** Beach and forest are the two views offered from the rooms of this hotel from its scenic location in the middle of a park just south of Holbæk Fjord. The pastel rooms are filled with flower prints and landscape paintings. Service is warm and attentive. ⊠ *Kalundborgvej 58, DK–4300* ☎ *59/43–06–16* 🖷 *59/43–32–76* ⊕ *www. hotelstrandparken.dk* ⇗*31 rooms* ♢ *Restaurant, billiards, meeting room* ▤ *AE, MC, V.*

Skibby

12 *26 km (16 mi) northeast of Holbæk, 65 km (40 mi) northwest of Copenhagen.*

Skibby is the main town of the little peninsula situated between Roskilde Fjord and Isefjord.

Four kilometers (2½ mi) east of Skibby is **Selsø Slot** (Selsø Castle), constructed in 1576 and reworked in 1734. The castle portrays life as it was for the aristocrats and their servants in the 1800s. The museum here displays original 17th-century interiors, as well as Renaissance furniture, weapons, clothes, domestic items, toys, and a collection of drawings. The altarpiece from 1605 and the pulpit from 1637 in the castle church exhibit Renaissance elements. ✉ *Selsøvej 30A* ☎ *47/52–01–71* 🌐 *www.selsoe.dk* 🎫 *Dkr 40* ⏲ *May–mid-June and mid-Aug.–Oct., weekends 1–4; mid-June–mid-Aug., daily 11–4.*

off the beaten path

JÆGERSPRIS SLOT – At the north end of the peninsula stands this medieval castle. The Baroque southern wing is from the 17th century and the rest of the castle, save for the 15th-century northern wing, is from 1722–46. King Frederik VII maintained his residence here in the 19th century and the decor in the southern wing reflects this. The tomb of his wife, the Countess Danner, is in the castle's park. To the north extends Nordskoven, a forest of 100-year-old oaks. To see the castle, you must join a guided tour and may not simply walk around on your own. Tours begin at the top of the hour and last for 50 minutes. ✉ *Slotsgården 15, Jægerspris* ☎ *47/53–10–04* 🌐 *www.museer.fa.dk* 🎫 *Dkr 35* ⏲ *Apr.–Oct., Tues.–Sun. 11–4.*

Where to Stay & Eat

$$–$$$ ✕ **Sønderby Kro.** This typical countryside inn sits next to the village's duck pond and serves remarkably tasty veal dishes, curried herring, shrimp. The restaurant is perhaps best known for its smørrebrød. ✉ *Sønderby Bro 2* ☎ *47/52–01–33* 💳 *No credit cards* ⏲ *Closed Mon.*

$ 🏨 **Hotel Skuldelev Kro.** In the middle of the countryside, this inn has a peaceful environment in a beautiful location. Rooms are adequate even for families. Some rooms are available for nonsmokers. ✉ *Østerg. 2B, DK–4050 Skuldelev* ☎ *47/52–03–08* 📠 *47/52–08–93* 🌐 *www.hotel-skuldelevkro.dk* *32 rooms with bath* *Restaurant, outdoor pool, some pets allowed, no-smoking rooms* 💳 *AE, DC, MC, V.*

Roskilde

13 *31 km (19 mi) southeast of Skibby, 36 km (22 mi) west of Copenhagen (on Rte. 156).*

Roskilde is Sjælland's second-largest town and one of its oldest, having been founded in 998. The town is named for Roars Kilde, a Viking king. Today Roskilde has a bustling smelting and machinery industry and two prominent academic institutions, Roskilde University and the Danish Center for Energetic Research of Risø.

Fodor'sChoice ★

Roskilde was the royal residence in the 10th century and became the spiritual capital of Denmark and northern Europe in 1170, when Bishop Absalon built the **Domkirke** (cathedral) on the site of a church erected 200 years earlier by Harald Bluetooth, the Viking founder of the town. Overwhelming the center of town, the current structure took more than 300 years to complete and thus provides a one-stop crash course in Danish architecture. Inside are an ornate Dutch altarpiece and the tombs—rang-

VIKING VICTUALS

THE STOCK IMAGE of ruddy-cheeked Vikings feasting around a wooden table, tearing into oversized drumsticks with their bare hands and gulping down frothy mugs of mead may whiff of Hollywood epics, but it isn't so far off the mark. The Vikings were hearty eaters, loved their mead, and didn't use plates or utensils, except for the knives that they pulled from their sheaths, and occasionally wooden spoons. Legend has it that Skål!, the bottoms-up toast that is roared across Denmark dinner tables, came from the Vikings, who used to drink from skulls.

While the Vikings' primitive table manners likely raised a few eyebrows, the cuisine itself was exceptionally developed. For all their seafaring fame, the Viking society was highly agricultural. They lived in communal farming settlements, and harvested barley, oat, and wheat, and a wide array of herbs and root vegetables, from rosemary and tarragon to parsnips and leeks. They also raised cattle, sheep, goats, pigs, ducks, and geese. They were avid hunters, roaming Denmark's wild countryside with their bows and arrows to hunt bear, wild boar, elk, and reindeer. Along the rich Scandinavian coastline, they speared seals and whales and collected seabird eggs. The thick inland forest yielded nuts, berries, and wild plants. The Vikings flavored soups with nettles and forest onions, and for dessert they topped graham flour pancakes with juicy bilberries. As for libations, they concocted everything from elderflower juice to the ever-popular honey-based mead.

The 300-year-long Viking era dates, appropriately enough, from its first raid on a small British island in the 8th century. It was, after all, the Viking's prowess at plundering and pillaging that brought them their well-deserved infamy. Wizard seamen and cunning conqueror, the Vikings swiftly plied the seas in their souped-up ships, rigged with massive sails and powered by muscled oarmen. England became their favorite stomping grounds, but the rest of Europe was also prey. The Vikings penetrated the Frankish empire via its rivers, from the Elbe in Germany to the Seine in France, toppling Hamburg, Bordeaux, and Paris along the way. Conquering works up a fierce appetite, and the Vikings prepared their feasts with the same zeal with which they razed the countryside.

If art is the reflection of life—or, more accurately, what is important in life—then the celebration of food and drink were central to the Viking existence. Viking-era tapestries unfold with rollicking feast scenes, often in commemoration of battles won—and gold and silver confiscated. A 70-meter-long Viking tapestry (on display in Bayeux, France) illustrates the legendary exploits of William the Conqueror, a descendent of the Viking chieftain Rollo. Depicted in detail is William's famous victory at the Battle of Hastings in 1066, which granted him control of England. No less prominent is the pre-battle banquet, a boisterous affair of spit-roasted chickens, free-flowing mead, and piping hot loaves of bread, suggesting that a proper feast is the necessary precursor to emerging victorious in war. Even passing through the Pearly Gates called for a drink. In Viking-era stone carvings, warrior heroes are presented with a drinking horn upon entering Valhalla, the heroes' afterlife presided over by the great Norse God Odin.

For a taste of Viking life, try this at home:

Wild Boar in Bilberry Sauce

2 lb wild boar meat	butter
2 carrots	2 onions
2 tablespoons honey	fresh ginger
1 cup stock	salt and pepper

In a frying pan, brown the wild boar meat and then place into a large pan. Peel and slice carrots and onions. Add carrots, onions, honey, ginger, and stock to the pan. Add a bit of salt and pepper. Cover and simmer over low heat for about 1 hour, or until meat reaches 167°F.

ing from opulent to modest—of 38 Danish monarchs. Predictably, Christian IV is interred in a magnificent chapel with a massive painting of himself in combat and a bronze sculpture by Thorvaldsen. In modest contrast is the newest addition, the simple brick chapel of King Frederik IX, who died in 1972, outside the church. In November 2000, his wife Queen Ingrid joined him in his tomb at the foot of the cathedral. On the interior south wall above the entrance is a 16th-century clock depicting St. George charging a dragon, which hisses and howls, echoing throughout the church and causing Peter Døver, "the Deafener," to sound the hour. A squeamish Kirsten Kiemer, "the Chimer," shakes her head in fright but manages to strike the quarter-hours. Around the altar are the Kannikekoret, the wooden choir stalls carved in 1420. Each seat is topped with a panel depicting a Biblical scene. Behind the altarpiece is the alabaster and marble sarcophagus of Queen Margrethe I, who died in 1412. ⊠ *Domkirkestr. 10* ☎ *46/35–16–24* ⊕ *www.roskildedomkirke.dk* ▣ *Dkr 15* ☉ *Apr.–Sept., weekdays 9–4:45, Sat. 9–noon, Sun. 12:30–4:45; Oct.–Mar., Tues.–Sat. 10–3:45, Sun. 12:30–3:45.*

Less than 1 km (½ mi) north of the cathedral, on the fjord, is the modern **Vikingeskibshallen** (Viking Ship Museum), containing five Viking ships sunk in the fjord 1,000 years ago. Submerged to block the passage of enemy ships, they were discovered in 1957. The painstaking recovery involved building a watertight dam and then draining the water from that section of the fjord. The splinters of wreckage were then preserved and reassembled. A deep-sea trader, warship, ferry, merchant ship, and fierce 92½-foot man-of-war attest to the Vikings' sophisticated and aesthetic boat-making skills. ⊠ *Vindeboder 12* ☎ *46/30–02–00* ⊕ *www. vikingeskibsmuseet.dk* ▣ *Dkr 60* ☉ *Daily 10–5.*

Where to Stay & Eat

$$$ ✕ **Svogerslev Kro.** Three kilometers (2 mi) west of Roskilde is the village of Svogerslev, a peaceful location for this traditional thatch-roof Danish inn. Exposed wooden beams make the interior a cozy place to tuck into the hearty Danish fare. The menu includes a vegetarian option as well as some international dishes such as Wiener schnitzel and steak. ⊠ *Hovedg. 45, Svogerslev* ☎ *46/38–30–05* ▭ *AE, DC, MC, V.*

★ $ ✕ **Club 42.** This popular Danish restaurant spills out onto the sidewalk in summer while inside the roof opens over the dining room. The fare is typically Danish, including smørrebrød and spare ribs, which are simply prepared and served with potato salad. ⊠ *Skomagerg. 42* ☎ *46/ 35–17–64* ▭ *MC, V.*

$$$$ ▥ **Hotel Prindsen.** In downtown Roskilde, this 100-year-old hotel is popular with business guests for its convenient location. The elegant dark-wood lobby leads to the plain but homey and comfortable rooms. Downstairs, the restaurant and grill La Bøf serves up fish, and next door there is a cushy bar. ⊠ *Alg. 13, DK–4000* ☎ *46/30–91–00* ▤ *46/ 30–91–50* ⊕ *www.prindsen.dk* ⟿ *76 rooms, 3 suites* ⌂ *Restaurant, cafeteria, minibars, bar, meeting rooms, some pets allowed, no-smoking rooms* ▭ *AE, DC, MC, V.*

¢ ▥ **Roskilde Vandrerhjem.** This youth hostel, perfect for budget travelers, is on Roskilde Fjord, which is close to the town's green areas. Guests have use of the kitchen. ⊠ *Vinderboder 7, DK–4000* ☎ *46/35–21–84* ▤ *46/32–66–90* ⊕ *www.rova.dk* ⟿ *152 beds, 40 showers* ⌂ *Restaurant, laundry facilities* ▭ *No credit cards.*

Nightlife & the Arts

For one weekend at the end of June, Roskilde holds one of Europe's biggest rock-music gatherings, the **Roskilde Festival** (⊕ www.roskilde-festival.dk). Some 75,000 people show up every year to enjoy the outdoor concerts.

When town's youth are in the mood for live rock, they head to **Gimle** (✉ Ringstedg. 30 ☎ 46/35–12–13) on the weekends. At **Bryggergården** (✉ Alg. 15 ☎ 46/35–01–03), or the Draft Horse, adults have a late supper and beer in cozy surroundings. During the summer, **Café Mulle Rudi** (✉ Djalma Lunds Gård 7 ☎ 46/37–03–25) is an arty spot with indoor and outdoor seating and live jazz.

Sports & the Outdoors

GOLF   **Roskilde Golf Klub** (✉ Margrethehåbvej 116 ☎ 46/37–01–81) has an 18-hole golf course with views of the twin-peak Roskilde Cathedral and the surrounding forest.

TOURS   Boat excursions depart from the town's docks for dual-purpose (sightseeing and transportation) routes on Roskilde Fjord. The boats occasionally make stops at Frederikssund and Frederiksværk, but most passengers are there for a fun and scenic boat ride. Some refreshments can be purchased onboard. **Saga Fjord** (☎ 46/75–64–60 ⊕ www.sagafjord.dk) operates more-sightseeing-oriented trips. **Viking Ruten** (☎ 47/38–87–50 ⊕ www.vikingruten.dk) operates a regular run up to Frederikssund with stops along the way.

Shopping

CRAFTS   Between Roskilde and Holbæk is **Galleri Kirke Sonnerup** (✉ Englerupvej 62, Såby ☎ 46/49–25–77), with a good selection of pottery, glass, clothing, and woodwork produced by more than 50 Danish artists.

Lejre

⑭ *10 km (6 mi) west of Roskilde, 40 km (25 mi) west of Copenhagen.*

Archaeological digs unearthing the times of the Vikings show that Lejre has had a glorious past. During the 10th century the town reigned as the kingdom's most sacred place.

FodorsChoice   The 50-acre **Lejre Forsøgscenter** (Lejre Archaeological Research Center) ★ compound contains a reconstructed village dating from the Iron Age and two 19th-century farmhouses. In summer a handful of hardy Danish families live here under the observation of researchers; they go about their daily routine—grinding grain, herding goats, eating with their hands, and wearing furs and skins—providing a clearer picture of ancient ways of life. In Bodalen (Fire Valley), children can try their own hand at such tasks as grinding corn, filing an ax, and sailing in a dugout canoe. ✉ *Slangealleen 2* ☎ *46/48–08–78* ⊕ *www.lejre-center.dk* ☐ *Dkr 75* ☉ *May–mid-June and mid-Aug.–mid-Sept., Tues.–Fri. 10–4, weekends 10–5; mid-June–mid-Aug., daily 10–5.*

Ledreborg Slot is one of Denmark's finest examples of 18th-century building and landscape architecture. Built in 1742, Ledreborg Castle is now owned by the eighth generation of the Holstein-Ledreborg family. The main building contains a remarkable collection of paintings and furniture from when it was first built. At the southern part there is an elaborate terraced garden in the 18th-century French style. ✉ *Ledreborg Allé 2* ☎ *46/48–00–38* ⊕ *www.ledreborgslot.dk* ☐ *Dkr 60* ☉ *May–mid-June and Sept., Sun. 11–5; mid-June–Aug., daily 11–5.*

Køge

⑮ *20 km (13 mi) southeast of Lejre, 47 km (29 mi) southwest of Copenhagen.*

The well-preserved medieval town of Køge began its existence as a fishing village dependent on the herring trade. Køge is also known for the witch hunts that took place in the early 17th century. Today, with about 40,000 inhabitants, this satellite town of Copenhagen exists as a center of trade. It links to the big city by suburban train.

In the 17th century and later during the Napoleonic wars, Køge was witness to many naval battles. The Danish and Swedish fleets clashed repeatedly in order to gain control over the sound, which was the gateway to trade with the Baltic Sea.

Køge Museum is in a centrally located 17th-century merchant's house. On display are mementos and items belonging to Hans Christian Andersen, local costumes, and artifacts including an executioner's sword and a 13th-century stone font. The legend of the font is that it had to be removed from the town church after a crippled woman committed an unsavory act into it, hoping her bizarre behavior would cure her. Also on exhibit are 16th-century silver coins from a buried treasure containing more than 2,000 coins. The stash was found in the courtyard of Langkildes Gård. ⊠ *Nørreg. 4* ☎ *56/63–42–42* 🖅 *Dkr 25* ⊙ *June–Aug., daily 11–5; Sept.–May, Tues.–Fri. 1–5, Sat. 11–3, and Sun. 1–5.*

Kunstmuseet Køge Skitsesamling (Art Museum Køge Sketches Collection) has changing exhibitions and an extensive permanent collection of sketches, sculpture, and other modern Danish art. ⊠ *Nørreg. 29* ☎ *56/67–60–20* 🖅 *Dkr 30* ⊙ *Tues.–Sun. 10–5; Wed. 10–8.*

The old part of Køge is filled with 300 half-timber houses, all protected by the National Trust; it is a lovely area for a stroll. At the end of Kirkestræde is the 15th-century **Skt. Nicolai Kirke** (St. Nicholas Church). Once a lighthouse, its floor is now covered with more than 100 tombs of Køge VIPs. Carved angels line the church's walls, but most have had their noses struck off—a favorite pastime of drunken Swedish soldiers in the 1700s. ⊠ *Kirkestr. 26* ☎ *56/65–13–59* 🖅 *Free* ⊙ *Mid-June–Aug., weekdays 10–4, Sat. 10–noon; Sept.–mid-June, weekdays 10–noon. Tower tours mid-June–mid-Aug., weekdays every 30 min. 10–1:30.*

off the
beaten
path

VALLØ SLOT – About 8 km (5 mi) south of Køge stands Vallø Slot, a large castle in Renaissance style from 1586. It was burnt down by a fire in 1893 and promptly rebuilt. The castle is surrounded by moats and reinforced with towers. Since 1737 noble families have used Vallø Slot for rest and relaxation. The gardens, the only part open to the public, are known for their roses and exotic plants. ⊠ *Slotsg. 3, Vallø* ☎ *56/26–74–13* 🖅 *Free* ⊙ *Daily 8–sunset.*

Where to Stay & Eat

$$$$ ╳ **Horizonten Restaurant.** For a great view, sit at the terrace overlooking the harbor. Horizonten's interior is modern and often decorated with exhibitions of local artists. The food here includes a mixture of Italian, French, Spanish, and Danish cuisine. Any of the grilled-fish dishes on the menu are a good option, but the seafood-and-fish platter is the highlight. Lunch is served only by prior reservation. ⊠ *Havnen 29A* ☎ *56/63–86–28* ▤ *MC, V* ⊙ *Closed Mon.; Jan. and Feb., closed Sun.*

$$$ 🏨 **Hotel Hvide Hus.** Built in 1966 and overlooking the Bay of Køge, the White House Hotel has fantastic views. The hotel is brightly decorated in a contemporary Danish style. ⊠ *Strandvejen 111, DK–4600* ☎ *56/65–36–90* 🖷 *56/66–33–14* ⊕ *www.hotelhvidehus.dk* 🛏 *127 rooms, 1 suite* ⚐ *Restaurant, cafeteria, sauna, bar, meeting room, some pets allowed, no-smoking rooms* ▤ *AE, DC, MC, V.*

$ 🏨 **Hotel Vallø Slotskro.** Near Vallø Slot and surrounded by the castle's
FodorśChoice beautifully landscaped grounds, this rural inn is a pleasant place to spend
★ a couple of days. The rooms are charming, some of them have beds with

canopies, and the service is personable. ✉ *Slotsg. 1, DK–4600* ☎ *56/ 26–70–20* 🖷 *56/26–70–71* 🌐 *www.valloeslotskro.dk* ➴ *11 rooms, 7 with bath* 🍴 *Restaurant, bar, some pets allowed, no-smoking rooms* 🚫 *AE, DC, MC, V.*

Nightlife & the Arts

Even if the name suggests another thing, **Hugo's Vinkælder** (Hugo's Winecellar; ✉ Brog. 19, courtyard ☎ 56/65–58–50) is an old beer pub, which was opened in 1968 on the ruins of a medieval monastery cellar. It is a favorite gathering spot for locals. There are beers from all over the world and sandwiches to go with them. On Saturday there is live jazz until midnight. It's closed Sunday.

> **en route** Twenty-four kilometers (15 mi) south of Køge near Rødvig, the Stevns Klint chalk cliffs make a good stop. The 13th-century **Højerup Kirke** sits on the cliffs. Over time as the cliffs eroded, first the cemetery and then part of the church toppled into the sea. The church has now been restored and the cliffs below have been bolstered by masonry to prevent further damage. ✉ *Højerup Byg., Stevns Klint, Store Heddinge* ☎ *56/50–36–88* 🕾 *Dkr 15* ⊙ *Daily 11–5.*

Møn

📍 ⑯ *77 km (47 mi) south of Køge, 122 km (75 mi) south of Copenhagen.*

The whole island of Møn is pocked with nearly 100 Neolithic burial mounds, but it is most famous for its dramatic chalk cliffs, the northern **Møns Klint,** which is three times as large as Stevns Klint. Circled by a beech forest, the milky-white 75-million-year-old bluffs plunge 400 feet to a small, craggy beach—accessible by a path and more than 500 steps. Wear good walking shoes and take care; though a park ranger checks the area for loose rocks, the cliffs can crumble suddenly. Once there, Danish families usually hunt for fossils of cuttlefish, sea urchins, and other sea life. The cliffs are an important navigational marker for ships as an unusual landmark on south Sjælland's otherwise flat topography.

Just inland from the northern section of the Møns Klint is **Liselund Slot,** a delightful 18th-century folly. Antoine de la Calmette, the island's sheriff and a royal chamberlain, took his inspiration from Marie-Antoinette's *Hameau* (*Hamlet*) at Versailles and built the Liselund Castle in 1792 for his beloved wife. The thatch-roof palace, complete with English gardens, combines a Norwegian country facade with elegant Pompeiian interiors. In this lovely setting, Hans Christian Andersen wrote his fairy tale *The Tinder Box.* The palace has been open to the public since 1938. This castle is not to be confused with a hotel of the same name. ✉ *Langebjergvej 4, Borre* ☎ *55/81–21–78* 🕾 *Dkr 30* ⊙ *Tours (Danish and German only) May–Oct., Tues.–Fri. 10:30, 11, 1:30, and 2; weekends also 3 and 3:30.*

Møn's capital, **Stege,** received its town charter in 1268. A third of the island's 11,500 inhabitants live here. Stege began as a small fishing village and it expanded slowly around a castle erected in the 12th century. By the 15th century, Stege was a commercial center for fishermen, peasants, and merchants. It was in this wealthy period that the town was encircled with moats and ramparts. The fortified town had three entranceways, each of them controlled with the help of a gate tower. One of these gates, **Mølleporten,** raised around 1430, is still standing.

The **Møns Museum** in Stege showcases antiques and local-history exhibitions and is well worth a stop. ✉ *Storeg. 75, Stege* ☎ *55/81–40–67* ⊕ *www.aabne-samlinger.dk/moens* ✇ *Dkr 30* ☉ *May–Oct., daily 10–4.*

One of the island's medieval churches noted for its naive frescoes, **Fanefjord Kirke** may have been completed by a collaborative group of artisans. The whimsical paintings include scholastic and biblical doodlings. The church also maintains an original 13th-century aisle. The Fanefjord church is 12½ km (8 mi) southwest of Stege. Other churches in the area famed for their frescoes include the ones in Elmelunde and Keldby. ✉ *Fanefjord Kirkevej 51, Askeby* ☎ *55/81–70–05* ☉ *Apr.–Sept., daily 7–4; Oct.–Mar., daily 8–4.*

Ten kilometers (6 mi) west of Stege is **Kong Asgers Høj** (King Asger's Hill), Denmark's biggest passage grave (a collection of upright stones supporting a horizontal stone slab to make a tomb) that dates from the early Stone Age. A 26-foot-long hall precedes the 32-foot grave chamber. During its history, the passage grave has periodically been used as a common grave for locals.

Where to Stay & Eat

$–$$ ✕▥ **Præstekilde Hotel.** On a small island close to the capital, this hotel has a splendid view of Stege Bay from the middle of the golf course. The service is efficient while maintaining the warmth of rural areas. The restaurant serves good French-inspired Danish food. The small, simply equipped rooms are decorated in light colors, giving a bright impression on sunny days. ✉ *Klintevej 116, DK–4780 Keldby* ☎ *55/86–87–88* ▤ *55/ 81–36–34* ⊕ *www.praestekilde.dk* ➷ *46 rooms with bath, 4 suites* ♨ *Restaurant, minibars, 18-hole golf course, indoor pool, sauna, billiards, meeting rooms, some pets allowed, no-smoking rooms* ▤ *AE, DC, MC, V.*

★ **$$** ▥ **Liselund Ny Slot.** In a grand old manor on an isolated estate, this modern hotel offers refined accommodations without being stodgy. The staircase and frescoed ceilings have been preserved and the rooms are fresh and simple, with wicker furnishings and pastel color schemes. Half the rooms overlook the forest and a pond filled with swans. The downstairs restaurant serves Danish cuisine. ✉ *Langebjergvej 6, DK–4791 Borre* ☎ *55/81–20–81* ▤ *55/81–21–91* ➷ *15 rooms* ♨ *Restaurant, meeting room* ▤ *AE, DC, MC, V.*

¢ ▥ **Pension Bakkegården.** Between the view of the Baltic Sea and the Klinteskov forest, this small hotel possesses the best qualities of the island. From here it is a simple and relaxing 20-minute stroll through the beech forest to see the cliffs of Møn. Partial board is available upon request. ✉ *Busenevej 64, Busene, DK–4791 Borre* ☎ *55/81–93–01* ▤ *55/ 81–94–01* ⊕ *www.bakkegaarden64.dk* ➷ *12 rooms without bath* ♨ *Billiards* ▤ *No credit cards.*

Falster

⓱ *3 km (2 mi) south of Bogø; Nykøbing Falster is 49 km (30 mi) southeast of Stege, 134 km (83 mi) south of Copenhagen.*

Accessible by way of the striking Farø Bridge or the parallel Storstrømsbroen (Big Current Bridge) from Fredensborg, Falster is shaped like a tiny South America and has excellent blond beaches to rival those of its continental twin. Among the best are the southeastern Marielyst and southernmost Gedser. Almost everywhere on the island are cafés, facilities, and water-sports rentals. Falster is also one of the country's major producers of sugar beets.

The **Middelaldercentret** (Center for the Middle Ages), a reconstructed medieval village, invites school classes to dress up in period costumes and experience life a millennium ago. Daytime visitors can participate in activities that change weekly—from cooking to medieval knife-making to animal herding and, on weekends, folk dances and other cultural happenings. ✉ *Ved Hamborgskoven 2, Nykøbing Falster* ☎ *54/86–19–34* ⊕ *www.middelaldercentret.dk* 🎫 *Dkr 80* ☉ *May–Sept., daily 10–4.*

Where to Stay & Eat

$$$–$$$$ ✕ **Czarens Hus.** This stylish old inn dates back more than 200 years, when it was a guest house and supply store for area farmers and merchants. Deep-green walls, gold trim, and chandeliers set the backdrop for antique furnishings. The specialty of the house is Continental European–Danish cuisine, which translates as creative beef and fish dishes, often served with cream sauces. Try the Zar Beuf (calf tenderloin in a mushroom-and-onion cream sauce). ✉ *Langg. 2, Nykøbing Falster* ☎ *54/85–28–29* ☰ *AE, DC, MC, V* ☉ *Closed Sun.*

★ **$$–$$$** 🏨 **Hotel Falster.** This sleek and efficient hotel accommodates conference guests as well as vacationers with its comfortable yet businesslike demeanor. Rustic brick walls and Danish antiques mix with sleek Danish-design lamps and sculpture. Rooms are done in dark wood and modular furniture. ✉ *Stubbekøbingvej 150, DK–4800 Nykøbing Falster* ☎ *54/85–93–93* 🖷 *54/82–21–99* ⊕ *www.hotel-falster.dk* ↘ *68 rooms, 1 suite* ☖ *Restaurant, bar, gym, meeting room, some pets allowed, no-smoking rooms* ☰ *AE, DC, MC, V.*

Sports & the Outdoors

GOLF The 18-hole **Sydsjælland Golf Klub** (✉ Præstø Landevej 39–Mogenstrup, DK–4700 Næstved ☎ 55/76–15–55) is more than 25 years old, and the park course is lined with a number of small lakes and streams. The highest accepted handicap is 36.

Lolland

⓲ *Sakskøbing is 19 km (12 mi) west of Nykøbing Falster and 138 km (85 mi) southwest of Copenhagen.*

The history of Lolland dates back more than 1,000 years, to a man named Saxe, who sat at the mouth of the fjord and collected a toll. He later cleared the surrounding land and leased it. It became known as Saxtorp and eventually Sakskøbing, the island's capital. Though most people head straight for the beaches, the area (accessible by bridge from Nykøbing Falster) has a few sights, including a water tower with a smiling face and an excellent car museum near the central 13th-century Ålholm Slot (closed to the public). The **Ålholm Automobile Museum** is northern Europe's largest, with more than 200 vehicles. ✉ *Ålholm Parkvej 17, Nysted* ☎ *54/87–19–11* ⊕ *www.aalholm.dk* 🎫 *Dkr 75* ☉ *Mid-May–Aug., daily 10–5; Sept.–mid-Oct., weekends 10–4.*

The **Knuthenborg Safari Park,** 8 km (5 mi) west of Sakskøbing and also on Lolland, has a drive-through range where you can rubberneck at tigers, zebras, rhinoceroses, giraffes, and areas where you can mingle with and pet camels, goats, and ponies. Besides seeing 20 species of animals, children can marvel at Småland's to-scale relief map of southern Sjælland or play on the jungle gym, minitrain, and other rides. ✉ *Birketvej 1, Maribo, Bandholm* ☎ *54/78–80–88* ⊕ *www.knuthenborg.dk* 🎫 *Dkr 95* ☉ *Late Apr.–late Sept., daily 9–5; late Sept.–late Oct., weekends 9–5.*

Where to Stay

$$ 🏨 **Lalandia.** This massive water-park hotel has an indoor pool, beachside view, and lots of happy families. On the southern coast of Lolland, about 27 km (16 mi) southwest of Sakskøbing, the modern white apartments, with full kitchen and bath, accommodate up to eight people. There are three family-style restaurants—a steak house, Italian buffet, and pizzeria. ⊠ *Rødbyhavn, DK–4970 Rødby* ☎ *54/61–05–00* 🖷 *54/61–05–01* ⊕ *www.lalandia.dk* 🛏 *636 apartments* ⟁ *3 restaurants, indoor pool, sauna, 9-hole golf course, 5 tennis courts, health club, playground, bar, meeting room* ▤ *AE, DC, MC, V.*

¢ 🖬 **Hotel Saxkjøbing.** Behind its yellow half-timber facade, this comfortable hotel is short on character and frills, but the rooms are bright, sunny, and modern, if very simply furnished. In the town center, the hotel is convenient to everything. Its family-style restaurant serves pizzas, steaks, and salads. ⊠ *Torvet 9, DK–4990 Sakskøbing* ☎ *54/70–40–39* 🖷 *54/ 70–53–50* 🛏 *24 rooms with bath* ⟁ *Restaurant, billiards, bar, meeting room* ▤ *AE, DC, MC.*

Ringsted

⑲ *95 km (59 mi) north of Sakskøbing (Lolland), 68 km (42 mi) southwest of Copenhagen (via Køge).*

During the Middle Ages Ringsted became one of the most important Danish towns by growing around a church and a nearby 12th-century Benedictine abbey. The abbey was partially destroyed by a fire in the beginning of the 1900s. Nowadays Ringsted is known for being "the town in the middle," the traffic junction of Sjælland.

☾ The spirit of fairy tales is tangible at **Eventyrlandet** (Fantasy World), where a life-size, animated model of Hans Christian Andersen tells his stories via a recorded tape playing in Danish, English, and German. Children enjoy Santa World and Cowboy Land while adults can discover the Adventure Gardens, where Moorish, Japanese, and Roman ornaments dot the well-preserved gardens. ⊠ *Eventyrvej 13, DK–4100 Ringsted* ☎ *57/61–19–30* ⊕ *www.fantasy-world.dk* 🖾 *Dkr 70* ☾ *June–Aug., Oct.–Dec., 2nd wk of Feb., and Easter, daily 10–5.*

Sct. Bendts Kirke (St. Benedict's Church) is the only evidence left of the existence of the Benedictine monastery that thrived here in the 12th century. Inside, four Danish kings are buried, including Valdemar I who died in 1182. ⊠ *Sct. Bendtsg. 3* ☎ *57/61–40–19* ☾ *May–mid-Sept., daily 10–noon and 1–5; mid-Sept.–Apr., daily 1–3.*

---

off the beaten path

SORØ – Eighteen kilometers (11 mi) west of Ringsted is the town of Sorø, known for **Akademiet,** founded in 1623 by King Christian IV. The Academy was established in the abbey, which had been built by Bishop Absalon in 1142 and abandoned after the Lutheran reformation. The educational importance of the town increased thanks to the Danish writer Ludvig Holberg, who donated his whole inheritance to the academy after his death in 1754. The academy is on the banks of Sorø Sø (Lake Sorø) inside an extensive park. Not far from here is **Klosterkirke,** a Roman church built in the 12th century as a part of a Cistercian abbey. In this church are the remains of Bishop Absalon.

☾ **BONBON-LAND** – Children adore this park in the tiny southern Sjælland town of Holme-Olstrup between Rønnede and Næstved, 30 km (19 mi) south of Ringsted. Filled with rides and friendly costumed grown-ups, BonBon-Land is an old-fashioned playland, with a few eating and drinking establishments thrown in for adults. ⊠ *Gartnervej 2, DK–4684 Holme-Olstrup* ☎ *55/53–07–00*

⊕ *www.bonbonland.dk* ⊠ *Dkr 150* ⊙ *Mid-May–mid-June and Aug., daily 9:30–5; mid-June–July, daily 9:30–8.*

Where to Stay

$$ ⊞ **Skjoldenæseholm.** Any point of the island can be reached by car within an hour from this luxurious hotel in the very center of Sjælland. Luxury prevails, from the Jacuzzi in the suites to the surrounding lush park and forest. Cottages for groups and families, one of them placed by the 15th hole in the nearby golf course, are available to rent. ⊠ *Skjoldenæsvej 106, DK–4174 Jystrup Midsjælland* ☎ *57/52–81–04* ⊟ *57/52–88–55* ⊕ *www.skj.dk* ↝ *38 rooms, 5 suites* ⏃ *Restaurant, bar, billiards, meeting room* ⊟ *AE, DC, MC, V.*

Sports & the Outdoors

CANOEING   Just 8 km (5 mi) south of Sorø is the Suså (Sus River) where you can arrange canoe trips that last an hour, a day, or as long as a week. Call **Suså Kanoudlejning** (☎ 57/64–61–44) for more information on canoe rentals.

Shopping

In Næstved, 25 km (16 mi) south of Ringsted, the **Holmegaards Glassværker** (Glass Workshop; ⊠ Glassværksvej 52–Fensmark, Næstved ☎ 55/54–62–00) sells seconds of glasses, lamps, and occasionally glass art, with reductions of up to 50%.

Halsskov

㉑ *48 km (30 mi) west of Ringsted, 110 km (69 mi) southwest of Copenhagen.*

Europe's third-longest tunnel-bridge, Storebæltsbro—the entire fixed-link length of which is 18 km (11 mi)—links Halsskov, on west Sjælland, to Nyborg, on east Fyn. Rail traffic traverses the west bridge and tunnel while auto traffic passes on the east-and-west bridge.

The **Storebæltsbro og Naturcenter** (Great Belt Bridge and Nature Center), which details the tunnel-bridge construction process, includes videos and models and makes for an informative stop. ⊠ *Storebæltsvej 88, Halsskov Odde, Korsør* ☎ *58/35–01–00* ⊠ *Dkr 25* ⊙ *Mid-Apr.–mid-Oct., daily 10–5.*

> **off the beaten path**

TRÆLLEBORG – Viking enthusiasts will want to head 18 km (11 mi) northeast from Halsskov to Slagelse to see its excavated Viking encampment with a reconstructed army shelter. No longer content to rely on farmer-warriors, the Viking hierarchy designed the geometrically exact camp within a circular, moated rampart, thought to be of Asian inspiration. The 16 barracks, of which there is one model, could accommodate 1,300 men. ⊠ *Trælleborg Allé 4, Hejninge, Slagelse* ☎ *58/54–95–16* ⊠ *Dkr 35* ⊙ *Apr.–mid-Oct., Sat.–Thurs. 10–5.*

Sjælland & Its Islands A to Z

AIRPORTS

🛈 Kastrup International Airport ☎ 32/31-32-31 ⊕ www.cph.dk is Sjælland's only airport.

BIKE TRAVEL

Sjælland's flat landscape allows easy biking, and in summer, touring this way can be a delightful experience. Most roads have cycle lanes, and tourist boards stock maps detailing local routes. For more biking information, call the Danish Cycling Association, the Danish Tourist Board, or the bicycle tour operator Bike Denmark. 🚲 **Bike Denmark** ✉ Olaf Poulsens Allé 1A, DK-3480 Fredensborg ☎ 48/48-58-00 🖷 48/48-59-00 ⊕ www.bikedenmark.com. **Danmarks Turistråd** (Danish Tourist Board) ✉ Vesterbrog. 6D, Vesterbro, DK-1620 Copenhagen ☎ 33/11-14-15 🖷 33/93-14-16 ⊕www.visitdenmark.com. **Dansk Cyklist Forbund** (Danish Cyclist Federation) ✉ Rømersg. 7, Downtown DK-1362 Copenhagen ☎ 33/32-31-21 🖷 33/32-76-83 ⊕ www.dcf.dk.

CAR TRAVEL

Highways and country roads throughout Sjælland are excellent, and traffic—even around Copenhagen—is manageable most of the time. As elsewhere in Denmark, take care to give right-of-way to the bikes driving to the right of the traffic. Sjælland is connected to Fyn, which is connected to Jylland, by the Storebæltsbroen, and it is connected to Malmö in Sweden by Øresund Bridge, which ends in Copenhagen.

BRIDGES 🚉 **Storebæltsbroen** ✉ Storebæltsvej 70, DK-4220 Korsør ☎ 70/15-10-15 🖷 58/30-30-80. **Øresundsbroen** ✉ Vester Søg. 10, Downtown DK-1601 Copenhagen ☎ 33/41-60-00 🖷 33/93-52-04.

BOAT & FERRY TRAVEL

There are several DSB and Scandlines car ferries from Germany. They connect Kiel to Bagenkop, on the island of Langeland (from there, drive north to Spodsbjerg and take another ferry to Lolland, which is connected to Falster and Sjælland by bridges); Puttgarden to Rødbyhavn on Lolland; and Travemünde and Warnemünde to Gedser on Falster. If you are driving from Sweden, take a car ferry from Hälsingborg to Helsingør. Molslinien runs routes between Jylland and Sjælland, linking Kalundborg and Havnebyen to Århus, and Havnebyen to Ebeltoft.

The ScanRail Pass, for travel anywhere within Scandinavia (Denmark, Sweden, Norway, and Finland), and the Interail and EurailPasses are valid on some ferry crossings. Call the DSB Travel Office for information. 🚢 **DSB** ☎ 70/13-14-16 international, 70/13-14-15 domestic ⊕ www.dsb.dk. **Mols-Linien** ☎ 70/10-14-18 🖷 89/52-52-90 ⊕www.molslinien.dk. **Scandinavian Seaways Ferries** (DFDS) ✉ Skt. Annæ Pl. 30, Sankt Annæ DK-1295 Copenhagen ☎ 33/42-33-42 🖷 33/42-33-41 ⊕ www.dfds.com. **Scandlines** ☎ 33/15-15-15 🖷 35/29-02-01 ⊕ www.scandlines.dk.

EMERGENCIES

For police, fire, or ambulance assistance anywhere in Denmark, dial 112. 🏥 **Major Hospitals Helsingør Sygehus** ✉ Esrumvej 145, Helsingør ☎ 48/29-29-29. **Køge Amts Sygehus** ✉ Lykkebækvej 1, Køge ☎ 56/63-15-00. **Roskilde Amts Sygehus** ✉ Køgevej 7-13, Roskilde ☎ 46/32-32-00. 🏥 **24-Hour Pharmacies Hillerød** ✉ Slotsg. 26 ☎ 48/26-56-00 🖷 48/24-23-85. **Roskilde** ✉ Dom Apotek, Alg. 52 ☎ 46/32-32-77 🖷 46/32-88-22.

SPORTS & THE OUTDOORS

FISHING Sjælland's lakes, rivers, and coastline teem with plaice, flounder, cod, and catfish. You can buy a fishing license for one day for Dkr 25; for one week for Dkr 75; or for one year for Dkr 100. Along Sjælland's coast it can be bought at any post office. Elsewhere, check with the local tourist office for license requirements. It is illegal to fish within 1,650 feet of the mouth of a stream.

TRAIN TRAVEL

Sjælland's extensive rail network will get you where you need to go in much less time than the cumbersome bus system. Most train routes, whether international or domestic, are directed to and through Copenhagen. Routes to north and south Sjælland almost always require a transfer at Copenhagen's main station. Every town in Sjælland has a central train station, usually within walking distance of hotels and sights. The only part of the island not connected to the DSB network is the sliver of northwestern peninsula known as Sjællands Odde. Trains leave from Holbæk to Højby, where you can bus to the tip of the point. For information, call the private railway company Arriva. Two vintage trains dating from the 1880s run from Helsingør and Hillerød to Gilleleje.

The Copenhagen Card, which includes train and bus transport as well as admission to some museums and sites, is valid within the HT bus and rail system, which extends north to Helsingør, west to Roskilde, and south to Køge. However, the Copenhagen Card is valid for a limited time, so it's only worthwhile if you're planning a nonstop, intense sightseeing tour.

Arriva ☎ 70/27-74-82 ⊕ www.arrivatog.dk. **DSB** ☎ 70/13-14-16 international, 70/13-14-15 domestic ⊕ www.dsb.dk. **HT Bus** ✉ Gammel Køge Landevej 3, DK-2500 Valby ☎ 36/13-14-15 🖷 36/13-18-97 ⊕ www.ht.dk. **Vintage trains** ☎ 48/30-00-30.

TOURS

The turn-of-the-20th-century *Saga Fjord* gives tours of the waters of the Roskildefjord from April through September; meals are served on board. Schedules vary; call ahead for schedules and information. Another option is *Viking Ruten*.

Check with the local tourism boards for general sightseeing tours in the larger towns or for self-guided walking tours. Most tours of Sjælland begin in Copenhagen. For information, call Copenhagen Excursions. The Afternoon Hamlet Tour (5 hours) includes Frederiksborg Castle and the exterior of Fredensborg Palace and Kronborg Castle. The seven-hour Castle Tour of North Sjælland visits Frederiksborg Castle and the outside of Fredensborg Palace, and stops at Kronborg Castle. The six-hour Roskilde Vikingland Tour includes the market and cathedral, Christian IV's Chapel, and the Viking Ship Museum.

Copenhagen Excursions ✉ Artillerivej 147, DK-2300 Copenhagen ☎ 32/54-06-06 🖷 32/57-49-05 ⊕ www.cex.dk. **Saga Fjord** ✉ Store Valbyvej 154, DK-4000 Roskilde ☎ 46/75-64-60 🖷 46/75-63-60 ⊕ www.sagafjord.dk. **Viking Ruten** ✉ Sydkajen, DK-3600 Frederikssund ☎ 47/38-87-50 🖷 47/38-87-51 ⊕ www.vikingruten.dk.

VISITOR INFORMATION

The Fiskeridirektoratet has information about fishing licenses and where to buy them.

Danmarks Turistråd (Danish Tourist Board) ✉ Vesterbrog. 6D, Vesterbro, DK-1620 Copenhagen ☎ 33/11-14-15. **Det grønne Sjælland** (Zealand Naturally) ⊕ www.sjaelland.com. **Fiskeridirektoratet** ✉ Stormg. 2, Downtown, DK-1470 Copenhagen ☎ 33/96-30-00 🖷 33/96-39-03 ⊕ www.fd.dk. **Fredensborg Turistinformation** ✉ Slotsg. 2, DK-3480 ☎ 48/48-21-00 🖷 48/48-04-65 ⊕ www.visitfredensborg.dk. **Frederiksdal Kanoudlejning** ✉ Nybrovej 520, DK-2800 Lyngby ☎ 45/85-67-70 🖷 45/83-02-91. **Helsingør Turistbureau** ✉ Havnepl. 3, DK-3000 ☎ 49/21-13-33 🖷 49/21-15-77 ⊕ www.visithelsingor.dk. **Hillerød Turistbureau** ✉ Slangerupg. 2, DK-3400 ☎ 48/24-26-26 🖷 48/24-26-65 ⊕ www.hillerodturist.dk. **Holbæk Turistbureau** ✉ Jernbanepl. 3, DK-4300 ☎ 59/43-11-31 🖷 59/44-27-44 ⊕ www.holbaek-info.dk. **Hornbæk Turistinformation** ✉ Vestre Stejlebakke 2A, DK-3100 ☎ 49/70-47-47 🖷 49/70-41-42 ⊕ www.hornbaek.dk. **Køge Turistbureau** ✉ Vesterg. 1, DK-4600 ☎ 56/67-60-01 🖷 56/65-59-84 ⊕ www.koegeturist.dk. **Nykøbing Falster Turistinformation** ✉ Østergåg. 7, DK-4800 ☎ 54/85-13-03 🖷 54/85-10-05 ⊕ www.tinf.dk. **Møn Turistbureau** ✉ Storeg. 2, DK-4780 Stege ☎ 55/86-04-00 🖷 55/81-48-46 ⊕ www.moen-touristbureau.dk. **Næstved Turistbureau** ✉ Det Gule Pakhus, Havnen 1, DK-4700 ☎ 55/72-11-22 🖷 55/72-16-67 ⊕ www.visitnaestved.com. **Odsherreds Turistbureau**

✉ Svanestr. 9, DK-4500 Nykøbing Sjælland ☏ 59/91-08-88 🖷 59/93-00-24 ⊕ www.odsherred.com. **Midtsjællands Turistcenter** ✉ Sct. Bendtsg. 6, DK-4100 Ringsted ☏57/62-66-00 🖷57/62-66-10 ⊕www.met-2000.dk. **Roskilde Festival** ✉Havsteensvej 11, DK-4000 Roskilde ☏ 46/36-66-13 🖷 46/32-14-99 ⊕ www.roskilde-festival.dk. **Roskilde Turistbureau** ✉ Gullandsstr. 15, DK-4000 ☏ 46/31-65-65 🖷 46/31-65-60 ⊕ www.destination-roskilde.dk. **Sakskøbing Turistbureau** ✉ Torveg. 4, DK-4990 ☏ 54/70-56-30 🖷 54/70-53-90 ⊕ www.lolland-falster.dk. **Slagelse Turistbureau** ✉ Løveg. 7, DK-4200 ☏ 58/52-22-06 🖷 58/52-86-87 ⊕ www.vikingelandet.dk.

2

FYN & THE CENTRAL ISLANDS

3

FODOR'S CHOICE

Brandts Klædefabrik, *artists' community in Odense*

Bregninge Mølle, *windmill restaurant in Tåsinge*

Egeskov Slot, *castle in Kværndrup*

Falsled Kro, *restaurant in Millinge*

Hesselet, *hotel in Nyborg*

Hotel Ydes, *Odense*

Marie Louise, *restaurant in Odense*

Valdemars Slot, *castle in Troense*

HIGHLY RECOMMENDED

RESTAURANTS   Den Grimme Ælling, *Odense*

Hos Grethe, *Ærøskøbing*

Rudolf Mathis, *Kerteminde*

HOTELS   Missionhotellet Stella Marris, *Svendborg*

SIGHTS   Ærøskøbing, *island of Ærø*

De 7 Haver, *gardens in Ebberup*

Hans Christian Andersen Hus, *museum in Odense*

Marstal

NIGHTLIFE   Café Anthon, *Nyborg*

Updated by
Eduardo López
de Luzuriaga

CHRISTENED THE GARDEN OF DENMARK by its most famous son, Hans Christian Andersen, Fyn (Funen) is the smaller of the country's two major islands. A patchwork of vegetable fields and flower gardens, the flat-as-a-board countryside is relieved by beech glades and swan ponds. Manor houses and castles pop up from the countryside like magnificent mirages. Some of northern Europe's best-preserved castles are here: the 12th-century Nyborg Slot, travel pinup Egeskov Slot, and the lavish Valdemars Slot. The fairy-tale cliché often attributed to Denmark springs from this provincial isle, where the only place with modern vigor or stress seems to be Odense, its capital. Trimmed with thatch-roof houses and green parks, the city makes the most of the Andersen legacy but surprises with a rich arts community at the Brandts Klædefabrik, a former textile factory turned museum compound.

Exploring Fyn & the Central Islands

Towns in Fyn are best explored by car. It's even quick and easy to reach the smaller islands of Langeland and Tåsinge—both are connected to Fyn by bridges. Slightly more isolated is Ærø, where the town of Ærøskøbing, with its colorfully painted half-timber houses and winding streets, seems caught in a delightful time warp.

WHAT IT COSTS In kroner				
$$$$	**$$$**	**$$**	**$**	**¢**
RESTAURANTS over 180	141–180	121–140	90–120	under 90
HOTELS over 1,500	1,200–1,500	1,000–1,200	700–1,000	under 700

Restaurant prices are for a main course at dinner. Hotel prices are for two people in a standard double room, including service charge and tax.

Timing

Wednesday and Saturday are market days in towns across Fyn throughout the summer. Often held in the central square, these morning markets sell fresh produce, flowers, and cheeses. Castle concerts are held throughout the summer months at Egeskov, Nyborg, and Valdemars castles and the rarely opened Krengerup manor house near Assens.

Nyborg

 1 *136 km (85 mi) southwest of Copenhagen (including the bridge across the Great Belt), 30 km (19 mi) southeast of Odense.*

Like most visitors, you should begin your tour of Fyn in Nyborg, a 13th-century town that was Denmark's capital during the Middle Ages. The city's major landmark, the moated 12th-century **Nyborg Slot** (Nyborg Castle), was the seat of the Danehof, the Danish parliament from 1200 to 1413. It was here that King Erik Klipping signed the country's first constitution, the Great Charter, in 1282. In addition to geometric wall murals and an armory collection, the castle houses changing art exhibits. ✉ *Slotsg. 34* ☎ *65/31–02–07* ⊕ *www.museer-nyborg.dk* ⊠ *Dkr 30; Dkr 45 combined ticket with Nyborg Museum* ☺ *Mar.–May and Sept.–mid-Oct., Tues.–Sun. 10–3; June and Aug., Tues.–Sun. 10–4; July, Tues.–Sun. 10–5.*

The **Nyborg Museum** occupies Mads Lerches Gård, a half-timber merchant's house from 1601, and provides an insight into 17th-century life. In ad-

dition to furnished period rooms, there's a small brewery. ⊠ *Slotspl. 11*
☎ *65/31–02–07* ⊕ *www.museer-nyborg.dk* ⊠ *Dkr 30, Dkr 45 combined
ticket with Nyborg Slot* ⊘ *Mar.–May and Sept.–Oct., Tues.–Sun. 10–3;
June and Aug., Tues.–Sun. 10–4; July, Tues.–Sun. 10–5.*

Every Tuesday at 7 PM in July and August, look and listen for the **Nyborg Tappenstreg** (Nyborg Tattoo), a military march accompanied by music
that winds through the streets in the center of town. This ceremony dates
from the mid-17th century, when officers would march through the streets,
rounding up all the soldiers from the bars and beer halls to return them
to the barracks. The word "tattoo" has its roots in the old Dutch word
"taptoo" (or "taptoe"), which means to close the tap of a barrel; the
variant "taps" obviously claims the same etymology.

Where to Stay & Eat

$–$$$ ✕ **Central Cafeen.** In a 200-year-old town house in the center of town,
this warm-tone restaurant with velvet seats has been open since 1854.
To many a Nyborg native, there's nowhere better in town for a Danish
smørrebrød lunch or hearty dinner. Evidence of the customers' affec-
tion lines the walls and shelves, from old Carlsberg and Tuborg caps
worn by the deliverymen to ancient shop scales—all gifts from happy
diners after they retired or closed down their businesses. The menu in-
cludes roasted salmon with spinach and boiled potatoes, and fried pork
with parsley sauce. Round out the meal with a plate of fresh Fyn cheeses
served with radishes and chives. In summer, you can dine in the out-
door courtyard, surrounded by the neighborhood's yellow, half-timber
houses. ⊠ *Nørreg. 6* ☎ *65/31–01–83* ☐ *AE, DC, MC, V* ⊘ *Closed Sun.
Oct.–June.*

$–$$$ ✕ **Danehofkroen.** Outside Nyborg Slot, this family-run restaurant does
a brisk lunch business, serving traditional Danish meals to tourists who
enjoy a view of the castle and its tree-lined moat. The menu is basic meat
and potatoes, with such dishes as *flæskesteg* (sliced pork served with
the crisp rind). ⊠ *Slotspl.* ☎ *65/31–02–02* ⚑ *Reservations essential* ☐ *V*
⊘ *Closed Mon. and Oct.–May.*

$$$$ ⊞ **Hesselet.** A modern brick slab outside, this hotel is a refined Anglo-
Fodor'sChoice Asian sanctuary on the inside. Guest rooms have cushy, contemporary
★ furniture, most with a splendid view of the Storebæltsbro. ⊠ *Chris-
tianslundsvej 119, DK–5800* ☎ *65/31–30–29* ⊟ *65/31–29–58* ⊕ *www.
hesselet.dk* ⇌ *43 rooms, 4 suites* ⚐ *Restaurant, indoor pool, bar, meeting room* ☐ *AE, DC, MC, V.*

$$$ ⊞ **Nyborg Strand.** This large hotel complex, owned by the Best West-
ern hotel chain, sprawls along the shoreline 1½ km (1 mi) east of Ny-
borg's city center. The Nyborg Strand caters to the conference crowd,
with numerous meeting rooms and an antiseptic lobby that reverber-
ates with the din of noisy groups. However, the seaside location can't
be beat, and the summer rates, particularly for families, are surprisingly
low, especially considering the hotel's lovely location. ⊠ *Østerøvej 2,
DK–5800* ☎ *65/31–31–31* ⊟ *65/31–37–01* ⊕ *www.nyborgstrand.dk*
⇌ *228 rooms* ⚐ *Restaurant, indoor pool, bar, meeting rooms, some
pets allowed (fee)* ☐ *AE, DC, MC, V.*

Nightlife & the Arts

★ Take on the Nyborg night at the popular **Café Anthon** (⊠ Mellemg. 25
☎ 65/31–16–64), a laid-back bar in the heart of town, with live jazz,
blues, or rock on Friday and Saturday nights. The quirky decor includes
an upright piano with a built-in aquarium and an old grandfather clock
in the corner. The walls are hung with all sorts of instruments, from ac-
cordions to cellos to electric guitars, many of which were gifts from mu-
sicians who have played here.

The hub of travel on the island of Fyn is the city of Nyborg, though many head straight for Odense and its Hans Christian Andersen–related sights. Three fairy-tale castles grace the southern edges of Fyn, and Det Fynske Øhav (The Fyn Archipelago), consisting of the small islands of Langeland, Tåsinge and Ærø, combines cultural heritage and natural beauty.

Numbers in the text correspond to numbers in the margin and on the Fyn & the Central Islands map.

3

**If you have
3 days**

Starting in **Nyborg** ① ►, seek out Nyborg Slot, the city's main attraction, and move on to **Ladby** ③ to see the *Ladbyskibet,* a preserved Viking ship. End your first day in ▦ **Kerteminde** ② with a dinner and a stroll. In the morning travel to ▦ **Odense** ④ and spend the rest of the day brushing up on your fairy tale knowledge and Hans Christian Andersen trivia, as well as visiting Brandts Klædefabrik, a vibrant artists' compound. On day three, make sure to swing by **Kværndrup** ⑧ and splendid Egeskov Slot before returning to Nyborg.

**If you have
5 days**

Spend your first day canvassing the sights of ▦ **Odense** ④ ►; by the end of the day you should have a good impression of H. C. Andersen's native town. Find your way southwest to **Assens** ⑤ the next morning to see the beautiful public garden there, and continue on towards ▦ **Svendborg** ⑦, stopping in **Faaborg** ⑥ for dinner. Stay in ▦ **Tåsinge** ⑨ for two nights, using is as a base for day excursions to **Langeland** ⑩ and Valdemars Slot. On the fifth day route your northward trek through **Kværndrup** ⑧ and Egeskov Slot, ending your day in Nyborg.

Shopping

ANTIQUES Many of Fyn's manor houses and castles now double as antiques emporiums. The largest is **Hindemae** (⊠ Hindemaevej 86, Ullerslev ☏ 65/ 35–32–60), which lies 12 km (7 mi) west of Nyborg. The site is only open to the public during auctions.

Kerteminde

② *21 km (13 mi) north of Nyborg, 20 km (13 mi) northeast of Odense.*

Kerteminde is an important fishing village and popular summer resort. The pastel paints and red roofs of the town's houses contrast with the cool blues of the nearby ocean, which supports recreational fishing, swimming, and other watersports in the summer. On Langegade, walk past the neat half-timber houses to Møllebakken and the **Johannes Larsen Museet**, dedicated to the work of the Danish painter (1867–1961). Across from a strawberry patch and a century-old windmill, the artist built a large country villa that has been perfectly preserved, right down to the teacups. In front is a sculpture of a woman done by Kai Nielsen. Local legend has it that one night, after a particularly wild party in Copenhagen, its legs were somehow broken off. An ambulance was called, and once it arrived, the enraged driver demanded that the artists pay a fine. A chagrined Larsen paid, and in return kept Nielsen's wounded sculpture. ⊠ *Møllebakken 14* ☏ *65/32–11–77* ⊕ *www.kert-mus.dk* ☏ *Dkr*

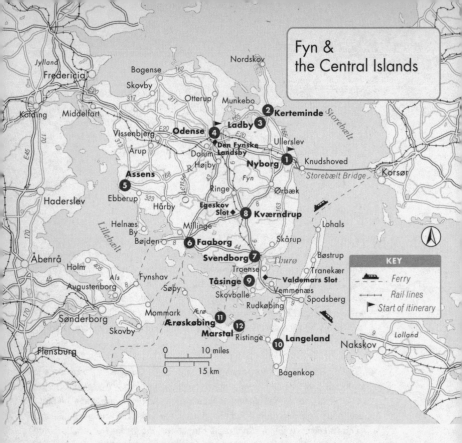

Fyn &
the Central Islands

50 ⊙ June–Aug., daily 10–5; Mar.–May, Sept., and Oct., Tues.–Sun. 10–4; Nov.–Feb., Tues.–Sun. 11–4.

Where to Eat

★ $$$$ ✕ **Rudolf Mathis.** This busy harborside restaurant is topped by two chimneys, which are needed to ventilate the open grills where popular fish dishes are broiled. Favorites are catfish with butter, fennel, and Pernod sauce, and grilled turbot in green-pepper–and–lime sauce. ⊠ *Dosseringen 13, 13 km (8 mi) northeast of Odense on Rte. 165* ☎ *65/32–32–33* ⊟ *AE, DC, MC, V* ⊙ *Closed Mon. and Jan.–Feb.*

$$$–$$$$ ✕ **Gittes Fiskehus.** Dine to the gentle sounds of lapping water at this friendly fish restaurant that extends out over Kerteminde's small canal amid colorful, bobbing fishing boats. Dishes include shrimp smothered in garlic, cream, rum, and Pernod, or the "Hemingway steak," a plate of blue marlin, the fish protagonist of *The Old Man and the Sea.* An additional dining room is housed inside a permanently moored boat that sits alongside the restaurant. Come summer, diners spill out onto the deck to enjoy their seafood under the sun. ⊠ *Hindsholmvej 5* ☎ *65/32–12–38* ⊟ *MC, V* ⊙ *Closed Sun.–Tues. No lunch Sept.–May.*

$ ✕ **Tornøes Hotel.** Steps from Kerteminde's harbor is this comfortable hotel with basic rooms, many of which have partial views of the waterfront. The handsome restaurant has pale yellow walls and matching tablecloths, and serves contemporary Danish fare, including a set "Kerteminde menu" of fried sole as well as crepes with ice cream and strawberries for dessert. Café Wenzel, a lively café-bar with light meals, has a pool table, and live music on the weekends. ⊠ *Strandg. 2, DK–5300* ☎ *65/32–16–05* 🖷 *65/32–48–40* ⊕ *www.tornoeshotel.dk*

⮑ *30 rooms, 2 suites with bath* ⮑ *Restaurant, bar, some pets allowed* ⊟ *AE, DC, MC, V.*

¢ ⊞ **Danhostel Kerteminde Vandrehjem.** South of Kerteminde, this well-maintained hostel is surrounded by a peaceful patch of woodland and is just a few minutes' walk from the beach. Families flock here in summer, drawn by the low prices and a plethora of outdoor activities that awaits just beyond the front door, from hiking to biking to swimming. The rooms are outfitted in typical Danish hostel style, with sturdy wooden bunks and basic showers. An industrial-size kitchen and cafeteria—built to feed the large school groups that come through—serves breakfast. Sheets and towels also cost extra. If you pay by credit card, you'll have to pay a surcharge. ⊠ *Skovvej 46, DK–5300 Kerteminde* ☎ *65/ 32–39–29* 🖷 *65/32–39–24* ⊕ *www.danhostel.dk* ⮑ *30 rooms with shower* ⊟ *MC, V.*

Shopping

CERAMICS   Just a few miles west of Kerteminde is **Bjørnholt Keramik** (⊠ Risingevej 12, Munkebo ☎65/97–40–90), where you can watch ceramics being made.

> **off the beaten path**

ROMSØ – The 250-acre, pristine island of Romsø, just a half-hour ferry ride from Kerteminde, attracts nature-lovers, hikers, and bird-watchers. A hardwood forest blankets half the island, making it something of a rarity among Denmark's islands, only a few of which have forests. More than 170 species of birds have been recorded here, and during their breeding season (March through June) part of the island is closed to visitors. Deer roam freely through the wooded areas, and hiking trails crisscross the island (bicycles are not allowed). Romsø's population peaked at 50 after World War I, but after the lighthouse closed in 1973, the population dwindled to just a handful of residents. Bring all supplies that you might need, as there are no accommodations or food on the island. Camping is not permitted. A high-speed **passenger boat** (☎ 65/32–13–77 for reservations with Leif Hansen) connects Kerteminde with Romsø. The cost is around Dkr 100 roundtrip. The boat operates only in the summer months, usually from June through August. Schedules change frequently so call ahead.

Ladby

❸   *4 km (2½ mi) south of Kerteminde, 16 km (10 mi) east of Odense.*

The village of Ladby is best known as the home of the 1,100-year-old remains of the *Ladbyskibet.* This ship belonging to a Viking chieftain was buried along with the hunting dogs and horses he would need for Valhalla—the afterlife. Today you can see a massive hull-shaped indentation in the ground where the excavation took place. All the wooden parts of the ship disintegrated centuries ago, but exhibited at the site are the ship's anchor, and also the remains of the horses and hunting dogs. A replica of the ship (in real size) was in the works until the project stalled because of practical and financial difficulties; if and when it's completed, it will be shown alongside the burial site. ⊠ *Vikingevej 123* ☎ *65/32–16–67* ⊕ *www.kert-mus.dk* 🎫 *Dkr 25* ⊙ *June–Aug., daily 10–5; Mar.–May, Sept., and Oct., Tues.–Sun. 10–4; Nov.–Feb., Wed.–Sun. 11–3.*

Odense

▶ ❹ *20 km (12 mi) southwest of Ladby on Route 165, 144 km (90 mi) west of Copenhagen.*

It's no coincidence that Odense, the capital of Fyn and third largest city in Denmark, is reminiscent of a storybook village—much of its charm is built upon the legend of its most famous son, author Hans Christian Andersen. The town is named after another famous Scandinavian, Odin, the king of the Nordic gods. When you're in town, first see the flourishing Kongens Have (King's Garden) and 18th-century Odense Castle, now a government building. If you walk east on Østre Stationsvej to Thomas B. Thriges Gade and Hans Jensens Stræde, you'll come to

★ the **Hans Christian Andersen Hus** (H. C. Andersen House), which sits amid half-timber houses and cobbled streets. Inside, the storyteller's life is chronicled through his photographs, drawings, letters, and personal belongings. The library has Andersen's works in more than 100 languages, and you can listen to fairy tales on tape. ⊠ *Hans Jensens Str. 37–45* ☎ *66/13–13–72 Ext. 4601* ⊕ *www.odmus.dk* ☜ *Dkr 35* ⊙ *Mid-June–Aug., daily 9–7; Sept.–mid-June, Tues.–Sun. 10–4.*

☾ The **Børnekulturehuset Fyrtøjet** (Children's Culture House, The Tinderbox) museum includes walk-through fairy-tale exhibits as well as studios where children can draw and write their own tales and plays and then dress up and perform them. ⊠ *Hans Jensen Str. 21* ☎ *66/14–44–11* ⊕ *www.fyrtoejet.com* ☜ *Dkr 50* ⊙ *Feb.–Dec., Tues.–Sat. 10–3.*

The sleek **Carl Nielsen Museum** creates multimedia exhibits of the life and work of Denmark's most famous composer (1865–1931) and of his wife, the sculptor Anne Marie Carl-Nielsen (yes, that's the way she took his name). ⊠ *Claus Bergs G. 11* ☎ *66/13–13–72 Ext. 4601* ⊕ *www. odmus.dk* ☜ *Dkr 25* ⊙ *Nov.–Mar., Thurs.–Fri. 4–8, weekends noon–4; Apr.–May and Sept.–Oct., Thurs.–Sun. noon–4; June–Aug., Tues.–Sun. noon–4.*

Møntergården, Odense's city museum, occupies four 17th-century row houses adjacent to a shady, cobbled courtyard. Exhibits range from Middle Age interiors to coverage of Denmark's Nazi occupation to an extensive and impressive collection of ancient coins from all over the world. ⊠ *Overg. 48–50* ☎ *66/13–13–72 Ext. 4601* ⊕ *www.odmus.dk* ☜ *Dkr 25* ⊙ *Tues.–Sun. 10–4.*

The stately **Skt. Knuds Kirke,** built from the 13th to the 15th century, is the only purely Gothic cathedral in Denmark. The intricate wooden altar covered with gold leaf was carved by German sculptor Claus Berg. Beneath the sepulchre are the bones of St. (King) Knud, killed during a farmers' uprising in 1086, and his brother. ⊠ *Toward the pedestrian zone of Skt. Knuds Kirkestræde, in front of Andersen Park.*

In the diminutive **Hans Christian Andersens Barndomshjem** (H. C. Andersen's Childhood Home), the young boy and his parents lived in three tiny rooms. The rooms are outfitted with rustic, period furnishings (chairs, lamps, a table) and little else, befitting a humble abode of the early 1800s. ⊠ *Munkemøllestr. 3–5* ☎ *66/13–13–72 Ext. 4601* ☜ *Dkr 15* ⊙ *June–Aug., daily 10–4; Sept.–May, Tues.–Sun. 11–3.*

Near the center of town is the elegant **Fyns Kunstmuseum** (Funen Art Museum), which displays a large and varied collection of Danish art, from the 18th century to the present. Featured artists include Jens Juel, Vilhelm Hammershøj, P. S. Krøyer, and Robert Jacobsen. The museum's highlight is its comprehensive collection of Fyn artists, from Johannes

Larsen to Peter Hansen. ⊠ *Jernbaneg. 13* ☏ *66/13–13–72 Ext. 4601* ⊕ *www.odmus.dk* ⊠ *Dkr 30* ⊙ *Tues.–Sun. 10–4.*

For something completely different, head just west of the center of town to the **Superbowl Odense,** an indoor entertainment center with bowling alleys, a restaurant, and a go-cart track. ⊠ *Grønøkken 3* ☏ *66/19–16–40.*

Odense River Cruises (☏ 65/95–79–96) operates several boat trips on the Odense Å River from Filosofgangen. You can catch a boat (May through mid-August, daily on the hour 10–5, returning 35 minutes later) down-river to the Fruens Bøge (Lady's Beech Forest) and then walk down Erik Bøghs Sti (Erik Bøgh's Footpath) to **Den Fynske Landsby** (the Fyn Village). Among the country's largest open-air museums, it includes 25 farm buildings and workshops, a vicarage, a water mill, and a theater, which in summer stages adaptations of Andersen's tales. Afterward, cruise back to the town center or catch Bus 42, and walk down the boutique- and café-lined pedestrian street Vestergade (Kongensgade running perpendicular to the town hall), which in summer is abuzz with street performers, musicians, and brass bands. ⊠ *Sejerskovvej 20* ☏ *66/13–13–72 Ext. 4601* ⊕*www.odmus.dk* ⊠*Dkr 35* ⊙ *Apr.–mid-June and mid-Aug.–Oct., Tues.–Sun. 10–5; mid-June–mid-Aug., daily 9:30–7; Nov.–Mar., Sun. 11–3.*

Occupying a former textile factory, the four-story artist compound **Brandts Klædefabrik** houses the **Museet for Fotokunst** (Museum of Photographic Art), **Danmarks Grafiske Museum** (Danish Graphics Museum), **Dansk Presse Museum** (Danish Press Museum), and **Kunsthallen** (Art Gallery). National and international exhibits shown here vary widely, but the photography museum and the art gallery gravitate toward especially experimental work. The press museum chronicles the history of Denmark's printing trade, and houses lithography, bookbinding, and papermaking workshops. ⊠ *Brandts Passage 37 and 43, north of the river and parallel to Kongensgade* ☏ *66/13–78–97* ⊕ *www.brandts.dk* ⊠ *Combined ticket Dkr 50; photography museum Dkr 25; graphics museum Dkr 25; press museum Dkr 25; art gallery Dkr 30* ⊙ *July and Aug., daily 10–5; Sept.–June, Tues.–Sun. 10–5.*

FodorśChoice
★

off the beaten path

HOLLUFGÅRD – This 16th-century manor houses the city's archaeological department. The house has reopenened after a renovation and its grounds contain a completely renovated old barn and adjacent buildings showing special exhibits, including the archaeological find of the month and an ecology display. Nearby are a sculpture garden and a sculpture center, where you can see an artist at work. Take Bus 61 from the railway station on Østre Stationsvej 10 km (6 mi) south of Odense. ⊠ *Hestehaven 201* ☏ *66/13–13–72 Ext. 4601* ⊠ *Dkr 25* ⊙ *Apr.–Oct., Tues.–Sat. 10–4; Nov.–Apr., Sun. 10–4.*

Where to Eat

$$$$ ✕ **LPC** (La Petite Cuisine). This romantic little restaurant, tucked in the Brandts Passage, can accommodate about 40 diners. The southern French specialties change every day according to what can be purchased fresh at the market. Typical dishes include Asian-inspired marinated duck breast, grilled skewered salmon or catfish with vegetables, and white mocha parfait for dessert. Dishes can be combined in three- to five-course menus. ⊠ *Brandts Passage 13* ☏ *66/14–11–00* ⚑ *Reservations essential* ▭ *DC, MC, V.*

$$$–$$$$ ✕**Marie Louise.** Headed by the illustrious chef Michel Michaud, this is
FodorśChoice considered one of Fyn's—if not Denmark's—finest French restaurants.
★ The elegant whitewashed dining room glitters with crystal and silver.
The French-Danish menu typically offers such specialties as scalloped
salmon with bordelaise sauce and grilled veal with lobster cream sauce.
Business and holiday diners are sometimes treated to gratis extras—such
as quail's-egg appetizers or after-dinner drinks. ⊠ *Lottrups Gaard,
Vesterg. 70–72* ☎ *66/17–92–95* ▤ *AE, DC, MC, V* ☾ *Closed Sun.
and Mon.*

$$$–$$$$ ✕**Restaurant Under Lindetræet.** The snug corner restaurant, situated in
the same cozy, cobblestoned neighborhood as the Hans Christian An-
dersen House, serves homestyle Danish fare, including grilled redfish with
boiled potatoes. Copper pots and Andersen-style paper cutouts hang on
the wall, alongside a portrait of the great man himself. Old-fashioned
lamps shed light onto the tables, which are set with gold-rim plates. Bur-
gundy velvet drapes divide parts of the dining room, making dining an
intimate experience. ⊠ *Ramsherred 2* ☎ *66/12–92–86* ⋒ *Reserva-
tions essential* ▤ *MC, V* ☾ *Closed Sun.–Mon.*

$$–$$$$ ✕**Klitgaard.** Named after its young owner-chef, Jacob Klitgaard, this
chic, cool-tone restaurant serves a changing menu of innovative French-
Italian fusion fare. The season drives the menu; market-fresh produce
graces every dish, from the young Fyn lamb with green asparagus to the
lightly salted trout served with an herb mousse. Stuffed quail is seasoned
with rosemary and accompanied by an endive salad; a fricassee of scallops and asparagus is enveloped in a tangy lemon sauce. The fresh cuisine is complemented by a soothing decor of tan walls, hardwood floors,
and cane furniture that glow softly under recessed lights. ⊠ *Gravene 4*
☎ *66/13–14–55* ⋒ *Reservations essential* ▤ *DC, MC, V* ☾ *Closed Sun.
and Mon.*

$$$ ✕**Carlslund.** Ask most any Odense local where to find the best *æggek-
age* in town, and he'll probably point you in this direction. Cholesterol-
watchers, beware: æggekage is a rich dish consisting of a fluffy,
cream-whipped, parsley-speckled omelet topped with either bacon strips
or pork rinds. Dab on some mustard and scoop it up with hunks of rye
bread. It's traditionally washed down with shots of aquavit. The place
also serves an extensive Danish menu of fish and meat dishes. Dating
from 1860, the cozy, low-ceiling restaurant sits amid a wooded park on
the outskirts of Odense. In summer, Carlslund sets up an outdoor stage
and hosts live jazz on the weekends, drawing hundreds. ⊠ *Fruens Bøge
Skov 7* ☎ *66/91–11–25* ⋒ *Reservations essential* ▤ *DC, MC, V.*

$–$$$ ✕**Den Gamle Kro.** Built within the courtyards of several 17th-century homes,
this popular restaurant has walls of ancient stone topped by a sliding glass
roof. The French-Danish menu includes fillet of sole stuffed with salmon
mousse and Châteaubriand with garlic potatoes, but there's also inexpensive smørrebrød. ⊠ *Overg. 23* ☎ *66/12–14–33* ▤ *DC, MC, V.*

$–$$$ ✕**Franck A.** Overlooking the pedestrian street, this spacious, stylish
café–restaurant–bar with exposed brick walls is Odense's answer to
Copenhagen's trendy venues—minus the pretension. Hipsters and
media types (it's a favorite with the folks from the local TV station)
mingle over cocktails but, this being Odense, informality prevails.
You're just as likely to sit next to families and older couples lingering
over coffee. A rack of newspapers and Tintin comic books invites those
who want to settle in for an afternoon read. Brunch is served all day;
try the salmon–and–cherry-tomato omelet. The lunch and dinner
menu of global cuisine runs the gamut from Thai chicken curry to hefty
grilled burgers. Live music (usually Thursday through Saturday nights)
draws a toe-tapping crowd. On Thursday, Franck A. often hosts a pop-

ular '80s music night, with lively cover bands. ⊠ *Jernbaneg. 4* ☎ *66/ 12–57–27* 🖃 *MC, V.*

★ ¢–$ ✕ **Den Grimme Ælling.** The name of this chain restaurant means "the ugly duckling," but inside it's simply homey, with pine furnishings and a boisterous family ambience. It's extremely popular with tourists and locals alike, thanks to an all-you-can-eat buffet heaped with cold and warm dishes. ⊠ *Hans Jensens Str. 1* ☎ *65/91–70–30* 🖃 *DC, MC.*

¢–$ ✕ **Målet.** A lively crowd calls this sports club its neighborhood bar. The schnitzel is served in a dozen creative ways from traditional schnitzel with sautéed potatoes and peas to Indian curry schnitzel with rice, chutney, and pineapple. After the steaming plates of food, watching and discussing soccer are the chief delights of the house. ⊠ *Jernbaneg. 17,* ☎ *66/ 17–82–41* ⚬ *Reservations not accepted* 🖃 *No credit cards.*

Where to Stay

$$$ 🏨 **Clarion Hotel Plaza.** A five-minute walk from the train station, this stately hotel dates from 1915 and overlooks Odense's leafy central park, Kongens Have. An old-fashioned wooden elevator takes you up to the ample, comfortable rooms outfitted in traditional dark-wood furniture. Adjoining the pale-green lobby is the glass-walled Restaurant Rosenhaven, which serves contemporary Danish fare, including wild rabbit wrapped in cabbage and topped with honey and berry preserves, and lemon-accented fillet of sole served in a puff pastry with a tarragon and saffron aspic. ⊠ *Østre Stationsvej 24, DK–5000* ☎ *66/11–77–45* 🖶 *66/ 14–41–45* ⊕ *www.hotel-plaza.dk* ⤳ *68 rooms* ⚬ *Restaurant, fitness center, sauna, bar, meeting rooms* 🖃 *AE, DC, MC, V.*

$$$ 🏨 **Radisson SAS–Hans Christian Andersen Hotel.** Around the corner from the Hans Christian Andersen House, this blocky brick conference hotel has a plant-filled lobby and ample rooms done up in warm shades of red and yellow. In the fall and winter, you have to battle your way through large conference groups to get to your room, but in summer it's half the normal price, and relatively quiet. ⊠ *Claus Bergs G. 7, DK–5000* ☎ *66/ 14–78–00 or 800/33–3333* 🖶 *66/14–78–90* ⊕ *www.radissonsas.com* ⤳ *145 rooms* ⚬ *Restaurant, sauna, bar, casino* 🖃 *AE, DC, MC, V.*

$–$$$ 🏨 **First Hotel Grand Odense.** More than a century old, with renovated fin-de-siècle charm, this imposing four-story, brick-front hotel greets guests with old-fashioned luxury. The original stone floors and chandeliers lead to a wide staircase and upstairs guest rooms that are modern with plush furnishings and sleek marble bathrooms. ⊠ *Jernabaneg. 18, DK–5000* ☎ *66/11–71–71* 🖶 *66/14–11–71* ⊕ *www.firsthotels.com* ⤳ *138 rooms with bath, 3 suites* ⚬ *Restaurant, room service, sauna, bar, some pets allowed, no-smoking rooms* 🖃 *AE, DC, MC, V.*

¢ 🏨 **Hotel Ydes.** This well-kept, bright, and colorful hotel is a good bet
Fodor'sChoice for students and budget-conscious travelers tired of barracks-type ac-
★ commodations. The well-maintained rooms are spotless and comfortable. ⊠ *Hans Tausens G. 11, DK–5000* ☎ *66/12–11–31* 🖶 *66/12–14–13* ⊕ *www.ydes.dk* ⤳ *25 rooms with bath* ⚬ *Café* 🖃 *MC, V.*

Nightlife & the Arts

CAFÉS & BARS Odense's central arcade is an entertainment mall, with bars, restaurants, and live music ranging from corny sing-alongs to hard rock. For a quiet evening, stop by **Café Biografen** (⊠ Brandts Passage ☎ 66/13–16–16) for an espresso, beer, or light snack, or settle in to see one of the films screened here. The **Air Pub** (⊠ Kongsg. 41 ☎ 66/14–66–08) is a Danish pub that caters to a thirty- and fortysomething crowd, with meals and a small dance floor. At the **Boogie Dance Café** (⊠ Nørreg. 21 ☎ 66/ 14–00–39), a laid-back crowd grooves to pop, disco, and '60s music. In the heart of town is **Franck A** (⊠ Jernbaneg. 4 ☎ 66/12–57–27), a spirited café-restaurant with arched windows overlooking the pedestrian street. Live music on the weekends—from pop to jazz—draws a stylish crowd, as does the popular '80s night on Thursday. The specialty at **Klos Ands** (✉ Vineg. 76 ☎ 66/13–56–00) is malt whiskey.

CASINO   Fyn's sole casino is in the slick glass atrium of the **SAS Hans Christian Andersen Hotel** (✉ Claus Bergs G. 7, Odense ☎ 66/14–78–00), where you can play blackjack, roulette, and baccarat.

JAZZ CLUBS   **Dexter's** (✉ Vinderg. 65 ☎ 66/13–68–88) has all kinds of jazz—from Dixieland to fusion—Friday and Saturday nights. **Grøntorvet Café and Bar** (✉ Sortebrødre Torv 9 ☎ 66/14–34–37) presents live jazz at 5 PM Thursday and 2 PM Saturday.

THEATER   **Den Fynske Landsby** stages Hans Christian Andersen plays from mid-July to mid-August. In summer the young members of the **Hans Christian Andersen Parade** present a pastiche of the bard's fairy tales in a couple of different languages at Lotzes Have, an herb garden behind the Hans Christian Andersen Museum.

Sports & the Outdoors

GOLF   There are two major golf attractions and another smaller course near Odense for golf enthusiasts. Although the island appears to be flat, subtle hills provide excellent, challenging terrain for the golfer. Courses are well-groomed, with a number of natural water hazards. Golf has become an extremely popular sport in Denmark, so it would be wise to call ahead of time to inquire about starting times and the dates of tournaments. It's also very easy to find someone to play with—just ask in the clubhouse. **Odense Eventyr Golfklub** (✉ Falen 227 ☎ 66/65–20–15), 4 km (2½ mi) southwest of Odense, has three nine-hole courses, one of which is entirely composed of challenging par-3s. The **Odense Golf Klub** (✉ Hestehaven 200 ☎ 65/95–90–00), 6 km (4 mi) southeast of Odense, has 27 holes on relatively flat ground with some woods. **Blommenlyst** (✉ Vejruplundvej 20 Blommenlyst ☎ 65/96–71–20) is a pleasant nine-hole course with a driving range and putting greens, 12 km (7 mi) west of Odense.

Shopping

Odense's compact city center is bustling with clothing, furniture, and shoe stores, and a Magasin department store. The main shopping strips are Vestergade and Kongensgade. Rosengårdcentret, one of Northern Europe's largest malls, is 5 km (3 mi) west of Odense. It has more than 125 shops and food outlets, including trendy clothing stores; jewelry, woodwork, and antique shops; a multiplex cinema; and a post office.

Denmark is well known for its paper mobiles and cutouts, inspired, in part, by Hans Christian Andersen. Using a small pair of scissors and white paper, he would create cutouts to illustrate his fairy tales. Today, replicas of Andersen's cutouts are sold at several Odense gift stores. Also popular are mobiles, often depicting Andersen-inspired themes, like swans and mermaids. Uniquely Danish—and light on the suitcase—they make great gifts to take home.

Jam-packed with mobiles, cutouts, and Danish flags and dolls, **Klods Hans** (✉ Hans Jensens Str. 34 ☎ 66/11–09–40) opened just after World War II to cater to all the American soldiers on leave who wanted to bring back Danish gifts. For fine replicas of Scandinavian Viking jewelry, head to **Museums Kopi Smykker** (✉ Klareg. 3 ☎ 66/12–06–96). Each piece, in either sterling silver or gold, comes with a printed leaflet explaining its Viking origins. Among the offerings are silver bracelets of various weights, once used by the Vikings as currency; pendants of the Nordic god "Odin," Odense's namesake; and a Viking "key to Valhalla." A modest selection of antiques is for sale at **Hønnerup Hovgård** (✉ Hovgårdsvej 6, Hønnerup ☎ 64/49–13–00); take Exit 55 to Route 161 toward Middelfart; follow the signs to Hønnerup.

Assens

❺ *38 km (24 mi) southwest of Odense.*

★ Near the quiet town of Assens is one of the most extraordinary private gardens in Denmark: Tove Sylvest's sprawling **De 7 Haver** (The Seven Gardens). A privately owned botanical United Nations, the gardens represent the flora of seven European countries, including many plants rare to Denmark. ✉ *Å Strandvej 33, Ebberup* ☎ *64/74–12–85* ⊕ *www.visit-vestfyn.dk* ✆ *Dkr 45* ☉ *Apr.–Oct., daily 10–6.*

On the same street as Seven Gardens is the **Hviids Have,** a 1-acre Japanese garden complete with elegant ponds traversed by rough-plank walkways, as well as stone settings and modest amounts of greenery. ✉ *Å Strandvej 33, Ebberup* ☎ *64/74–11–02* ⊕ *www.visit-vestfyn.dk* ✆ *Dkr 30* ☉ *May–Oct., daily 10–6.*

off the beaten path

TERRARIET – Children may appreciate this detour 18 km (11 mi) northeast to Fyn's Terrarium, where they can examine all kinds of slippery and slithery creatures, including snakes, iguanas, alligators, and the nearly extinct blue frog. ✉ *Kirkehelle 5, Vissenbjerg* ☎ *64/47–18–50* ⊕ *www.reptil-zoo.dk* ✆ *Dkr 50* ☉ *May–Aug., daily 10–6; Sept.–Apr., daily 10–4.*

Faaborg

❻ *30 km (18 mi) south of Odense (via Rte. 43).*

The beaches surrounding this lovely 13th-century town are invaded by sun-seeking Germans and Danes in summer. Four times a day you can hear the dulcet chiming of a carillon, the island's largest. In the town center is the controversial *Ymerbrønden* sculpture by Kai Nielsen, depicting a naked man drinking from an emaciated cow's udder while it licks a baby.

The 1725 **Den Gamle Gaard** (Old Merchant's House) chronicles the local history of Faaborg through furnished interiors and exhibits of glass and textiles. ✉ *Holkeg. 1* ☎ *62/61–33–38* ⊕ *www.fkm.nu* ✆ *Dkr 30* ☉ *Mid-May–Aug., daily 10:30–4:30; Apr.–mid-May, Sept., and Oct., weekends 11–3.*

The **Faaborg Museum for Fynsk Malerkunst** (Fyn Painting Museum) has a good collection of turn-of-the-20th-century paintings and sculpture by the Fyn Painters, a school of artists whose work captures the dusky light of the Scandinavian sun. ✉ *Grønneg. 75* ☎ *62/61–06–45* ⊕ *www.faaborgmuseum.dk* ✆ *Dkr 35* ☉ *Apr.–Oct., daily 10–4; Nov.–Mar., Tues.–Sun. 11–3.*

Where to Stay & Eat

$–$$$ ✕ **Vester Skerninge Kro.** Midway between Faaborg and Svendborg, this traditional inn is cluttered and comfortable. Pine tables are polished from years of serving hot stews and homemade *medister pølse* (mild grilled sausage) and æggekage. ✉ *Krovej 9, Vester Skerninge* ☎ *62/24–10–04* ☰ *AE, MC, V* ☉ *Closed Tues., Oct.–Mar.*

$$$$ ✕ **Falsled Kro.** Once a smuggler's hideaway, the 500-year-old Falsled
FodorśChoice Kro is one of Denmark's most elegant inns. A favorite among well-heeled
★ Europeans, it has appointed its cottages sumptuously with European an-

tiques and stone fireplaces. The restaurant combines French and Danish cuisines, using ingredients from markets in Lyon and its own garden. ⊠ *Assensvej 513, DK–5642 Millinge, 13 km (8 mi) northwest of Faaborg on Millinge-Assens Hwy.* ☎ *62/68–11–11* 📠 *62/68–11–62* ⊕ *www.falsledkro.dk* ⇨ *19 rooms, 8 suites* ⚭ *Restaurant, cafeteria, bar, some pets allowed* ▤ *AE, DC, MC, V.*

$$–$$$$ ✕▥ **Steensgård Herregårdspension.** A long avenue of beeches leads to this 700-year-old moated manor house, 7 km (4½ mi) northwest of Faaborg. The rooms are elegant, with antiques, four-poster beds, and yards of silk damask. The fine restaurant serves Danish classics crafted from the wild game from the manor's own reserve. ⊠ *Steensgård 4, DK–5642 Millinge* ☎ *62/61–94–90* 📠 *62/61–78–61* ⊕ *www. herregaardspension.dk* ⇨ *15 rooms, 13 with bath* ⚭ *Restaurant, tennis court, horseback riding* ▤ *AE, DC, MC, V* ☉ *Closed Feb.*

¢–$ ✕▥ **Hotel Faaborg.** Rising over Faaborg's rustic main square, this small hotel is housed in a brick town house. The rooms are basic and simply furnished. The corner rooms overlook the central square. The Danish menu at the spacious restaurant includes baked cod smothered in a tomato ratatouille sauce with oregano, shallots, garlic, and anchovies. Veal is topped with honey-fried apple slices and served with seasonal vegetables. On weekdays, it serves a decently priced lunch buffet, which includes herring, smoked salmon in a mustard sauce, and chicken salad. ⊠ *Torvet 13–15, DK–5600 Faaborg* ☎ *62/61–02–45* 📠 *62/61–08–45* ⊕ *www.hotelfaaborg.dk* ⇨ *10 rooms with bath* ⚭ *Restaurant, bar* ▤ *AE, DC, MC, V.*

★ $ ▥ **Hotel Færgegaarden.** For well over 150 years this spot has been a favorite of budget-conscious tourists and traveling artists with its traditional, dusty yellow and red facade. Newly refurbished, Færgegaarden offers elegantly modern rooms right on the medieval-era harbor front. ⊠ *Christian IXs Vej 31, DK–5600 Faaborg* ☎ *62/61–11–15* 📠 *62/ 61–11–95* ⊕ *www.hotelfg.dk* ⇨ *24 rooms with bath* ⚭ *Restaurant, some pets allowed* ▤ *AE, DC, MC, V.*

Nightlife & the Arts

Near the waterfront is **Bar Heimdal** (⊠ Havneg. 12 ☎ no phone), where Faaborg's fishermen crowd into booths and knock back cold ones after hauling in their nets. An inexpensive menu of simple Danish fare includes fillet of sole with tartar sauce and smoked ham with asparagus. In summer, the sunny outdoor terrace draws a mixed crowd of tourists and locals. Just off Faaborg's main square is the homey **Oasen Bodega** (⊠ Strandg. 2 ☎ 62/61–13–15), frequented by regulars who enjoy lingering while imbibing in the local brew. Most of the local residents sit by the wooden bar, and this can be a good place to strike up a conversation. **Tre Kroner** (⊠ Strandg. 1 ☎ 62/61–01–50) is a traditional watering hole with varied clientele and the enchantment of an inn from the turn of the 20th century. Perhaps Faaborg's most *hyggelig* hangout is the historic **Schankstube** (tap house; ⊠ Havneg. 12, ☎ 62/61–11–15), inside the harborside Hotel Færgegaarden. Housed in a former beer tap house, this small bar has worn wooden tables, yellow walls hung with richly colored paintings by Faaborg artists, and small windows with views of the harbor. The menu is traditional—*smørrebrød* and beer.

off the beaten path

LYØ, AVERNAKØ, AND BJØRNØ – A string of verdant little islands speckles the sea off Fyn's southern coast. Three of these islands—Lyø, Avernakø, and Bjørnø—are easily accessible by ferry from Faaborg. Lyø, just 4 km (2½ mi) long, has a year-round population of 150 residents and a tangle of hiking and biking trails that lure Fyn families in summer. In the center of the island sits Lyø village, a rustic assortment of half-timber houses and a church with a unique circular churchyard. Eight-km-long (5-mi-long) Avernakø is the hilliest and largest of the three islands, with several farmhouses, a pleasant little village, and a few meandering hiking trails. Bjørnø, 3 km (1½ mi) south of Faaborg, is the smallest island, both in population and size. What it lacks in human residents, however, it makes up with avian. A rich birdlife draws binocular-toting bird-watchers, particularly during the summer breeding season. If you wish to stay overnight on the islands, contact the Faaborg tourist office for information on local families who offer accommodation. The **Avernakø–Lyø ferry** (☎ 62/61–23–07 ⊕ www.oe-faergen.dk) travels five to seven times daily in summer from the Faaborg harbor. Travel time is about 30 minutes to Avernakø, and then another 30 minutes to Lyø, though the ferry sometimes arrives at Lyø first. The round-trip cost is about Dkr 85. The **Bjørnø ferry** (☎ 20/29–80–50) departs from Faaborg three to five times daily; the trip takes 20 minutes, and costs about Dkr 45.

Svendborg

❼ *25 km (15 mi) east of Faaborg (via Rte. 44 east), 44 km (28 mi) south of Odense.*

Svendborg is Fyn's second-largest town, and one of the country's most important cruise harbors. It celebrates its eight-centuries-old maritime traditions every July, when old Danish wooden ships congregate in the harbor for the circular Fyn *rundt,* or regatta. Play your cards right, and you might hitch aboard and shuttle between towns. Contact the tourist board or any agreeable captain. With many charter-boat options and good marinas, Svendborg is an excellent base from which to explore the hundreds of islands of the South Fyn archipelago.

On Fruestræde near the market square at the center of town is the black-and-yellow **Anne Hvides Gård,** the oldest secular structure in Svendborg and one of the four branches of Svendborgs Omegns Museum (Svendborg County Museum). This evocative exhibit includes 18th- and 19th-century interiors and glass and silver collections. ✉ *Fruestr. 3* ☎ *62/21–76–45* ⊕ *www.svendborgmuseum.dk* ✇ *Dkr 25* ☉ *Mid-June–Sept., Tues.–Sun. 10–5; Oct.–Dec., Wed.–Sun. 10–4.*

Bagergade (Baker's Street) is lined with some of Svendborg's oldest half-timber houses. At the corner of Grubbemøllevej and Svinget is the **Viebæltegård,** the headquarters of the Svendborg County Museum and a former poorhouse. You can wander through dining halls, washrooms, and the "tipsy clink," where, until 1974, inebriated citizens were left to sober up. ✉ *Grubbemøllevej 13* ☎ *62/21–02–61* ⊕ *www.svendborgmuseum.dk* ✇ *Dkr 40* ☉ *June–Sept., Tues.–Sun. 10–5; Oct.–May, Tues.–Sun. 10–4.*

Changing contemporary-art exhibits are showcased at the two-story **SAK Kunstbygningen** (SAK Art Exhibitions), a skylit gallery-museum just to the west of the city center. The museum's highlight is the small collection of sculptures by Svendborg native Kai Nielsen. One of Denmark's most popular sculptors, Nielsen is best known for his sensual figures of women in languid repose and chubby angelic babies playing together. Nielsen's sculptures are displayed in a sun-drenched octagonal gallery with views over a leafy garden. His works are exhibited all over Denmark, most famously in Copenhagen's Ny Carlsberg Glyptotek. Here, his "Water Mother" fountain sculpture depicts a voluptuous woman reclining atop a lily pond, while a half-dozen plump, adorable babies crawl out of the water and over her curves, suckling at her breasts and dozing between her thighs. ☒ *Vesterg. 27–31* ☎ *62/22–44–70* ☜ *Dkr 25* ⊘ *Tues.–Sun. 11–4.*

need a break?

In the heart of Svendborg, tucked behind the main street of Brogade, is a small, cobblestone courtyard surrounded by red half-timber houses. Dating from 1650, this charming square used to house Svendborg's general store. **Vintapperiet** (☒ Brog. 37 ☎ 62/ 22–34–48), a snug, low-ceiling wine bar and shop, now occupies the square, and here you can taste your way—by the glass or by the bottle—through a range of top-notch French and Italian wines. Wine barrels line the entranceway; the small dining room, with less than a half dozen tables, overlooks the courtyard. They serve a light menu to complement the wines, including pâté and pungent cheese with hunks of bread, and olives. It is open for lunch only, and closed on Sunday; in winter it's also closed on Monday.

Where to Stay & Eat

$$$ ✕ **Svendborgsund.** In a harborside building dating from 1682, this warm, maritime-theme restaurant serves traditional Danish cuisine, including pork tenderloin heaped with grilled onions and mushrooms and served with potatoes and pickled cucumbers. The extensive smørrebrød lunch menu includes marinated herring topped with egg yolk and fried fillet of plaice with shrimp, caviar, and asparagus. The summertime terrace is an inviting spot to soak up sun, beer, and the waterfront views. ☒ *Havnepl. 5* ☎ *62/21–07–19* ▱ *AE, DC, MC, V* ⊘ *Closed Sun. Oct.–Mar.*

¢–$$ ✕ **Hotel Ærø.** A hodgepodge of ship parts and nautical doodads, this dimly lighted restaurant and inn looks like it's always been here. Brusque waitresses take orders from serious local trenchermen. The menu is staunchly old-fashioned, featuring *frikadeller* (fried meatballs), fried *rødspætte* (plaice) with hollandaise sauce, and dozens of smørrebrød options. ☒ *Brog. 1, Ærøfærgen (at the Ærø ferry), DK–5700* ☎ *62/21–07–60* 🖷 *62/21–06–78* ⊕ *www.hotel-aeroe.dk* ▱ *DC, MC, V.*

★ **$** ▥ **Missionhotellet Stella Marris.** Southwest of Svendborg, this lovely seaside villa dates from 1904. An old-fashioned English-style drawing room, complete with piano, stuffed chairs, and an elegant chandelier, overlooks the villa's spacious gardens; follow a path through the greenery and you can dive right off the private pier into the sea. Each of the rooms has its own color scheme; one room has flowery wallpaper and white lace curtains, while another has a simple tan-and-rose decor. Bathrooms are basic and include a shower only. The hotel is part of Missionhotel, a Christian hotel chain in operation since the early 1900s. The Stella Marris is one of the few Missionhotels that still maintains an alcohol- and smoke-free environment. ☒ *Kogtvedvænget 3, DK–5700* ☎ *62/21–38–91* 🖷 *62/21–41–74* ⊕ *www.stellamaris.dk* ⇋ *25 rooms, 19 with bath* ⚬ *Dining room* ▱ *AE, DC, MC, V.*

Nightlife & the Arts

BARS & LOUNGES A diverse crowd congregates at **Banjen** (☒ Klosterpl. 7 ☎ 62/21–35–40) to hear live rock and blues. The popular blues shows, usually Friday and Saturday nights, attract all ages. Adjoining the bar is La Tumba nightclub, which throbs with dance music on the weekends. The beer flows freely at the cavernous pub **Børsen** (☒ Gerritsg. 31 ☎ 62/22–41–41), in a building dating from 1620. A young rowdy crowd of tourists and locals packs the place nightly. If this isn't your scene, skip the evening and stop by in the quieter early afternoon instead, when you can better enjoy your beer amid the old-style pub atmosphere.

Chess (⊠ Vesterg. 7 ☎ 62/22–17–16) is popular with a young crowd that comes for the live bands. **Crazy Daisy** (⊠ Frederiksg. 6 ☎ 62/21–67–60) attracts a casual, over-21 crowd that dances to oldies and rock on Saturday night; a younger crowd pours in on Friday. The restaurant **Oranje** (⊠ Jessens Mole ☎ 62/22–82–92), an old sailing ship moored in the harbor, sometimes has live jazz in summer. Tucked back from the street, **Barbella Nightclub** (⊠ Vesterg. 10A ☎ 62/22–47–83) is a dimly lit bar with dark-rose walls and long wooden tables. A casual vibe and friendly staff draws a mixed-age crowd that mingles over cocktails, cheap bar grub (open-face sandwiches and meatballs), and live music in the evenings—jazz on Thursday; rock, pop, or classical on Friday and Saturday nights. On the first Sunday of the month, the club has live jazz starting at around noon. (It's closed the other Sundays of the month.)

CAFÉS In the heart of town is the spacious **Under Uret Café** (⊠ Gerritsg. 50 ☎ 62/21–83–08), playfully decorated with oversize watches on the wall—"Under Uret" means "under watch." For prime people-watching, settle in at one of the outdoor tables. The café menu includes brunch, club sandwiches, burritos, and a range of salads, from Greek to Caesar. Come nightfall, there's live music ranging from soul to rock.

Shopping

Svendborg's **city center** is bustling with shops, particularly on Gerritsgade and Møllergade, which are peppered with clothing stores, gift shops, and jewelers. For colorful, hand-blown glassworks head to **Glas Blæseriet** (⊠ Brog. 37A ☎ 62/22–83–73), which shares a half-timber courtyard in the center of town with the wine restaurant Vintapperiet. Glassblower Bente Sonne's lovely nature-inspired creations—in pale greens, oranges, and blues—are decorated with seashells, starfish, lizards, fish, and lobsters. You can watch Sonne blowing glass weekdays 10–3:30. On Saturday the shop is open 10–3:30 with no glass-blowing demonstration.

Kværndrup

❽ *15 km (9 mi) north of Svendborg, 28 km (18 mi) south of Odense.*

Fodor'sChoice The moated Renaissance **Egeskov Slot,** one of the best-preserved island-
★ castles in Europe, presides over this town. Peaked with copper spires and surrounded by Renaissance, baroque, English, and peasant gardens, the castle is still a private home, though visitors can see a few of the rooms, including the great hall, the hunting room, and the Riborg Room, where the daughter of the house was locked up from 1599 to 1604 after giving birth to a son out of wedlock. The castle also has an antique vehicle museum. ⊠ *Kværndrup, 15 km/9 mi north of Svendborg* ☎ *62/27–10–16* ⊕ *www.egeskov.com* 🎟 *Castle and museum Dkr 135* ☉ *Castle May, June, Aug., and Sept., daily 10–5; July, daily 10–7; Museum June and Aug., daily 10–6; July, daily 10–8 (Wed. open until 11 PM); May and Sept., daily 10–5.*

Tåsinge

❾ *3 km (2 mi) south of Svendborg (via the Svendborg Sound Bridge), 43 km (27 mi) south of Odense.*

Tåsinge Island is known for its local 19th-century drama involving Elvira Madigan and her married Swedish lover, Sixten Sparre. The drama is featured in the 1967 Swedish film *Elvira Madigan*. Preferring heavenly union to earthly separation, they shot themselves and are now buried in the island's central Landet churchyard. Brides throw their bouquets on the lovers' grave.

Fodor'sChoice
★

Troense is Tåsinge's main town, and one of the country's best-preserved maritime villages, with half-timber buildings and their hand-carved doors. South of town is **Valdemars Slot** (Valdemars Castle), dating from 1610, one of Denmark's oldest privately owned castles. You can wander through almost all of the sumptuously furnished rooms, libraries, and the candlelit church. There's also an X-rated 19th-century cigar box not to be missed. A yachting museum, with gleamingly restored yachts and skiffs, along with ship models and historical dioramas, explores Denmark's extensive yachting history. ⊠ *Slotsalleen 100, Troense* ☎ *62/ 22-61-06* ⊕*www.valdemarsslot.dk* ⊠*DKr 55* ☉ *May–Aug., daily 10–5; Sept., Tues.–Sun. 10–5; Apr. and Oct., weekends 10–5. Call to confirm opening hours.*

Where to Stay & Eat

$$$$
✕ **Lodskroen.** This whitewashed, thatch-roof restaurant opened its doors in 1774 to serve as an inn for passing sailors. For the past 30 years, it has been run by the husband-and-wife team of Hans and Kirsten Dahlgaard, who treat diners as if they were guests in their own home. In fact, diners are asked to not order more than two main dishes per table because, as a placard explains, "the cook, who is also the hostess, is always alone by the kitchen range and the food is never pre-prepared." The French-inspired Danish menu includes fillet of plaice stuffed with mushrooms, peppers, and herbs. For dessert, try the figs pickled in a sweet sherry and served with whipped cream. A surcharge is applied to credit cards. ⊠ *Troense Strandvej 80, Troense* ☎ *62/22–50–44* ☐ *MC, V* ☉ *Closed Mon.–Thurs. Feb., Nov., and Dec.; closed Jan. No lunch weekdays.*

¢–$$
Fodor'sChoice
★

✕ **Bregninge Mølle.** If you've ever wondered what the inside of a windmill looks like, this is your chance to find out. Within the Bregninge windmill, built in 1805, circular stairs lead to this restaurant's three levels, each with 360-degree views of the surrounding sea and Tåsinge countryside. On a clear day, you can see the southern tip of Jylland and the islands of Langeland and Thurø. The traditional Danish menu features *frikadeller* (fried meatballs) served with rice and peas, and æggekage. ⊠*Kirkebakken 19, Bregninge* ☎*62/22–52–55* ☐*MC, V* ☉ *Closed mid-Oct.–Mar.*

$
✕ **Hotel Troense.** Dating from 1908, this harborside hotel has bright, simply furnished rooms with fringed white bedcovers. One-third of the rooms look toward the harbor. The restaurant, with rose walls and a fireplace, serves a Danish menu with such dishes as salmon served with spinach topped with almonds. It also offers a couple of vegetarian dishes, including a pie stuffed with seasonal vegetables. The smørrebrød lunch menu includes open-face sandwiches of herring, salmon, eggs, liver pâté, or shrimp. The hotel often has discounted weekend deals that include breakfast and dinner. ⊠ *Strandg. 5, DK–5700 Troense* ☎ *62/ 22–54–12* 🖶 *62/22–78–12* ⊕ *www.hoteltroense.dk* 🛏 *30 rooms with bath* ⚙ *Restaurant, bar* ☐ *AE, DC, MC, V.*

$
✕ **Valdemars Slot.** The castle's guest rooms are not enormous, but they are nicely decorated in beige, ochre, light-green, and light-blue tones. Some have a view out to the north; others look out onto the adjacent yard and palace garden. Down below, a domed restaurant is ankle-deep in pink carpet and aglow with candlelight. Fresh French and German ingredients and wild game from the castle's reserve are the menu staples. Venison with cream sauce and duck breast *à l'orange* are typical of the French-inspired cuisine. A second eatery, Æblehaven, serves inexpensive sausages and upscale fast-food. ⊠ *Slotsalleen 100, DK–5700 Troense* ☎ *62/22–59–00* 🖶 *62/22–72–67* ⊕ *www.valdemarsslot.dk* 🛏 *8 rooms, 1 suite* ⚙ *2 restaurants* ☐ *MC, V.*

¢ ▣ **Det Lille Hotel.** This red half-timber, thatch-roof family house–turned–small hotel has eight snug rooms (none with bath or shower) with pale green walls and flowery curtains. The well-tended back garden blooms brilliantly in summer. A breakfast of homemade bread and jam is included. You can rent a bike for around Dkr 50 per day. ⊠ *Badstuen 15, DK–5700 Troense* ☎ *62/22–53–41* 🖷 *62/22–25–41* ⊕ *www.detlillehotel.dk* ⌁ *8 rooms, 3 with bath* ♿ *Dining room* ▤ *MC, V* ☉ *Closed Nov.–Mar.*

Shopping

For delicate hand-blown glass, visit **Glasmagerne** (⊠ Vemmenæsvej 10, Tåsinge ☎ 62/54–14–94).

Langeland

🔟 *16 km (10 mi) southeast of Troense, 64 km (40 mi) southwest of Odense.*

Reached by a causeway bridge from Tåsinge, Langeland is the largest island of the southern archipelago, rich in relics, with smooth, tawny beaches. Bird-watching is excellent on the southern half of the island, where migratory flocks roost before setting off on their cross-Baltic journey. To the south are Ristinge and Bagenkop, two towns with good beaches; at Bagenkop you can catch the ferry to Kiel, Germany.

Sports & the Outdoors

FISHING Langeland has particularly rich waters for fishing, with cod, salmon, flounder, and gar. For package tours, boat rentals, or fishing equipment, contact **Ole Dehn** (⊠ Sønderg. 22, Tranekær ☎ 62/55–17–00).

Ærøskøbing

★ ⑪ *30 km (19 mi) south of Svendborg, 74 km (46 mi) south of Odense, plus a one-hour ferry ride, either from Svendborg or Langeland.*

The island of Ærø, where country roads wind through fertile fields, is aptly called the Jewel of the Archipelago. About 27 km (16 mi) southeast of Søby on the island's north coast, the storybook town of Ærøskøbing is the port for ferries from Svendborg. Established as a market town in the 13th century, it did not flourish until it became a sailing center during the 1700s. Today, Ærøskøbing is a bewitching tangle of cobbled streets lined with immaculately preserved half-timber houses. Stop by the red 17th-century home at the corner of Vestergade and Smedegade, considered to be one of the town's finest examples of its provincial architecture. Ærøskøbing is a bastion of small-town Denmark: every morning, the whistling postman, in a red jacket and black-and-gold cap, strides the streets and delivers the mail; the friendly mayor pedals home for lunch and waves to everyone on the way.

As you wander through town, you'll notice that many of the homes display a pair of ceramic dogs on their windowsills. Traditionally, these were used by sailors' wives to signal to outsiders—and, as rumor has it, potential suitors—the whereabouts of their husbands. When the dogs were facing in, it meant that the man of the house was home, and when the dogs were facing out, that he was gone. Ironically, these ceramic dogs were brought home, usually from the Orient, by the sailors themselves, who had received them as "gifts" from prostitutes they had been with. The prostitutes gave these ceramic dogs as a cover-up, so that it appeared that they were selling souvenirs rather than sex.

Ferries provide the only access to Ærø. The ferry from Svendborg to Ærøskøbing takes 1 hour, 15 minutes. In addition, there's a one-hour ferry from Faaborg to Søby, a town on the northwest end of the island; and a shorter one from Rudkøbing—on the island of Langeland—to Marstal, on the eastern end of Ærø.

History is recorded in miniature at the **Flaskeskibssamlingen** (Bottle-Ship Collection), thanks to a former ship's cook known as Peter Bottle, who painstakingly built nearly 2,000 bottle ships in his day. The combination of his life's work and the enthusiastic letters he received from fans and disciples around the world makes for a surprisingly moving collection. ✉ *Smedeg. 22, Ærøskøbing* ☎ *62/52–29–51* 💲 *Dkr 30* ☺ *May–Oct., daily 10–4; Nov.–Apr., Tues.–Fri. 1–3, weekends 10–2.*

Ærø Museum houses numerous relics—including some from the Stone Age—culled from archaeological digs on the island. Also displayed are antique domestic furnishings from the homes of skippers on the island. Call ahead or check at the tourist office, because nonsummer hours can vary. ✉ *Brog. 3–5, Ærøskøbing* ☎ *62/52–29–50* 💲 *Dkr 20* ☺ *May–mid-Oct., weekdays 10–4, weekends 11–3; mid-Oct.–Apr., weekdays 10–3.*

The two-story half-timber **Hammerichs Hus** (Hammerich's House) was once the home of sculptor Gunnar Hammerich. Today it features reconstructed period interiors of ancient Ærø homes, including antique maritime paintings, furniture, and porcelain pieces. ✉ *Gyden 22, Ærøskøbing* ☎ *65/52–29–50* 💲 *Dkr 20* ☺ *Mid-June–mid-Sept., weekdays noon–4.*

Where to Stay & Eat

★ ¢–$$ ✕ **Hos Grethe.** In the heart of town is this amiable restaurant, run by long-time local Grethe. The dining room, with low white ceilings and a black-and-white checkered floor, is nicknamed the *kongelogen* (the royal box) because of the royal portraits, past and present, that line the walls. Grethe is famous for her steaks, thick-cut and juicy, which come with large salads. In summer, the outside terrace and beer garden overflow with day-trippers from the mainland. ✉ *Vesterg. 39* ☎ *62/52–21–43* ▭ *MC, V* ☺ *Closed Oct.–May. No lunch Apr.–mid-June and mid-Aug.–Sept.*

¢–$ ✕▣ **Det Lille Hotel.** Six large, simply furnished rooms make up the second floor of this friendly *lille* (little) hotel. Flowery curtains frame small windows that overlook the garden below. Dating from 1865, the building once housed the offices of Ærø's farmer's journal. It later became a boarding house. On the bottom floor are a popular restaurant and bar, both of which draw a daily crowd of regulars (reservations are essential for the restaurant). Paintings of ships and schooners hang on the walls, and a collection of old porcelain coffee- and teapots lines the shelves. A brick-floor terrace opens up in summer, and from here you can catch glimpses of the sea through the trees. The Danish menu includes fried plaice topped with butter sauce and pork fillet with tomatoes, mushrooms, and a white-wine cream sauce. The snug bar is decorated with a ship wheel and lanterns. ✉ *Smedeg. 33, DK–5970* ☎ *62/52–23–00* ⇴ *6 rooms without bath* ⌂ *Restaurant* ▭ *MC, V.*

$$$ ▣ **Ærøhus Marina.** A half-timber building with a steep red roof, the Ærøhus looks like a rustic cottage on the outside and an old, but overly renovated, aunt's house on the inside. Hanging pots and slanted walls characterize the public areas, and pine furniture and cheerful duvets keep the guest rooms simple and bright. The garden's five cottages have small terraces. ✉ *Vesterg. 38, DK–5970* ☎ *62/52–10–03* ▤ *62/52–21–23* ⊕ *www.aeroehus-hotel.dk* ⇴ *67 rooms, 56 with bath* ⌂ *Restaurant, bar, some pets allowed* ▭ *V.*

¢ ▣ **Pension Vestergade 44.** Rising over Ærøskøbing's main street are two superbly maintained patrician homes. Standing side by side, they are mirror images of each other, built by two ship captains, brothers, who wanted to raise their families in identical surroundings. One of the homes has been converted into this small hotel that has been lovingly restored by its owners, a friendly British-German couple, to recapture all of the building's former charms. A clawfoot iron stove heats up the breakfast room that overlooks a sprawling back garden with clucking chickens who lay the eggs for breakfast. White lace curtains frame the windows and an antique wooden plate rack displays blue-and-white English porcelain dishes. The beautifully appointed rooms, each with their own color scheme, have naturally sloping floors and vintage wooden towel racks laden with fluffy, bright-white towels. If you want to pedal around town, they'll lend you a bike. ⊠ *Vesterg. 44, DK 5970* ☎ *62/52–22–98* ⌁ *6 rooms without bath* ⚬ *Dining room.*

Nightlife & the Arts

Of Ærøskøbing's few bars, one of the most popular is **Arrebo** (⊠ Vesterg. 4 ☎ 62/52–28–50), with yellow walls, wooden tables, and local art on the walls. On the weekends, it hosts live music, from blues to rock to jazz. A bell dangles at one end of the bar, and in the sailor tradition, whoever rings it must buy the whole bar a round of drinks.

Shopping

Ærøskøbing is sprinkled with a handful of craft and gift shops. Unfortunately, there are virtually no more bottle-ship makers on the island. Instead, the labor-intensive curiosities are made in Asia and modeled on original ærø bottle-ship designs. For souvenir bottle-ships, head to **Kolorit** (⊠ Torvet 1A ☎ 62/52–25–23), a small gift shop crammed with Danish mementos.

Marstal

★ ⑫ *10 km (6 mi) southeast of Ærøskøbing, 40 km (25 mi) south of Svendborg, 84 km (52 mi) south of Odense. From Svendborg, it's a one-hour ferry ride to Ærøskøbing; from Langeland it's a 45-min ferry ride to Marstal.*

Southeast of Ærøskøbing, past a lush landscape of green and yellow hills rolling toward the sea, is the sprightly shipping town of Marstal. From its early fishing days in the 1500s to its impressive rise into a formidable shipping port in the 1700s, Marstal's lifeblood has always been the surrounding sea. At its seafaring height, in the late 1800s, Marstal had a fleet of 300 ships. During this heady time, the Marstal government couldn't expand the harbor fast enough to accommodate the growing fleet, so Marstal's seamen took it upon themselves to extend its port. Working together in the winter season, they built the 1-km (½-mi) stone pier—still in use today—by rolling rocks from the fields, along the ice, and onto the harbor. They began in 1835 and completed the pier in 1841.

Today, Marstal is home port to 50 vessels, from tall-masted schooners to massive trawlers. Much of the town's activity—and its cobbled streets—radiates from the bustling port. A nautical school, first established in the 1800s, is still going strong, with more than 150 students. In a nod to its seafaring heritage, the Marstal harbor is one of the few places in the world still constructing wooden ships.

Marstal's winding streets are dotted with well-preserved skipper's homes. **Maren Minors Hjem** (Maren Minor's Home) was once the genteel abode of successful Marstal seaman Rasmus Minor, who eventually settled in the United States. The house has been carefully restored inside and out to look just as it did in the 1700s, including vintage art and furniture.

Opening hours vary from year to year, so check with the tourist office. ⊠ *Teglg. 9* ☏ *62/53–24–25* ✉ *Free* ⏱ *June–Aug., Tues.–Sun. 11–3.*

Spread out over three buildings, the sprawling **Marstal Søfartsmuseum** (Marstal Maritime Museum) offers a rich and fascinating account of Marstal's formidable shipping days. Thirty-five showrooms are jam-packed with maritime memorabilia, including more than 200 ship models, 100 bottle-ships, navigation instruments, and a collection of maritime paintings by artist Carl Rasmussen. He was born in Ærøskøbing and made his name painting Greenland sea- and landscapes. Wandering the museum is like exploring a massive ship: step aboard large-scale decks and hulls and command the gleaming ship wheels like a Marstal captain. Mind your head as you climb up and down the steep ship stairs that connect many of the rooms. "Back on land," you can duck into the low-ceiling parlors of a skipper's house, meticulously reproduced with period furnishings. Long-time museum director and Marstal historian Erik B. Kromann is a font of maritime information, and will enthusiastically take you on a tour of the museum if you ask. The museum shop is bursting with nifty gifts, including key chains made from maritime rope knots. ⊠ *Prinsensg. 1* ☏ *62/53–23–31* ⊕ *www.marmus.dk* ✉ *Dkr 40* ⏱ *July, daily 9–8; June and Aug., daily 9–5; May and Sept., daily 10–4; Oct.–Apr., Tues.–Fri. 10–4, Sat. 11–3.*

Where to Stay & Eat

¢ ✕⊠ **Marstal.** Mere paces from the waterfront is this homey locals' favorite, with wooden ceilings, dim lighting, and a ship's wheel on the wall. The homestyle Danish dishes include minced steak with peas, potatoes, and béarnaise sauce, and smoked salmon served with asparagus and scrambled eggs. Another favorite is mussels-and-bacon on toast. The cozy bar draws a friendly pre- and post-dinner crowd of dockworkers. Above the restaurant are eight very basic rooms, none with bath, and two with partial views of the harbor. ⊠ *Dronningestr. 1A, DK–5960* ☏ *62/ 53–13–52* ↴ *8 rooms without bath* ⚙ *Restaurant, bar* ▭ *MC, V* ⏱ *Closed Sept.–May.*

$ ⊡ **Ærø Strand.** On the outskirts of Marstal lies this holiday hotel that caters to the island's summer tourists. Blond-wood and dark-blue tones adorn the comfortable rooms. In the center of the hotel is a heart-shape pool and, for the after-hours crowd, a popular nightclub disco. ⊠ *Egehovedvej 4, DK–5960* ☏ *62/53–33–20* 🖷 *62/53–31–50* ⊕ *www.hotel-aeroestrand.dk* ↴ *100 rooms with bath, 20 suites* ⚙ *Restaurant, tennis court, indoor pool, gym, sauna, nightclub* ▭ *AE, DC, MC, V.*

Nightlife & the Arts

Marstal's night scene is sedate, but when locals want a beer they head to the informal **Café Victor** (⊠ Kirkestr. 15 ☏ 62/53–28–01), with its yellow walls and a brass-lined bar. Here you can also tuck into simple Danish dishes, such as fillet of sole with french fries.

Shopping

The maritime paintings of Marstal artist Rita Lund are popular throughout the island, gracing the walls of several restaurants and decorating the sunny sitting rooms of the ferries that shuttle between Svendborg and Ærø. For a further look, visit Rita Lund's **Galleri Humlehave** (⊠ Skoleg. 1 ☏ 62/53–21–73) which, appropriately enough, is near the Marstal harbor. Her extensive collection includes paintings of crashing waves, ships at sea, and Ærø during the four seasons.

Fyn & the Central Islands A to Z

BIKE TRAVEL

With their level terrain and short distances, Fyn and the Central Islands are perfect for cycling. A bike trip around the circumference of the main island, stopping at the series of delightful port towns that ring Fyn like a string of pearls, is a wonderful way of spending a few days. The Odense tourist office has a helpful map of cycle routes in and around Odense. You can rent bikes through City Cykler in Odense or at several hotels around the islands. Contact Fyntour for longer cycling tour packages that include bike rental, hotel accommodations, and a half-board (breakfast and one meal) meal plan.

🖪 **City Cykler** ⊠ Vesterbro 27, Odense ☎ 66/13-97-83 ⊕ www.citycykler.dk. **Fyntour** ⊠ Svendborgvej 83-85, DK-5260 Odense ☎ 66/13-13-37 🖶 66/13-13-38 ⊕ www.fyntour.dk.

BUS TRAVEL

Buses are one of the main public-transportation options in the area. Timetables are posted at all bus stops and central stations. Passengers buy tickets on board and pay according to the distance traveled. If you plan on traveling extensively by bus, ask at any bus station about a 24-hour bus pass, which cuts costs considerably. Contact Fynbus for more information about routes between cities. Odense Bytrafik runs the bus system within Odense.

🖪 **Fynbus** ⊠ Odense Bus Station ☎ 63/11-22-33 🖶 63/11-22-99. **Odense Bytrafik** (Odense City Transport) ☎ 65/51-29-29 🖶 66/19-40-27.

CAR TRAVEL

From Copenhagen, take the E20 west to Halsskov, near Korsør, and drive onto the Great Belt bridge, which costs about Dkr 250 per car. You'll arrive near Nyborg, which is 30 minutes from either Odense or Svendborg.

The highways of Fyn are excellent, and small roads meander beautifully on two lanes through the countryside. A trip around the circumference of the island can be done in a day, but stopping for a night or two at one of the enchanting port towns can be fun, and offers the chance to meet some of the locals. Traffic is light, except during the height of summer in highly populated beach areas.

EMERGENCIES

For fire, police, or ambulance anywhere in Denmark, dial 112. Lægevagten is the service for house calls, but will also dispatch an ambulance in case of emergencies. Trained phone personnel are generally able to judge whether a house call would be sufficient. The doctor's visits are made according to a priority list, with serious illnesses and sick children at the top of the list. Falck is the emergency road service, for towing vehicles in trouble or in case of accidents.

🖪 **Lægevagten** (Emergency Doctor) ☎ 65/90-60-10, 4 PM-7 AM. **Falck** ☎ 70/10-20-30 ⊕ www.falck.dk. **Odense University Hospital** ⊠ Søndre Blvd. 29, Odense ☎ 66/11-33-33. **Ørnen Apoteket** ⊠ Vesterg. 80, Odense ☎ 66/12-29-70.

TOURS

Few towns offer organized tours, but check the local tourist offices for step-by-step walking brochures. The Hans Christian Andersen Tours are full-day tours to Odense that depart from Copenhagen's Rådhus Pladsen. (Six of 11 hours are spent in transit.) Call ahead because departure days and times may vary. The two-hour Odense tour departs from the local tourist office. Contact Fyntour or Odense Tourist Office for details about prices and times of tours. Most itineraries include the exteriors of the Hans Christian Andersen sites and the cathedral and the guides are generally more than willing to answer questions about the area or Denmark as a whole. Odense Tourist Office also offers one-hour tours of the Italian Gothic Odense City Hall. Inside is a long memorial wall commemorating famous Fyn citizens. The local calendar of events often presents interesting activities at the city's sites, so it would be wise to call one of the tourist offices to inquire about any events.

🔊 **Fyntour** ✉ Svendborgvej 83–85, Odense ☎ 66/13-13-37 🌐 www.fyntour.dk. **Odense Tourist Office** ✉ Vesterg. 2 Odense ☎ 66/12-75-20 🌐 www.odenseturist.dk.

TRAIN TRAVEL
Direct trains from Copenhagen's main station depart for the 90-minute trip to Odense's train station about hourly from 5 AM to 10:30 PM, every day. The Odense station is central, close to hotels and sites. Large towns in the region are served by intercity trains. The Nyborg–Odense–Middelfart and the Odense–Svendborg routes are among the two most important. You can take the train to Odense direct from Copenhagen Airport.

RESERVATIONS   A reservation, which is required during rush hour, costs an additional Dkr 15.

🔊 **DSB Train Booking and Information** ☎ 70/13-14-15 🌐 www.dsb.dk.

VISITOR INFORMATION
For central Odense, the Odense Eventyrpas (Adventure Pass), available at the tourism office and the train station, affords admission to sites and museums and free city bus and train transport. The cost for a 48-hour pass is Dkr 150; for a 24-hour pass, Dkr 110.

🔊 **Assens Touristbureau** ✉ Damg. 22, DK-5610 Assens ☎ 64/71-20-31 🖶 64/71-49-39 🌐 www.visit-vestfyn.dk. **Egeskov Touristbureau** ✉ Egeskov 1, DK-5772 Kværndrup ☎ 62/27-10-46 🖶 62/27-10-48. **Fyntour** ✉ Svendborgvej 83–85, DK-5260 Odense ☎ 66/13-13-37 🌐 www.fyntour.dk. **Faaborg Touristbureau** ✉ Banegårdspl. 2A, DK-5600 Faaborg ☎ 62/61-07-07 🖶 62/61-33-37 🌐 www.visitfaaborg.dk. **Kerteminde Touristbureau** ✉ Strandg. 1B, DK-5300 Kerteminde ☎ 65/32-11-21 🖶 65/32-18-17 🌐 www.kerteminde-turist.dk. **Langeland Touristforeningen** ✉ Torvet 5, DK-5900 Rundkøbing ☎ 62/51-35-05 🖶 62/51-43-35 🌐 www.langeland.dk. **Marstal Touristbureau** ✉ Havneg. 5, DK-5960 Marstal ☎ 62/52-13-00 🖶 62/53-25-17 🌐 www.arre.dk. **Nyborg Touristbureau** ✉ Torvet 9, DK-5800 Nyborg ☎ 65/31-02-80 🖶 65/31-03-80 🌐 www.nyborgturist.dk. **Odense Touristbureau** ✉ Vesterg. 2, DK-5000 Odense ☎ 66/12-75-20 🖶 66/12-75-86 🌐 www.odenseturist.dk. **Sydfyns Touristbureau** ✉ Centrumpl. 4, DK-5700 Svendborg ☎ 62/21-09-80 🖶 62/22-05-53 🌐 www.visitsydfyn.dk. **Ærø Touristbureau** ✉ Vesterg. 13, DK-5970 Ærøskøbing ☎ 62/52-13-00 🖶 62/52-14-36 🌐 www.arre.dk.

JYLLAND

FODOR'S CHOICE

Bryggeriet Sct. Clemens, *restaurant-pub in Århus*

Den Gamle Arrest, *hotel in Ribe*

Hotel Dagmar, *Ribe*

Legoland, *Billund*

Schackenborg Slotskro, *hotel in Møgeltønder*

Seafood, *restaurant in Marselisborg*

Tilsandede Kirke, *church in Skagen*

Trapholt Museum for Moderne Kunst, *Kolding*

HIGHLY RECOMMENDED

RESTAURANTS Admiralen, *Kolding*

Café Nanas Stue, *Fanø*

Duus Vinkjælder, *Aalborg*

HOTELS Royal Hotel, *Århus*

Sønderho Kro, *Sønderho*

Saxildhus Hotel, *Kolding*

Molskroen, *Ebeltoft*

SIGHTS Den Gamle By, *open-air museum in Århus*

Jens Bang Stenhus, *17th-century merchant's house in Aalborg*

Ribe

Skagen Museum, *Skagen*

NIGHTLIFE Café Under Masken, *Århus*

Updated by
Eduardo López
de Luzuriaga

JYLLAND (JUTLAND), Denmark's western peninsula, is the only part of the country naturally connected to mainland Europe; its southern boundary is the frontier with Germany. In contrast to the smooth, postcard-perfect land of Fyn and Sjælland, this Ice Age–chiseled peninsula is bisected at the north by the craggy Limfjord and spiked below by the Danish "mountains." Himmelbjerget, the zenith of this modest range, peaks at 438 feet. Farther south, the Yding Skovhøj plateau rises 568 feet—modest hills just about anywhere else.

Hunters first inhabited Denmark, in southern Jylland, some 250,000 years ago. You can see flint tools and artifacts from this period locked away in museums, but the land holds more-stirring relics from a later epoch: after 1,000 years, Viking burial mounds and stones still swell the land, some in protected areas, others lying in farmers' fields, tended by grazing sheep.

The windswept landscapes filmed in *Babette's Feast,* the movie version of the Karen Blixen (Isak Dinesen) novel, trace the west coast northward to Skagen, a luminous, dune-covered point. To the east, facing Fyn, Jylland is cut by deep fjords rimmed with forests. The center is dotted with castles, parklands, and the famed Legoland. Denmark's oldest and youngest towns, Ribe and Esbjerg, lie in southwest Jylland. In Ribe's medieval town center is the country's earliest church; modern Esbjerg, perched on the coast, is the departure point for ferries to nearby Fanø, an island of windswept beaches and traditional villages. Århus and Aalborg, respectively Denmark's second- and fourth-largest cities, face east and have nightlife and sights to rival Copenhagen's.

WHAT IT COSTS In kroner					
	$$$$	**$$$**	**$$**	**$**	**¢**
RESTAURANTS	over 180	141–180	121–140	90–120	under 90
HOTELS	over 1,500	1,200–1,500	1,000–1,200	700–1,000	under 700

Restaurant prices are for a main course at dinner. Hotel prices are for two people in a standard double room, including service charge and tax.

Kolding

❶ *71 km (44 mi) northwest of Odense (via the Little Belt Bridge), 190 km (119 mi) west of Copenhagen.*

Lying in Jylland's heartland, the lively town of Kolding is a pleasing blend of old and new, with a historical center of cobbled streets and brightly painted half-timber houses that give way to industrial suburbs.

The well-preserved **Koldinghus,** a massive stonework structure that was once a fortress, then a royal residence in the Middle Ages, is today a historical museum. In the winter of 1808, during the Napoleonic Wars, Spanish soldiers set fire to most of it while trying to stay warm. ✉ *Rådhusstr.* ☎ *76/33–81–00* ⊕ *www.koldinghus.dk* 💰 *Dkr 50* ⊙ *Daily 10–5.*

Fodor'sChoice ★ Just east of town is the **Trapholt Museum for Moderne Kunst** (Trapholt Museum of Modern Art), one of Denmark's largest—and most highly acclaimed—modern-art museums outside Copenhagen. Rising over the banks of the Kolding Fjord, this sprawling white complex has been artfully incorporated into its natural surroundings, affording lovely views

4

Nearly three times the size of the rest of Denmark, with long distances between towns, the peninsula of Jylland can easily take at least several days, even weeks, to explore. If you are pressed for time, concentrate on a single tour or a couple of cities. Delightful as they are, the islands are suitable only for those with plenty of time, as many require an overnight stay.

Numbers in the text correspond to numbers in the margin and on the Jylland map.

If you have 3 days

After reaching 🖼 **Århus** ⑪ ▶ by boat, car, train or plane, allow yourself a day to see the city's sights; be sure not to miss Den Gamle By. On the second day travel to 🖼 **Ribe** ④, stopping on the way to visit the Trapholt Museum for modern art in **Kolding** ①. On the way back to Århus on the third day, stop by Legoland in **Billund** ⑦, where both children and adults can easily spend several hours.

If you have 7 days

Base yourself in 🖼 **Århus** ⑪ ▶ and spend the first day around town savoring the city's lively café and nightlife scene. Leave early the next morning and journey all the way north to Skagen, stopping for lunch in **Aalborg** ⑭ at one of the restaurants along the bustling Jomfru Ane Gade. As you arrive in 🖼 **Skagen** ⑮, notice the beautiful, unique light that inspired its own school of painting; stop by the town's museum to see this ethereal quality portrayed on canvas. On your second day in Skagen, explore the beaches of the northern coastline, marvelling at the power and size of the sand dunes at Tilsandede Kirke and the Råbjerg Mile. After a second night in Skagen, make your way to 🖼 **Viborg** ⑬ and enjoy a quiet evening in this old town. On the fifth day head straight for **Billund** ⑦ and Legoland's modular wonders. 🖼 **Ribe** ④ is a good town to find overnight accommodations, but you might also pass appealing-looking inns along the way. Get up early to see Ribe's church and Viking museum on the morning of the sixth day and, if the weather is good, drive to **Rømø** ③ or take a ferry to **Fanø** ⑥, and wander out onto these islands' wild, expansive beaches. On the way, grab lunch in nearby **Esbjerg** ⑤. Spend the last day working your way back to Århus, stopping in for a brief peep at the Trapholt Museum in **Kolding** ①.

of the fjord and parkland from its soaring floor-to-ceiling windows. An extensive collection of 20th-century Danish paintings is displayed in the light-filled galleries; it includes works by Anna Ancher, Richard Mortensen, Aksel Jørgensen, and Franciska Clausen. A true highlight is the furniture collection, housed in a specially designed annex that is accessed via a circular ramp topped by a skylight. The superbly displayed collection includes the largest assemblage of Danish-designed chairs in the world, offering a unique historical overview of the birth and popularization of Danish furniture design. Best of all, you can try out any of the hundreds of chairs for yourself thanks to the museum's philosophy that art should be experienced with all the senses, from visual to tactile. Sink into an Arne Jacobsen egg chair, or play with Nanna Ditzel's children's stools; when you're bored of sitting, turn the stool on its side, and it becomes a nifty toy that can be rolled along the ground. Also on display are numerous furnishings by prolific designer Hans J. Wegner, including a rounded, blond-wood chair entitled "The Chair." The museum keeps its furniture storage room open to the public, so you can peruse the entire collection even when it's not officially on display. The Danish ceramics collection, one of the largest in Denmark, is also well worth a look. Check out the one-of-a-kind ceramics by Danish artist Axel Salto, whose pieces often resemble living organisms. ⊠ *Æblehaven 23* ☎ *76/30–05–30* ⊕ *www.trapholt.dk* ⊠ *Dkr 50* ⊙ *Daily 10–5.*

Where to Stay & Eat

★ **$$$$**   ✕ **Admiralen.** Across from the harbor is this elegant seafood restaurant, with pale yellow tablecloths, white walls, and blue-suede chairs. It serves excellent fish dishes, including grilled salmon with spinach and steamed lemon sole with scallops. Pigeon with mushrooms, apples, and a basil gravy is another option. ⊠ *Toldbodeg. 14* ☎ *75/52–04–21* ⊟ *AE, DC, MC, V.*

$$$–$$$$ ✕ **Radisson SAS Hotel Koldingfjord.** This impressive neoclassical hotel has mahogany floors and pyramid skylights. It's five minutes from town and faces the Kolding Fjord and 50 acres of countryside. The rooms vary in size (with 39 in a separate annex), but all have pale-wood furnishings and bright prints. The motto of the excellent French-Danish restaurant is "good food is art"; expect well-presented seafood dishes, as well as intriguing vegetarian options. ⊠ *Fjordvej 154, DK–6000 Strandhuse* ☎ *75/51–00–00* ☐ *75/51–00–51* ⊕ *www.koldingfjord.dk* ↵ *134 rooms, 9 suites* ☐ *Restaurant, tennis court, indoor pool, sauna, billiards, bar* ⊟ *AE, DC, MC, V.*

★ **$$–$$$**   ✕ **Saxildhus Hotel.** Just steps from the train station, this has long been Kolding's premier hotel. Its rooms come in a range of styles, some with old-fashioned mahogany four-poster beds and others with more-contemporary furnishings. The restaurant serves top-notch Danish dishes, including fried plaice with parsley sauce and potatoes. ⊠ *Jernbaneg. 39, Banegårdspl., DK–6000* ☎ *75/52–12–00* ☐ *75/53–53–10* ⊕ *www.saxildhus.dk* ↵ *80 rooms, 7 suites* ☐ *Restaurant, bar, some pets allowed, no-smoking rooms* ⊟ *AE, DC, MC, V.*

Nightlife & the Arts

In the heart of town, on Lilletorv (Little Square), is the stylish and amiable **Den Blå Café** (⊠ Slotsg. 4 ☎ 75/50–65–12), with British and American rock and blues music playing to a backdrop of film posters. In the afternoons, locals sidle up to the picture windows overlooking the square and enjoy coffee and warm baguette sandwiches or chips and guacamole. In the evening, beer and cocktails flow freely, and on the weekends, there's live jazz on the terrace.

Shopping

Kolding's town center is a jumble of walking streets dotted with clothing and jewelry stores and ice cream shops. The two-story **Bahne** (⊠ Sønderg. 9 ☎ 75/50–56–22) sells all the big names in Danish design, from Stelton and Georg Jensen tableware to functional wooden furniture made by the Danish design firm Trip Trap.

Tønder

❷ *105 km (66 mi) southwest of Kolding, 195 km (122 mi) southwest of Århus.*

Just 4 km (2½ mi) north of the German border, the historical town of Tønder has long been closely allied with its southern neighbor. In 1864, Tønder was annexed by Germany. After Germany's defeat in World War I, plebiscites were held in the area, and Tønder chose to become reunited

4

Jylland Summerhouses

When summer vacation rolls around, Danes make beelines for the beach and the forest, knowing instinctively to frolic on long summer days in preparation for the long winter ahead. Jylland, with its vast meadows, forests, and windswept coastlines, is a popular getaway. To make these excursions more convenient and economical, many vacationing Danes own or rent houses in the Jylland countryside. Calling these homes "summerhouses" is a bit of a misnomer, since Danes retreat to these residences in any season—even at Christmas. The houses are usually available for rent when their owners aren't using them, and tourists have caught on quickly. Because visitors from northern Germany have developed such an affinity for the summerhouses, it's now specified in Danish law that it's illegal to sell the residences to foreigners.

The properties that you might find through a rental agency or tourist office vary from luxurious villas with spas and saunas, to basic cottages, where you might have to entertain yourself by reading, hunting for mushrooms, or buying fresh fish on the beach or at the local harbor. Depending on what landscape you prefer, you could choose to rent a house in the wilder regions of western and northern Jylland, the more sheltered area around the Limfjorden, or southern Jylland, where you could take day trips to northern German towns and cities such as Hamburg or Lübeck. For more information on prices and house rental agencies, *see* Lodging *in* Smart Travel Tips.

Fishing

Whether you prefer stream, river, lake, or coastal waters, Jylland is the best region of Denmark for anglers. The peninsula has more than 14 times as much flowing stream water and twice as much coastline as Sjælland. Depending on whether you choose fresh- or saltwater fishing, you can cast for brown trout, salmon, grayling, garfish, turbot, mackerel, plaice, and many other less plentiful species. If you're in the Vejle area, you'll have plenty of opportunity to fish in Gudenåen, a legendary spot . . . literally. The story goes that where the river springs up from the earth, a young man, Gudar, once snatched a young girl and ran with her, following windy roads to lose his pursuers. The girl's father asked a wise man for help, and the wise man called upon all the creeks and brooks of the region to follow Gudar's circuitous path. Near the town of Randers, the summoned waters caught up with him and drowned him. The young girl was saved, but not before the longest river in Denmark, the Gudenå, was formed. The salmon population in this river has come back strong in recent years after being nearly decimated by a damming project upstream.

---

with Denmark. Nevertheless, Tønder is still home to a small but important German community, with a German kindergarten and library.

Tønder received its official municipal charter in 1243, making it one of Denmark's oldest towns. Amble back in time among the winding cobbled streets in the heart of town, where half-timber gabled houses, many with intricately carved doors, lean up against small old-fashioned shops.

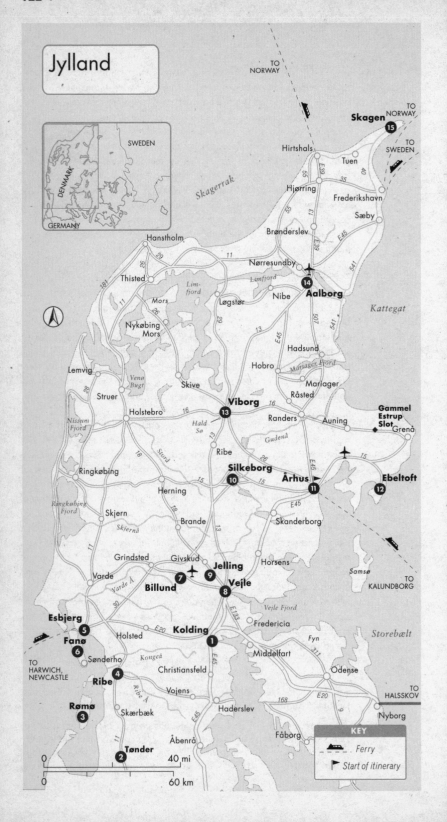

Jylland

SWEDEN

DENMARK

GERMANY

TO
NORWAY

Skagerrak

TO NORWAY

Skagen **15**

TO SWEDEN

Hirtshals

Tuen

55 E39 40

Hjørring 35

Frederikshavn

E39 13

Brønderslev Sæby

E45

Hanstholm

26 29 11

Nørresundby 541

Limfjord

Thisted 181

Nibe 14 **14** Aalborg

Mors 26 Løgstør

Limfjord Kattegat

Nykøbing
Mors 29

13

507 541

Lemvig

Venø
Bugt

Struer 28

Skive

E45 Hadsund

Hobro

Muriager Fjord

Mariager

Råsted

Gammel
Estrup
Slot

Holstebro 16 Viborg **13** 16 Randers Auning Grenå

Nissum
Fjord

Hald
Sø 13

Gudenå

Ribe 26

18 Stora

Ringkøbing

Silkeborg

15 **10** 15

E45 15

Århus **11**

Ebeltoft **12**

Herning

Ringkøbing
Fjord

Skjern 18 Brande 13 Skanderborg E45

Skjernå

11

Grindsted Givskud Jelling **9**

Horsens Samsø TO
KALUNDBORG

Varde **7** Vejle **8**

Varde Å Billund

Vejle Fjord

30

Esbjerg **5**

Fanø **6**

Holsted E20 Kolding **1** Fredericia

Fyn Storebælt

TO HARWICH,
NEWCASTLE

Sønderho

Kongeå

Middelfart 311

E45

Ribe **4**

Christiansfeld

Odense E20 TO
HALSSKOV

Rømø **3**

Vojens

168 9

Skærbæk

Haderslev

Nyborg

Åbenrå

0

Tønder **2**

40 mi

Fåborg

KEY

Ferry

0 60 km

Start of itinerary

The town is surrounded by low-lying marshes, and has been subject to major floods throughout its history. To combat the floods, a series of protective dikes was built in the 16th century. The result was double-edged: though Tønder was now safe from the sea, it also lost its natural harbor and waterways and, most importantly, its shipping industry. So, the town turned its sights inward, to the Tønder women's sewing rooms, and built itself up as the "lace capital of the world." In the 18th century, lacemaking became Tønder's most lucrative export, and at its height more than 12,000 women and girls were working as lacemakers. Throughout town are the stately gated homes once owned by successful lace merchants.

Tønder comes vibrantly alive in the last week of August for the **Tønder Folk Music Festival** (☎ 74/72–46–10 ⊕ www.tf.dk), which has been drawing folk music–lovers from all over the world since 1974. Big names and local acts perform everything from blues, zydeco, and gospel to the more traditional Irish, Scottish, and American folk tunes. Reserve hotel rooms well in advance, as the town fills up to capacity during this time.

Founded in 1923, the **Tønder Museum** has amassed an impressive collection of South Jylland arts and crafts. The extensive lace exhibit includes delicate doilies and baptismal gowns. In another room, intricately etched silverware is displayed alongside antique furnishings. A highlight is the collection of hand-painted glazed Dutch tiles brought back by sailors during the 17th and 18th centuries. The tiles served as ballast for the ships, and were then used to decorate the home. Tønder's old water tower, connected to the museum via a glass corridor, houses the world's largest collection of chairs designed by Tønder native Hans J. Wegner, one of Denmark's best-known furniture designers. The 40-meter (130-foot) tower with eight sun-drenched decks is the ideal showroom for Wegner's chairs and furnishings, which range from a rope and ash-wood circle chair to his Y-chair, made of beech wood with a plaited paper yarn seat. The skylit top deck, above which sits the old water-tower lantern, displays a massive circular table, designed by Wegner's daughter. Around the table sit 25 of Wegner's most popular chair, a rounded blond-wood design that he called simply "The Chair," which brought Wegner worldwide recognition, particularly in the United States, after both Kennedy and Nixon each sat in one during a television interview. Settle into one and enjoy the 360-degree views of Tønder's red rooftops and surrounding green marshland that unfold to the sea. If you're in the market for some Tønder lace, you can buy some in the small museum store. ⊠ *Kongevej 51* ☎ *74/72–89–89* ⊕ *www.tonder-net.dk/museerne* ⊡ *Dkr 35* ☉ *June–Aug., daily 10–5; Sept.–May, Tues.–Sun. 10–5.*

Lace-lovers will be richly rewarded at the **Drøhses Hus,** a well-preserved 1672 town house with exhibits of lace and lacemaking. In summer, lacemakers often work their trade inside the house. ⊠ *Storeg. 14* ☎ *74/72–49–90* ⊡ *Dkr 20* ☉ *Apr.–Dec., weekdays 10–5, Sat. 10–1.*

Where to Stay & Eat

$$$–$$$$
FodorsChoice
★

×⊞ **Schackenborg Slotskro.** This elegant hotel is the official royal inn of the nearby Schackenborg Castle, the residence of Prince Joachim and his wife Princess Alexandra. Stay at the inn, and you can say that while in Denmark, you were a guest of the Danish royal family (albeit a paying guest). Alexandra personally decorated the rooms in rich blues, greens, and reds; each has a large, sparkling bathroom and views of the castle. The castle and inn are 4 km (2½ mi) west of Tønder, in the small village of Møgeltønder. Though the castle is not open to the public, you can roam about the lush grounds that are surrounded by a moat. Møgeltønder's narrow cobbled main street, lined with lime trees, rose gardens, and lovely brick and half-timber houses, has been rightfully named "Denmark's most beautiful village street." The inn's highly acclaimed restaurant serves superb Danish-French cuisine, including beef tournedos with foie gras, cherry tomatoes, and potatoes topped with a truffle sauce. ⊠ *Slotsg. 42, DK–6270 Møgeltønder* ☎*74/73–83–83* ⊟*74/73–83–11* ⊕ *www.slotskro.dk* ⊅ *25 rooms, 2 suites* ⅏ *Restaurant, bar, some pets allowed, no-smoking rooms* ⊟ *AE, DC, MC, V.*

Sports & the Outdoors

Biking trails crisscross Tønder's lush and flat countryside. The tourist office has helpful cycling maps that detail the bike routes in the area. You can rent bikes at **Top Cycler** (⊠ Jernbaneg. 1C ☎ 74/72–18–81).

Shopping

Since 1671, **Det Gamle Apotek** (The Old Pharmacy; ⊠ Østerg. 1 ☎ 74/72–51–11) has dispensed medicine to Tønder's townspeople. In 1989, the pharmacy was converted into a Danish gift and crafts center, but the entire building, both inside and out, was left intact. The beautifully carved front entranceway opens onto a vintage interior lined with pharmaceutical artifacts and medicine jars. Craft items for sale include antique stationery and pens, and handmade candles, glassware, and ceramics. From March to September, the cellar bursts with Danish Christmas items, from tree decorations and festive paper cutouts to elves and angels.

Rømø

❸ *34 km (21 mi) northwest of Tønder, 30 km (19 mi) southwest of Ribe.*

The lush island of Rømø boasts one of Denmark's widest beaches, which unfurls along the island's sunny western coast. Rømø has just 850 permanent residents, but masses of vacationing German and Danish families increase this number tenfold in summer. A 10-km (6-mi) causeway crosses green fields and marshy wetlands to connect Rømø to the mainland. A varied birdlife lives here, feeding off the seaweed and shellfish washed up by the tides. Summer houses dot the island; most of Rømø's services and accommodations are in and around the village of Havneby, 8 km (5 mi) south of the causeway, and in the camping and shopping complex of Lakkolk, in the west.

The 18th century was a golden age in Rømø's seafaring history, when more than 50 local sailors were appointed captains of Dutch and German whaling expeditions to Greenland. Upon their return, the newly prosperous captains built lavish farmsteads, such as **Kommandørgård** (Captain's House), in Toftum, 2 km (1 mi) north of the causeway. Part of the Danish National Museum, this stately, thatch-roof–and–brick farmhouse, dating from 1874, has been meticulously restored, with opulent period furnishings including brass-lined chests and marble-top tables. Blue-and-white glazed Dutch tiles cover the walls, alongside hand-painted rococo panels and doors. ⊠ *Juvrevej 60, Toftum* ☎*74/75–52–76* ⊕ *www.natmus.dk* ⊠ *Dkr 20* ◷ *May–Sept., Tues.–Sun. 10–6; Oct., Tues.–Sat. 10–3.*

Just north of the Captain's House, in the tiny village of Juvre, is a **whale jawbone fence** built in 1772. Lacking wood and stone, villagers constructed this fence from the whalebones that Rømø captains brought back from Greenland.

Off the main road south of the causeway rises the whitewashed, 18th-century **Rømø Kirke** (Rømø Church), dedicated to St. Clemens, the patron saint of fisherman and sailors. Inside are several hand-painted ship models. The churchyard gravestones, brought back by Rømø captains, are made of Greenlandic stone and carved with depictions of ships. ✉ *Havnebyvej 152* ☎ *no phone* ⏱ *Tues.–Fri. 8–4.*

Where to Stay & Eat

$–$$ ✕⌂ **Hotel Færgegaarden.** In the costal village of Havneby, this holiday hotel has basic rooms with white bedspreads and flowery pillows. The cozy maritime-theme restaurant, with a brick fireplace, Dutch-tile walls, and model ships, serves simple Danish-French fare, including fried plaice with butter sauce. ✉ *Vesterg. 1, DK–6792 Havneby* ☎ *74/75–54–32* 🖷 *74/75–58–59* ⊕ *www.faergegaarden.dk* 🛏 *35 rooms* ⚫ *Restaurant, pool, bar* ⊟ *AE, DC, MC, V.*

Ribe

★ ❹ *60 km (36 mi) southwest of Kolding, 150 km (103 mi) southwest of Århus.*

In the southwestern corner of Jylland, the country's oldest town is well worth the detour for its medieval center preserved by the Danish National Trust. From May to mid-September, a night watchman circles the town, recalling its history and singing traditional songs. If you want to accompany him, gather at the main square at 10 PM.

The **Ribe Domkirke** (Ribe Cathedral) stands on the site of one of Denmark's earliest churches, built around AD 860. The present structure, which dates from the 12th century, is built of a volcanic tufa stone, transported by boats from quarries in Cologne, France. Note the Cat Head Door, said to be for the exclusive use of the devil. The 14th-century brick bell tower once clanged out flood and fire warnings to Ribe's citizens, and today affords sweeping views of the town's red slate rooftops and surrounding marshes. ✉ *Torvet 15* ☎ *75/42–06–19* 🎫 *Dkr 12* ⏱ *May–Sept., Mon.–Sat. 10–5, Sun. noon–5; Oct. and Apr., Mon.–Sat. 11–4, Sun. noon–3; Nov.–Mar., Mon.–Sat. 11–3, Sun. noon–3. Call first to confirm hrs.*

The **Ribes Vikinger** (Ribe Viking Museum) chronicles Viking history with conventional exhibits of household goods, tools, and clothing. There's a multimedia room with an interactive computer screen where you can search for more Viking information in the form of text, pictures, and videos. ✉ *Odinspl.* ☎ *76/88–11–33* ⊕ *www.ribesvikinger.dk* 🎫 *Dkr 50* ⏱ *June–Aug., daily 10–6; Apr., May, Sept., and Oct., daily 10–4; Nov.–Mar., Tues.–Sun. 10–4.*

Take Bus 57 (confirm with the driver) from the railway station across the street from the Ribes Vikinger. The bus travels 2 km (1 mi) south and arrives at the **Viking Center,** an outdoor exhibit detailing how the Vikings lived day-to-day, with demonstrations about homes, food, and crafts. ✉ *Lustrupvej 4, Lustrupholm* ☎ *75/41–16–11* ⊕ *www.ribevikingecenter.dk* 🎫 *Dkr 60* ⏱ *May, June and Sept., weekdays 11–4; July and Aug., daily 11–4:30.*

Where to Stay & Eat

¢–$ ✕ **Sælhunden.** The 300-year-old canal-side "Seal Tavern" barely holds a dozen tables, but its cosiness draws both wayfarers and locals. The only seal mementos left are a few skins and pictures, but you can still order a "seal's special" of cold shrimp, sautéed potatoes, and scrambled eggs or—an old Danish favorite—fat strips of pork served with cream gravy and boiled potatoes (only served on winter Wednesdays). Console yourself in summer with *rød grød med fløde* (red porridge with cream); the pronunciation of this dessert—which defies phonetic spelling—

is so difficult that Danes get a kick out of making foreigners pronounce it. ⊠ *Skibbroen 13* ☎ *75/42–09–46* ▭ *DC, MC, V* ☉ *Closed after 8:45 PM.*

$$–$$$
Fodor'sChoice
★
✕⊡ **Hotel Dagmar.** In Ribe's quaint center, this cozy half-timber hotel encapsulates the charm of the 16th century—with stained-glass windows, sloping wooden floors, and carved chairs. The lavish rooms have antique canopy beds, fat armchairs, and chaise longues. The fine Danish-French restaurant serves such specialties as fillet of salmon in sorrel cream sauce. For drinks and light meals, descend into the atmospheric cellar restaurant-bar, with beamed ceilings and colorfully tiled pillars. ⊠ *Torvet 1, DK–6760* ☎ *75/42–00–33* 🖷 *75/42–36–52* ⊕ *www.hoteldagmar.dk* ⊷ *48 rooms* ⚙ *Restaurant, bar, meeting room, some pets allowed* ▭ *AE, DC, MC, V.*

$–$$
Fodor'sChoice
★
⊡ **Den Gamle Arrest.** Spend the night in the clink at "The Old Jail," a simple yet cozy hotel housed in what was Ribe's main jail from 1893 to 1989. The artist-owner has done a brilliant job of modernizing the cells into comfortably habitable rooms, while preserving all the prison details. The cells, which used to house five prisoners, have been creatively refashioned into single and double rooms with lofts in which the bed can be stored during the day. The tiny windows, once covered with mesh-like gratings so that prisoners couldn't see outside, now offer glimpses of blue sky. The original prison gates, with iron bars and padlocks, still serve as the entrances into the hallways. The prison dungeons have been converted into a sprawling gift shop with handmade Danish crafts, from inventive candles and glassware to hundreds of Christmas decorations. The former guardroom, which opens onto the prison yard–turned–terrace, is now a clothing store with fashions by Danish designers. ⊠ *Torvet 11, DK–6760* ☎ *75/42–37–00* 🖷 *75/42–37–22* ⊕ *www.dengamlearrest.dk* ⊷ *11 rooms, 2 with bath* ⚙ *Café.*

¢
⊡ **Danhostel Ribe.** In the town center, this plain, redbrick hostelry has six- and four-bed family rooms arranged in clusters of two, each with its own private bath and toilet in a small hallway. There are also double rooms with private bath and eight four-bed rooms with completely private facilities. They are functional and childproof, with pine bunks and industrial carpeting. A kitchen is available. ⊠ *Ribehallen, Skt. Pedersg. 16, DK–6760* ☎ *75/42–06–20* 🖷 *75/42–42–88* ⊕ *www.danhostel-ribe.dk* ⊷ *152 beds in 40 shared rooms, 38 with bath* ⚙ *Cafeteria* ▭ *No credit cards* ☉ *Closed Dec. and Jan.*

Shopping

Antikgaarden (⊠ Overdammen 5 ☎ 75/41–00–55) has a varied collection of Danish antiques, including old Royal Copenhagen plates. **Idé Butik Aps** (⊠ Overdammen 4 ☎ 75/42–14–14) sells Danish crafts ranging from paper cutouts and glassware to figurines of Danish *nisser* (elves). For amber jewelry, head to **Rav I Ribe** (⊠ Nedderdammen 32 ☎ 75/42–03–88), one of the largest amber purveyors in town.

Esbjerg

❺ *35 km (22 mi) northwest of Ribe, 145 km (90 mi) southwest of Århus.*

The thriving port town of Esbjerg is the capital of South Jylland and Denmark's fifth largest city. Esbjerg's nerve center is its formidable harbor, crowded with fishing trawlers, tankers, and ferries. Scandinavian Seaways operates ferries from here for the 20-hour journey to Harwich, England.

Founded in 1868, Esbjerg is Denmark's youngest town, with a pleasant mish-mash of architectural styles, including stately turn-of-the-20th-century brick government buildings. The fortified **water tower** (⊠ Havneg.

22 ☎ 75/12–78–11) was built in a medieval German design. Climb to the top (admission is Dkr 10) for splendid views of Esbjerg and the sea. Reigning over Esbjerg's central square is a statue of Christian IX, who was in power when Esbjerg was founded.

The highlight at the **Esbjerg Museum** is its amber collection, one of the largest in Denmark. The west coast of Jylland is well-known for being rich in amber. Detailed exhibits trace the history of amber along the Jylland coast over a whopping 10,000-year period. ⊠ *Torveg. 45* ☎ *75/ 12–78–11* ⊕ *www.esbjergmuseum.dk* 🔤 *Dkr 30, free Wed.* ☉ *June–Aug., daily 10–4; Sept.–May, Tues.–Sun. 10–4.*

The **Esbjerg Kunstmuseum** (Esbjerg Art Museum) showcases a fine collection of Danish contemporary art, including works by Richard Mortensen. Innovative temporary exhibits feature up-and-coming Danish artists, and have included a retrospective of Danish mobile art and avant-garde sculptures and installations. ⊠ *Havneg. 20* ☎ *75/13–02–11* 🔤 *Dkr 30* ☉ *June–Dec., daily 10–4.*

One of Esbjerg's most striking sights is the giant whitewashed sculpture by Danish artist Svend Wiig Hansen entitled *Menesket ved Havet* (*Man Meets Sea*), depicting four 19-foot-tall men staring solemnly out to sea.

Where to Stay & Eat

$$$ ✕ **Sand's Restauration.** Founded in 1907, this warm, dimly lit restaurant is one of Esbjerg's oldest. The creative Danish menu includes garlic-marinated ostrich steak with red-wine gravy and panfried haddock drizzled with a sweet-and-sour sauce. The original owners collected more than 50 works of art by West Jylland artists, which now cover the walls. ⊠ *Jyllandsg. 32* ☎ *75/12–02–07* ▤ *MC, V* ☉ *Closed Sun.*

¢–$ 🏨 **Palads Cab Inn.** In the heart of Esbjerg is this budget hotel, affiliated with the popular Cab-Inn Copenhagen chain. The rooms have pale green walls and purple flowery bedspreads, and all are equipped with a TV and telephone. The smaller "cabin" rooms are also comfortable and clean. Breakfast, included in the price, is served in a colossal, high-ceiling dining room that once served as a ballroom. ⊠ *Skoleg. 14, DK–6700* ☎ *75/ 18–16–00* 🖷 *75/18–16–24* ⊕ *www.cabinn.dk* 📫 *107 rooms with bath* 🍴 *Cafeteria, bar, no-smoking rooms* ▤ *AE, DC, MC, V.*

Nightlife & the Arts

Pubs dot Esbjerg's main drag, Skolegade. In the center of town is the friendly restaurant-bar **Dronning Louise** (⊠ Torvet 19 ☎ 75/13–13–44), named after Queen Louise, the wife of Christian IX. The bar has red-leather chairs and a wall lined with bookshelves. In the upstairs club, a DJ spins dance tunes on Friday and Saturday nights. Esbjerg locals flock to the live Saturday-afternoon jazz sessions that start at 1 PM. In summer, the jazz is performed on a terrace that faces the main square. The adjoining restaurant serves light lunches (burgers, club sandwiches, and chicken wings) and a Danish dinner menu of meat and fish dishes.

Fanø

6 *30 km (19 mi) northwest of Ribe, plus 12-min ferry from Esbjerg, 153 km (96 mi) southwest of Århus, plus 12-min ferry from Esbjerg.*

During the 19th century, this tiny island had an enormous shipbuilding industry and a fleet second only to Copenhagen's. The shipping industry deteriorated, but the proud maritime heritage remains. Today, Fanø is a summer oasis for legions of Danes and other Northern Europeans. Silky sand beaches unfold along the west coast, buffered by windswept dunes and green reeds. Cars are allowed on the beach, and it's well worth taking a ride along the flat sandy coast between the ferry port in Nordby, Fanø's capital, and the traditional town of Sønderho, in the south. Spinning along the white sandy expanse is like crossing a desert; only the dark blue sea off in the distance reminds you of your island whereabouts. The beach is so level and wide that the military used to train here. In the off season, when the summer visitors have packed up and returned home, the Fanø shore becomes a tranquil retreat, hauntingly silent save for the rustle of reeds and the far-off squawk of a bird.

The old-fashioned village of Sønderho, 13 km (8 mi) south of Nordby, has tiny winding lanes and thatch-roof cottages decorated with ships' relics, figureheads, painted doors, and brass lanterns. You may even see people wearing the traditional costumes, especially on Sønderhodag, a town festival held on the third Sunday in July.

Fanø's annual kite festival, held in mid-June, draws scores of aficionados who fill the sky with hundreds of their colorful, swooping kites.

Where to Stay & Eat

★ **$–$$** ✕ **Café Nanas Stue.** This half-timber farmhouse restaurant, dating from 1854, doubles as the **Fanø Flisemuseum** (Fanø Tile Museum). The walls and old-fashioned wooden cupboards are lined with glazed Dutch tiles, brought back by Danish sailors from the 17th to 19th centuries. The handmade tiles, usually in blue and white, depict everything from bible stories and ships at sea to frolicking children. After their introduction to Denmark in the 1600s, the tiles became a characteristic part of most Fanø homes. The restaurant is a favorite among locals, who gather around the wooden tables to tuck into traditional Danish fare, including smørrebrød and pepper steak topped with a cognac sauce. Round out the meal with a taste of their specialty drink, a potent aquavit flavored with orange, vanilla, and coffee beans. In summer, local musicians perform traditional Fanø folk music on the violin, guitar, bagpipe, and harmonica. Inquire at the tourist office for a schedule. ⊠ *Sønderland 1* ☎ *75/16–40–25* ▤ *MC, V* ☺ *No dinner Sun. Closed Mon. Aug.–Sept.; closed Mon.–Thurs. Oct.–May.*

★ **$$–$$$** ✕▢ **Sønderho Kro.** In the heart of Sønderho, this 270-year-old thatch-roof inn is one of Jylland's finest, its charm preserved with painted doors and beamed ceilings. Rooms are jazzed up with four-poster beds, elegant tapestries, and gauzy curtains. The French-Danish restaurant serves excellent seafood. ⊠ *Kropl. 11, DK–6720, Sønderho* ☎ *75/16–40–09* ▤ *75/16–43–85* ⊕ *www.sonderhokro.dk* ➷ *14 rooms with bath* ♨ *Restaurant, some pets allowed* ▤ *AE, DC, MC, V* ☺ *Closed Feb. and weekdays Nov.–Jan.*

Billund

❼ *101 km (63 mi) southwest of Århus.*

🏵 Billund's claim to fame is **Legoland**, an amusement park in which everything is constructed from 45 million plastic Lego bricks. Among its incredible structures are scaled-down versions of cities and villages, working harbors and airports, the Statue of Liberty, a statue of Sitting Bull, Mt. Rushmore, a safari park, and Pirate Land. Grown-ups might marvel at toys from pre-Lego days, the most exquisite of which is Titania's Palace, a sumptuous dollhouse built in 1907 by Sir Neville Wilkinson for his daughter. The Lego empire is expanding: the company's goal is to open one park globally every three years, but Danes maintain that theirs, the original, will always be the best. The park also has a massive theme building–ride–restaurant extravaganza that's much better ex-

FodorsChoice ★

perienced than described. It all takes place within the massive Castle-land, where guests arrive via a serpentine dragon ride. Most everything inside is made of the ubiquitous bricks, including the wizards and war-locks, dragons, and knights that inhabit it. At the Knight's Barbecue, waiters in Middle Ages garb hustle skewered haunches of beef, "loooong sausages," and typical fare of the period. ⊠ *Normarksvej 9* ☎ *75/ 33–13–33* ⊕ *www.legoland.dk* ⊠ *Dkr 170* ☉ *Apr., May, Sept., and Oct., weekdays 10–6, weekends 10–8; June and late Aug., daily 10–8; July–mid-Aug., daily 10–9.*

Vejle

❽ *40 km (25 mi) east of Billund, 73 km (46 mi) southwest of Århus.*

Vejle is beautifully positioned on a fjord on the east coast, amid forest-clad hills. You can hear the time of day chiming on the old **Dominican monastery clock**; the clock remains, but the monastery long ago gave way to the town's imposing 19th-century city hall.

In the town center, at Kirke Torvet, is **Skt. Nikolai Kirke** (St. Nicholas Church). In the left arm of the cross-shaped church, lying in a glass Empire-style coffin, is the body of a bog woman found preserved in a peat marsh in 1835; she dates to 500 BC. The church walls contain the skulls of 23 thieves executed in the 17th century. ⊠ *Kirke Torvet* ☎ *75/ 82–41–39* ☉ *May–Sept., weekdays 9–5, Sat. 9–noon, Sun. 9–11:30.*

Where to Stay & Eat

$$$$ 🏨 **Munkebjerg Hotel.** Seven kilometers (4½ mi) southeast of town and sur-rounded by a thick beech forest and majestic views of the Vejle Fjord, this elegant hotel attracts guests who value their privacy. Beyond the rus-tic lobby, rooms furnished in blond pine and soft green overlook the for-est. There are also two top-notch French-Danish restaurants and a swank casino. ⊠ *Munkebjergvej 125, DK–7100* ☎ *75/42–85–00* ☎ *75/72–08–86* ⊕ *www.munkebjerg.dk* ⤳ *149 rooms, 3 suites* ☼ *3 restaurants, cafe-teria, tennis court, indoor pool, gym, sauna, bar, casino, meeting room, some pets allowed, no-smoking rooms* ☰ *AE, DC, MC, V.*

$ 🏨 **Park Hotel.** Centrally located and offering very spacious rooms con-sidering the small stature of this establishment, the pleasant service caps off an overall enjoyable experience and ensures return visits from its patrons. A bountiful breakfast is included in the price, and the restau-rant is good though perhaps a bit thin on variety. ⊠ *Orla Lehmannsg. 5, DK–7100* ☎ *75/82–24–66* ☎ *75/72–05–39* ⊕ *www.park-hotel.dk* ⤳ *33 rooms with bath* ☼ *Restaurant, bar, some pets allowed* ☰ *AE, DC, MC, V.*

Nightlife

The casino at the **Munkebjerg Hotel** (⊠ Munkebjergvej 125 ☎ 75/ 72–35–00) has blackjack, roulette, baccarat, and slot machines.

Jelling

❾ *10 km (6 mi) northwest of Vejle (via Rte. 18), 83 km (52 mi) southwest of Århus.*

In Jelling, two 10th-century burial mounds mark the seat of King Gorm and his wife, Thyra. Between the mounds are two **Runestener** (runic stones), one of which is Denmark's certificate of baptism, showing the oldest known figure of Christ in Scandinavia. The inscription explains that the stone was erected by Gorm's son, King Harald Bluetooth, who brought Christianity to the Danes in 960.

The most scenic way to get to Jelling is via the **vintage steam train** that runs from Vejle every Sunday in July and the first Sunday in August. Call the Jelling tourist office for schedules.

Silkeborg

❿ *60 km (38 mi) north of Jelling, 43 km (27 mi) west of Århus.*

At the banks of the River Gudenå begins Jylland's lake district. Stretching southeast from Silkeborg to Skanderborg, the area contains some of Denmark's loveliest scenery and most of its meager mountains, including the 438-foot **Himmelbjerget**, at Julsø (Lake Jul), 15 km (10 mi) southeast of Silkeborg. You can climb the narrow paths through the heather and trees to the top, where an 80-foot tower stands sentinel. It was placed there on Constitution Day in 1875 in memory of King Frederik VII.

In late June, jazz-lovers from all over Europe come to celebrate Silkeborg's **Riverboat Jazz Festival** (☎ 86/80–16–17 ⊕ www.riverboat.dk), with live jazz performed on indoor and outdoor stages.

The best way to explore the lake district is by water, as the Gudenå winds its way some 160 km (100 mi) through lakes and wooded hillsides down to the sea. Take one of the excursion boats or the world's last coal-fired paddle steamer, *Hjejlen*, which departs in summer from Silkeborg Harbor. Since 1861 it has paddled its way through narrow stretches of fjord, where the treetops meet overhead, to the foot of the Himmelbjerget. ⊠ *Havnen* ☎ *86/82–07–66* 🎟 *Dkr 90* ☉ *Mid-June–Aug.*

The **Silkeborg Museum** houses the city's main attractions: the 2,200-year-old Tollund Man and Elling Girl, two bog people preserved by the chemicals in the soil and water. Discovered in 1950, the Tollund Man remains the best-preserved human face from the Iron Age. He was killed by strangulation—the noose remains around his neck—with a day's worth of stubble that can still be seen on his hauntingly serene face. ⊠ *Hovedgårdsvej 7* ☎ *86/82–14–99* ⊕ *www.silkeborgmuseum.dk* 🎟 *Dkr 40* ☉ *May–mid-Oct., daily 10–5; mid-Oct.–Apr., Wed. and weekends noon–4.*

Where to Eat

$$$–$$$$ ✕ **Aalekroen.** Also known as Onkel Peters Hus (Uncle Peter's Place), this spot is noted for its house specialties, fried eel and seafood. The grilled meat dishes are also an excellent choice. This old inn stands at the shore of a scenic lake, an aspect that adds to dining pleasure. ⊠ *Julsøvænget 5* ☎ *86/84–60–33* 🖃 *AE, DC, MC, V* ☉ *Closed Mon.*

Århus

▶ **⓫** *40 km (24 mi) east of Silkeborg.*

Århus is Denmark's second-largest city, and, with its funky arts and college community, one of its most pleasant. Cutting through the center of town is a canal called the Århus Å (Århus Creek). It used to run underground, but was uncovered a few years ago. Since then, an amalgam of bars, cafés, and restaurants has sprouted along its banks, creating one of Denmark's most lively thoroughfares. At all hours of the day and night, this waterfront strip is abuzz with crowds that hang out on the outdoor terraces and steps down to the creek.

The tourist office has information about the **Århus Pass,** which includes passage on buses, free or discounted admission to museums and sites, and tours. A one-day pass is Dkr 97, a two-day pass is Dkr 121, and a seven-day pass is Dkr 171.

The town comes most alive during the first week of September, when the **Århus Festival** (☎ 89/40–91–91 ⊕ www.aarhusfestuge.dk) begins, combining concerts, theater, and art exhibitions with beer tents and sports. The **Århus International Jazz Festival** bills international and local greats in early or mid-July. In July, the **Viking Moot** draws aficionados to the beach below the Museum of Prehistory at Moesgård. Activities and exhibits include market booths, ancient defense techniques, and rides on Viking ships.

The **Rådhus** is probably the most unusual city hall in Denmark. Built in 1941 by noted architects Arne Jacobsen and Erik Møller, the pale Norwegian-marble block building is controversial but cuts a startling figure when illuminated in the evening. ⊠ *Park Allé* ☎ *89/40–67–00* ☜ *City hall Dkr 10, tower Dkr 5* ⊙ *Guided tours (in Danish only) mid-June–early Sept., weekdays at 11; tower tours weekdays at noon and 2.*

Rising gracefully over the center of town, the **Århus Domkirke** (Århus Cathedral) was originally built in 1201 in a Romanesque style but was later expanded and redesigned into a Gothic cathedral in the 15th century. Its soaring, whitewashed nave is one of the longest in Denmark. The cathedral's highlights include its chalk frescoes, in shades of lavender, yellow, red, and black that grace the high arches and towering walls. Dating from the Middle Ages, the frescoes depict biblical scenes, including the valiant St. George slaying a dragon and saving a maiden princess in distress. Also illustrated is the poignant death of St. Clement who drowned from an anchor tied around his neck. Nonetheless, he became the patron saint of sailors. Climb the tower for bird's-eye views of the rooftops and thronged streets of Århus. ⊠ *Bispetorv* ☎ *86/20–54–00* ⊕ *www.aarhus-domkirke.dk* ☜ *Tower Dkr 10* ⊙ *Jan.–Apr. and Oct.–Dec., Mon.–Sat. 10–3; May–Sept., Mon.–Sat. 9:30–4.*

★ Don't miss the town's open-air museum, known as **Den Gamle By** (Old Town). Its 70 half-timber houses, mill, and millstream were carefully moved from locations throughout Denmark and meticulously re-created, inside and out. ⊠ *Viborgvej* ☎ *86/12–31–88* ⊕ *www.dengamleby.dk* ☜ *Dkr 45–Dkr 75 depending on season and activities* ⊙ *June–Aug., daily 9–6; Apr., May, Sept., and Oct., daily 10–5; Jan., daily 11–3; Feb., Mar., Nov., and Dec., daily 10–4. Grounds always open.*

Just south of the city is **Marselisborg Slot** (Marselisborg Castle), the palatial summer residence of the royal family. The changing of the guard takes place daily at noon when the Queen is staying in the palace. When the royal family is away (generally in the winter and spring), the palace grounds, including a sumptuous rose garden, are open to the public. ⊠ *Kongevejen 100* ☎ *no phone* ☜ *Free.*

In a 250-acre forest south of Århus is the **Moesgård Forhistorisk Museum** (Prehistoric Museum), with exhibits on ethnography and archaeology, including the famed Grauballe Man, a 2,000-year-old corpse so well preserved in a bog that scientists could determine his last meal. In fact, when the discoverers of the Grauballe Man stumbled upon him in 1952, they thought he had recently been murdered and called the police. The Forhistorisk vej (Prehistoric Trail) through the forest leads past Stone- and Bronze Age displays to reconstructed houses from Viking times. ⊠ *Moesgård Allé (Bus 6 from the center of town)* ☎ *89/42–11–00* ⊕ *www.moesmus.dk* ☜ *Dkr 45* ⊙ *Apr.–Sept., daily 10–5; Oct.–Mar., Tues.–Sun. 10–4.*

☺ If you are in Århus with children, visit its provincial **Tivoli**, with rides, music, and lovely gardens. ⊠ *Skovbrynet* ☎ *86/14–73–00* ☜ *Dkr 35* ⊙ *Late Apr.–mid-June, daily 2–10; mid-June–early Aug., daily 1–11.*

Where to Stay & Eat

$$$–$$$$ ✕ **Restaurant Margueritten.** Tucked into a cobbled courtyard, this cheery restaurant is housed in former stables, which accounts for the low wood-beam ceiling. Well-worn wooden tables and tan walls round out the warm atmosphere. Contemporary Danish fare includes guinea fowl stuffed with tiger shrimp and marinated in tandoori and yogurt, and chicken breast served with Italian ham. ⊠ *Guldsmedg. 20* ☎ *86/19–60–33* ⊟ *AE, DC, MC, V.*

$$–$$$$ ✕ **Seafood.** Just south of town is Marselis Harbor, a bustling little sail-
FodorsChoice boat cove surrounded by waterfront restaurants and cafés that draw big
★ crowds on sunny summer weekends. Here you'll find Seafood, one of the best seafood restaurants in Århus. Its signature dish, which draws moans of delight from diners, is a seafood bouillabaisse heaped with tiger prawns, squid, Norwegian lobster, and mussels, and served with aioli on the side. Other dishes include oven-baked catfish with aspara-gus and warm ginger butter. The restful interior has light-blue walls. ⊠ *Havnevej 44, Marselisborg* ☎ *86/18–56–55* ⊟ *AE, DC, MC, V* ✆ *Closed Sun. Sept.–Apr.*

$$$ ✕ **Prins Ferdinand.** Sitting on the edge of Old Town, this premier Dan-ish-French restaurant is named after the colorful Århus-based Prince Fred-erik (1792–1863), who was much loved despite his fondness for gambling and carousing about town. Here, elegant crystal chandeliers hang over large round tables with crisp linen tablecloths and ceramic plates cre-ated by a local artist. Vases of sunflowers brighten the front room. Grilled turbot is topped with a cold salsa of radishes, cucumber, and dill. Cabbage, foie gras, and new potatoes accompany a venison dish. A daily vegetarian option is offered, and might include grilled aspara-gus with potatoes, olives, and herbs. ⊠ *Viborgvej 2* ☎ *86/12–52–05* ⊟ *AE, DC, MC, V* ✆ *Closed Sun.–Mon.*

¢–$$ ✕ **Bryggeriet Sct. Clemens.** At this popular pub, you can sit among cop-
FodorsChoice per kettles and quaff the local brew, which is unfiltered and without ad-
★ ditives, just like in the old days. Between the spareribs and Australian steaks, you won't go hungry either. ⊠ *Kannikeg. 10–12* ☎ *86/13–80–00* ⊟ *AE, DC, MC, V.*

$$$ ✕▣ **Philip.** Occupying a prime spot along the canal, this hotel offers an original—but pricey—concept in lodging. Eight former studio apartments have been converted into luxury suites, each outfitted in its own sump-tuous style. Suites have original white wood-beam ceilings, elegant wooden furniture imported from France and Italy, huge gleaming bath-rooms, and views of the canal. The plush restaurant, with dark hard-wood floors and brass candleholders, serves a blend of cuisines that may include cannelloni stuffed with Serrano ham, Danish feta, and crayfish and served with truffles and new potatoes. ⊠ *Åboulevarden 28, DK–8000* ☎ *87/32–14–44* 🖷 *87/32–69–55* ⊕ *www.hotelphilip.dk* ➷ *8 suites* ♨ *Restaurant, bar* ⊟ *DC, MC, V.*

★ $$$$ ▣ **Royal Hotel.** In operation since 1838, Århus's grand hotel has wel-comed such greats as musicians Arthur Rubinstein and Marian Ander-son. Well-heeled guests enter through a stately lobby appointed with sofas, modern paintings, and a winding staircase. Plush rooms vary in style and decor, but all have velour and brocade furniture and marble bath-rooms. ⊠ *Store Torv 4, DK–8100* ☎ *86/12–00–11* 🖷 *86/76–04–04* ⊕ *www.hotelroyal.dk* ➷ *98 rooms, 7 suites* ♨ *Restaurant, cafeteria, sauna, bar, casino, some pets allowed* ⊟ *AE, DC, MC, V.*

$ ▣ **Hotel Guldsmeden.** Small and intimate, this hotel with a personal touch is housed in a renovated 19th-century town house. The soothing rooms are dressed in cool greens and yellows and have teak shelves. The sunny garden blooms with flowers in summer, and the outdoor terrace is just the spot to enjoy the organic breakfast of fruit, muesli, toast, and marmalade. ⊠ *Guldsmedg. 40, DK–8000* ☎ *86/13–45–50* 🖷 *86/13–76–76* ⊕ *www.hotelguldsmeden.dk* 🖘 *20 rooms, 14 with bath* ♘ *Bar, some pets allowed* ⊟ *AE, DC, MC, V.*

¢ 🖸 **Danhostel Århus.** As in all Danish youth and family hostels, the rooms here are clean, bright, and functional. The secluded setting in the woods near the fjord is downright beautiful. Unfortunately, the hostel can get a bit noisy. Guests may use the kitchen. ⊠ *Marienlundsvej 10, DK–8100* ☎ *86/16–72–98* 🖷 *86/10–55–60* ⊕ *www.hostel-aarhus.dk* 🖘 *138 beds in 30 shared rooms, 11 with private shower* ♘ *Dining room* ⊟ *AE, MC, V* ☉ *Closed mid-Dec.–mid-Jan.*

Nightlife & the Arts

There's no better time to visit Århus than during the 10-day **Århus Festival Week** in early September, when jazz, classical, and rock concerts are nonstop, in addition to drama, theater, and dance.

BARS, LOUNGES & DISCOS   As in most other towns, the local discos come and go with remarkable frequency; stop by at a local café for the latest on what's happening. A prime spot to start—and perhaps end—your night is along the Århus Å, which is thronged with bars and cafés. **Carlton** (⊠ Rosensg. 23 ☎ 86/20–21–22) is a classy bar and restaurant, presided over by a carousel horse. Sip cocktails in the front bar–café, or dine on contemporary Danish fare in the dining room. The friendly **Café Jorden** (⊠ Badstueg. 3 ☎ 86/19–72–22) has a brass-and-wood bar and a heated outdoor terrace with a red awning. Students and young professionals mix with the chatty bar staff, who like to sing along to the pop and rock classics. The ★ **Café Under Masken** (Under the Mask Café; ⊠ Bispeg. 3 ☎ 86/18–22–66), next door to the Royal Hotel, is the personal creation of Århus artist Hans Krull, who also designed the unique iron sculptures that grace the entrance to the hotel. The surreal bar is crammed with every type of mask imaginable, from grinning Balinese wooden masks to black-and-yellow African visages. Pygmy statues and stuffed tropical birds and fish line the shelves. Everything was collected by Krull and other bar patrons. The back wall is one long aquarium filled with exotic fish. As the bar manager puts it, "Everyone's welcome. This bar is a no-man's-land, a place for all the 'funny fish' of the world." If that's not enough of a draw, consider that the drink prices are the lowest in town, and more than 30 kinds of beer are on offer. The **Hotel Marselis** (⊠ Strandvejen 25 ☎ 86/14–44–11) attracts a varied crowd to its two venues: the **Beach Club**, with danceable rock and disco, and the more elegant **Nautilus** piano bar. **Sidewalk** (⊠ Åboulevarden 56–58 ☎ 86/18–18–66) has a large waterfront terrace that draws crowds on warm nights; in the equally lively interior you can sip cocktails at the long bar or graze on tapas and light meals, including hummus with olives and salad topped with soy-roasted chicken and spinach pasta.

CASINO   The **Royal Hotel** (⊠ Store Torv 4 ☎ 86/12–00–11), the city's casino, offers blackjack, roulette, baccarat, and slot machines.

JAZZ CLUBS   For jazz, head to **Bent J's** (⊠ Nørre Allé 66 ☎ 86/12–04–92), a small club with free-admission jam sessions three times a week and occasional big-name concerts. **Café Brasserie Svej** (⊠ Åboulevarden 22 ☎ 86/12–30–31), on the canal, hosts live jazz acts on Sunday at 1 PM. **Lion's Pub** (⊠ Rosensg. 21 ☎ 86/13–00–45) showcases live jazz on Friday night (mid-August through May) in its downstairs club, which is lined with black-and-white photos of jazz greats. A small stage faces several long tables that fill up with toe-tapping jazz aficionados.

The state-of-the-art **Musikhuset Århus** (Århus Concert Hall; ⊠ Thomas Jensens Allé 2 ☎ 89/40–40–40) has a splendid glass foyer housing palm trees and a fine Danish-French restaurant. The concert hall showcases theater, opera, ballet, and concerts of all kinds, from classical music to rock. In summer it often hosts free musical and theater performances on its outdoor stages; ask at the tourist office for a schedule.

Shopping

Stylish yet laid-back, Århus is a grand place to shop. Søndergade, the main pedestrian strip through town, is lined with clothing, jewelry, and home-furnishing stores. As befits a student town, Århus also has its "Latin Quarter," a jumble of cobbled streets around the cathedral, with boutiques, antiques shops, and glass and ceramic galleries. At the **Bülow Duus Glassworks** (⊠ Studsg. 14 ☎ 86/12–72–86), you can browse among delicate and colorful glassworks from fishbowls to candleholders. **Folmer Hansen** (⊠ Sønderg. 43 ☎ 86/12–49–00) is packed with Danish tableware and porcelain, from sleek Arne Jacobsen–designed cheese cutters, ice buckets, and coffeepots to Royal Copenhagen porcelain plates. For the best selection of Georg Jensen designs, head to the official **Georg Jensen** (⊠ Sønderg. 1 ☎ 86/12–01–00) store. It stocks Jensen-designed and -inspired watches, jewelry, table settings, and art nouveau vases.

Ebeltoft

⑫ *45 km (28 mi) east of Århus.*

Danes refer to Ebeltoft—a town of crooked streets, sloping row houses, and crafts shops—as Jylland's nose. In the middle of the main square is Ebeltoft's half-timber **Det Gamle Rådhus** (Old Town Hall), said to be the smallest town hall in Denmark. Dating from 1789, it served as the town hall until 1840; today it is an annex of the Ebeltoft Museum, with historical exhibits displayed in its traditionally decorated rooms. The mayor still receives visitors here, and couples come from all over Denmark to be married in the quaint interior.

Near the town hall is the **Ebeltoft Museum**, which holds the Siamesisk Samling (Siamese Exhibit), a motley collection of Thai artifacts—from silks and stuffed lemurs to mounted tropical insects—brought back by explorer and Ebeltoft local Rasmus Havmøller. The museum also encompasses the nearby well-preserved dye-works factory, where the Ebeltoft peasants had their wool dyed until 1925. In summer, dyeing demonstrations are often held. ⊠ *Juulsbakke 1* ☎ *86/34–55–99* 🖙 *Dkr 25 (includes the town hall)* ⊙ *June–Aug., daily 10–5; Sept.–mid-Oct., Apr., and May, Sat.–Thurs. 11–3; mid-Oct.–Dec., Feb., and Mar., weekends 11–3.*

Danish efficiency is on display beside the ferry at the **Vindmølleparken,** one of the largest windmill parks in the world. Sixteen wind-powered mills on a curved spit of land generate electricity for 600 families. ⊠ *Færgehaven* ☎ *86/34–12–44* 🖙 *Free* ⊙ *Daily.*

You can't miss the **Frigate Jylland,** dry-docked on the town's main harbor. The renovation of the three-masted tall ship was financed by Danish shipping magnate Mærsk McKinney Møller, and it's a testament to Denmark's seafaring days of yore. You can wander through to examine the bridge, gun deck, galley, captain's room, and the 10½-ton pure copper and pewter screw. Don't miss the voluptuous Pomeranian pine figurehead. ⊠ *Strandvejen 4* ☎ *86/34–10–99* ⊕ *www.fregatten-jylland. dk* 🖙 *Dkr 60* ⊙ *Mid-June–Aug., daily 10–7; Apr.–mid-June, Sept., and Oct., daily 10–6; Nov.–Mar., daily 10–5.*

CloseUp

JUL-TIDE IN DENMARK

T COULD BE THE BLANKET of snow on thatched roofs, or the dancing flames of candles flickering behind frosted window panes. It might be the pungent aroma of roast goose wafting from the kitchen, or perhaps the giggling group of rosy-cheeked children in red clogs catching snowflakes in their mittens. If Denmark is the land of all that's cute and hygellig (the catch-all Danish term for cozy), then a Danish Christmas (Jul) just about epitomizes the country's charm.

It is on December 1 that Danish children are permitted to open the first little window on their advent calendars, a signal that the Christmas season has officially begun. A seasonal staple, the colorful advent calendar (also called nativity calendar) has 25 windows, behind which lies a Christmas scene and, more importantly, a chocolate. The calendar culminates on December 25th, usually with a depiction of the birth of baby Jesus—and the largest chocolate of the lot.

The Danes' penchant for home decoration blossoms during the holidays. Delicate paper cutouts of snowflakes and reindeer dangle from ceilings. Wreathes heavy with berries hang on front doors, and red and white candles set living rooms aglow.

As any Danish child knows, when you can't find a sock, or if the milk suddenly spills as if an invisible hand pushed it, then it means that the mischievous Christmas nisser (elves) are up to their tricks again. Pranksters at heart, the nimble nisser can wreak havoc on a household—that is, unless they're left a bowl of porridge or some other Christmas goodie, which Danish kids make sure to do. And what goodies to choose from— candy stores and bakeries are bursting with marzipan of all shapes and sizes, drizzled with chocolate and sprinkles in every hue of the rainbow. The windows are piled high with glistening wienerbrød, Denmark's decadent, flaky pastry—often oozing with creamy fillings—that knows no equal.

Christmas is officially celebrated on the evening of December 24. Families gather 'round the table for a Christmas feast, which may be roast duck or goose stuffed with oranges or prunes, or pork roasted in its own juices. No Danish meal is complete without the omnipresent rød kål, boiled, vinegary red cabbage, and kartoffler (potatoes). The choice for dessert is unanimous: the Christmas meal always ends with ris å l'amande, a thick and creamy rice pudding. Hidden within its fluffy folds is an almond, and whoever finds it receives a gift—and, some believe, good luck for the rest of the year.

A properly decorated Danish Christmas tree is a sight to behold, bedecked in handmade decorations—from gold-paper angels to brightly painted wooden figures—and strung (but of course) with miniature Danish flags. Purists still decorate their trees with white candles, which are lit for the next phase of the evening. Dancing around the tree, the perfect antidote to falling into a post-feast stupor, is the bonding highlight of the night. Family and guests hold hands and skip and sway around the tree, singing Danish carols. All worries and differences are forgotten as they engage in this refreshingly primary act of sharing, just as generations have before them. The circle breaks when the children can't bear the temptation a moment longer, and scamper over to the gifts piled high under the tree. This is when a Danish Christmas ends like any other, kids sitting among reams of ribbons and ripped paper, while the adults sip their spiked eggnog, remembering when happiness was what you got for Christmas.

The small, light, and airy **Glasmuseum** is on the Ebeltoft harbor, a perfect setting for the collection, which ranges from the mysterious symbol-laden monoliths of Swedish glass sage Bertil Vallien to the luminous gold pavilions of Japanese artist Kyohei Fujita. Once a customs and excise house, the museum has a glass workshop where international students come to study. The shop sells functional pieces, art, and books. ⊠ *Strandvejen 8* ☎ *86/34–17–99* ⊕ *www.glasmuseet.dk* ⊡ *Dkr 40* ⊙ *Jan.–June and Aug.–Dec., daily 10–5; July, daily 10–7.*

Where to Stay & Eat

★ **$$$$** ✕🏠 **Molskroen.** Perched on the coast northwest of Ebeltoft, in a sunflower-yellow, half-timber manor house from 1923, is this swanky inn and restaurant. The ample rooms are tastefully decorated in cool tones with four-poster beds and Bang & Olufsen televisions. The large, gleaming bathrooms, done up with designer fixtures, could easily grace the pages of an interior-design magazine. Half the rooms overlook the water. Acclaimed young chef Jesper Koch heads the restaurant, which serves fine French fare with an imaginative twist. Roasted duck is stuffed with apricots, figs, and dates and drizzled in a sauce of rum and raisins. Marinated cod sashimi comes with mussels and dill salad. Four brightly colored, original Warhol prints of famous queens—including Queen Margerethe, of course, and Queen Nomi of Swaziland—lend a dazzling touch to the blond-wood floors and pale orange walls. Large picture windows overlook the lush garden, through which a path winds to the private beach. The adjoining sitting room is perfect for a post-dinner brandy and cigar in front of the fireplace. ⊠ *Hovedg. 16, DK–8400* ☎ *86/36–22–00* 🖨 *86/36–23–00* ⊕ *www.molskroen.dk* ⇱ *18 rooms, 3 suites* ♨ *Restaurant, beach, bar* ⊟ *AE, DC, MC, V* ⊙ *Restaurant closed Mon.–Tues. Oct.–Mar.*

Viborg

⑬ *22 km (36 mi) north of Silkeborg, 66 km (41 mi) northwest of Århus.*

Viborg dates back at least to the 8th century, when it was a trading post and a place of pagan sacrifice. Later it became a center of Christianity, with monasteries and an episcopal residence. The 1,000-year-old **Hærvejen,** the old military road that starts near here, was once Denmark's most important connection with the outside world; today it lives on as a bicycle path. Legend has it that in the 11th century, King Canute set out from Viborg to conquer England; he succeeded, of course, and ruled from 1016 to 1035. You can buy reproductions of a silver coin minted by the king, embossed with the inscription "Knud, Englands Kong" (Canute, King of England).

Built in 1130, Viborg's **Domkirke** (cathedral) was once the largest granite church in the world. Only the crypt remains of the original building, which was restored and reopened in 1876. The dazzling early-20th-century biblical frescoes are by Danish painter Joakim Skovgard. ⊠ *Sct. Mogensg. 4* ☎ *87/25–52–50* ⊡ *Free* ⊙ *June–Aug., Mon.–Sat. 10–5, Sun. noon–5; Apr., May, and Sept. Mon.–Sat. 11–4, Sun. noon–4; Oct.–Mar., Mon.–Sat. 11–3, Sun. noon–3.*

Where to Stay & Eat

$$$ ✕ **Brygger Bauers Grotter.** A former brewery dating from 1832, this cozy, cavernous underground restaurant has arched wooden ceilings, old paintings depicting Viborg history, and beer barrels lining the back wall. The contemporary Danish menu includes a hearty beef stew served with rice, and chicken breast stuffed with Gorgonzola. ⊠ *Sct. Mathiasg. 61* ☎ *86/61–44–88* ⊟ *MC, V.*

$$$ 🏨 **Palads Hotel.** This large hotel near the center of town has ample, simply furnished rooms done up in a rose decor. A third of the rooms are designed for longer stays and have kitchenettes. ✉ *Sct. Mathiasg. 5, DK–8800* ☎ *86/62–37–00* 📠 *86/62–40–46* 🌐 *www.hotelpalads.dk* 🛏 *99 rooms, 19 suites* 👌 *Bar, kitchenettes (some), sauna, some pets allowed, no-smoking rooms* 🍴 *AE, DC, MC, V.*

Aalborg

⑭ *80 km (50 mi) northeast of Viborg, 112 km (70 mi) north of Århus.*

The gentle waters of the Limfjord cut off the top segment of Jylland completely. Perched on its narrowest point is Aalborg, Denmark's fourth-largest city. The town, founded in 692, is the gateway between north and mid-Jylland. The city is a charming combination of new and old; twisting lanes filled with medieval houses and, nearby, broad modern boulevards.

★ The local favorite site is the magnificent 17th-century **Jens Bang Stenhus** (Jens Bang's Stone House), built by a wealthy merchant. Chagrined he was never made a town council member, the cantankerous Bang avenged himself by caricaturing his political enemies in gargoyles all over the building and then adding his own face, its tongue sticking out at the town hall. The five-story 1624 building has a vaulted stone beer-and-wine cellar, Duus Vinkælder, one of the most atmospheric in the country. ✉ *Østeråg. 9.*

The Baroque **Budolfi Kirke** (Budolfi Cathedral) is dedicated to the English St. Botolph. The stone church, originally made of wood, has been rebuilt several times in its 800-year history. It includes a copy of the original spire of the Rådhus in Copenhagen, which was taken down about a century ago. The money for the construction was donated to the church by a generous local merchant and his sister, both of whom, locals say, had no other family on which to lavish their wealth. ✉ *Gammel Torv.*

Next to Budolfi Kirke is the 15th-century **Helligåndsklosteret** (Monastery of the Holy Ghost). One of Denmark's best-preserved monasteries—and perhaps the only one that admitted both nuns and monks—it is now a home for the elderly. During World War II the monastery was the meeting place for the Churchill Club, a group of Aalborg schoolboys who became world famous for their sabotage of the Nazis, even after the enemy thought they were locked up. ✉ *C. W. Obels Pl., Gammel Torv* ☎ *98/12–02–05* 🕑 *Guided tours mid-June–mid-Aug. at 1:30.*

In the center of the old town is **Jomfru Ane Gade,** named, as the story goes, for an aristocratic maiden accused of being a witch, then beheaded. Now the street's fame is second only to that of Copenhagen's Strøget. Despite the flashing neon and booming music of about 30 discos, bars, clubs, and eateries, the street attracts a thick stream of pedestrian traffic and appeals to all ages.

The only Fourth of July celebrations outside the United States annually blast off in nearby **Rebild Park,** a salute to the United States for welcoming some 300,000 Danish immigrants. The tradition dates back to 1912.

Just north of Aalborg at Nørresundby (still considered a part of greater Aalborg) is **Lindholm Høje,** a Viking and Iron Age burial ground where stones placed in the shape of a ship enclose many of the site's 682 graves. At its entrance there's a museum that chronicles Viking civilization. ✉ *Vendilavej 11* ☎ *96/31–04–28* 🏛 *Museum Dkr 30; burial ground free* 🕑 *Easter–mid-Oct., daily 10–5; mid-Oct.–Easter, Tues.–Sun. 10–4.*

The blocky marble-and-glass structure of the **Nordjyllands Kunstmuseum,** (Museum of Contemporary Arts of North Jutland) was designed by architects Alvar and Elissa Aalto and Jacques Baruël; the building was completed in 1972. The gridded interior partition system allows the curators to tailor their space to each exhibition, many of which are drawn from the museum's permanent collection of 20th-century Danish and international art. On the grounds there is also a manicured sculpture park and an amphitheater that hosts occasional concerts. ⊠ *Kong Christians Allé 50* ☎ *98/13–80–88* ⊕ *www.nordjyllandskunstmuseum.dk* ⊠ *Dkr 30* ☉ *Easter–mid-Oct., daily 10–5; mid-Oct.–Easter, Tues.–Sun. 10–4.*

The **Aalborg Historical Museum** contains the well-preserved underground ruins of a medieval Franciscan friary, including a walled cellar and the foundations of the chapel. Enter via the elevator outside the Salling department store. ⊠ *Alg. 19* ☎ *96/31–04–10* ⊕ *www.aahm.dk* ⊠ *Dkr 30* ☉ *Weekdays 10–5.*

Where to Stay & Eat

$$$ ✕ **Benzon's.** Light and bright on an old cobble street, this is one of the most popular eateries in town. Downstairs is a French-style bistro, with marble-top tables, engraved mirrors, and windows overlooking Jomfru Ane Gade. The upstairs is elegant and quiet. The French menu includes lobster-and-cognac soup for two, sliced roast duck with Waldorf salad, and beef fillet. ⊠ *Jomfru Ane G. 8* ☎ *98/16–34–44* ▭ *AE, DC, MC, V.*

$–$$$ ✕ **Spisehuset Kniv og Gaffel.** In a 400-year-old building parallel to Jomfru Ane Gade, this busy restaurant is filled with oak tables, crazy slanting floors, and candlelight; the year-round courtyard is a veritable greenhouse. Young waitresses negotiate the mayhem to deliver inch-thick steaks, the house specialty. ⊠ *Maren Turisg. 10* ☎ *98/16–69–72* ▭ *DC, MC, V* ☉ *Closed Sun.*

★ ¢–$$ ✕ **Duus Vinkjælder.** Most people come to this cellar—part alchemist's dungeon, part neighborhood bar—for a drink, but you can also get a light bite. In summer enjoy smørrebrød; in winter sup on grilled specialties such as frikadeller and *biksemad* (a meat-and-potato hash), and the restaurant's special liver pâté. ⊠ *Østeråg. 9* ☎ *98/12–50–56* ▭ *DC, V* ☉ *Closed Sun.*

$$$ ▣ **Helnan Phønix.** In a central and sumptuous old mansion, this hotel is popular with vacationers as well as business travelers. The rooms are luxuriously furnished with plump chairs and polished, dark-wood furniture; in some the original wooden ceiling beams are still intact. The Brigadier restaurant serves excellent French and Danish food. ⊠ *Vesterbro 77, DK–9000* ☎ *98/12–00–11* ▤ *98/10–10–20* ⊕ *www.helnan.dk* ⇌ *219 rooms, 2 suites* ⚘ *Restaurant, gym, bar, meeting room, some pets allowed, no-smoking rooms* ▭ *AE, DC, MC, V.*

Nightlife & the Arts

BEER & WINE CELLARS
Consider a pub crawl along the famed **Jomfru Ane Gade,** wildly popular for its party atmosphere but also for its rock-bottom drink prices, which are much lower than anywhere else in Denmark. Opt for the house drink of the night (usually a Danish beer), and you'll often pay one-third of the normal cost. The street has become overrun by the pre-teen crowd, but increasingly the bars are enforcing age restrictions, with an eye to drawing more-mature crowds. Dimly lit and atmospheric, **Duus Vinkjælder** (⊠ *Østeråg. 9* ☎ *98/12–50–56*) is extremely popular, one of the most classic beer and wine cellars in all of Denmark. It's an obligatory stop for anyone who wants a taste of Aalborg's nightlife. **Rendez-Vous** (⊠ *Jomfru Ane G. 5* ☎ *98/16–88–80*) has a pleasant outdoor terrace with black and brown wicker chairs. Thursday through Satur-

day, it opens its upstairs dance floor, which attracts 18- to 25-year-olds with standard disco.

CASINO   The city's sole casino is at the **Radisson SAS Limfjord Hotel** (⊠ Ved Stranden 14–16 ☎ 98/16–43–33).

MUSIC & DISCOS   Aalborg doesn't have a regular jazz club, but local musicians get together at least once a week for jam sessions. Ask the tourist board for details.

Gaslight (⊠ Jomfru Ane G. 23 ☎ 98/10–17–50) plays rock and grinding dance music to a young crowd. If you're here in the fall or winter, head to the harborside **Kompasset** (⊠ Vesterbådehavn ☎ 98/13–75–00), where live jazz is paired with a Saturday-afternoon lunch buffet. **Natsværmeren** (⊠ Ved Stranden 9 ☎ 98/11–60–22) is popular with a mature audience. **Vesterå 4** (⊠ Vesterå 4 ☎ 98/16–99–99), with pale gray walls and flickering orange candles, hosts live jazz performances several times a month.

Skagen

⑮   *88 km (55 mi) northeast of Aalborg, 212 km (132 mi) north of Århus.*

At the windswept northern tip of Jylland is Skagen (pronounced *skane*), a very popular summer beach area for well-heeled Danes. The long beaches and blue light, soft as silk and enhanced by reflections in the calm sea, have inspired painters and writers alike. The 19th-century Danish artist Holger Drachmann (1846–1908) and his friends, including the well-known P. S. Kroyer and Michael and Anna Ancher, founded the Skagen School of painting, which sought to capture the special quality of

★   light here. You can see their efforts on display in the **Skagen Museum.** The museum store offers the best selection in town of posters, postcards, and other souvenirs depicting the Skagen paintings. ⊠ *Brøndumsvej 4* ☎ *98/44–64–44* ⊕ *www.skagensmuseum.dk* ⊠ *Dkr 60* ⊙ *June–Aug., daily 10–6; May and Sept., daily 10–5; Apr. and Oct., Tues.–Sun. 11–4; Nov.–Mar., Wed.–Fri. 1–4, Sat. 11–4, Sun. 11–3.*

Michael and Anna Ancher are Skagen's—if not Denmark's—most famous artist couple, and their meticulously restored 1820 home and studio, **Michael og Anna Ancher's Hus** (Michael and Anna Ancher's House), is now a museum. Old oil lamps and lace curtains decorate the parlor; the doors throughout the house were painted by Michael. Anna's studio, complete with easel, is awash in the famed Skagen light. More than 240 paintings by Michael, Anna, and their daughter, Helga, grace the walls. ⊠ *Markvej 2–4* ☎ *98/44–30–09* ⊕ *www.anchershus.dk* ⊠ *Dkr 40* ⊙ *May–Sept., daily 10–5 (until 6 late-June–mid-Aug.); Apr. and Oct. daily 11–3; Nov.–Mar., weekends 11–3.*

Danes say that in Skagen you can stand with one foot on the Kattegat, the strait between Sweden and eastern Jylland, the other in the Skagerrak, the strait between western Denmark and Norway. The point is so

Fodor'sChoice   thrashed by storms and roiling waters that the 18th-century **Tilsandede**
★   **Kirke** (Sand-Buried Church), 2 km (1 mi) south of town, is completely covered by dunes.

Even more famed than the Buried Church is the west coast's dramatic **Råbjerg Mile,** a protected migrating dune that moves about 33 feet a year and is accessible on foot from the Kandestederne.

Where to Stay & Eat

$$–$$$ ✕▨ **Strand Hotel.** In the old part of Skagen, this bright and romantic hotel is the perfect foil to the wild, windy sea- and sandscapes nearby. Filled with gently curved wicker furnishings, painted woods, and orig-

inal art, the hotel's rooms are simple and restful; the staff is friendly and accommodating. Sømærket, the traditional Danish fish restaurant, is open only between April and October, but breakfast, which includes healthful and fortifying fresh breads and berries, is available year-round. ⊠ *Jeckelsvej 2, DK–9990* ☎ *98/44–34–99* 🖷 *98/44–59–19* ⊕ *www. strandhotellet.glskagen.dk* 🗦 *21 rooms, 6-person house* ♿ *Restaurant, meeting room* ⊟ *AE, DC, MC, V.*

$ ✕🖵 **Brøndums Hotel.** A few minutes from the beach, this 150-year-old gabled inn is furnished with antiques and Skagen School paintings, and although it is charming, it is beginning to show its age. The very basic 21 guest rooms in the main building are old-fashioned and include wicker chairs, Oriental rugs, and pine four-poster beds. The 25 annex rooms are more modern. The fine French-Danish restaurant, where the Skagen School often gathered, has a lavish cold table. Brøndums Hotel became associated with the Skagen School early on: Anna Ancher was the daughter of Eric Brøndum, the hotel proprietor. ⊠ *Anchersvej 3, DK–9990* ☎ *98/44–15–55* 🖷 *98/45–15–20* ⊕ *www.broendums-hotel. dk* 🗦 *47 rooms, 19 with bath, and 3 suites* ♿ *Restaurant, bar, meeting room, some pets allowed* ⊟ *AE, DC, MC, V.*

Shopping

Skagen's artistic heritage and light-drenched landscapes continue to draw painters and craftspeople, making for excellent souvenir shopping opportunities. For colorful, innovative handblown glass, head for **Glaspusterblæser** (⊠ Sct. Laurentii Vej 33 ☎ 98/44–58–75), a large glassblowing workshop housed in what was once Skagen's post office. The amber store and workshop **Ravsliberen I Skagen** (⊠ Sct. Laurentii Vej 6 ☎ 98/44–55–27) sells top-quality amber jewelry, including pieces with insects trapped inside. You can buy miniature replicas of figureheads, ships' "guardian angels," at **Trip Trap** (⊠ Sct. Laurentii Vej 17A ☎ 98/44–63–22), a branch of the popular Danish home-decorating chain.

Jylland A to Z

AIRPORTS & TRANSFERS

Jylland has regional hubs in Aalborg, Århus, and Billund, which handle mainly domestic and some European traffic. Billund Airport, 2 km (1 mi) southwest of downtown, is the largest and on the arrival end of flights from major European, Scandinavian, and Danish airports.

🛪 Airports **Aalborg Airport** ☎ 98/17-11-44 ⊕ www.aal.dk **Århus Airport** ☎ 87/75-70-00 ⊕ www.aar.dk. **Billund Airport** ☎ 76/50-50-50 ⊕ www.billund-airport.dk.

TRANSFERS Hourly buses run between the Århus airport and train station. The trip takes around 45 minutes and costs Dkr 60. Bus 212 runs from Århus airport to Randers (60 minutes) and Ebeltoft (20 minutes). A taxi ride from the airport to central Århus takes 45 minutes and costs well over Dkr 300.

From Billund airport there are buses to Århus (Radisson-Sas Hotel, Dkr 130), Esbjerg, Kolding, Vejle, Odense, and the Legoland Hotel near the airport.

Taxi and bus routes connect Aalborg airport with the city. A taxi costs around Dkr 175 and takes roughly 20 minutes. Nordjyllands Trafikselskab has buses connecting the airport to towns near Aalborg, and the company Flybusnord runs routes to Sæby and Frederikshavn.

🚍 **Flybusnord** ☎ 98/43-30-00 ⊕ www.flybusnord.dk. **Nordjyllands Trafikselskab** ☎ 98/11-11-11.

BIKE TRAVEL

Jylland has scores of bike paths, and many auto routes also have cycle lanes. Keep in mind that distances feel much longer here than elsewhere in the country, and that even these humble hills are a challenge for children and novice cyclists. Consider prearranged package holidays, which range from island day trips to eight-day excursions. Among the offices that can help with bike tips are the visitor information offices in the different towns. Bike rentals are available in most towns from the tourism board, which can also supply maps and brochures. Contact Visit Nord for routes and tour packages in North Jylland.

In the west, the Vestkyst-stien (west-coast path) goes from Skagen in the north to Bulbjerg in the south. In the east, the Vendsyssel-stien (winding path) goes from Frederikshavn to the mouth of the Limfjord. The Østkyst-stien (east-coast path) follows and leads to the south of the Limfjord. In the south, much of the 1,000-year-old Hærvejen (Old Military Road) has been converted into a network of scenic cycling lanes. It's signposted for all 240 km (145 mi) through the center of Jylland, from Padborg in the south to Viborg in the north.

🚲 **Visit Nord** ☎ 96/96-12-00 ⊕ www.visitnord.dk.

BOAT & FERRY TRAVEL

More than 20 ferry routes still connect the peninsula with the rest of Denmark (including the Faroe Islands), as well as England, Norway, and Sweden, with additional connections to Kiel and Puttgarden, Germany, the Baltics, Poland, and Russia. For most ferries you can get general information and make reservations by calling FDM (Danish Motoring Association). Other major routes include those of Scandinavian Seaways, which links England's Harwich to Esbjerg in the southwest. There are ferries from Göteborg (3¼ hours), on Sweden's west coast and Oslo, Norway (10 hours), to Frederikshavn in the northeast. Call Stena Line for both. For direct Sjælland to Jylland passage, you can take a car-ferry hydrofoil from Sjælland's Odden to Ebeltoft (45 minutes) or Århus (1 hour). You can also take the slower, but less expensive, car ferry from Kalundborg (on Sjælland) to Århus (2 hours 40 minutes). Both ferries travel five times daily on weekdays, and slightly less on the weekends. For ferry schedules and information, call Mols-Linien.

🚢 **FDM** ☎ 70/11-60-11. **Mols-Linien** ☎ 70/10-14-18 🖶 89/52-52-90 ⊕ www.molslinien.dk. **Scandinavian Seaways** ☎ 79/17-79-17 Esbjerg, 33/42-30-00 Copenhagen ⊕ www.dfdsseaways.dk. **Stena Line** ☎ 96/20-02-00 ⊕ www.stenaline.com.

BUS TRAVEL

Bus and train travel inside Denmark is made more convenient by way of "Bus/Tog Samarbejde," a comprehensive route and schedule information source. Bus tickets are usually sold onboard the buses immediately before departure. Ask about discounts for children, senior citizens and groups.

Intercity buses are punctual and slightly cheaper but slower than trains. You can buy tickets on the bus and pay according to destination. For schedules and fares, call the local tourist office, as a network of different bus companies covers the peninsula. Thinggaard Buses traverse Jylland from north to south, between Frederikshavn and Esbjerg, with stops in Aalborg and Viborg; a one-way ticket between Frederikshavn and Esbjerg costs around Dkr 245. Abildskou buses travel between Kastrup Airport on Sjælland to Ebeltoft and Århus. The trip lasts about 3 hours and 45 minutes, similar to the train; a one-way ticket is Dkr 230.

Schedules for most bus travel within towns are posted at all bus stops and fares are usually about Dkr 15.

Abildskou ⊠ Graham Bellsvej 40, Århus ☎ 70/21-08-88 ⊕ www.abildskou.dk. **Bus/ Tog Samarbejde** ⊕ www.rejseplan.dk. **Thinggaard Bus** ☎ 70/10-00-20 ⊕ www. thinggaard-bus.dk.

CAR TRAVEL

Although train and bus connections are excellent, sites and towns in Jylland are widely dispersed, and the peninsula is best explored by car. Whether you decide to take speedy, modern highways or winding old roads, traffic is virtually nonexistent.

Getting around Denmark these days is much easier than in the past thanks to bridges that connect the kingdom to both Sweden and the Continent; that said, it's best to confirm all passage with either a local tourist board or FDM before setting out, to avoid confusion caused by ferry mergers and discontinued routes. Although there are several ferry connections to other parts of Denmark and Europe, most travelers drive north from Germany, or arrive from the islands of Sjælland or Fyn. Ferry prices can get steep and vary according to the size of the vehicle and the number of passengers.

From Copenhagen or elsewhere on Sjælland, you can drive the approximately 110 km (69 mi) across the island, then cross the world's second-longest suspension bridge, the Storebæltsbro (Great Belt Bridge), to Knudshoved. You then drive the 85 km (53 mi) across Fyn and cross from Middelfart to Fredericia, Jylland, over the Lillebæltsbro (Little Belt Bridge). There are more choices, since two bridges link Middelfart to Fredericia. The older, lower bridge (2 km/1 mi) follows Route 161, whereas the newer suspension bridge (1 km/½ mi) on E20 is faster.
FDM ☎ 70/11-60-11.

EMERGENCIES

For ambulance, fire, or police anywhere in Denmark, dial 112. You can contact local pharmacies in Aalborg or Århus for information on emergency doctors.
Aalborg ⊠ Budolfi Apotek, Alg. 60 ☎ 98/12-06-77. **Århus** ⊠ Løve Apoteket, Store Torv 5 ☎ 86/12-00-22.

SPORTS & THE OUTDOORS

CANOEING Canoes can be rented (about Dkr 220 per day) in the lake district, Limfjord, and at almost all lakes and rivers. One- to three-day package tours are available throughout the region, with either camping or hostel accommodation. Local tourist boards can provide more information.

FISHING The lake district is a great place for fishing and angling. License requirements vary and package tours are also available; contact any local tourist office for details.

TOURS

Guided tours are few and far between, although some local tourism offices do provide them. Check with the individual city tourism offices— especially the one in Århus—for tips, reservations, and brochures that describe walking tours and scenic routes.

TRAIN TRAVEL

DSB makes hourly runs from Copenhagen to Frederikshavn, in northern Jylland, stopping in Fredericia (2½ hours), Århus (3½ hours), and Aalborg (4¾ hours) along the way. The trip includes train passage across the Storebæltsbro between Korsør, on west Sjælland, and Nyborg, on east Fyn. A one-way trip from Copenhagen to Frederikshavn is about Dkr 320. For long trips, the DSB trains are fast and efficient, with superb views of the countryside. Smaller towns do not have inter-city trains, so you have to switch to buses once you arrive.

DSB ☎ 70/13-14-15 ⊕ www.dsb.dk.

VISITOR INFORMATION

At the Århus tourist office, check out the Århus Pass, which includes bus travel, free or discounted admission to museums and sites, and tours.

Aalborg ✉ Østeråg. 8 ☎ 98/12-60-22 🖷 98/16-69-22 ⊕ www.visitaalborg.com. **Århus** ✉ Park Allé 2 ☎ 89/40-67-00 ⊕ www.visitaarhus.com. **Ebeltoft** ✉ Strandvejen 2 ☎ 86/34-14-00 ⊕ www.visitdjursland.com. **Esbjerg** ✉ Skoleg. 33 ☎ 75/12-55-99 🖷 75/12-27-67 ⊕ www.visitesbjerg.com. **Fanø** ✉ Færgevej 1, Nordby ☎ 75/16-26-00 🖷 75/16-29-03 ⊕ www.fanoeturistbureau.dk. **Jelling** ✉ Gormsg. 23 ☎ 75/87-13-01 🖷 75/82-10-11 ⊕ www.visitvejle.com. **Kolding** ✉ Akseltorv 8 ☎ 76/33-21-00 🖷 76-33-21-20 ⊕ www.visitkolding.dk. **Mid-Jylland** ⊕ www.midtjylland.dk. **North Jylland Tourist Office** ⊕ www.visitnord.dk. **South and Southeast Jylland Tourist Information** ☎ 75/83-59-99 🖷 75/83-45-67 ⊕ www.visitsouth-eastjutland.com. **Ribe** ✉ Torvet 3 ☎ 75/42-15-00 🖷 75/42-40-78 ⊕ www.ribetourist.dk. **Rømø** ✉ Havnebyvej 30 ☎ 74/75-51-30 🖷 74/75-50-31 ⊕ www.romo.dk. **Silkeborg** ✉ Åhavevej 2A ☎ 86/82-19-11 🖷 86/81-09-83 ⊕ www.silkeborg.com. **Skagen** ✉ Sct. Laurentii Vej 22 ☎ 98/44-13-77 🖷 98/45-02-94 ⊕ www.skagen-tourist.dk. **Tønder** ✉ Torvet 1 ☎ 74/72-12-20 🖷 74/72-09-00 ⊕ www.visittonder.dk. **Vejle** ✉ Banegårdspl. 6 ☎ 75/82-19-55 🖷 75/82-10-11 ⊕ www.visitvejle.com. **Viborg** ✉ Nytorv 9 ☎ 87/25-30-75 🖷 86/60-02-38 ⊕ www.viborg.dk/turisme.

BORNHOLM

5

FODOR'S CHOICE
Østerlars Kirke, *church in Østerlars*
Strandhotellet, *hotel in Sandvig*

HIGHLY RECOMMENDED
RESTAURANTS   Fyrtøjet, *Rønne*
Strøgets Spisehûz, *Rønne*

HOTELS   Hotel Østersøen, *Svaneke*

SIGHTS   Gudhjem
Hammershus
Landsbrugs Museum, *Gudhjem*

Updated by
Eduardo López
de Luzuriaga

CALLED THE PEARL OF THE BALTIC for its natural beauty and winsomely rustic towns, Bornholm, 177 km (110 mi) southeast of Sjælland, is geographically unlike the rest of Denmark. A temperate climate has made this 588-square-km (235-square-mi) jumble of granite bluffs, clay soil, and rift valleys an extravagance of nature. Rich plantations of fir bristle beside wide dunes and vast heather fields; lush gardens teem with fig, cherry, chestnut, mulberry, and blue-blooming Chinese Emperor trees; and meadows sprout 12 varieties of orchids. Denmark's third-largest forest, the Almindingen, crowns the center; the southern tip is ringed with some of Europe's whitest beaches.

During the Iron and Bronze ages, Bornholm was inhabited by seafaring and farming cultures that peppered the land with burial dolmens and engravings. From the Middle Ages to the 18th century, the Danes battled the Swedes for ownership of the island, protecting it with strongholds and fortified churches, many of which still loom over the landscape. Bornholm's unique round churches—whitewashed splendors topped with black conical roofs—are a sight to behold. Considered to be some of the finest examples of Scandinavian medieval architecture, the churches imbue the island landscape with a lovely, stylized simplicity.

Today Bornholmers continue to draw their livelihood from the land and sea—and increasingly from tourism. Chalk-white chimneys rise above the rooftops, harbors are abob with painted fishing boats, and in spring and summer fields blaze with amber mustard and grain.

Few people come to Bornholm to stay indoors. Long, silky beaches, gentle hills, and lush forests make this a summer haven for walking, hiking, and swimming—particularly for families, many of whom take their summer vacations by packing provisions and children onto bikes, and cycling throughout the island.

Bornholm is famous throughout Scandinavia for its craftspeople, especially glassblowers and ceramicists, whose work is often pricier in Copenhagen and Stockholm. In the center of each town (especially Gudhjem and Svaneke) you can find crafts shops and *værksteder* (workshops). When you're on the road, watch for KERAMIK signs, which direct you to artists selling from home.

WHAT IT COSTS In kroner				
	$$$$	**$$$**	**$$**	**$**	**¢**
RESTAURANTS	over 180	141–180	121–140	90–120	under 90
HOTELS	over 1,500	1,200–1,500	1,000–1,200	700–1,000	under 700

Restaurant prices are for a main course at dinner. Hotel prices are for two people in a standard double room, including service charge and tax.

Rønne

▶ ❶ *190 km (120 mi) southeast of Copenhagen (7 hrs by ferry from Køge or 3 hrs from Ystad, Sweden).*

Bornholm's capital, port, and largest town is Rønne, a good starting point for exploring northward or eastward. East of Nørrekås Harbor on Laksegade is an enchanting area of rose-clad 17th- and 18th-century houses, among them the tile-roof **Erichsens Gård** (Erichsen's Farm). The home of the wealthy Erichsen family, whose daughter married the Danish poet Holger Drachmann, it includes paintings by Danish artist Kristian Zahrtmann, period furnishings, and a lovely garden. ⊠ *Lakseg. 7* ☎ *56/ 95–87–35* ⊕ *www.bornholmsmuseer.dk/erichs* 🖼 *Dkr 30* ⊙ *Mid-May–mid-Oct., Mon.–Sat. 10–5.*

Near Store Torv, the main square, is the **Bornholm Museum,** which puts on local geological and archaeological exhibits in addition to regular displays of more than 4,500 pieces of ceramics and glass. The museum also displays 25 18th-century Bornholmure (Bornholm Clocks), as characteristic of the island as smoked herring. In 1744, a Dutch ship was wrecked on Bornholm, and the English grandfather clocks it carried became the models for the island's clocks. ⊠ *Skt. Mortensg. 29* ☎ *56/ 95–07–35* ⊕ *www.bornholmsmuseum.dk* 🖼 *Dkr 35* ⊙ *Mid-Apr.–mid-Oct., Mon.–Sat. 10–5; mid-Oct.–mid-Apr., Mon.–Sat. 1–4.*

Bornholm has long been recognized for its beautiful ceramics. **Hjorths Fabrik** (Hjorth's Factory), founded in 1859 by ceramicist Lauritz Hjorth, is one of Bornholm's oldest ceramics factories, and is today a "working ceramics museum." Follow the "route of clay" through the old factory and workshops, from the mixer and the kiln to the painting and decorating rooms. Along the way you see the ceramicists at work, casting, glazing, decorating, and firing, and you can observe how a lump of raw clay slowly takes shape on the potter's wheel, blossoming into a lovely vase or bowl. (Note that the ceramicists take a lunch break from about noon to 1.) The museum displays ceramics made at Hjorths factory since 1859, from Greek Revival pieces of the mid-1800s to ceramic apothecary jars from 1930–50. Many of the ceramic pieces dating from the mid- to late 1900s were made by Ulla and Marie Hjorth, sisters of the factory's founder. The museum shop sells a wide range of Hjorth ceramics, from its distinctive stoneware to old-fashioned pharmacy jars. ⊠ *Krystalg. 5* ☎ *56/95–01–60* ⊕ *www.bornholmsmuseer.dk/hjorths* 🖼 *May–Oct. Dkr 30; Nov.–Apr. Dkr 10* ⊙ *May–Oct., Mon.–Sat. 10–5 (factory closed Sat.); Nov.–Apr., weekdays 1–5, Sat. 10–1 (exhibits and shops only).*

Where to Stay & Eat

★ **$$$** ✕ **Fyrtøjet.** Overlooking the Strøget, this bright and spacious restaurant offers an ample dinner buffet with soup, salad, a selection of fish dishes (usually smoked salmon and cod), and beef. The lunchtime herring and fish buffet is a hit with summer crowds as is the restaurant's inviting interior of pale yellow walls, blue tablecloths, and wooden floors. The house specialty is *granitbøf,* a hefty slab of beef served on a heated Bornholm granite-and-iron tray. While the beef is cooking on the hot granite, it's flambéed with whiskey. You pour the accompanying cold sauce (usually béarnaise) over the meat when it's suitably done. The former owner patented this unique tray. ⊠ *Store Torveg. 22* ☎ *56/95–30–12* 🖃 *AE, DC, MC, V* ⊙ *No lunch Jan.–Mar.*

$–$$ ✕ **Rådhuskroen.** With exposed timbers, comfortable armchairs, and close-set tables, this restaurant provides a softly lit change from Rønne's busy streets. The menu highlights substantial beef dishes such as pepper steak with wine and cream sauce, but you can also choose from a couple of local fish specialities—try the poached Baltic salmon or grilled fillet of sole, both served with lobster sauce. ⊠ *Nørreg. 2* ☎ *56/ 95–00–69* 🖃 *AE, DC, MC, V.*

★ **¢–$$$** ✕ **Strøgets Spisehūz.** When the hunger pangs hit, Rønne locals head for this friendly, family-owned restaurant at the end of Strøget. The hearty Danish fare includes beef with cognac sauce and potatoes, and smoked salmon sprinkled with lemon. The mood is casual, with hanging plants,

5

Bornholmers don't have a lot of positive words for material goods, but when it comes to expressing nature, the language is abundant. Bornholm, dubbed the Sunshine island, generally has a better climate than the rest of Denmark, so a bicycle can make a great form of transportation if you are so inclined; if not, these tours car be accomplished in a car, as well. Moreover, bringing a tent for beachside camping allows you more time to explore the beautiful coastline as well as the lush inland forests of the island. If you are pressed for time, you should choose between the north and east coasts, rather than trying to cram it all in on a whirlwind tour. If you have a week, a full island loop with excursions inland is more feasible.

Numbers in the text correspond to numbers in the margin and on the Bornholm map.

If you have 3 days

Begin day one in **Rønne** ❶ ▶, where you will have arrived by ferry. Beforehand, you should choose to explore either the island's north or east coast. If you decide on the north coast, hop on your bike early and peddle up to the fortress ruins of **Hammershus** ❷, where you will continue on to **Hammeren** ❸ and end your lengthy day in 🏨 **Allinge** ❹. Spend the next day at **Gudhjem** ❺, giving yourself plenty of time to see the sights and sample the local smoked herring. On the third day cycle back to Rønne, heading home through the **Rø Plantage** ❻. If you're up for it, you could make a small detour (10 km) to visit **Østerlars** ❼ to see the largest traditional church on Bornholm.

If you should wish to go eastward from Rønne, aim for 🏨 **Svaneke** ❽ on the first day, stopping in the forest at **Almindingen** ❿ to rest your legs. On the second day move on to **Neksø** ❾; stock up on food and drink and spend the rest of the day on the southern beaches swimming and tanning. On the third day follow the southern shoreline back to Rønne.

If you have 6 days

From **Rønne** ❶ ▶, follow the northern three-day route laid out above as far as 🏨 **Gudhjem** ❺, where you should spend your second night. Swing by the **Rø Plantage** ❻ on your way to **Østerlars** ❼, and on to 🏨 **Svaneke** ❽, where you will spend two nights, taking the fourth day for an excursion to the woods at **Almindingen** ❿. On the fifth day drive to **Neksø** ❾ for a quick stopover, then look for a perfect strip of sand along the shore between Snogebæk and Pedersker, where you can while away the afternoon. Either stay and camp there or return to Svaneke for its hotel accommodations. On the sixth and last day, turn west toward Rønne, driving through **Åkirkeby** ⓫ to view the island's oldest church and to **Nylars** ⓬ where you'll see another round church, typical of the island's architecture.

---

little Danish flags, paper napkins, and pink and purple curtains. ⊠ *Store Torveg. 39* ☎ *56/95–81–69* ▤ *MC, V* ⊙ *Closed Mon.*

$$$ 🏨 **Radisson SAS Fredensborg.** Along a curve of forest near a small beach, this hotel sets the island's standard for luxury. The glass-and-tile lobby is spare and sunny, the staff pleasant and eager. The dozen ample apartments have full kitchens, and guest rooms have modern furniture and balconies overlooking the sea. The rustic restaurant, De Fem Ståuerne, serves traditional French-Danish food. ⌧ *Strandvejen 116, DK–3700* ☎ *56/95–44–44* 🖷 *56/95–03–14* ⊕ *www.bornholmhotels.dk* ⌑ *72 rooms with bath, 4 suites, 12 apartments* ⅋ *Restaurant, room service, tennis court, hot tub, sauna, bar, meeting room, some pets allowed, no-smoking rooms* ⊟ *AE, DC, MC, V.*

$$ 🏨 **Hotel Griffen.** One of Bornholm's largest and most modern hotels is just off a busy street near the Rønne harbor. Three stories tall with plenty of windows, it has wonderful views—the sea on one side and Rønne on the other. Rooms have every modern convenience. ⌧ *Nordre Kystvej 34, DK–3700* ☎ *56/95–51–11* 🖷 *56/95–52–97* ⊕ *www.bornholmhotels. dk* ⌑ *142 rooms, 2 suites with bath* ⅋ *Restaurant, room service, cable TV, indoor pool, sauna, bar, dance club, meeting room, some pets allowed, no-smoking rooms* ⊟ *AE, DC, MC, V.*

$ 🏨 **Hotel Hoffmann.** This modern but somewhat institutional hotel has comfortable rooms, a third of which look out on the Rønne harbor. Highlights include a sunlit interior courtyard where you can enjoy a drink from the bar, and a full-service gym (popular with Rønne locals) with all the latest exercise equipment as well as a sauna and massage center. The gym fee for hotel guests is Dkr 40 (for nonguests, it's Dkr 50). ⌧ *Nordre Kyst 32, DK–3700* ☎ *56/95–03–86* 🖷 *56/95–25–15* ⊕ *www. bornholmhotels.dk* ⌑ *85 rooms with bath* ⅋ *Sauna, gym, bar, meeting room, some pets allowed, no-smoking rooms* ⊟ *AE, DC, MC, V.*

¢ 🏨 **Sverres Hotel.** Near the harbor in a building dating from 1850, this cheery hotel has simple, clean rooms. Enjoy a morning meal in the sunny breakfast room. Contented guests have covered the walls with artwork and drawings; the former owner, a jazz musician, sounded his own note by leaving behind his collection of jazz memorabilia. ⌧ *Snellemark 2, DK–3700* ☎ *56/95–03–03* 🖷 *56/95–03–92* ⊕ *www.sverres-hotel.dk* ⌑ *20 rooms, 10 with bath* ⅋ *Dining room* ⊟ *AE, DC, MC, V.*

¢ ⚠ **Galløkken Camping.** This site is just a short walk from the Rønne center, near an old military museum. The open grounds are surrounded by a perimeter of trees. The shower and cooking facilities are good. ⌧ *Strandvejen 4, DK–3700 Rønne* ☎ *56/95–23–20* ⊕ *www.gallokken. dk* ⅋ *Flush toilets, laundry facilities, showers, drinking water, kitchen, general store, playground.*

Nightlife & the Arts

Bornholm's nightlife is limited to a handful of discos and clubs in Rønne, which open and close frequently as tastes change. For live jazz on the weekends, head for the atmospheric **Doctor Jazz** (⌧ Snellemark 26 ☎ no phone), outfitted with an ample stage surrounded by round tables and jazz instruments hanging on the walls. At the ever-popular **O'Malley Irish Pub** (⌧ Store Torveg. 2 ☎ 56/95–00–16), a friendly crowd of locals and tourists mingles with frothy pints in hand.

Shopping

Bornholm is famous for its quality ceramics, and Rønne, as the island's capital city, offers the widest variety. The island's history of ceramics starts in 1773 when ceramicist Michael Andersen established a factory in Rønne. Today, his legacy lives on at the large factory-turned-shop **Michael Andersen Bornholmsk Keramik** (⌧ Lille Torv 7 ☎ 56/95–00–01 ⊙ weekdays 10–5:30, Sat. 10–3) on a small square near the center of town. The shop's wide selection includes the distinctive *krakelering* ceramics, where the surface of the ceramics is covered with a web of tiny black lines that give the pieces a cracked look. Ceramicists still work in the back studio, and the store sells a range of ceramics.

The distinctive clocks, or Bornholmures, sold on the island are all handmade and hand painted with round (or sometimes rectangular) faces. The

Fresh & Smoked Seafood

Fishing has been a major industry in Bornholm since the Middle Ages, when inhabitants fished large quantities of herring in the Baltic Sea and preserved it by means of drying and salting. In recent years, times have been hard, but the island is still famous for its seafood. Some of the best herring in the country comes from the waters around Bornholm and the locals have their own special recipes for pickling or curing the fish. Salmon and cod are also prevalent; inquire about local specialties. The northern and eastern coasts are dotted with fishing harbors and most of them have a local smokehouse with an excellent selection of fish. After the day's catch has been brought in and cleaned, the fish are taken to the smokehouse and hung side by side on large spears in smoking chambers above red-hot alderwood for eight or nine hours. A number of smokehouses double as informal eateries, or there will be a vendor nearby. A local specialty is called Sol over Gudhjem (Sun over Gudhjem, named for the town where the first smokehouse was built in 1886), a smoked herring served with raw egg yolk, radishes, and onions on rye. Another item to try is smoked herring eaten Bornholmer style, which is taking the fish by the tail, holding it above your mouth, and eating the whole thing, starting with the head.

Hiking

In contrast to the rest of Denmark, Bornholm is hilly and rugged. Marked trails crisscross the island, including three 4-km (2½-mi) hikes through the Almindingen Forest and several more through its Ekkodalen (Echo Valley). The northern coastline is beautiful but a rocky and more strenuous walk. Ask for a map, routes, and tips from any tourism office. The *Bornholm Green Guide,* available in shops and tourism offices, offers suggestions for walking and hiking tours.

Swimming

Beach worshipers thrive in Bornholm. The swimming and sunning are best in the south, between Pedersker and Snogebæk, where the dunes are tall and the beaches wide. Dueodde beach, blanketed in fine, white sand, unfolds along Bornholm's southern edge. As elsewhere in Denmark, topless bathing is common and nude bathing is tolerated.

---

new-style clocks have a modern touch: on the hour they play classics such as Mozart or Verdi and some even sound the hour with Stephen Sondheim or Andrew Lloyd Webber. Antique versions are the costliest, with prices from Dkr 10,000 to Dkr 80,000 and up. A handmade custom clock costs Dkr 37,000 on average. Reproductions modeled on original clocks are custom-made by **Bornholmerure** (⊠ Torneværksvej 26 ☎ 56/95–31–08).

You can pick up unusual gifts and one-of-a-kind clothing made of hand-printed textiles at **Bente Hammer** (⊠ Nyker Hovedg. 32 ☎ 56/96–33–35).

Hammershus

★ ❷ *8 km (5 mi) north of Jons Kapel, 30 km (19 mi) north of Rønne.*

The **fortress of Hammershus,** now in ruins, was once northern Europe's largest stronghold. The hulking fortress was begun in 1255 by the archbishop of Lund (Sweden), and became the object of centuries of strug-

gle between Denmark and Sweden. In 1658 Danes under Jens Kofoed killed its Swedish governor, and the castle was given back to Denmark. Used until 1743, it was quarried for stone to fortify Christiansø and that island's buildings. The government finally intervened in 1822, and the site is now a mass of snaggle-toothed walls and towers atop a grassy knoll. Occasionally, concerts and other performances are held here. 🎫 *Free.*

Nightlife & the Arts

Special events don't happen nearly often enough, but check with the Bornholm's **Main Tourist Office** (☎ 56/95–95–00 ⊕ www.bornholminfo.dk) to see if any are planned at or near Hammershus. The ruins add a spectacular dimension to classical music and the performing arts.

Hammeren

❸ *5 km (3 mi) north of Hammershus, 36 km (23 mi) north of Rønne.*

This knuckle of land jutting from the island's northern tip is nearly separated from the island by a deep rift valley and the Hammer Sø (Hammer Lake). Despite constant Baltic winds, rare plants and trees grow on the warm, granite-scattered Hammeren (the Hammer), including radiant anemones. Look across the water south of the tip to the stone formation known as the Camel Heads.

---

en route   A little more than 3 km (2 mi) southeast of Hammeren is **Madsebakke,** the largest collection of Bronze Age rock carvings in Denmark. They are presumed to be ceremonial carvings, which ancient fishermen and farmers hoped would bring good weather and bountiful crops. The most interesting of them depicts 11 ships, including one with a sun wheel, an ancient type of sun dial.

Allinge

4 *3 km (2 mi) east of Madsebakke, 21 km (13 mi) north of Rønne.*

In Allinge and its twin town Sandvig you'll find centuries-old neighborhoods and, particularly in Allinge, half-timber houses and herring smokehouses sprouting tall chimneys. Just south is a wood that the islanders call **Trolleskoven** (Trolls' Forest). Legend says that fog comes from the brew in the troll's kitchen and that when the trolls are brewing something they leave their little abodes under the cover of fog to wander the forest looking for trouble. The most mischievous is the littlest troll, Krølle Bølle, who has become a mascot of sorts for Bornholm. His likeness is everywhere—especially in souvenir shops.

Where to Stay

$–$$ 🏨 **Strandhotellet.** Romantic charm is the draw at this venerable hotel on
Fodor'sChoice a corner across from the harbor. A white arched entry leads into a
★ stone-and-whitewashed lobby. Rooms are furnished in plain beech furniture with woolen covers and pastel colors. ⊠ *Strandpromenaden 7, Sandvig DK–3770* ☎ *56/48–03–14* 🖷 *56/48–02–09* ⊕ *www. strandhotellet.dk* ↩ *52 rooms, 1 suite with bath* ♧ *Restaurant, bar* ▭ *MC, V.*

¢ 🏕 **Sandvig Familie Camping.** Pleasantly close to the beach, most of the camping sites here have a view of the water. The large kitchen and bathing facilities are well maintained. ⊠ *Sandlinien 5, DK–3770* ☎ *56/48–04–47 or 56/48–00–01* ♧ *Showers, kitchen, playground* ☉ *Closed Nov.–Mar.*

| en route | Eight kilometers (5 mi) southeast of Allinge along the coastal path are the grottoes and granite cliffs of the **Helligdomsklipperne** (Cliffs of Sanctuary), which contain a well-known rock formation best seen from the boats that sail the nearby waters in summer. In the Middle Ages, people used to visit these waters, believing that they had healing powers—hence the name. The **Helligdomsklipperne boat** (☎ 58/48–51–65) departs several times daily in the summer from the Gudhjem harbor. The round-trip costs Dkr 60. Just southeast of the Helligdomsklipperne, a pastoral coastal path leads to the tiny, preserved **Døndalen Forest.** Its fertile soil bears a surprising profusion of Mediterranean vegetation, including fig and cherry trees. During rainy periods look for a waterfall at the bottom of the dale. |

Gudhjem

★ **5** *18 km (11 mi) east of Allinge, 33 km (21 mi) northeast of Rønne.*

At the height of summer, Gudhjem (God's Home) is perhaps the most tourist-packed town on Bornholm. Tiny half-timber houses and gift shops with lace curtains and clay roofs line steep stone streets that loop around the harbor. The island's first smokehouses still produce alder-smoked golden herring.

★ ☙ Walk down Brøddegade, which turns into Melstedvej; here you'll find the **Landsbrugs Museum** (Agricultural Museum) and Melstedgård, a working farm. The farm includes the well-kept house and garden of a 19th-century family who lived here. Notice the surprisingly bright colors used on the interior of the house, and leave time to visit the old shop where you can buy locally produced woolen sweaters, wooden spoons, and even homemade mustard. ⊠ *Melstedvej 25* ☎ *56/48–55–98* ⊕ *www. bornholmsmuseer.dk/melstedg* 🎟 *Dkr 30* ☉ *Mid-May–mid-Oct., Tues.–Sun. 10–5.*

Just up the hill from Gudhjem's waterfront is the **Oluf Høst Museet,** with a collection of paintings by Bornholm artist Oluf Høst, including his series of a whitewashed Bornholm farm called Bognemark, which he depicted with glowing splashes of oranges and reds from the setting sun. Høst and other modernist Bornholm artists are well known for their ability to capture Bornholm's natural light. The museum is in Høst's home, which he built in 1929 out of two fisherman's cottages and lived in until his death in 1966. It's easy to see why Høst found artistic inspiration here. At the top of the house's leafy, rock-strewn garden are lovely views over the colorful cottages of Gudhjem. ✉ *Løkkeg. 35* ☎ *56/ 48–50–38* ⊕ *www.ohmus.dk* ✉ *Dkr 40* ⊙ *Mid-June–mid-Aug., daily 11–5; mid-Aug.–Sept., Tues.–Sun. 11–5; mid-Apr.–mid-June and early Oct., Tues.–Sun. 1–5.*

> **off the beaten path**

BORNHOLMS KUNSTMUSEUM – If you follow the main road, Hellidomsvej, out of Gudhjem in the direction of Allinge/Sandvig, you'll come to Bornholm's art museum, an excellent example of the Danes' ability to integrate art, architecture, and natural surroundings. Built by the architectural firm of Fogh and Følner, the white-painted brick, granite, and sandstone building is centered by a thin stream of "holy" trickling water that exits the building and leads the visitor to a walkway and overlook above the Helligdomsklipperne. Throughout, the walls of the museum are punched with picture windows overlooking nearby grazing cows and the crashing Baltic: a natural accompaniment to the art. Most of the works are by Bornholmers, including a body of modernist work by Oluf Høst, Karl Esaksen, and Olaf Rude. The museum also displays some sculpture and glass, as well as a survey of more historical paintings. Check out the restaurant and shop. ✉ *Hellidomsvej 95* ☎ *56/48–43–86* ⊕ *www.bornholms-kunstmuseum.dk* ✉ *Dkr 35* ⊙ *May, Sept., and Oct., Tues.–Sun. 10–5; June–Aug., daily 10–5; Nov.–Apr., Tues. and Thurs. 1–5, Sun. 10–5.*

CHRISTIANSØ – A 45-minute boat ride northeast from Gudhjem will bring you to the historic island of Christiansø. Though it was originally a bastion, the Storetårn (Big Tower) and Lilletårn (Little Tower) are all that remain of the fort, built in 1684 and dismantled in 1855. The barracks, street, and gardens, for which the earth was hauled here by boat, have hardly changed since that time. They remain under the jurisdiction of the defense ministry, making this a tiny tax-free haven for its 100 inhabitants. Nearby, the rocky, uninhabited island of **Græsholmen** is an inaccessible bird sanctuary— the only place in Denmark where the razorbill and guillemot breed.

Where to Stay & Eat

¢–$ ✗ **Café Klint.** Locals flock to this red, half-timber harborside restaurant, where the portions of good 'ole Danish fare are generous and the prices are low. Dishes include smoked salmon with spinach, fillet of sole with remoulade, or a plate heaped with different kinds of herring. In the summer, tables are set out on the terrace. In the winter, the restaurant changes its name to Vinter Klint (Winter Klint), and you can't get cozier than sitting in the low-ceiling dining room, surrounded by pine-green walls, and perhaps warmed by a glass or two of the house wine. ✉ *Ejnar Mikkelsensvej 20* ☎ *56/48–56–26* ⊟ *MC, V.*

$–$$ ▦ **Jantzens Hotel.** Founded in 1872, this bright-yellow building with white shutters and wrought-iron balconies is Gudhjem's oldest hotel. The front windows face the sea, and the backyard gives way to a sunny, idyllic terrace and rose garden. Much of the hotel has been lovingly restored, with an eye to recapturing its turn-of-the-20th-century ambience. Rooms are outfitted with hardwood floors, pale green walls, and rattan furniture. The balconies have views over Gudhjem's yellow and red houses, clustered against a backdrop of the blue Baltic. The bathrooms are small and basic, but all rooms are equipped with a refrigerator. The hotel's interior is still a work in progress; so far half the rooms have been restored, so ask when booking. What was once a pavilion and tea terrace is now utilized by the restaurant, Andi's Kokken, which includes on its French-Danish menu such dishes as mussels in a mild curry sauce with capers, and venison with shallots and mushrooms. Dessert might be fresh blueberries, hand-picked by the chef from the nearby fields. The restaurant is closed Mondays and November through April. ⊠ *Brøddeg. 33, DK–3760* ☎ *56/48–50–17* 🖷 *56/48–57–15* ⊕ *www.jantzenshotel.dk* 🛏 *18 rooms with bath* ♻ *Restaurant, some pets allowed (fee)* ☰ *MC, V* ☯ *Closed Nov.–Apr.*

¢ 🏠 **Danhostel Gudhjem.** In a half-timber 100-year-old former manor house, this hostel in the middle of Gudhjem offers single- to eight-bed rooms of standard Danish hostel style: pine bunks and industrial carpeting. There are six kitchens available for use. ⊠ *Løkkeg. 7, DK–3760* ☎ *56/48–50–35* 🖷 *56/48–56–35* ⊕ *www.danhostel-gudhjem.dk* 🛏 *50 rooms without bath* ♻ *Restaurant, laundry facilities* ☰ *MC, V.*

Shopping

Baltic Sea Glass (⊠ Melstedvej 47 ☎ 56/48–56–41), on the main road just on the outskirts of town, offers high-quality, bright, and imaginative decanters, glasses, candlesticks, and one-of-a-kind pieces, including an old-fashioned contraption to catch flies. In town, see the delicate porcelain bowls of **Per Rehfeldt** (⊠ Salenevej 1 ☎ 56/48–54–13). Unique, hand-thrown ceramic work is available from and by **Julia Manitius** (⊠ Holkavej 12 ☎ 56/48–55–99).

Rø Plantage

❻ *6 km (4 mi) southwest of Gudhjem, 24 km (15 mi) northeast of Rønne.*

Rø Plantation is dense forest that serves as a quiet foil to the hubbub of Gudhjem. A century ago it was a heather-covered grazing area, but after stone dikes were erected to keep the cattle out, spruce, pine, larch, and birch were cultivated. The cool refuge now consists largely of saplings and new growth—the result of devastating storms in the late '50s and '60s.

Rø Golfbane (⊠ Spellingevej 3 ☎ 56/48–40–50) has won various European and Scandinavian awards for its natural beauty—and challenges. Its 18 holes are set close to the coastal cliffs and have views of the sea. It has a pro shop and a restaurant.

Østerlars

❼ *5 km (3 mi) east of Rø Plantage, 22 km (14 mi) northeast of Rønne.*

Fodor'sChoice The standout attraction here is the **Østerlars Kirke.** The largest of the is-
★ land's four round churches, it was built in about 1150; extensions, including the buttresses, were added later. Constructed from boulders and slabs of limestone, the whitewashed church was part spiritual sanctuary, part fortification, affording protection from enemy armies and pirates. Inside is the island's only painted tympanum, with a faded image of a cross and decorative foliage. Several Gothic wall paintings—including depictions of the Annunciation and Nativity—have survived from the 1300s. ⊠ *Gudhjemsvej 28* ☎ *56/49–82–64* 🎫 *Dkr 6* ☯ *May–mid-Oct., Mon.–Sat. 9–5.*

off the
beaten
path

KIRSTEN CLEMANN'S CERAMIC STUDI – Bornholm, with its Baltic Sea location and wide-open skies, has been drawing artists to its shores for the past century. Kirsten Clemann has been here for several decades, creating her fanciful, one-of-a-kind ceramic designs in a clay-spattered studio adjoining her home, just west of the small, blink-and-you'll-miss-it town of Østermarie, 5 km (3 mi) southeast of Østerlars. As Clemann tells it, it took awhile to be accepted into the island community, but now her pieces are proudly displayed in restaurants and craft shows across Bornholm—and across the globe. Clemann works out of her pleasantly chaotic studio, where she creates turtles; hens; birdbaths; and delicate, floating ceramic balls for ponds. She usually works with the colors of blue and rose. Clemann's large, unique reliefs are often snapped up by German buyers; the pieces may depict rows of dancing women twirling their umbrellas, or be covered with protruding glazed ceramic fish heads, inspired by a display at a fish market. Clemann's other passion is her garden, which is teeming with blooming bushes and flowers and is strewn with her ceramic creations. Call ahead. ⊠ *Almindingensvej 84, 2½ km (1½ mi) west of Østermarie* ☎ *56/47–27–05.*

Svaneke

❽ *21 km (13 mi) east of Østerlars, 49 km (31 mi) northeast of Rønne.*

The coastal town of Svaneke, Denmark's easternmost settlement, is an enchanting hamlet of 17th- and 18th-century houses, winding cobbled streets, and a harbor sliced from the rocky earth. Once a fishing village, it is now immaculately preserved and the site of a thriving artists' community.

Bornholm's smoked herring is famous throughout Scandinavia, and no visit to the island is complete without sampling it for yourself—preferably in the manner of the Danes, who eat it outside on a sunny terrace, with a cold Carlsberg in hand. For more than 35 years, Hjorth Hansen has been smoking herring at **Hjorths Røgeri** (Hjorth's Smokehouse), 2 km (1 mi) south of Svaneke. Every morning at 6 AM, Hjorth hauls in big baskets of elmwood, lights a fire, and begins smoking the fresh herring, tending to the fire with a long pole wrapped with rags at one end. Five hours later, he serves up plates of warm, smoked herring in the adjoining terrace. Hjorth works from late April to October. The best time to watch him in action is around 10 AM, in the last hour of the smoking process. ⊠ *Brugsebakken 18, Årsdale,* ☎ *56/49–61–10* ⊘ *Late Apr.–Oct.*

Where to Stay & Eat

¢–$$ ✕ **Bryghuset.** Microbreweries are a new concept in the land of Carlsberg, but the idea is catching on, and Svaneke's Bryghuset (Brew House) is one of the first. All the beer is brewed on the premises, in a massive copper brew kettle linked by piping to the kitchen. The menu is based on the concept that food should compliment the beer. The house specialty is Bryggerben ("Brewer's bone"), a messy, finger-licking plate of spareribs smothered in barbecue sauce, which can be enjoyed at one of the long wooden tables set under the beam ceilings or on the large summer terrace. Also on offer is a platter of Christiansø herring served with egg, rye bread, and butter. At Easter and Christmas, try the stronger festive brew. ⊠ *Torvet 5* ☎ *56/49–73–21* ☐ *MC, V* ⊘ *Closed Jan.*

$$ ✕⊡ **Siemsens Gaard.** Built in a 270-year-old merchant house, this U-shape hotel with a gravel-courtyard café overlooks the harbor. The inside is cushy with sofas below severe black-and-white prints and antiques. The rooms differ, but all have stripped pine and soft colors. The bright,

modern restaurant serves French-Danish food, with a menu of 75 dishes—from club sandwiches to smoked Baltic salmon to smørrebrød. The restaurant is closed from November to May. ⊠ *Havnebryggen 9, DK–3740* ☎ *56/49–61–49* 🖷 *56/49–61–03* ⊕ *www.siemsens.dk* ⊂▷ *51 rooms with bath* ☼ *Restaurant, café, some pets allowed, no-smoking rooms* ⊟ *AE, DC, MC, V.*

Shopping

Stroll through the boutiques in the central Glastorvet in Svaneke. Among them is the studio of **Pernille Bülow** (⊠ Glastorvet, Brænderigænget 8 ☎ 56/49–66–72), one of Denmark's most famous glassblowers. Her work is sold in Copenhagen's best design shops. Even if you buy directly from her studio, don't expect bargains—though you may be lucky to find seconds—but do expect colorful, experimental work.

Neksø

❾ *9 km (5½ mi) south of Svaneke, 48 km (30 mi) northeast of Rønne.*

Neksø (or Nexø) bustles with tourists and locals who shop and live around its busy harbor, lined with fishing boats from throughout the Baltics and Eastern Europe. It might seem like a typical 17th-century town, but it was rebuilt almost completely after World War II, when the Russians bombed it to dislodge stubborn German troops who refused to surrender—three days after the rest of Denmark had been liberated. The Russians lingered on the island until April 1946.

Wander down to the harbor to find the **Neksø Museum,** housed in a mustard-yellow building that was once the town's courthouse. The museum has a fine collection of fishing and local history exhibits and maritime memorabilia. ⊠ *Havnen* ☎ *56/49–25–56* ⊕ *www.bornholmsmuseer. dk* ▨ *Dkr 15* ⊙ *May–Oct., Tues.–Sun. 10–4.*

The **Andersen Nexøs Hus** contains photographs and mementos of Danish author Martin Andersen Hansen (1909–55), who changed his last name to Nexø after his beloved town. A complicated man and vehement socialist, he wrote, among other works, *Pelle the Conqueror,* set in Bornholm at the turn of the 20th century, when Swedish immigrants were exploited by Danish landowners. The story was turned into an Academy Award–winning film. ⊠ *Ferskesøstr. 36* ☎ *56/49–45–42* ⊕ *www.bornholmsmuseer.dk/manexo* ▨ *Dkr 20* ⊙ *Mid-May–Oct., weekdays 10–4, Sat. 10–2.*

Where to Eat

$$–$$$ ✕ **Tre Søstre.** Facing Nexø's bustling harbor, this spacious restaurant, housed in a converted storage warehouse, is named after a 19th-century Danish ship *The Three Sisters,* a model of which hangs on the wall. The creatively decorated interior (right down to the plates and the candlesticks) pays tribute to Bornholm's artists. The lavender, pale-orange, and sea-green vases of Svaneke glassblower Pernille Bülow grace the window sills, providing a bright and delicate contrast to the restaurant's rustic furnishings. Hanging from the ceiling is a playful, blue-and-green ceramic fish, created by long-time Bornholmer Kirsten Clemann. The Danish menu includes grilled salmon with spinach and hollandaise sauce, and fried scampi flavored with cognac, garlic, and curry. ⊠ *Havnen 5* ☎ *56/49–33–93* ⊟ *AE, DC, MC, V* ⊙ *Closed Sept.–May.*

Shopping

For exquisite woodwork see **Bernard Romain** (⊠ Rønnevej 54 ☎ 56/48–86–66).

Almindingen

🔟 *23 km (14 mi) west of Neksø, 27 km (17 mi) northeast of Rønne.*

The lush Almindingen, Denmark's third-largest forest, is filled with ponds, lakes, evergreens, and well-marked trails, and it blooms with lily of the valley in spring. Within it, the oak-lined **Ekkodalen** (Echo Valley)— where children love to hear their shouts resound—is networked by trails leading to smooth rock faces that soar 72 feet high. At the northern edge, near the road to Østermarie, once stood one of Bornholm's most famous sights: seven evergreens growing from a single trunk. The plant succumbed to old age in 1995, but you may still be able to see the remains of its curious trunk.

Sports & the Outdoors

HIKING Check with the tourist board for a map showing three 4-km (2½-mi) hikes through the Almindingen Forest and several more through its Echo Valley. The *Bornholm Green Guide,* available in shops and tourism offices, offers walking and hiking routes.

Åkirkeby

⓫ *5 km (3 mi) south of Almindingen, 16 km (9 mi) east of Rønne.*

Åkirkeby is the oldest town on the island, with a municipal charter from 1346. The town's church, the **Åkirke,** is Bornholm's oldest and largest, dating from the mid-12th century. Though it is not one of the more typical round churches, its walls and tower were well suited for defense. The altarpiece and pulpit are Dutch Renaissance pieces from about 1600, but the carved sandstone font is as old as the church itself. ✉ *Torvet* ☎ *56/97–41–03* 💷 *Dkr 10* 🕙 *Mon.–Sat. 10–4.*

Nylars

⓬ *8 km (5 mi) west of Åkirkeby, 9 km (6 mi) east of Rønne.*

Like the Østerlars church, the round **Nylars Kirke** dates from 1150. The chalk paintings from the Old Testament on its central pillar are the oldest on the island, possibly dating from 1250. Even older are the runic stones on the church's porch. Both are of Viking origin. ✉ *Kirkevej* ☎ *56/ 97–20–13* 💷 *Suggested donation Dkr 5* 🕙 *Mid-May–mid-Sept., Mon.–Sat. 9–5.*

Bornholm A to Z

AIRPORTS
The Bornholms Lufthavn airport is 5 km (3 mi) south of Rønne at the island's southwestern tip.
🇫 Bornholms Lufthavn ☎ 56/95-26-26 ⊕ www.slv.dk/bornholm.

BIKE TRAVEL
Biking is eminently feasible and pleasant on Bornholm, thanks to a network of more than 200 km (125 mi) of cycle roads, including an old railway converted to a cross-island path. Rentals of sturdy two-speeds and tandems are available for about Dkr 50 a day at more than 20 different establishments all over the island—near the ferry; at the airport; and in Allinge, Gudhjem, Hasle, Pedersker (near Åkirkeby), Rønne, Svaneke, and most other towns.
🇫 Bike Rentals **Bornholms Cykeludlejning** ✉ Nordre Kystvej 5, Rønne ☎ 56/ 95-13-59. **Cykel-Centret** ✉ Sønderg. 7, Rønne ☎ 56/95-06-04.

BOAT & FERRY TRAVEL

The *Bornholmstrafikken* car ferry from Copenhagen's Kvæsthusbro Harbor (near Nyhavn) departs at 11:30 PM year-round; from late January to mid-March, it departs only on Wednesday, Friday, and Sunday. From late June to mid-August, there are also departures at 8 AM on Monday, Wednesday, Friday, and weekends. During the rest of the year, there is often one weekly 8:30 AM departure, usually on Tuesday or Friday. Call for details. The night trip takes seven hours, and the day trip takes six hours. To avoid delays, make reservations. Comfortable sleeping bunks in a massive hall are also available for an extra charge. At this writing, the public operators of the ferry line were discussing changes in overall service in conjunction with a privatization plan. The schedule above should be valid until 2005, but it would be wise to double check as the fate of the line may be determined in the interim.

With the opening of the Øresund Bridge between Copenhagen and Malmö, *Bornholmstrafikken* has increased its ferry departures from Ystad, which lies 57 km (36 mi) southeast of Malmö. There are two to four departures from Ystad to Rønne daily, on either the high-speed ferry (1 hr 20 min), or the conventional ferry (2½ hrs).

Nordbornholms Turistbureau (North Bornholm Tourist Board) is the agent for a summer ferry that links Neu Mukran and Fährhafen Sassnitz on the island of Rügen in Germany. Scandlines, a competing company, offers passage aboard the ferry to Fährhafen Sassnitz. Prices vary according to the number of people traveling and the size of the vehicle. There is also a boat between Swinoujscie, Poland and Rønne (7 hrs); call Polferries in Poland.

🛈 **Bornholmstrafikken** ☎ 56/95-18-66 ⊕ www.bornholmferries.dk. **Nordbornholms Turistbureau** ☎ 56/48-00-01 ⊕ www.bornholmsbookingcenter.dk. **Polferries** ✉ Norgesvej 2 Rønne ☎ 56/95-10-69, 48/943-552-102 in Poland ⊕ www.polferries.com. **Scandlines** ☎ 33/15-15-15 ⊕ www.scandlines.dk.

BUS TRAVEL

The *Bornholmerbussen* (Bornholm Bus) No. 866 runs from Copenhagen's main station, travels across the Øresund Bridge to Malmö, in Sweden, and then continues to Ystad, where it connects with a ferry to Rønne. The trip takes around three hours. Buses depart two to four times daily, usually once in the morning and several times in the afternoon and evening. Call Bornholmerbussen for more details.

Though bus service is certainly not as frequent as in major cities, there are regular connections (with BAT, see below) between Bornholm towns. Schedules are posted at all stations, and you can usually pick one up on board. The fare is Dkr 8.50 per zone, or you can buy a klip kort (punch ticket) of 10 tickets for Dkr 68. A 24-hour bus pass costs Dkr 110.

🛈 **Bornholmerbussen** ☎ 44/68-44-00. **BAT** (Bornholm Municipality Traffic Company) ☎ 56/95-21-21 ⊕ www.bat.dk.

CAR RENTAL

Rønne's Hertz agency is near the ferry arrivals and departures area. The Avis branch is also nearby.

🛈 **Avis** ✉ Snellemark 19, Rønne ☎ 56/95-22-08 **Hertz** ✉ Munch Petersens Vej 1, Rønne ☎ 56/91-00-12.

CAR TRAVEL

There are excellent roads on the island, but be alert for cyclists and occasional leisurely paced cows.

EMERGENCIES

The general emergency number for ambulance, accident, or fire anywhere in Denmark is 112.

Bornholm's Central Hospital ⊠ Sygehusvej, Rønne ☎ 56/95-11-65. **Rønne Apotek** (Rønne Pharmacy) ⊠ Store Torveg. 12, Rønne ☎ 56/95-01-30.

SPORTS & THE OUTDOORS

FISHING   Cod, salmon, and herring fishing are excellent in season, though better from a boat than from shore. Licenses cost Dkr 25 per day, Dkr 75 per week, and Dkr 100 per year. Contact the tourist office for details and information on charter trips.

TOURS

Klippefly can arrange a 20- to 40-minute aerial tour in a Cessna or Piper plane that covers either the entire coast or the northern tip.

The BAT (Bornholm Municipality Traffic Company) offers some inventive summer tours. All are available Tuesday through Friday, from mid-July until early August. All begin at the red bus terminal at Snellemark 30 in Rønne at 10 AM and cost Dkr 110. (You can also buy a 24-hour bus card for Dkr 110, or a five- or seven-day card for Dkr 390, good for both the regional buses and the tours.) Tour prices do not include some Dkr 5–Dkr 10 admissions or lunch at a herring smokehouse. The five-hour tour aboard the Kunsthåndværkbussen (Arts and Crafts Bus) includes stops at glass, pottery, textile, and silver studios. In summer, different studios are visited each day. The Havebussen (Garden Bus) visits sights that illustrate the ways in which the island's exquisite flora and fauna are being preserved. The Veteranbussen (Veteran Bus), a circa World War II Bedford, connects some of Bornholm's oldest industries, including a clockmaker, water mill, and Denmark's last windmill used for making flour.

From mid-June to mid-September, boats to the Helligdomsklipperne (Sanctuary Cliffs) leave Gudhjem at 10:30, 1:30, and 2:30, with extra sailings from mid-June to mid-August. Call Thor Båd. Boats to Christiansø depart from Svaneke at 10 AM daily year-round; May to September daily at 10:20 from Gudhjem, and at 1 from Allinge; and between mid-June and August, an additional boat leaves Gudhjem weekdays at 9:40 and 12:15. Call Christiansø Farten for additional information.

BAT (Bornholm Municipality Traffic Company) ☎ 56/95-21-21 ⊕ www.bat.dk. **Christiansø Farten** ⊠ Ejnar Mikkelsensvej 25, Gudhjem ☎ 56/48-51-76 ⊕ www.christiansoefarten.dk. **Klippefly** ⊠ Søndre Landevej 2, Rønne ☎ 56/95-35-73 ⊕ www.bornholmerguiden.dk/klippefly. **Thor Båd** ⊠ Melstedvej 17, Gudhjem ☎ 56/48-51-65.

TRAIN TRAVEL

A DSB Intercity train travels two to five times a day from Copenhagen's main station, across the Øresund Bridge to Malmö, and then to Ystad, where it connects with a ferry to Rønne.

DSB ☎ 70/13-14-15 ⊕ www.dsb.dk.

VISITOR INFORMATION

The main tourist office in Rønne operates a Web site with area listings.

Bornholm Tourist Office ⊠ Nordre Kystvej 3, DK-3700 Rønne ☎ 56/95-95-00 ☐ 56/95-95-68 ⊕ www.bornholminfo.dk. **Allinge-Nordbornholms Turistbureau** ⊠ Kirkeg. 4, DK-3770 Allinge ☎ 56/48-00-01 ☐ 56/48-00-20 ⊕ www.bornholmsbookingcenter.dk. **Åkirkeby** ⊠ Torvet 2, DK-3720 Åkirkeby ☎ 56/97-45-20 ☐ 56/97-58-90 ⊕ www.sydborn.dk. **Gudhjem** ⊠ Åbog. 9 DK-3760 Gudhjem ☎ 56/48-52-10 ☐ 56/48-52-74. **Hasle** ⊠ Havneg. 1 DK-3790 Hasle ☎ 56/96-44-81 ☐ 56/96-41-06 ⊕ www.hasle-turistbureau.dk. **Nexø** ⊠ Søndre Hammer 2A DK-3730 Nexø ☎ 56/49-70-79 ☐ 56/49-70-10 ⊕ www.nexoe-dueodde.dk. **Svaneke** ⊠ Storeg. 24, DK-3740 Svaneke ☎ 56/49-70-79 ☐ 56/49-70-10 ⊕ www.nexoe-dueodde.dk.

THE FAROE ISLANDS

6

FODOR'S CHOICE

Skansin Guesthouse, *Tórshavn*

HIGHLY RECOMMENDED

HOTELS   Hotel Föroyar, *Tórshavn*

SIGHTS   Kirkjubøur

Listasavn Føroya, *art gallery in Tórshavn*

Vestmanna

Viðareiði

Updated by
Eduardo López
de Luzuriaga

THE 18 FAROE ISLANDS (Føroyar in Faroese; Færøerne in Danish) rise up out of the North Atlantic as the extended knuckle of a volcanic archipelago. All but one—Lítla Dímun—are inhabited by a population totaling 46,000 people and twice as many sheep. For obvious reasons, Føroyar means "Islands of the Sheep." The native Faroese live by fishing, fish farming, and shepherding.

Situated 300 km (188 mi) northwest of Scotland, 430 km (270 mi) southeast of Iceland, and 1,300 km (812 mi) northwest of Denmark, the fjord-chiseled islands support little vegetation besides short grasses and moss. The climate is oceanic: humid, changeable, and stormy, with surprisingly mild temperatures—52°F in summer, 37°F in winter—and a heavy annual rainfall of 63 inches.

Of their 1,399 square km (540 square mi), only 6% is fertile, the rest rough pasture—an Eden for 70 breeding and 120 migratory species of birds, among them thousands of gannets, auks, and puffins. Beneath azure skies and rugged, mossy mountains, villages of colorful thatch-roof houses cling to hillsides while large trawlers and small fishing boats glide in and out of their harbors. Religious and proud, the Faroese have built churches in nearly every settlement.

Catholic monks from Ireland were the first to settle the islands in the middle of the 7th century, but they died out without leaving a trace and were replaced by Norwegian Vikings, who settled the land about AD 800. It was here that the Løgting (parliament) met for the first time in AD 900 in Tórshavn, where it still meets today. In 1035 the islands came under Norwegian rule and remained so until 1380 when Olaf III of Denmark became king of both Denmark and Norway. Under the Danish crown, the islands have had a home-rule government since 1948, with their own flag and language. The roots of the Faroese language are in Old West Norse. Most people speak English but a Danish dictionary can be helpful to the visitor. Danish is the second language.

It's difficult for visitors to understand the isolation or the practical relationship the Faroese have with the natural world. Dubious outsiders, for example, accuse locals of cruelty during the traditional pilot-whale harvests. An essential foodstuff, the sea mammals are killed in limited numbers to reduce the islands' dependence on imported meat. The profit factor is eliminated: whale meat is not sold—it's given away to the townspeople in equal portions on a per capita basis. The hunt is also an important social bond involving both the young and the old.

After having plunged into a severe depression at the beginning of the 1990s, the islands have recovered well and are enjoying a healthy economy again. The unemployment rate stands at 3%, tourism is increasing at an annual rate of 10%–15%, and international oil companies believe there is oil in the region. If they strike it rich, the Faroese, who currently receive Dkr 650,000 from Denmark each year, could become economically independent. However, many people fear that the black gold will irrevocably change the face of their islands. Oil or not, the autonomous government is committed to achieving independence from Denmark.

Exploring the Faroe Islands

Tórshavn on the island of Streymoy is the largest city in the Faroes and makes for a good touring base; the town of Klaksvík on the island of Borðoy is also a pleasant place to overnight. Efficient bus and ferry service is the best way to travel between towns, but be prepared for service interruptions during inclement weather.

If you are visiting the islands for only a short period of time, seek out a satisfactory room in Tórshavn and then make day trips from there. If you stay more than a few days, endeavor to get an impression of both the northern and the southern ends of the archipelago: the islands to the north are mountainous and lined with sheer cliffs, while the islands to the south are milder both in climate and topography.

Numbers in the text correspond to numbers in the margin and on the Faroe Islands map.

6

If you have 3 days Find suitable accommodations in ⊠ **Tórshavn** ① ⚑ and use the city as a base of operations, making excursions to more remote points on the island of Streymoy. Spend your first day in Tórshavn, soaking in the atmosphere of a North Atlantic outpost. Rise early the next day and travel to **Vestmanna** ③, where you can take a boat tour to get a closer look at the area's bustling avian life, or you can travel on to **Saksun** ④ to take in the view from another unique coastal vantage point. On the third day venture south to **Kirkjubøur** ②, which was once the ecclesiastical hub of the Faroe Islands; the remains of Magnus Cathedral and the still-standing St. Olaf's Church testify to this fact.

If you have 7 days With a week to spend in the Faroe Islands, you should do as much island-hopping as possible, though to be safe (especially in the off-season) you should route yourself back through Tórshavn, so you can minimize the chances of getting stranded far from the capital and missing your flight off the Faroes. Be flexible at all times, and if taking the longer ferry trips early in the week seems more prudent, don't hesitate to rearrange this itinerary upon arrival. Spend your first day and night in ⊠ **Tórshavn** ① ⚑, getting settled and taking a quick walking tour of the city. On the second day, catch the afternoon bus to ⊠ **Klaksvík** ⑥, and spend the night there. Get an early start on the third day and find your way to ⊠ **Viðareiði** ⑦ on the island of Viðoy, the most scenically stunning of the Faroe Islands. Nature-lovers and hikers will want to overnight here and spend as much time as possible exploring. However, you could also make it a long day trip and return to Klaksvík for another night. On the fourth day, make your way back to Tórshavn, where you should look for a ferry to take you to either Tvøroyi or Vágur on the island of Suðuroy on the morning of the fifth day. Spend the fifth and sixth nights in ⊠ **Vágur** ⑪, exploring the island by daylight. Return to Tórshavn either late on the sixth day or early on the seventh. If you have a proclivity for the rugged landforms of the northern islands, you can forgo the trip to Suðuroy for a three-day jaunt to **Mykines** ⑨ by way of Vágar.

Because you can experience the full range of Faroese seasons in the span of just a few hours, a good rain jacket and sunglasses are necessities. If you intend to do any hiking, bring a sturdy pair of hiking boots.

About the Hotels

The amenities and services of the few hotels and hostels on the islands vary widely, but you can usually count on a clean, simple room. The islands' best hotels are in Tórshavn and near Vagar Airport. In the smaller villages you can find accommodation at the local bed-and-breakfasts.

Most hotels beyond the island of Streymoy are closed from the early fall to the late spring. Faroese weather patterns are capable of whipping up strong winds and heavy rains that discourage all but the hardiest would-be campers. If you do intend to camp, make sure to choose your site carefully and set up the tent securely. Camping is permitted only in the archipelago's many registered campgrounds or on private land with the permission of the land owner.

WHAT IT COSTS In kroner					
	$$$$	$$$	$$	$	¢
RESTAURANTS	over 180	141–180	121–140	90–120	under 90
HOTELS	over 1,500	1,200–1,500	1,000–1,200	700–1,000	under 700

Restaurant prices are for a main course at dinner. Hotel prices are for two people in a standard double room, including service charge and tax.

Timing

From May to September, the islands' storminess abates a bit, allowing boats and ferries to operate fairly regularly throughout the archipelago. Any journeys beyond the island of Streymoy and Eysturoy are best left to the long—if not warm—days of summer. During the dead of winter, when an average of 25 days per month are marked by precipitation, travelers to the farther flung islands like Mykines should prepare to be stranded by storms and budget their time accordingly. Transportation is not the only reason to favor the summer season; when the weather is foul on the Faroe Islands, it is truly unpleasant to venture outside, but to enjoy the islands' stark natural beauty, outside is exactly where you'll want to be when you visit.

Tórshavn

▶ ❶ *1,343 km (839 mi) northwest of Copenhagen, 2 hrs by plane.*

Most visitors begin their explorations on the largest and most traveled island of Streymoy, which, though carved by sheer cliffs and waterfalls, has good roads and tunnels. On the northern end of the island are bird sanctuaries and a NATO base. On its southeastern flank is one of the world's tiniest capitals, Tórshavn, named for the Viking god Thor. Centrally located, Tórshavn has a population of 16,000. St. Olaf's Day, July 29, is named for the Norwegian king who brought Christianity to the islands in the 14th century. Celebrations include rowing competitions and group dances in the form of a chain—a sort of North Atlantic ring dance.

The rugged **Tinganes** is a small peninsula between the east and west bays that was the site of both the old trading post and the meetings of the local parliament (*tinganes* means "assembly place"). Here you can see some of the town's oldest buildings, dating from the 17th and 18th centuries, and some old warehouses, which today house the government offices. At the end of the docks is **Skansin,** a fort built in 1580 by Magnus Heinason to protect the town against pirates; after many reconstructions, it assumed its present form in 1790. The British navy used this site as its Faroe headquarters during World War II, and two guns from that era remain.

Down from the Tinganes is Old Main Street, lined with small 19th-century houses and crossed by twisting streets. You'll come to the slate **Havnar Kirkja** (Tórshavn's Church), rebuilt many times in its 200-year

The Faroe Islands

TO
ICELAND

Viðareiði
7
Viðoy
Fugloy

Kunoy
Kalsoy
Hattarvík

Gjógv
Húsar
Kunoy

Eiði
5
Svínoy
Slættaratindur
Syðradalur

Haldarsvík
Fuglafjørður
Hvannasund

Saksun
4
Norðskáli
Klaksvík
6
Eysturoy
Leirvík
Borðoy

Vestmanna
3

Fjallavatn
Vágar
Streymoy
Strendur

Mykines
9
Oyrargjógv
Tóftir

Sørvágur
Sandavágur

Sørvágsvatn
8
Nólsoy
Bøsdalafossur
Miðvágur
Tórshavn
1

Velbastaður
Nólsoy
Koltur
Hestur
Kirkjubøur
2

Hestur

Skopun

Sandoy
TO
SHETLAND
ISLANDS

Sandur
10

Skúvoy
Skúvoy

ATLANTIC
OCEAN

Stóra Dímun

Lítla Dímun
TO
DENMARK

Tvøroyri

Øravík
Suðuroy
Vágur
11

0   20miles

0   30km

history. Inside is a model of a ship salvaged from an 18th-century wreck, the ship's bell, and an altarpiece dating from 1647.

There are very few trees on the islands. **Viðalundin Park,** a walk up Hoydalsvegur, is the pride of the town—a rare cultivated oasis of green trees in a land where storms and strong winds flatten most tall vegetation.

Atop a hill in the center of town, **Kongaminnið** (King's Memorial) is an obelisk commemorating the visit King Christian IX paid to the island in 1874. Christian IX was the first representative of the still-reigning Glucksborger family to serve as Denmark's king. ⊠ Norðrari Ringvegur, just off R. C. Effersøes gøta.

★ **Listasavn Føroya** (National Art Gallery) has a permanent exhibition, which provides an overview of contemporary Faroese arts. Special attention is paid to the painter Mykines and also to Tróndur Patursson, known for his painted-glass sculptures. ⊠ Gundadalsvegur 9 ☎ 298/31–35–79 ⊕ www.art.fo ☒ Dkr 25 ⊙ June–Aug., Mon.–Fri. 11–5, weekends 2–6; Sept.–mid-Dec. and mid-Jan.–May, Tues.–Fri. 2–5, weekends 2–6.

The Museum of Natural History, **Føroya Náttúrugripasavn,** highlights the central role played by nature in Faroese history. It also portrays the islanders' point of view on the controversial issue of pilot-whale hunting. ⊠ V. U. Hammershaimbsgøta 13 ☎ 298/31–23–00 ⊕ www.ngs. fo ☒ Dkr 20 ⊙ June–Aug., weekdays 11–4, weekends 3–5; Sept.–May, Sun. 3–5.

Where to Stay & Eat

★ **$$** ✕ 🖭 **Hotel Föroyar.** Five minutes by car from Tórshavn center, this Best Western hotel has a splendid view of the Old Town and the Isle of Nólsoy. Island specialties are to be found in the restaurant. All rooms have TVs and phones and some have access for the disabled. ⊠ Við Oyggjarvegur, FO–110 ☎ 298/31–75–00 🖨 298/31–60–19 ⊕ www. hotelforoyar.fo ↪ 108 rooms, 4 suites ◊ Restaurant, minibars, billiards, Ping-Pong, bar, meeting rooms ☐ AE, DC, MC, V.

$$ ✕ 🖭 **Hotel Hafnia.** In the middle of Tórshavn, this modern business hotel offers big-city ambience and a view of the town from the roof terrace. The restaurant serves Faroese, Danish, and French cuisine. All rooms are comfortably appointed with TVs, telephones, and desks. Some rooms are specifically suited for travelers with disabilities. ⊠ Áarvegur 4–10, FO–110 ☎ 298/31–32–33 🖨 298/31–52–50 ⊕ www.hafnia.fo ↪ 57 rooms, 4 suites ◊ Restaurant, minibars, hair salon, sauna, meeting rooms ☐ AE, DC, MC, V.

¢ 🖭 **Bládýpi.** Its central location makes this guesthouse/youth hostel especially appropriate if you want to enjoy Tórshavn's nightlife. The guest house has rooms sleeping up to four people; the youth hostel has dormitory rooms. Breakfast is not included, but guests may use the kitchen. ⊠ Dr. Jakobsensgøta 14–16, FO–100 ☎ 298/31–19–51 🖨 298/ 31–94–51 ⊕ www.farhostel.fo ↪ 12 rooms without bath ◊ Dining room ☐ No credit cards ⊙ Closed for individuals Sept.–Apr. Open year-round for groups.

¢ 🖭 **Skansin Guesthouse.** This is a warm and welcoming alternative for
★ those who would like to experience Faroese hospitality within the modesty and personality of a private home. The Restorffs, your hosts, offer expert advice and assistance in planning activities. All rooms have TVs and sinks. Guests may use the kitchen. ⊠ Jekaragøta 8, FO–110 ☎ 298/ 31–22–42 🖨 298/31–06–57 ↪ 11 rooms without bath ◊ Refrigerators ☐ No credit cards.

ç ▣ **Youth Hostel Tórshavn.** Next door to the Hotel Föroyar is this clean and simple hostel. The view over Tórshavn's harbor is expansive. Shuttle buses run into town from the hostel, or you can stroll 15 minutes to get there. ⊠ *Við Oyggjarvegin, FO–100* ☎ *298/31–89–00* 🖨 *298/34–59–50* ⊕ *www.farhostel.fo* ↩ *22 rooms without bath* ⊟ *AE, DC, MC.*

Nightlife & the Arts

The little nightlife that exists in Tórshavn is concentrated in the very center of town and is at its height in summer. Frequented by friendly locals, **Café Natur** (⊠ Áarvegur 7 ☎ 298/31–26–25) has a rowdy Faroese atmosphere complete with live pop and rock music on weekends. Eat, drink, and sing karaoke at the youth-filled **Club 20** (⊠ Tinghúsvegur 8 ☎ 298/31–56–28). On summer weekends the club remains open until 4 AM. Adults flock to **Club Kaggin** (⊠ Dalavegur 1 ☎ 298/31–41–70) on Friday and Saturday nights for dancing and live rock music.

At the northern tip of Tórshavn, **Norðurlanda Húsið.** (Nordic House; ⊠ Norðari Ringvegur, FO–110 ☎ 298/31–79–00, ⊕ www.nlh.fo) built in 1983 to promote Nordic culture in the region, hosts exhibitions, concerts, and theater throughout the year.

Shopping

You won't knock yourself out shopping in Tórshavn but you can find original Faroese knitwear, Viking-style jewelry, stamps, and even stuffed birds.

Shop at **Føroyskt Heimavirki** (⊠ Kongabrúgvin ☎ 298/31–17–67) for hand-knit woolen items based on centuries-old Faroese patterns. Decorated with Tróndur Patursson's colorful stained-glass sculptures, **SMS Shopping Center** (⊠ Trapputrøðin ☎ 298/31–30–41) is a mall with more than 30 shops as well as a bank and post office.

Kirkjubøur

★ ❷ *13 km (8 mi) south of Tórshavn.*

From Tórshavn, a bus takes you to Kirkjubøur, a tiny town populated by about 60 people. The townsfolk live in black houses with red window frames and green grass roofs perched on hillsides around the tiny, often fog-shrouded harbor. At the southern tip of the island of Streymoy, Kirkjubøur was a spiritual and cultural center of the island in the Middle Ages.

A particularly ambitious priest, Bishop Erlendur, built a cathedral in the town in the 13th century—there is some controversy over whether or not it was ever completed—and the ruins of the Gothic **Magnus Cathedral** still stand. Inside the church is a large stone tablet engraved with an image of Christ on the cross, flanked by the Virgin Mary and Mary Magdalene, and an inscription to St. Magnus and St. Thorlak. During restoration work in 1905, the tablet was removed to reveal well-preserved relics of the saints. In 1538, after the Reformation, the episcopal see was dissolved and with it the town's power.

Just next door to the Magnus Cathedral is the restored **St. Olaf's Church,** which dates from 1111 and is now the only church from that time still in use. Most of its sculptures have been removed to Copenhagen, leaving little to see, but there's a hole in the north wall that once allowed lepers standing outside to watch the mass and receive the Eucharist. The altarpiece is the work of the most famous painter of the islands, Sámal Mykines. The interior of the cathedral is only open for the 11 AM service on Sunday.

Near the church is **Roykstovan,** a former farmhouse now in use as a museum. Legend has it that the lumber for the building came drifting to the town, neatly numbered and bundled, from the Sogne Fjord in Norway. Inside are the traditional Faroese one-main-room living quarters and a dozen other rooms. It's been in the same family for the last 16 generations, and it is here that foreign dignitaries are welcomed to the town. The large split-log building is said to be about 900 years old and is the oldest cabin in Europe. ☎ *298/32–80–89* ☺ *June–Aug., Fri.–Wed. 2–5; Sept.–May by appointment only.*

Vestmanna

★ ❸ *49 km (30 mi) northwest of Tórshavn.*

On the western coast of Streymoy, this town of 1,200 inhabitants is easily accessible from Tórshavn by bus. Once there, you can take a boat tour through narrow channels and see thousands of nesting birds, including puffins and kittiwakes. Although the bird life is the big draw, the sheep life is nearly as fascinating. In the spring sheep are hoisted with ropes 2,310 feet up to graze atop the sheer cliffs, and in the fall they are caught and brought back down.

Saksun

❹ *47 km (30 mi) northwest of Tórshavn.*

Among the fjords slicing the northern end of Streymoy is the tiny town of Saksun, one of the most popular excursions on the islands. The town and its scattered sod-and-thatch-roof houses are idyllically situated on a small bay sheltered on both sides by steep, imposing cliffs leading into a long, narrow fjord. Saksun swarms with great skuas, large brown seabirds prone to low dives. As you unwittingly near their nests, you will certainly notice their cantankerous presence. Not far from the village are two picturesque lakes, Pollur and Saksunarvatn, both perfect for trout and salmon fishing. The valley has gushing waterfalls and fantastic hiking.

Visit the **Dúvugarðar Museum** for a re-creation of Faroese living conditions in the 19th century and a portrait of the islands' history since the Middle Ages. ☎ *289/31–07–00* ☺ *Jun.–Aug., Fri.–Wed. 2–5.*

Eiði

❺ *52 km (32 mi) northwest of Tórshavn.*

The island of Eysturoy, just east of Streymoy, is connected to the latter by a bridge and bus service. The center of activity is the town of Eiði, which lies to the northwest amid a spectacular landscape. Looking northwest from town, you can see two 250-foot cliffs, a part of local mythology: one night an Icelandic giant and his wife came to carry the islands to Iceland to provide food for their land. They put the islands into a sack but she dropped them, giving the islands their cracked topography. Once the sun rose, the giants were petrified and transformed into the bluffs.

Due east of Eiði is the islands' highest point, the 2,910-foot **Slættaratindur** mountain. To the south, on the shores of the **Skálafjørður,** the longest fjord in the archipelago, the majority of the island's 10,500 people live.

Where to Stay

¢ 🏨 **Hotel Eiði.** Perched on a hilltop in a village near the sea, this slightly dated hotel is small and clean, with a TV in every room. ⊠ *FO–470* ☎*298/42–34–56* 🖷*298/42–32–00* 🛏*16 rooms, 12 with bath* ⚐*Restaurant, cafeteria, minibars* ▤ *AE, DC, MC, V* ☺ *Closed Sept.–Apr.*

¢ ⊞ **Gjáargarður.** This youth hostel occupies a prime position on the north end of the island, with nearby access to the ocean and the mountains. Built in traditional Faroese style, the foundation is stone, the exterior wooden walls painted black, and the roof is thatch. Inside you'll find a combined kitchen and family room with a fireplace in the middle. Breakfast is not included, but guests have use of the Internet as well as the kitchen. Campsites are also available. ⊠ *FO–476 Gjógv* ☎ *298/ 42–31–71* 🖷 *298/42–35–05* ⊕ *www.gjaarhostel.dk* 🖎 *11 rooms, 10 with bath* ⚲ *Cafeteria, Ping-Pong, meeting room* ▭ No *credit cards* ⊙ *Closed mid-Aug.–mid-June.*

Klaksvík

❻ *75 km (47 mi) northeast of Tórshavn, 2 hrs by bus and ferry.*

The six islands in the far northeast region of the Faroese archipelago are gathered under the name of Norðoyar (Northern Islands). Three of them, Borðoy, Viðoy, and Kunoy are connected by causeways, while Fugloy, Svinoy, and Kalsoy are accessible only by passenger boat or helicopter.

Borðoy is reached by boat from Leirvík on eastern Eysturoy. On its southwest coast, nearly divided by two fjords, Klaksvík is the Faroes' second-largest town and most important fishing harbor; its fleet of sophisticated boats harvests cod, haddock, herring, and other fish.

Within Klaksvík, the baptismal font in the **Christianskirkjan** (Christian's Church) is a piece of carved granite thought to have been used in pagan rituals in Denmark 4,000 years ago. Suspended from the church roof is a 24-foot boat used by a former vicar to visit nearby towns; the boat—common in Danish churches—is a symbol that God is watching over the village fishermen. ☎ *289/45–57–70* ⊙ *May–Sept., Mon.–Sat. 11–noon and 2–3.*

Where to Stay

$ ⊞ **Klaksvíkar Sjómansheim.** Sheep graze on the front lawn of this big hotel; the back overlooks the colorful harbor. The staff is cheery and helpful, and rooms—request one with a harbor view—offer no-frills comfort. Toilets are in the hallways but all rooms have sinks. The restaurant serves generous portions of the homemade special of the day but doesn't have a liquor license. ⊠ *Vikavegur 38, FO–700* ☎ *298/45–53–33* 🖷 *298/ 45–72–33* 🖎 *31 rooms, 11 with bath* ⚲ *Restaurant, cafeteria, meeting rooms* ▭ No *credit cards.*

¢ ⊞ **Ferðamannaheimið Íbúð.** Housed in a former hotel built in 1945, this youth hostel and guesthouse is near a ferry slip and is surrounded by hiking trails. ⊠ *Garðavegur 31, FO–700* ☎ *298/45–75–55 or 298/ 28–79–65* 🖷 *298/45–75–55* ⊕ *www.farhostel.fo* 🖎 *12 rooms without bath* ▭ No *credit cards* ⊙ *Closed for individuals mid-Sept.–mid-May; for groups mid-Dec.–early Jan.*

Viðareiði

★ ❼ *18 km (11 mi) north of Klaksvík.*

The island of **Viðoy** is among the wildest and most beautiful of the islands, with mountains of 2,800 feet and sheer cliffs plunging into extremely rough, unnavigable waters. Amazingly, 600 people live here, many in the town of Viðareiði. Cape Enniberg, at its northernmost tip, reaches 2,460 feet; it's the world's highest cape rising directly from the sea. From the town of Viðareiði you can take a boat tour to see many seabirds nesting on cliff walls, including kittiwakes and puffins—endearing little black-and-white birds with enormous orange beaks. The Faroese have

CloseUp

FAROESE FLAVORS

VEGETARIANS AND PICKY EATERS, be warned: the Faroe Islands offer a much different and more exotic culinary experience than the rest of Denmark. Faroese cuisine has a long history, and the islands' residents are specialists in a number of unconventional dishes. Because not many fruits and vegetables can nourish themselves on the islands' rocky soil, the principal ingredients in most dishes are meat (often lamb) and potatoes. However, to supplement these rather plain basics, the Faroese get quite creative. For instance, many kitchens still serve fried puffin—the richly colored national bird—and its eggs. Although the puffin is cute, the species is still abundant on the island, so if you can conquer your better instincts, give it a try. Still feeling adventurous? How about a meal of sheep's head, followed by dried cod and unleavened bread?

Perhaps the most controversial Faroese foodstuffs are the meat and blubber of pilot whales, which, in high season, venture in pods into the islands' bays and fjords. As soon as word of whale sightings reaches the community, hunters rush to the beaches and drive the whales shoreward to kill them, following centuries-old, time-honored rules. The catch is divided among the villagers and constitutes about 25% of their meat consumption. An average of nearly 1,000 whales die each year, but it is estimated that at least 100,000 populate the waters of Faroese. Animal-rights activists protest the annual Faroese whale hunt and slaughter on the grounds of cruelty, but the Faroese respond by citing the hunt's cultural value, whale meat's vital role in their diet, and the sustainability of their annual take.

---

a remarkable relationship with the puffins, harvesting them by the thousands for food and yet remaining careful not to diminish their numbers.

Where to Stay

¢ 🏨 **Hotel Norð.** In the tiny town of Viðareiði on the northern end of the island, this simple business hotel has beautiful surroundings and great bird-watching nearby. ⊠ FO–750 ☎ 298/45–12–44 🖷 298/45–12–45 ⇖ 15 rooms � Restaurant, billiards, meeting room ☰ MC, V ☉ Closed Sept.–May.

Miðvágur

❽ 18 km (11 mi) west of Tórshavn.

Vágar, the third-largest island in terms of area, takes its name from the three fjords that slice into it. There are also two major lakes on the island, Fjallavatn and Sørvágsvatn, the last of which is fed by the Bøsdalafossur, a 100-foot waterfall. The main town here is Miðvágur, an excellent perch for watching auks and gannets.

Where to Stay

$ 🏨 **Hotel Vágar.** Next to the airport, this hotel is small and standard. ⊠ FO–380 Sørvágur ☎ 298/33–29–55 🖷 298/33–23–10 ⊕ www.hotelvagar.fo ⇖ 26 rooms � Restaurant, minibars, meeting room ☰ AE, DC, MC, V ⦿.

¢ 🏨 **Á Giljanesi.** This youth hostel is just 10 minutes by bus from Vágar Airport. Guests have access to the kitchen, and meals are available on request. There is also camping. ⊠ FO–360 Sandavágur ☎ 298/33–34–65 🖷 298/33–29–01 ⊕ www.farhostel.fo ⇖ 11 rooms without bath � Dining room ☰ No credit cards.

Mykines

9 48 km (30 mi) west of Miðvágur (1 hr, 15 min by boat, 15 min by helicopter).

It's rough sailing to the tiny atoll of Mykines and only manageable when weather permits. In the town of the same name, population 19, the dwellings are roofed with sod. The town was placed here to be close to the **Mykineshólmur,** an islet swarming with thousands of puffins, which are harvested for food. You can get here by traversing the island northward on foot about 2 km (1 mi) from the boat landing in Sørvágur.

Where to Stay

¢ 🖼 **Kristianshús.** Stay at this small guest house with compact rooms to experience real Faroese home and native cuisine—fried puffin is available in the cafeteria. ✉ FO–388 ☎ 298/32–19–85 📠 298/31–09–85 ⇨ 11 rooms without bath ♿ Cafeteria ▤ No credit cards ⊙ Closed Sept.–Apr.

Sandur

10 25 km (16 mi) south of Tórshavn.

Sandoy, the fifth-largest island, lies to the south. Relatively fertile, it's named for the sandy white beaches of the town of Sandur, on its bay. Sheep graze on green hills, and the lakes north and west of town swell with auks, purple sandpipers, and great skuas. Puffin colonies dwell in the island's cliffs. You can visit the island of Sandoy as a day trip from Tórshavn.

Vágur

11 64 km (40 mi) south of Tórshavn.

The southernmost island, Suðuroy, is milder than the others, with cultivated green fields at its center and mountains along the coast. Ferries from Tórshavn dock either in Vágur or the quieter village of Tvøroyri.

Where to Stay

¢ 🖼 **Hotel Tvøroyri.** In the middle of town, this old hotel has simple, clean rooms, and minimal service. ✉ FO–800 Tvøroyri ☎ 298/37–11–71 📠 298/37–21–71 ⇨ 15 rooms, 2 with bath ♿ Cafeteria ▤ AE, V.

¢ 🖼 **Vallaraheimið Áargarður.** Overlooking the fjord of Trongisvágsfjørður, this youth hostel is centrally located for exploring the island of Suðuroy. Access to the kitchen is provided, and campsites are available. ✉ FO–827 Øravík ☎ 298/37–13–02 📠 298/37–20–57 ⊕ www.farhostel.fo ⇨ 15 rooms without bath ♿ Dining room, meeting room ▤ No credit cards.

The Faroe Islands A to Z

AIR TRAVEL

There are daily flights from Copenhagen to Vágar airport in Sørvágur, on the western island of Vágar. Delays due to heavy fog are common. The flight from Copenhagen takes about two hours.

CARRIERS For reservations, call either Atlantic Airways or Mærsk Air in Copenhagen. Both fly year-round between Copenhagen and the Faroe Islands and also from Billund in Jylland in the summer season. There are also connections available from Reykjavík (Iceland), Stavanger (Norway), Aberdeen (Scotland), and London on Atlantic Airways. Two weekly flights are also available from Reykjavík on Icelandair. Helicopter service is available in Vágar.

🔹 **Atlantic Airways** ☏ 45/32-50-47-00 in Denmark, 298/34-10-10 in the Faroes ⊕ www.atlantic.fo. **Helicopter Service (Atlantic Airways)** ☏ 298/34-10-60 **Icelandair** ☏ 800/223-5500, Ext. 2 prompt 1, in North America, 354/50-50-100 in Iceland, 45/33-70-22-00 in Denmark ⊕ www.icelandair.com. **Mærsk Air** ☏ 45/70-10-74-74 in Denmark, 298/34-00-60 in the Faroes ⊕ www.maersk-air.com.

AIRPORTS
🔹 **Vágar Airport** ✉ FO-380 Sørvágur ☏ 298/33-22-28 🖨 298/33-29-98 ⊕ www.slv.dk/vagar.

TRANSFERS From Vágar Airport, count on another 1½ hours to get to Tórshavn by bus and ferry. The SL Visitor Travelcard is a good value for exploring the islands; it affords free passage on all SL (the local transportation company) buses and ferries. Be sure to buy the card at the airport (or from your travel agent) to pay for the trip to Tórshavn.

BIKE TRAVEL
It's hard work peddling up and down the steep hills. The islands' roads aren't designed for safe cycling; many roads aren't paved and those that are don't have real shoulders. Nevertheless, if you're determined, renting a bike is an option. For information about routes and rentals, call J. W. Thomsen.

🔹 **J. W. Thomsen** ✉ Nólsoyar Páls gøta, FO-700, Klaksvík ☏ 298/45-58-58.

BOAT & FERRY TRAVEL
Every Saturday night in summer, from mid-May to mid-September, car ferries ply the waters between Hanstholm in Jylland and Tórshavn (34 hours). The same service is available from mid-October to mid-May with a different timetable. There is usually no ferry service between mid-September and mid-October. Call Smyril Line for more information. For information on frequent ferry service to all islands in the Feroese, call Strandfaraskip Landsins. The most remote areas are linked by mailboat and helicopter.

The SL Visitor Travelcard, which includes ferry and bus travel throughout the Faroes, is available from Strandfaraskip Landsins and costs around Dkr 400 for 4 days, Dkr 650 for 7 days, and Dkr 1,000 for 14 days.

🔹 **Smyril Line** ✉ Jónas Broncksgøta 37 FO-110 Tórshavn ☏ 45/96-55-03-60 or 45/33-16-40-04 in Denmark, 298/34-59-00 in the Faroes ⊕ www.smyril-line.com. **Strandfaraskip Landsins (SL)** ✉ Eystara Bryggja, FO-100 Tórshavn ☏ 298/34-30-00 🖨 298/34-30-01 ⊕ www.ssl.fo.

BUS TRAVEL
In towns, and between islands that are connected by bridges, there is regular bus service, and the drivers tend to be friendly toward perplexed travelers. For schedules and reservations, call Strandfaraskip Landsins in Tórshavn.

🔹 **Strandfaraskip Landsins** ☏ 298/34-30-30 ⊕ www.ssl.fo.

CAR RENTAL
Car rentals are available in Tórshavn and at Vágar Airport. Although cars are the most convenient method of travel on the islands, they are quite expensive to rent (Dkr 600–Dkr 900 per day).

🔹 **Avis** ☏ 298/31-35-35 in Tórshavn, 298/34-88-00 at the airport. **Hertz** ☏ 298/34-00-0730 in Tórshavn, 298/34-00-60 at the airport.

CAR TRAVEL

A network of two-lane asphalt roads has been built between towns, using tunnels and bridges. The roads are best on the nine main islands, but once outside towns, beware of untethered animals. Driving laws are the same as in Denmark. Speed limits are 50 kph (30 mph) in urban areas, 80 kph (50 mph) outside.

EMERGENCIES

For ambulance, fire, or police dial 112.

Hospital Landssjúkrahúsi◊ ⊠ J. C. Svvaboes gøta, Tórshavn ☎ 298/31-35-40.
Pharmacies Klaksví ⊠ Fornagar◊ur ☎ 298/45-50-55. **Runavík** ⊠ Hei◊avegur ☎ 298/44-93-66. **Tórshavn** ⊠ R. C. Effersøes gøta 31, by SMS shopping center ☎ 298/31-11-00.

TOURS

In addition to the local tours offered by many hotels, there are four main tour operators offering angling, city, hiking, and bird-watching tours: Flogfelag Føroyar, Tora Tourist Traffic, Smyril-Line and MB-Tours.

Besides the four operators mentioned above, there are two others specializing in the spectacular bird-cliffs of Vestmanna: Skúvadal and Palli Lamhauge. Other bird-watching tours are available on the islands of Nólsoy (guided by Jens Kjeld Jensen) and Koltur (guided by Koltur). Berg Hestar organizes horseback riding trips.

Berg Hestar ⊠ Vi◊ Oyggjarvegin, FO-100, Tórshavn ☎ 298/31-68-96 or 298/21-68-96. **Flogfelag Føroyar** ⊠ Áarvegur 6, FO-110, Tórshavn ☎ 298/34-00-10 ⊕ www.ff.fo. **Jens Kjeld Jensen** ⊠ FO-270, Nólsoy ☎ 298/32-70-64 🖷 298/32-70-54. **Koltur** ⊠ Koltursgar◊ur, FO-285, Koltur ☎ 298/29-92-70. **MB-Tours** ⊠ Bryggjubakki 2, FO-100, Tórshavn ☎ 298/32-21-21 ⊕ www.mb-tours.com. **Palli Lamhauge** ⊠ FO-350, Vestmanna ☎ 298/42-41-55 ⊕ www.sightseeing.fo. **Skúvadal** ⊠ FO-350, Vestmanna ☎ 298/42-43-05 ⊕ www.puffin.fo/skuvadal. **Smyril-Line** ⊠ Jonas Broncksgøta 37, FO-110, Tórshavn ☎ 298/34-59-00, 96/55-03-60 in Denmark ⊕ www.smyril-line.fo. **Tora Tourist Traffic** ⊠ Niels Finsensgøta 21, Box 3012, FO-110, Tórshavn ☎ 298/31-55-05 🖷 298/31-56-67 ⊕ www.tora.fo.

VISITOR INFORMATION

The helpful brochure *Faroe Islands Tourist Guide* is published by the Faroese Tourist Board.

Faroe Islands Tourist Board ⊠ Undir Bryggjubakka 17, Box 118, FO-110, Tórshavn ☎ 298/31-60-55 🖷 298/31-08-58 ⊠ Hovedvagtsg. 8, 2nd floor, DK-1103 Copenhagen ☎ 45/33-14-83-83 ⊕ www.tourist.fo. **Streymoy Kunningarstovan** (Streymoy Tourist Information) ⊠ Niels Finsens gøta 13, FO-110, Tórshavn ☎ 298/31-57-88 🖷 298/31-68-31 ⊕ www.kunning.fo.

GREENLAND

7

FODOR'S CHOICE

An excursion to the Greenland Ice Cap

HIGHLY RECOMMENDED

Hotel Igloo Village, *Kangerlussuaq/Søndre Strømfjord*

Updated by
Charles Ferro

WHEN ERIC THE RED DISCOVERED GREENLAND (Kalaallit Nunaat in Greenlandic, Grønland in Danish) a thousand years ago, his Norsemen thought they had reached the edge of the world. After it, there was only Ginnungagap, the endless abyss.

Greenland still commands awe from the growing number of tourists who venture off the usual Scandinavian path to explore the world's largest island. Measuring more than 2.1 million square km (1.3 million square mi), it's larger than Italy, France, Great Britain, Germany, and Spain combined. The coastal regions are sparsely populated with about 7,500 Danes and 48,000 Inuit—the indigenous people, whose roots can be traced to the native inhabitants of Canada's Arctic, and further back to the people of Alaska. More than 80% of the land is perpetually frozen beneath an ice cap that, at its deepest, reaches a thickness of 3 km (2 mi). If it melted, sea levels around the world would rise about 21 feet.

Greenland's first inhabitants probably arrived some 5,000 years ago from what is today Canada, which is only around 26 km (16 mi) away at the closest point. Inuit peoples continued to migrate to and roam across the island. Greenland's recorded history began at about the same time, in AD 982, when Eric and his Norse settlers claimed the land, but after 400 years of colonization they mysteriously disappeared. During this period Denmark and Norway were joined under the Danish crown, a union that muddled ownership of Greenland until 1933, when the International High Court awarded Denmark complete sovereignty. (Until 1997 every town had both a Greenlandic and a Danish name; today the Greenlandic names are used on modern maps with the Danish included in brackets.) Geographically isolated and increasingly politically independent, Greenlanders are intent on redefining their ethnic identity in a modern world. They refer to themselves as Inuit, in solidarity with native peoples of Canada, Alaska, and the former Soviet Union, and speak their own language in addition to Danish.

In 1979 Denmark granted Greenland home rule, vesting its tiny Landsting (parliament) in the capital Nuuk/Godthåb with power over internal affairs. Though Denmark continues to devolve power, it still administers foreign policy and provides financial aid to an economy based on fishing, animal husbandry, construction, and tourism.

The number of visitors has been growing at an impressive rate, from just 3,000 in 1993 to 18,000 in 1997, and then well over 30,000 in 2001. The island also garnered national attention when Crown Prince Frederik of Denmark completed a highly publicized dogsled trip across northern Greenland in early 2001. Relatively speaking, though, with still few tourists (almost all on package tours), Greenland remains one of the world's least developed regions. By its nature, the region is far more difficult to explore than dwarfed mother Denmark. Travel is possible only by airplane, helicopter or coastal boat, because there are few roads and no railroads. However, the southern and western towns—trimmed with building-block red-and-green houses and well-used harbors—have adequate hotels, airfields, and helicopter pads, and regular summertime ferry service. Man-made luxuries are few, but the rewards of nature are savagely beautiful. Below the Arctic Circle, the attractions include Norse ruins, Ice Age–gouged mountains, and jagged fjords. Farther north, dogsleds whip over icy plains, and ferries glide past icebergs as big as city blocks.

The country remains a wilderness that offers unique opportunities for hunting, fishing, hiking, skiing, dogsledding, and camping. True, some of this can be done on your own, but there are state-certified outfitters who cater to every need and are familiar with the characteristics of the wilderness in their territories. Their expertise can make all the difference. They know where the big fish lurk, where the big game can be found, and the safest routes to sites—this is especially important in winter. An outfitter makes it possible to get the very best out of a visit to this breathtaking country.

Because most travelers follow preset routes, towns and sites are arranged south to north in geographic order and not necessarily in the order they would be visited. Perhaps only one major museum or site is noted per village, but there is much more to see in Greenland's mercurial natural landscape. Venture along the wooden stairs and boardwalks that connect most private homes and provide inner-village walking paths. Cruise beneath the expanse of an iceberg and listen to it moan. Take a hike, a bike ride, or a motor-vehicle excursion to the inland ice and marvel at its magnitude. Rise at 3 AM to take a stroll through the summer sunshine. There is no private property in Greenland—nature is free for all to enjoy, and in Greenlandic fashion, it is best savored slowly. Those who love this island do not move through it at a clip; it's more gratifying to let it move you.

Exploring Greenland

Visitors cannot simply "explore" Greenland. There are few roads between towns, just a few ferry routes and a handful of airports or heliports. Even towns that appear just a hop-skip-and-a-jump away may be isolated except by foot, dog sled, or snowmobile—all types of transportation that should only be undertaken alone by experts. A visit to Greenland can be difficult to plan, so do your homework before departure. Consider it an absolute must to contact Greenland Tourism well before departure. The office has a wealth of information that will save time and money, and help the visitor get the best out of a trip.

Due to the size of the country, tourist literature proclaims that Greenland is really five lands in one, broken down into the four points of the compass and the Qaanaaq region in the far reaches of the polar north. Tourism is still relatively new, and some services can be irregular, but local tourism offices and central administration continue to refine conditions.

About the Restaurants
With few exceptions, most notably in Nuuk (which has slightly more variety), restaurants tend to serve typical Danish-style food, much of which is frozen and shipped in from Europe. Standards could be compared to mid-level European standards, though servings tend to be ample as visitors normally burn a lot of calories. Ask whether seafood on the menu is fresh or frozen, because fresh, locally caught fish is often delightful. You may be lucky enough to find a kitchen serving whale or musk ox, and while many may have reservations about the former, the latter is an unequivocal treat. Local delicacies can be difficult to find, but they are around if you look closely; most villages have congregation houses and sometimes local fare is served there. Prices tend to be at northern European levels, often with a premium.

About the Hotels
Hotel accommodations vary from European two- and three-star levels to unabashedly spartan. In any case, most tourists who venture to Greenland come for its natural beauty; spend most of the day outside; and use the room only as a place to sleep. For that reason, many hotels offer plain rooms at lower rates without many amenities, but the rooms

7

Dogsledding

For an exhilarating experience, sit in a sled and wrap up in reindeer pelts while a team of half-wild huskies pulls you across the ice. The dogs are harnessed in a fan shape rather than a straight line, so if one falls through the ice, the others will be spared. Though used as recreation by tourists, the dogsled is still a real means of transport for fishermen hauling their catch and hunters trekking across the land. March, April, and May are the best times to take a dogsled ride across the frozen plains because the temperatures are warmer and there's daylight. In summer the only place to dogsled is in the north at Qeqertarsuaq/Godhavn. Local hunter-guides also lead gentle trips from Uummannaq. The most relaxing routes are those across the flat ice. Trips on rougher terrain require dismounting the sled at certain points and walking.

Fishing

Fishermen can test the sea waters close to towns or angle from the banks of the fjords to find cod, halibut, or Arctic char. The thawed summer mountainscape is dotted with lakes and crossed by thousands of rivers and brooks, which are perfect for a fishing adventure. Outfitters can design a real adventure trip for the serious angler to insider spots teeming with trout and salmon. Ice fishing can be found in Ilulissat, where fishermen throw long lines down holes in the ice in hope of catching a Greenlandic shark. Call the local tourist office for details. Fishing licenses (Dkr 300) are available from the local police, major hotels, and tourism offices.

Hiking

Hiking in Greenland appears unlimited, but the tourist board does try to control hikers for their own safety. It's wiser to join an organized hike with an experienced guide than to attempt a solo expedition, as it's not uncommon for rescue crews to be dispatched in search of lost hikers. A sturdy pair of hiking shoes or boots is imperative, as are extra clothing and a survival kit. Even in the milder months the weather can change quickly. Hiking in the colder months is not advised for the inexperienced.

Organized excursions are available in Nuuk/Godthåb and Narsarsuaq for about Dkr 150 for a half day, Dkr 300 for a full day. In the past two years many new routes have opened to the visitor. For the most popular hiking areas in Greenland, up-to-date 1:100,000 topographic maps are available. In these areas, experienced hikers can find their way without a guide. One good source for finding maps is Saga Maps (www.sagamaps.com). To cross the polar ice cap or to enter Greenland's national parkland—which is larger than Germany and France combined—you must obtain a license. Contact the **Danish Polar Center** (✉ Strandg. 100H, Downtown DK–1401 Copenhagen ☎ 32/88–01–00 ☏ 32/88–01–01 ⊕ www.dpc.dk).

Wildlife

Watching animals could occupy much of your time in Greenland. Polar bears and walruses are prevalent in the northern reaches of the country, while reindeer stick to greener patches of land in the south. Musk oxen are ubiquitous and can even be seen upon landing at Kangerlussuaq Airport. Whale-watching tours are offered by all boat companies, though it is possible to spot these gentle giants swimming past from just about anywhere on the coast.

are clean and the beds generally comfortable. Reservations should be made well in advance, especially in the summer. It's also wise to reserve in the winter, as some smaller villages shut their tourist facilities in the off-season.

WHAT IT COSTS In kroner					
	$$$$	$$$	$$	$	¢
RESTAURANTS	over 180	141–180	121–140	90–120	under 90
HOTELS	over 1,500	1,200–1,500	1,000–1,200	700–1,000	under 700

Restaurant prices are for a main course at dinner. Hotel prices are for two people in a standard double room, including service charge and tax.

Timing

Greenland has two distinct seasons, summer and winter. In southern and western towns, the late-summer months remain the favorite of many travelers as temperatures climb to comfortable levels. The midnight sun— from mid-May to mid-July—north of the Arctic Circle and relatively mild temperatures allow visitors to plan their own outdoor adventures. For the native population, it's a time of celebration after a long winter, thus more events are staged at this time of year. In the south watch for local produce, which comes to market in late summer.

Winter temperatures range from cold-but-comfortable to numbingly frigid. Winter activities demand careful planning and it would be wise to contact the local tourist office at your destination well before departure. While winter is harsh, it does bring with it the mysterious magnificence of round-the-clock darkness and the singular beauty of an icy landscape where light is reflected in myriad shades on the snow-covered territory. The northern lights, or aurora borealis, only serve to make the atmosphere more surreal as they dance colorfully across a clear night sky about 100 km (63 mi) up in the ether. If you're planning a winter trip, be sure to research the performance of outdoor clothing designed for polar regions. There's a reason why the Greenlanders wear items like furs, sealskin anoraks, and leggings.

Narsarsuaq

❶ *4 hrs, 50 min northwest of Copenhagen by plane.*

Narsarsuaq, meaning Great Plain in English, aptly describes the wide, smooth land harboring one of Greenland's largest civilian airports. The town is accessible from Copenhagen, Reykjavík, and Kangerlussuaq by plane only, and from Nuuk/Godthåb by plane and boat—though such boats are booked months in advance.

Not far from the edge of town, you can take a 10-km (6-mi) boat ride from the Narsarsuaq harbor to an area where icebergs have broken off from a nearby glacier. There you are invited to collect glacial ice for the cocktails served on board.

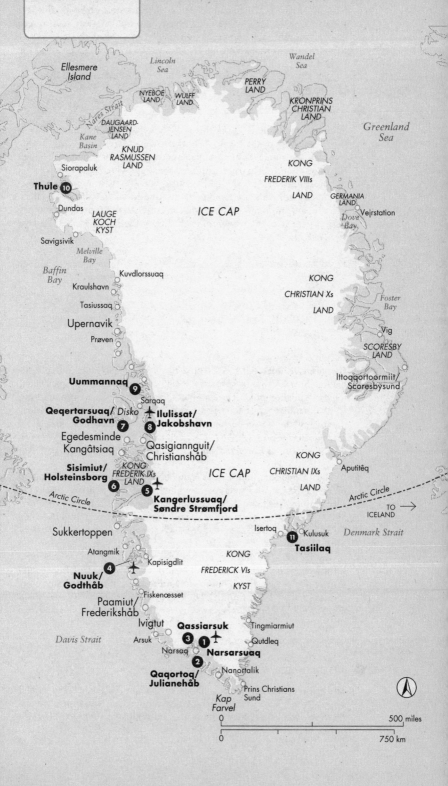

Greenland

Ellesmere
Island

Lincoln
Sea

Wandel
Sea

NYEBOE
LAND

WULFF
LAND

PERRY
LAND

KRONPRINS
CHRISTIAN
LAND

Greenland
Sea

Nares Strait

DAUGAARD-
JENSEN
LAND

Kane
Basin

KNUD
RASMUSSEN
LAND

KONG
FREDERIK VIIIs
LAND

GERMANIA
LAND

Vejrstation

Siorapaluk

ICE CAP

Dove
Bay

Thule ⑩

Dundas

LAUGE
KOCH
KYST

Savigsivik

Melville
Bay

Baffin
Bay

Kuvdlorssuaq

KONG
CHRISTIAN Xs
LAND

Foster
Bay

Kraulshavn

Tasiussaq

Vig

Upernavik

Prøven

SCORESBY
LAND

Ittoqqortoormiit/
Scoresbysund

Uummannaq ⑨

Sarqaq

Qeqertarsuaq/
Godhavn *Disko* ⑦ ⑧ ✈ **Ilulissat/
Jakobshavn**

Egedesminde
Kangâtsiaq

Qasigianguit/
Christianshåb

KONG
CHRISTIAN IXs
LAND

Aputitêq

**Sisimiut/
Holsteinsborg** ⑥

KONG
FREDERIK IXs
LAND

ICE CAP

✈ ⑤ **Kangerlussuaq/
Søndre Strømfjord**

Arctic Circle

Arctic Circle

TO
ICELAND →

Sukkertoppen

Isertoq

Denmark Strait

⑪ Kulusuk

Atangmik

KONG
FREDERIK VIs

Tasiilaq

Kapisigdlit

**Nuuk/
Godthåb** ④ ✈

KYST

Fiskenæsset

Paamiut/
Frederikshåb

Ivigtut

Qassiarsuk

Tingmiarmiut

Davis Strait

Arsuk

③ ✈ ①

Qutdleq

Narsaq

Narsarsuaq

②

Nanortalik

**Qaqortoq/
Julianehåb**

Prins Christians
Sund

*Kap
Farvel*

0 ——— 500 miles

0 ——— 750 km

Near Narsarsuaq is the point locals call **Hospitalsdalen** (Hospital Valley), a controversial area named for an alleged American hospital where Korean War wounded were said to have been hidden away so as not to weaken morale back home. Though history books deny the story, many locals swear it's true. Nothing remains of the hospital, so proof of the legend is unavailable here.

Qaqortoq/Julianehåb

❷ *6 hrs south of Narsarsuaq by ferry.*

With a population of 3,600, this is the largest town in southern Greenland—and one of the loveliest. In the town square is the island's only fountain, surrounded by half-timber and brightly colored houses. Though the oldest building in town is the cooper shop, which dates from 1797, the most interesting is the 1871 smithy, which now houses the **Julianehåb Museum.** Inside are handmade hunting tools, kayaks, Inuit clothing, and a furnished sod house you can enter. A traditional dwelling, its design kept it cozy and warm even during the harsh winter. 🖃 *Free* ☺ *Weekdays 11–4.*

> off the
> beaten
> path

HVALSEY CHURCH – A nice half-day excursion from Qaqortoq is the 14½-km (9-mi) sailboat ride to the well-preserved Hvalsey Church ruins, site of a well-attended Norse wedding in 1408—the community's last recorded activity before it mysteriously disappeared. As the church is close to a rocky beach, the hardy can opt for a frigid dip.

Where to Stay

$$$$ 🏨 **Sulisartut Højskoliat.** This school hosts Danish schoolchildren visiting for short sessions or semesters; it also serves as a hotel complex catering to all pocketbooks. The spot has various levels of accommodations, from dormitory-style to private, hotel-like rooms. Meals can be ordered and there are sleeping bags for rent. 🖂 *Box 132, DK–3920* 🕾 *299/64–24–66* 🖷 *299/64–29–73* ⊕ *www.sulisartut.gl* 🗺 *70 rooms, 41 with bath* ☖ *Cafeteria, laundry facilities, meeting rooms* 🖃 *AE, DC, MC, V.*

$ 🏨 **Hotel Qaqortoq.** Built in 1987, this hotel is among the more modern on the entire island. Its glass-and-white facade atop a hill overlooks the surrounding fjord and the town center. Rooms are simple but comfortable, all with private bath, TV, and phone. 🖂 *Box 155, DK–3920* 🕾 *299/64–22–82* 🖷 *299/64–12–34* 🗺 *50 rooms with bath* ☖ *Restaurant, billiards, bar* 🖃 *AE, DC, MC, V.*

¢ 🏨 **Siniffik Inn.** This inn is a dormitory-style spot for the traveler who simply needs a place to sleep and facilities for a bath. This fine option for the thrifty has shared bathroom and toilet facilities, a common living room, and a TV room. 🖂 *Box 172, DK–3920* 🕾 *299/64–27–28* 🖷 *299/64–23–28* 🗺 *26 beds* ☖ *Grocery* 🖃 *AE, DC, MC, V* ☺ *Closed Oct.–Apr.*

Qassiarsuk

❸ *30 min northwest of Narsarsuaq by boat.*

The main focus of the tiny village of Qassiarsuk is sheep breeding. Though there are few modern facilities in town, the **Norse ruins** are fascinating and include, for example, the **Brattahlíð**—1,000-year-old ruins of Eric the Red's farm.

The remains of **Tjodhilde Kirke** are especially intriguing: this was touted as the first Christian church on the North American continent (Greenland is considered part of North America geographically but part of Europe politically). It was from this point that Eric the Red's son, Leif Ericsson, began the expedition in AD 1000 that took him to Vinland, somewhere on the coast of North America. The first Greenlandic Ting (outdoor parliament), fashioned after those in Iceland, was also held here at about the same time.

Nuuk/Godthåb

❹ *1 hr, 25 min northwest of Narsarsuaq by small plane (15 hrs by ferry), 7 hrs east of Ottawa by plane.*

Nuuk/Godthåb, the capital of Greenland, is beautifully situated on a peninsula between two fjords. It was founded in 1728 by the Norwegian missionary Hans Egede; his harborside home is now the private residence of the island's home-rule premier. The university, the National Museum, and Greenland's only cultural center are also in town. The annual snow sculpture contest in March brings artists from near and far.

The centrally located **Landsmuseet** (National Museum) has a good permanent display of kayaks, costumes, and hunting weapons; an art exhibit; and the five 15th-century mummies of Qilakitsoq, one of Greenland's archaeological treasures. Among the most striking are a woman and child so well preserved that even their 500-year-old clothes are in pristine condition. ⊠ *Hans Egede Vej 8* ☎ *299/32–26–11* ⊕ *www.natmus.gl* ⊠ *Free* ⊗ *Tues.–Sun. 1–4.*

Where to Stay & Eat

$$$ ✕⌨ **Hotel Hans Egede.** This hotel is the largest in Greenland. The rooms are plain and functional but have such extras as minibars, TVs, VCRs, and phones. The sixth-floor Sky Top Restaurant, known for its lovely view of the fjords and its inventive nouveau Greenlandic menu, prepares local fish employing French methods. ⊠ *Box 289, DK–3900* ☎ *299/ 32–42–22* 🖷 *299/32–44–87* ⊕ *www.hhe.gl* ⟿ *108 rooms* ♿ *Restaurant, in-room VCRs, bar, dance club, meeting room* ⊟ *AE, DC, MC, V.*

$$ ⌨ **Sømandshjemmet Nuuk.** This is one of the oldest of the seaman's hotels that are found in many of Greenland's southern ports. It was at these establishments that the (mostly Danish) seamen spent their nights while their ships were being loaded or when the waters iced over. This particular example has been converted into a standard hotel, but it retains its atmosphere and history. ⊠ *Marinevej 3, Box 1021, DK–3900* ☎ *299/ 32–10–29* 🖷 *299/32–21–04* ⊕ *www.soemandshjem.gl* ⟿ *36 rooms with bath* ♿ *Cafeteria, meeting room* ⊟ *AE, DC, MC, V.*

Nightlife & the Arts

Katuaq (⊠ Skibshavnsvej ☎ 299/32–33–00) is the city's newest landmark and the country's only cultural center. A triangular-shape construction fronted by a wavy wall—inspired by the aurora borealis—contains spaces for concerts, exhibitions, theatrical performances, conventions, and cinema; it also has a café. Its residents include the Greenland Art School; the Nordic Institute on Greenland; and the Groenlandica Collection, a modern lending library with what is thought to be the largest collection of literature on the Arctic regions. The center is open weekdays 10–9:30 and on weekends 1:30–9:30. Performance schedules are available from the tourist office.

Shopping

Shopping is limited to native arts and these are sold in hotels, restaurants, and tourist offices all over Greenland. The arts and crafts are of very high quality and in the tradition of the Inuit. Probably the most popular souvenirs are the *tupilaks,* small distorted figures carved from animal tusks or teeth and meant to represent evil spirits. These amulets were worn primarily by hunters to keep away evil spirits. The idea was that if you already had an evil spirit, another one wouldn't come after you.

The Nuuk tourism office offers the 90-minute **Greenlandic Handicraft Shopping Tour** (☒ Box 199 ☏ 299/32–27–00), which stops at a few local artists' studios where you can purchase handicrafts.

Kangerlussuaq/Søndre Strømfjord

❺ *1 hr northeast of Nuuk/Godthåb by plane; 4 hrs, 20 min northwest of Copenhagen by plane.*

Kangerlussuaq/Søndre Strømfjord is at the head of one of the longest and deepest fjords in the world. The airport, Greenland's most vital, lies just 25 km (15 mi) from the ice cap. Until World War II, nobody lived here permanently, but Greenlanders would come in the spring to hunt reindeer. During the war, the U.S. Air Force chose its dry, stable climate for an air base, called Blue West Eight. The military moved out in the fall of 1992, selling the facilities to the local government for the sum of $1.

Where to Stay

$$$ 🏨 **Hotel Kangerlussuaq.** Just 10 minutes from the airport, this hotel is on the reclaimed U.S. Air Force base. The landing strip here serves as the town's airport and the former barracks have been converted to provide adequate rooms as well as conference facilities. The restaurant serves mainly European cuisine. The hotel also runs a hostel with considerably cheaper rooms (around Dkr 315 per person). ☒ *Box 1006, DK–3910* ☏ *299/84–13–00* 🖷 *299/ 84–14–43* ✈ *88 rooms* ♨ *Restaurant, laundry service, meeting rooms* ☰ *AE, DC, MC, V.*

★ ¢ 🏨 **Hotel Igloo Village.** This peculiar hotel offers visitors the novel opportunity to sleep in igloos on beds made of ice. Though the hotel exists only during the sub-zero winter, the bedding, consisting of an expedition-class sleeping bag tucked into musk ox skins, is guaranteed to keep you warm inside the igloo. In the bar you can relax with a drink served in a glass made of ice and enjoy the ice sculptures and candlelight that fills the space. ☒ *Adjacent to the airport* ☏ *299/84–11–80* 🖷 *299/84–12–84* ✈ *10 rooms* ♨ *Bar* ☰ *AE, DC, MC, V* ☻ *Closed Apr.–Nov.*

Sisimiut/Holsteinsborg

❻ *20 min west of Kangerlussuaq/Søndre Strømfjord by airplane.*

On the Davis Strait, this hilltop town is full of Danish-style wooden houses—a local luxury, as all wood is imported. Sisimiut, the second-largest town in Greenland with about 3,600 inhabitants, has become a center for winter tourism and is adapting to accommodate a growing influx of visitors. The area gets more snowfall than nearby towns, making it perfect for winter sports.

Sisimiut also marks the southernmost boundary for walrus hunting; the walrus, though extremely rare, is a popular game animal because of its valuable tusks. Sisimiut, like all other Greenlandic towns, has a "table" where local hunters and fishermen bring their catch—including walrus, whale, and local fish—to market. In all, the market consists of no more than a few tables, but it displays many of the ingredients that are staples of the local cuisine.

The Greenlandic name Sisimiut means Burrow People. There are many explanations of the source of this name; some people believe it refers to hunters who, during severe weather, burrow down in the snow and spend the night there.

On the outskirts of town is the archaeological site of **Asummiut**, where Inuits have made their homes for more than 4,000 years. Remnants of various prehistoric villages as well as Danish and Greenlandic whaling settlements have been uncovered here. To visit the site, contact the Sisimiut Museum. ⊠ *Near the airport* ☎ *299/86–50–87.*

In a cluster of old buildings dating back to 19th-century colonial times, the tiny **Sisimiut Museum** is a delight. It displays the anthropological history of Greenland, telling of the development of the hunter and trapper societies that evolved in harmony with the natural surroundings. The site also has Danish-inspired local art, old original colonial homes, and a post-colonization Greenlandic dwelling. An added benefit is the enthusiasm of the helpful, informed staff. ⊠ *Jukkorsuup aqq. 9, Box 308* ☎ *299/86–50–87* ⊕ *www.museum.gl/sisimiut* ⊠ *Dkr 25* ☯ *June–Aug., Tues.–Sun. 2–5; Sept.–May, Wed., Thurs., and Sun. 2–5.*

Where to Stay & Eat

$$$ ╳⚏ **Hotel Sisimiut.** The hotel has received four-star status in Greenland and provides excellent accommodation. Refurbished to a high standard, the rooms have telephones, TVs, and data ports. The restaurant is very large and is often used for conferences and sometimes as a nightclub. ⊠ *Box 70, DK–3911* ☎ *299/86–48–40* 🖷 *299/86–56–15* ⊕ *www.hotelsisimiut.gl* ➴ *39 rooms, 6 suites, 1 apartment with kitchen* ⚅ *Restaurant, in-room data ports, meeting rooms* ⊟ *AE, MC, V.*

$ ⚏ **Sømandshjemmet Sisimiut.** Situated on the harbor, The Seaman's Home provides basic lodging at a low price in a former sailors' boarding house. The cafeteria has simple, hearty fare at modest prices. ⊠ *Box 1015, DK–3911* ☎ *299/86–41–50* 🖷 *299/86–57–91* ⊕ *www.soemandshjem.gl* ➴ *40 rooms* ⚅ *Lounge, meeting rooms* ⊟ *AE, MC, V.*

Shopping

Shopping is not high on the list of things to do in Greenland. However, Sisimiut has a bigger selection than anywhere else on the giant island. Here you can find souvenirs such as handmade jewelry or hand-stitched leather goods. **Mersortarfik Panigiit** (⊠ Jaakunnguaq aqq. 19 ☎ 299/86–55–75) is primarily a leatherwork studio but also sells souvenirs. **Skindsystuen Natseq** (⊠ Paamaap Kuua 11 ☎ 299/86–43–55) is a co-op of sorts, selling leatherwork such as clothes, bags, and mittens from its studio. Keep an eye out for the traditional hand-stitched items. Occupying a converted warehouse, the **Society of Artists' workshop** (⊠ at the harbor ☎ 299/86–59–51) is a great place to see artists at work in their studios. It has no set hours, but you can find most artists in residence on weekdays.

Sports & the Outdoors

In summer there are great opportunities for fishing in the fjords, or getting an outfitted excursion to fishing spots known only to local residents. In the warmer months, it's also possible to take a week-long hiking and camping trip to Kangerlussuaq. All activities can be arranged through the local tourist office.

SKIING Locals and visiting skiers make good use of the Solbakken ski lift ½ km (⅓ mi) outside of town. A snowmobile taxi shuttles back and forth between the town and the ski lift for a fee, but you could also walk or ski there. The ski lift operates daily, but consult the tourist office just in case before setting out. Cross-country skiing tracks exist in the areas surrounding the town, although you should confer with the tourist office to find routes and be sure to inform your hotel where you plan to go and when you expect to return.

DOGSLEDDING   You can take a dogsled ride for just a few hours or go off on an overnight adventure; tiny shed-like cabins dot the countryside and many are free for overnight stays. These sites run on a first-come, first-served basis and are mostly used by hunters and trappers. Check with the Sisimiut tourist office before you set out.

Qeqertarsuaq/Godhavn

❼ *1 hr, 20 min west of Ilulissat by helicopter (8 hrs, 30 min by coastal boat; reserve far in advance).*

In the Disko Bugt (Disko Bay) sits the island of Qeqertarsuaq/Disko. The main town here is Qeqertarsuaq/Godhavn. Until 1950 this was the capital of northern Greenland; Nuuk/Godthåb served as the southern capital. Accessible by helicopter and ship, Godhavn is often booked to capacity by European tourists. It's the only area in Greenland with summertime dogsledding. Contact the tourist office for recommendations of tour operators specializing in such trips.

Ilulissat/Jakobshavn

❽ *45 min north of Kangerlussuaq/Søndre Strømfjord by plane.*

In the center of Disko Bay is Ilulissat/Jakobshavn, 300 km (185 mi) north of the Arctic Circle. At the tip of its fjord is the Northern Hemisphere's most productive glacier, calving 20 million tons of floes each day—equivalent, according to the Greenland tourist board, to the amount of water New York City uses in a year. For a humbling experience, take one of the helicopter tours encircling the glacier. A violent landscape of floating ice giants and dazzling panoramas, it's been inhabited by the Inuit for as long as 4,000 years. The town was founded in 1741 by a Danish merchant, Jakob Severin. Today the largest industry is shrimping, though in the winter dogsledders also fish for halibut along the fjord. From mid-May to mid-June, the sun doesn't set and the regular routine is ignored as people congregate at all hours to enjoy the sunny nights.

Visit the **Knud Rasmussens Fødehjem** (boyhood home of Knud Rasmussen); this Danish-Greenlandic explorer (1879–1933) initiated the seven Thule expeditions, which enhanced the knowledge of Arctic geography and Inuit culture. At the museum you can follow his explorations through photographs, equipment, and clothing. ▦ *Dkr 20* ◷ *Daily 10–4.*

Where to Stay & Eat

$$$ ✕▣ **Hotel Arctic.** This modern hotel, divided into two low-lying red buildings, is in the mountains on the edge of town and provides views of the icy fjord. Rooms are simple, with bathroom, phone, radio, and TV. The main dining room has panoramic views of the iceberg-filled harbor and serves fine beef and fish dishes. ⊠ *Box 1501, DK–3952* ☎ *299/94–41–53* 🖷 *299/94–40–49* ⊕ *www.hotel-arctic.gl* ⇋ *40 rooms* ⌂ *Restaurant, sauna, billiards, meeting room* ▭ *AE, DC, MC.*

$$$ ✕▣ **Hotel Hvide Falk.** The compact rooms in this central, moderate-size, two-story building are furnished with TVs and small desks, and have magnificent views of the icebergs and the Disko Mountains. The restaurant, which specializes in seafood—especially herring, cod, and salmon—

looks out over the bay and its loomin.g icebergs. The director of the hotel, Lars Rasmussen, is explorer Knud Rasmussen's grandson. ⊠ *Box 20, DK–3952* ☎ *299/94–33–43* 🖷 *299/94–35–08* ⊕ *www.greenland-guide. gl/hvidefalk* 🖙 *27 rooms* ⚲ *Restaurant, bar* ☴ *DC.*

Uummannaq

❾ *55 min north of Ilulissat/Jakobshavn by helicopter.*

The inhabitants of the town of Uummannaq—on the island of the same name—maintain Greenlandic traditions in step with modern European life. Their professional fields range from hunting to linguistics and they are as apt to drive dogsleds as sport-utility vehicles. The town lies beneath the magnificent hues and double domes of the granite Uummannaq Mountain, 3,855 feet high. Because the village is also perched on uneven stone cliffs, housing largely consists of brightly painted, freestanding cottages rather than the ugly Danish barracks that line some of Greenland's larger towns. Every April (if the weather cooperates, Uummannaq hosts the Drambuie World Ice Golf Championships.

The **Uummannaq Museum** gives a good overview of life on the island, with photographs and costumes of local hunters and displays on the nowdefunct mines of the area. Exhibits also detail the doomed 1930 expedition of German explorer and scientist Alfred Wegener, and there is a section on the Qilakitsoq mummies, found in a nearby cave in 1977 and now displayed in Nuuk/Godthåb. ⊠ *Alfred Berthelsen-ip aqq. B9* ☎ *299/95–15–18* 🖾 *Free* ⊙ *Weekdays 8–4.*

The **Uummannaq Church**, dating from 1937, is the only stone church in Greenland and is made from local granite. Next door are three sod huts, traditional Inuit dwellings that were occupied until just a few decades ago.

Where to Stay & Eat

$$$ ✕🖭 **Uummannaq Hotel.** This tidy harborside hotel and a nearby 10-room extension offer bright, compact rooms with white, Danish-design furniture. The fine restaurant serves local specialties, including polar bear, caribou, seal, and plenty of fish. ⊠ *Box 202, DK–3961* ☎ *299/95–15–18* 🖷 *299/95–12–62* 🖙 *32 rooms* ⚲ *Restaurant, bar* ☴ *AE, MC, V.*

Sports & the Outdoors

DOGSLEDDING Though there is plenty of **dogsledding** north of the Arctic Circle, the trips that set forth from Uummannaq are the most authentic, as local hunters do the mushing. The trips are also gentler, because the terrain here is especially smooth. Visitors sit comfortably in heavy, fur-lined sleighs that tear across the frozen fjord. Trips can be arranged at the Hotel Uummannaq and range from a few hours to several days of racing through the terrifying beauty of the landscape and sleeping in the shadows of towering icebergs.

Thule

❿ *2 hrs, 40 min north of Uummannaq by passenger-cargo plane; 1 hr, 45 min north of Kangerlussuaq/Søndre Strømfjord by plane.*

The northern reaches of Greenland are sparsely populated, with few accommodations in the scattered coastal outposts. The inhabitants of Thule were relocated to Qaanaaq when the U.S. Air Force established a base there. The extreme northern region is often called "the most original Greenland," as this is the cradle of the Inuit society of polar hunters. The surrounding landscape is simply breathtaking. The American **air base** at Thule, used for monitoring the Northern Hemisphere, is difficult but not impossible to visit. Check with the **Danish Ministry of Foreign Affairs** (✉ Asiatisk Pl. 2, DK–1448 Copenhagen ☎ 33/92–00–00). Also ask the **Royal Danish Embassy** (✉ 3200 Whitehaven St. NW, Washington, DC 20008-3683 ☎ 202/234–4300) about the feasibility of a visit.

Tasiilaq

⓫ *2 hrs west of Reykjavík by plane, connecting via helicopter from Kulusuk.*

Much of the east coast is empty. Most accessible are the town of Tasiilaq and, slightly farther northeast, the tiny village of Kulusuk. Both welcome day-trippers from Iceland, who are their most frequent visitors. Tours, arranged through Icelandair, are usually short and very well organized, offering an accurate (and relatively affordable) peek at Greenlandic culture and the natural splendor of the Arctic.

Where to Stay

$$$ 🏨 **Hotel Kulusuk.** On the coast close to the tiny town of Kulusuk, this hotel offers splendid views from each of its rooms. The accommodations and amenities here, like at most hotels in Greenland, are comparable to a decent North American motel room. ✉ *Box 1500, DK–3915* ☎ *299/98–69–93* 📠 *299/98–69–83* ⊕ *www.arcticwonder.com* 🛏 *34 rooms* ♿ *Restaurant, bar* 🚭 *AE, DC, MC, V.*

$$ 🏨 **Hotel Angmagssalik.** Perched on a mountain, with a lovely view of the town and harbor, this hotel is decorated with a simple wood interior, both in the guest rooms and common areas. ✉ *Box 117, DK–3900* ☎ *299/98–12–93* 📠 *299/98–13–93* ⊕ *www.arcticwonder.com* 🛏 *30 rooms, 18 with shower* ♿ *Restaurant, bar* 🚭 *AE, DC, MC, V.*

Greenland A to Z

AIR TRAVEL

Helicopters and small planes are the only way to connect small towns because inter-city roads are basically non-existent and there are no railroads. Flying over Greenland is not merely a way to get around; the grandeur of the icebergs comes into full view only from the window of an airplane or helicopter. Because of Greenland's highly variable weather, delays are frequent. Air Greenland is the only airline licensed for domestic flights on the island. Its modest fleet of helicopters and small planes is booked year-round, so make reservations well in advance. Confirm all flights, connections, and details with your local travel agent or airline representative before you leave home.

The most common points of departure for Greenland are Denmark and Iceland. If you're going by way of Iceland, Icelandair has flights from New York, Baltimore, Fort Lauderdale, and Orlando to Keflavík, Iceland, daily in summer.

From Copenhagen, Air Greenland has service to Kangerlussuaq/Søndre Strømfjord on weekdays from June through August, and four times weekly from September through May. The Air Greenland flight to Narsarsuaq runs on a weekly basis in the off-season, increasing in frequency to three times a week during peak summer months. For connections from North America, contact the Great Canadian Travel Company about charter flights.

🛫 Carriers & Charters **Air Greenland** ☎ 299/34-34-34 in Greenland, 32/31-40-88 in Denmark ⊕ www.airgreenland.gl. **Great Canadian Travel Company** ✉ 333 N. Michigan Ave., Suite 812, Chicago IL 60601 ☎ 204/949-0199 ⊕ www.greatcanadiantravel.

com. **Icelandair** ☎ 354/505-0300 in Iceland, 0207/874-1000 in the U.K., 800/223-5500 in North America, 33/70-22-00 in Denmark ⊕ www.icelandair.com.

AIRPORTS

The main international airport in Greenland is Kangerlussuaq/Søndre Strømfjord. Narsarsuaq has some international routes and hubs domestic service in the south. Kulusuk is the main airport for the east coast. Nuuk and Ilulissat also serve as domestic airports. Greenland also has ten heliports that service the coastal towns and islands in the southern half of the country; the pad at Aasiatt/Egedesminde provides access to Disko Bay. Air Greenland can provide a full roster of regular helicopter routes. ⚑ **Aasiatt/Egedesminde Heliport** ☎ 299/89-28-88 🖷 299/89-27-88. **Ilulissat Airport** ☎ 299/94-35-88 🖷 299/94-37-88. **Kangerlussuaq/Søndre Strømfjord Airport** ☎ 299/84-13-00 🖷 299/84-10-47. **Kulusuk Airport** ☎ 299/98-69-88 🖷 299/98-69-36. **Narsarsuaq Airport** ☎ 299/66-52-88 🖷 299/98-69-36. **Nuuk Airport** ☎ 299/34-34-34 🖷 299/32-72-88.

BOAT & FERRY TRAVEL

The most beautiful way to pass the distance between towns is by water. Local tourist offices offer various types of water excursions, for transportation or for sightseeing. Some cruise and coastal boats make frequent stops. You must reserve through a travel agency. Boat voyages, including luxury cruises, are also available from Canada's Frobisher Bay, Norway's Svalbard (archipelago), and Iceland. Contact Arctic Umiaq Line or Greenland Travel in Copenhagen.
⚑ **Arctic Umiaq Line** ✉ Box 608, DK-3900 Nuuk ☎ 299/32-52-11 🖷 299/32-32-11 ⊕ www.aul.gl. **Greenland Travel** ✉ Gammel Mønt 12, Copenhagen ☎ 33/13-10-11.

EMERGENCIES

Every community has its own fire, ambulance, and police numbers and dentist and doctor, all of which you may reach through your hotel. The best way to handle emergencies is to avoid danger in the first place. Don't take risks, ask for advice, and give your travel agent and hotel your itinerary so that they can reach you in case of emergencies—or if you don't show up when you're due. If you are taking medication, bring enough to last throughout your visit.
⚑ **Sana Dronning Ingrids Hospital** ✉ Nuuk ☎ 299/34-40-00.

WHERE TO STAY

BED-AND-BREAKFASTS In recent years the bed-and-breakfast has become popular in Greenland, especially in Nuuk/Godthåb. The system is centrally organized, and you should consult the Nuuk tourism office for information. The B&Bs generally have single or double rooms with access to a bathroom and kitchen. You can also expect to spend significantly less per night than in a standard hotel room.

Also contact the Nuuk tourism office about staying in turf cottages, which are (often reconstructed) relics of the way Greenlanders used to live. Nightly rates start at Dkr 625.

TOURS

On-the-spot excursions are available in most towns and range from about Dkr 250 for a half day to Dkr 600 for a full day, more for dogsledding, boat, and helicopter trips.

Because transportation and accommodations are limited, you may want to have all details of your trip—connections, accommodations, sightseeing, and meals—arranged by an experienced travel agent, tour organizer, or airline. It's also prudent to bring a copy of your tour contract and all confirmations. Tour packages range from one- to four-day east-coast excursions from Reykjavík by Icelandair to month-long excursions, which can include sailing, hiking, hunting, dogsledding (February to May), whale safaris, and iceberg-watching.

United States **Bennett of Scandinavia** ✉ 270 Madison Ave., New York, NY 10016 ☎ 800/221-2420. **Borton Overseas** ✉ 5412 Lyndale Ave. S., Minneapolis, MN 55419 ☎ 612/822-4640 🖷 612/843-0602 ⊕ www.bortonoverseas.com. **Eurocruises** ✉ 303 W. 13th St., New York, NY 10014 ☎ 800/688-3876. **Five Stars of Scandinavia** ✉ 13104 Thomas Rd., KPN, Gig Harbor, WA 98329 ☎ 253/857-4852 🖷 253/857-4978 ⊕ www.5stars-of-scandinavia.com. **Great Canadian Travel Company** ✉ 333 N. Michigan Ave., Suite 812, Chicago, IL 60601 ☎ 204/949-0199 ⊕ www.greatcanadiantravel.com. **Icelandair** ✉ Symphony Woods, 5950 Symphony Woods Rd., Columbia, MD 21044 ☎ 800/223-5500. **Katlin Travel Group** ✉ 15 Depot Sq., Lexington, MA 02173 ☎ 617/862-6229 🖷 781/674-2080 ⊕ www.katlintravel.com. **Quark Expeditions** ✉ 980 Post Rd., Darien, CT 06820 ☎ 203/656-0499. **ScanAm World Tours Inc.** ✉ 108 N. Main St., Cranbury, NJ 08512 ☎ 609/655-1600 🖷 609/555-1622 ⊕ www.scanamtours.com. **Scantours Inc.** ✉ 3439 Wade St., Los Angeles, CA 90006 ☎ 310/636-4656 🖷 310/390-0493 ⊕ www.scantours.com. **Taylor Travel** ✉ 818 North Tejom St., Colorado Springs, CO 80903 ☎ 719/636-3871 🖷 719/636-3879. **Travcoa** ✉ 2350 S.E. Bristol St., Newport Beach, CA 92660 ☎ 949/476-2538 or 800/992-2003.

Canada **Carlson Wagonlit Travel** ✉ Proctor & Gamble Bldg., 4711 Yonge St., Suite 701, North York, Ontario M2N 6K8 ☎ 416/730-0911 🖷 416/730-1986. **Great Canadian Travel Company Ltd.** ✉ 158 Fort St., Winnipeg, Manitoba R3C 1C9 ☎ 204/949-0199 🖷 204/949-0188 ⊕ www.greatcanadiantravel.com. **North Winds Arctic Adventures** ✉ Box 820, Iqaluit, NT X0A 0H0 ☎ 867/979-0551 🖷 868/979-0573 ⊕ www.northwinds-arctic.com. **Nunavut Tourism** ✉ Box 1450, Iqaluit, NT X0A 0H0 ☎ 819/979-6551 🖷 819/979-1261 ⊕ www.nunavuttourism.com. **Silami Voyages** ✉ 70 Dahlia St., Dorval, Quebec H9S 3N2 ☎ 514/633-0893 🖷 514/633-6415. **The Wilderness Adventure Company** ✉ R.R. #3 Parry Sound, Parry Sound, Ontario P2A 2W9 ☎ 705/746-1372 🖷 705/746-7048 ⊕ www.wildernessadventure.com.

Denmark **Arctic Adventure** ✉ Reventlowsg. 30, Vesterbro, DK-1651 Copenhagen ☎ 33/25-32-21 🖷 33/25-63-08 ⊕ www.arctic-adventure.dk. **Greenland Travel** ✉ Gammel Mønt 12, Downtown, DK-1004 Copenhagen ☎ 33/13-10-11 🖷 33/13-85-92 ⊕ www.greenland-travel.dk.

VISITOR INFORMATION

Greenland Tourism, the national board, is able to provide extensive information about the country. Consider it imperative to contact the office well before departure. There is a tourism office in almost every town, but brochures, maps, and specific information may be limited. Call ahead for an exact street address (a 299 access code must be dialed before all phone numbers when calling from outside Greenland).

Tourist Information **Greenland Tourism** ✉ Box 1139, DK-1010 Copenhagen ☎ 45/33-69-32-00 🖷 45/33-93-38-83 ⊕ www.greenland.com or www.gt.gl. **Greenland Travel** ✉ Gammel Mønt 12, Downtown, DK-1004 Copenhagen ☎ 33/13-10-11 🖷 33/13-85-92 ⊕ www.greenland-travel.dk. **Ilulissat/Jakobshavn** ✉ Box 272, DK-3952 Ilulissat ☎ 299/94-43-22 🖷 299/94-39-33. **Kangerlussuaq/Søndre Strømfjord** ✉ Box 49, DK-3910, Kangerlussuaq ☎ 299/84-10-98 🖷 299/84-14-98 ⊕ www.kangerlussuaqtourism.gl. **Nuuk/Godthåb** ✉ Box 199, DK-3900 Nuuk ☎ 299/32-27-00 🖷 299/32-27-10 ⊕ www.nuuk-tourism.gl. **Qaanaaq/Thule** ✉ Box 70, DK-3971 Qaanaaq ☎ 299/97-14-73 🖷 299/97-14-74 ⊕ www.turistqaanaaq.gl. **Qaqortoq/Julianehåb** ✉ Box 183, DK-3920 Qaqortoq ☎ 299/64-29-13 🖷 299/64-29-87. **Qeqertarsuaq/Godhavn** ✉ Box 175, DK-3953 Qeqertarsuaq ☎ 299/92-11-96 🖷 299/92-11-98 ⊕ www.qeqertarsuaq.gl. **Sisimiut/Holsteinsborg** ✉ Box 65, DK-3911 Sisimiut ☎ 299/86-48-48 🖷 299/86-56-22. **Tasiilaq** ✉ Box 112, DK-3913 Tasiilaq ☎ 299/98-13-11 🖷 299/98-17-11. **Uummannaq** ✉ Atuarfimmut B821, Box 200, DK-3961 Uummannaq ☎ 299/95-17-05 🖷 299/95-14-75.

UNDERSTANDING
DENMARK

THE UTTERLY DANISH PASTRIES OF DENMARK

THE FEAST BEFORE THE FAST

BOOKS & MOVIES

CHRONOLOGY

VOCABULARY

THE UTTERLY DANISH PASTRIES OF DENMARK

I BELIEVE above and beyond every gastronomic specialty a country offers, there is one, just one, perfect, delicious bit or bite or drop of something or another that sums up everything the country is and ever has been. As a transplanted American living in Denmark, I long thought the country's perfect bite was the smørrebrød, or open-face sandwiches: they are practical, well designed, and small—in essence everything Denmark is. Over time, however, I have revised my theory. Today, I believe that divine bite can be found in the pastries, the Danish pastries.

Take a stroll through Copenhagen, and before long you'll have to make an effort to pass up the bakeries, to steel yourself not to try one of the flaky sweets. But then again, why should you? A Danish pastry is effortlessly elegant, unobtrusively hedonistic, and often packed with a surprise—an edible metaphor of the Danish experience.

Imagine this: you are walking through Copenhagen, and you happen to meander off Strøget, the store-crammed and remarkably congested pedestrian spine. Immediately, you notice the pace of the city slows. Antique shops sidle up to cafés while, a block away, rows of half-timbered houses lined with thick squares of convex windows wiggle to nowhere. At the tip of Gammel Strand, literally the old beach, you spy a lone fisherwoman in worn shawls and head scarves hawking live eel and smoked herring. You wind back to the more-than-150-year-old La Glace, purported to be the oldest confectionery shop in Copenhagen. Decorous ladies in aprons serve you a dainty china pot of coffee and light, crisp, and exceedingly Danish, pastries.

Not just any sweets these—not French, nor Austrian—and certainly not those suspicious-looking pillows of white dough injected with Red Stuff you chance to order in the United States, but the real McCoy, made in the same way since the 19th century. It makes me wonder why the Danes don't lay claim to the name, and insist upon it as an appellation d'origine.

The first time I had a Danish pastry, at the source, was 14 years ago, when the Dane of my affections (my husband today) introduced me to Copenhagen. A late night of debauchery had turned into an early morning amble, when Jesper and his best friend, Jan Erik, assured me that pastries would cure all of our ails. Though most bakeries don't open until 6 AM, Jan Erik went to a side door and rapped on its top window. Shady conversation with a young, flour-dusted blade ensued, and paper bags and cash were quickly exchanged. (I was never clear if it was law or legend, but in those days, most Danes believed the police enforced regular shopping hours.) Prize in hand, we strolled to Peblinge Sø, one of the city's lakes, where we sat on a bench, drank from a carton of milk, and ate several flaky pastries topped with nuts and sugar icings and filled with marmalades and creams. As the sun rose, defining the ducks, swans, and occasional heron, I felt enormously happy just to be there.

Those who record such events mark the birth of the Danish pastry sometime at the end of the 19th century, when Danish bakers went on strike, demanding money rather than room and board as payment for their work. Their employers replaced them with Austrian bakers, who brought with them the mille-feuille, or puff pastry, which they learned to make from the French. Once the Danes were back at work, they adopted the continental dough, making it their own by adding yeast and sweet fillings.

It was a tradition at the time (and to a lesser degree today) for Danish bakers to travel abroad to add to their repertoire. This pastry cross-pollination helps explain why the yeast-risen puff pastry is called *Kopenhagener Geback*, literally "Copenhagen bread," in Austria, and Danish pastry in America. Ironically, the yeast-risen pastries are still called *wienerbrød*, or Vienna bread, in Denmark.

What makes Danish pastries special is the production process, which for most bakers is still done by hand. Essentially, the dough—milk, flour, eggs, butter, sugar, and yeast—is made, then chilled. It is then rolled into a rectangle, and, unapologetically, a slab of margarine or butter is put on the center third. The two ends of the dough are folded over the butter, and the process is repeated three times, until there are 27 layers in all.

Once the dough has been rolled and chilled, it is finally shaped into pretzel forms (called *kringle*), as well as braids, squares, triangles, fans, combs, swirls, pinwheels, horns, crescents, and wreaths, and filled with *remonce*, the stupefyingly rich butter, sugar, and nut (or marzipan) combination. The word remonce only sounds French; since it was very fashionable in 19th-century Denmark to give things French-ified names, a Danish baker is said to have invented the word. Ask for it in Paris, and, no doubt, you will be met with bewilderment.

In addition to the remonce, Danish bakers also fill their pastries with raisins, fruit compotes, and vanilla and—to a lesser degree—chocolate custards. As Gert Sørensen, the chief baker and owner of Konditoriet in Tivoli, says, "The final product should be crisp on the outside, juicy on the inside."

He should know: as one of the country's most respected pastry chefs, he has been educating and enlightening generations of young pastry stars. In fact, not just anyone can be a *konditor*, as they are known in Denmark. The rigorous education takes three years and seven months, and entails basic economics as well as an apprenticeship at a bakery, making wienerbrød daily. Danes are happy to consume the schoolwork, and do so at breakfast, after lunch, or with their afternoon coffee, especially on the weekends. Copenhagen alone boasts more than 150 of Denmark's 1,400 bakeries, the latter pulling in the equivalent of $727 million annually, about 20 percent of which is attributable to wienerbrød. At an average cost of 5 kroner (roughly 91 cents), I figure that's close to 30 million pastries a year.

Trying to pick the best of Copenhagen's—let alone Denmark's—pastries is like hunting down France's best truffle. Though Denmark's pastry chefs participate in a number of national and international pastry contests (and consistently rank among the world's best), nearly every Dane has found a bakery within a five-minute cycling radius of home that they claim to be the best in the land. My own allegiance is to the bakery named Bosse, in the neighborhood of Østerbro. I often find my bed-headed self wandering there on Saturday morning to buy a bagful of pastries with names like rum snail, marzipan horn, and my husband's favorite, a rum ball, essentially the sausage of pastries, all the leftover bits rolled together and often covered with chocolate sprinkles. My own favorites include the *spandauer*, a flat swirl of dough, centered with vanilla custard, and the marzipan horn, a crispy twirl of pastry rolled up with remonce. Even though these may not be the finest pastries in town, they are the genuine article, and uncommonly Danish.

But, there's much more to Danish pastries than wienerbrød. At La Glace the windows display delicate special-occasion cakes like those for baptisms, trimmed with marzipan pacifiers, cradles, and dolls. From her original 1920 pink, green, and gold tea room, proprietor Marianne Stagetorn Kolos explains that most guests come for her layer cakes, like the best-selling *Sportskage*, a mound of macaroons, whipped cream, and caramel chunks created and named for a play performed at the nearby Folketeatret in 1891. It's a Danish custom to name confections for events and personalities, but there was a time when ordering a miniature Sarah Bernhardt, a chocolate-truffle-covered macaroon named for the French actress, was an act of courage. During World War II, resistance fighters and sympathizers recognized one another by ordering the pastry as a "radio macaroon," since it resembles an old-fashioned radio knob. The name stuck.

Close by, on a quiet cobblestoned courtyard, is the Kransekagehuset, where confectioner Jørgen Jensen makes the marzipan cakes compulsory at any Danish wedding. Using 1 kilogram marzipan to 400 grams sugar to 200 grams egg whites, Jensen molds the dough into rings of varying sizes. Once baked, they are fashioned into cones or cornucopias, squiggled with white icing, decked with paper decorations, or filled with wrapped candies.

I know the *kransekage* intimately. At our wedding years ago, Jesper and I split the difference in our Italian-Armenian-American-Danish backgrounds, and ordered two cakes, one of which was a kransekage laced with Danish and American flags, and tiny, shiny-paper firecrackers that made a polite, little bang.

"It's something special," smiles Jensen. "It's something very Danish."

—Karina Porcelli

THE FEAST BEFORE THE FAST

JENS PETER NISSEN loves to behold his handiwork smashed to smithereens. "It's a pure delight to see," he says. It begins when youngsters in vividly colored costumes shriek with glee as they bash a wooden baton against the fruits of Nissen's labor. Princesses and pirates swing the baton with all of their might in an attempt to "knock the cat out of the barrel." The loud crack of wood striking wood punctuates the excited cries of the youngsters. One by one, they take a turn until one of the revelers succeeds in splintering the barrel and spilling the goodies inside. The lucky one will become the Cat King or Cat Queen of Fastelavn, the Danish Shrovetide celebration.

Nissen is one of the few remaining coopers who makes barrels for Fastelavn parties, as the art of barrel making has been pushed aside by the importation of cheaper wares. Using resilient beech wood, Nissen crafts several thousand barrels each season. In fact, he has even begun a "green barrel" project. "I can recoup around two-thirds of the staves from local customers and make new barrels," he says. The recycled staves are then re-assembled to face the onslaught of costumed kiddies the following Fastelavn.

Fastelavn Sunday, or Shrove Sunday, falls seven weeks before Easter at the time of the second new moon of the year, sometime during February or the first week of March. During this anxious late-winter period before the dawn of spring, agrarian societies saw their stores of food running low and felt considerable apprehension about the growing season to come. Thus, Danish Fastelavn evolved as a fertility rite, mixing practices and beliefs imported from other cultures. Like Carnival, Mardi Gras, and Shrovetide, Fastelavn also provided the final binge before the 40-day Lenten fast preceding Easter.

Centuries ago, Danish peasants gathered for Fastelavn festivities at the larger farms in their region. Provisions were gathered by donation from area farmers, and long days were spent in preparation. Since there was little farmwork to be done this time of year, landowners were liberal about al-lowing free time and the event sometimes lasted for a week. Beer and *akvavit* (brandywine) flowed generously, while pork and pigs' feet often featured in the menus alongside *Æggesøppe* (a concoction of eggs, sugar, and beer) and other baked goods. Behind the gaudy smorgasbords and conspicuous consumption, though, was a strong symbolism, with the ubiquitous and variously cooked egg signifying the holiday's obsession, fertility.

When the day of the feast arrived, people would gather dressed in costumes and ready for a blowout. Usually there was a hag, a ragamuffin, and a jester at each gathering, each playing a predetermined role in the festivities. Bacchus, the Greek god of wine, was a regular (and fitting) figure at most feasts. Some costumes revealed the revelers' "birthday suits," borrowing elements from fertility rites in other countries, where sowing seeds in the nude was thought to ensure a bountiful agricultural year. One common Fastelavn event was a women's footrace where the ladies would hike their skirts and reveal their bare bottoms—all for the sake of a good crop!

In the 16th century Danish rulers and clergy attempted to abolish what they called "the debauchery of Fastelavn." Outcries protesting the sinfulness of the spectacles echoed down through the years, but Fastelavn was too beloved a celebration to stamp out altogether. Although authorities managed to tame the celebrations, and particularly raucous traditions fell by the wayside, the spirit of Fastelavn has survived to the present day.

When Danish children try to "knock the cat out of the barrel," they are in effect jousting. In olden days and even up through the 19th century, a live cat was placed in a barrel suspended on a rope between two houses or trees. Cats, especially black ones, had the misfortune of being considered harbingers of bad luck. Riders on horseback would "tilt the barrel" until it shattered and the unlucky (and often deceased) cat was expelled. The rider who succeeded in liberating the cat would receive a "free ride" for the party or even a reprieve on taxes. Edible goodies gradually replaced the hapless felines, so that today the barrels are filled with an inanimate cargo of fruit, nuts, and sweets.

Outside Copenhagen on the island of Amager, many of the older traditions connected to Fastelavn have been preserved and draw thousands of spectators each year. At Store Magleby, 12 km from the capital on the outskirts of Dragør, the day-long festivities begin early Monday morning when riders dressed in top hats, white embroidered shirts and black vests gather to participate in a parade led by flagmen and a carriage full of musicians. The procession winds its way throughout the district where the burghers serve participants hot rum punch. In return, the hosts are toasted for their graciousness with a song.

Later in the day the mounted assembly meets for spectacular tilting of the barrel, as riders take turns steering their steeds under the hoisted cask. The audience gasps as each of the 25 to 30 "knights" swings a beautifully carved baton to whack the barrel at full gallop. The excitement of thundering hooves and gleaming horseflesh draws the imagination back to yesteryear. When the final stave has been bashed, the gathering elects a Barrel King who gets a wreath for his valor and a kiss from the Barrel Queen. The couple then opens the festive Barrel Ball with the first three dances and the revelry extends long into the night.

Traces of other traditions can also be seen in the family's celebration of Fastelavn.

Children start the day by looking under their beds where their parents have placed a *ris,* a small cluster of twigs decorated with colored paper and sweets. The twigs bear significance as an implement of punishment, as mock floggings used to mark the holiday, and their decorations symbolize hopes for a fruitful season ahead. The children then "beat" their parents out of bed with the twigs, singing a song in which they threaten to make mischief unless they are fed. The parents' duty is to then serve the youngsters Fastelavnsboller, a heated sweet bun.

After breakfast the kiddies don costumes ranging from fairy-tale princesses to modern-day superheroes. Many of them rattle coin boxes to get contributions from friends and family, a throwback to the days when the good burghers bore some of the cost of holiday festivities. But, of course, the real highlight of Fastelavn is "knocking the cat out of the barrel," in cobblestone courtyards and lawns on Sunday and again in school the following day. Children can't wait to get into their costumes and take a swipe at the barrel, making it certain that this tradition will live on for years to come.

"It's funny. I'm a fourth-generation cooper," says Jens Peter Nissen, "and my son told me recently that he was interested in becoming a cooper one day."

—Charles Ferro

BOOKS & MOVIES

Books

A History of the Vikings (Oxford University Press, 1984) recounts the story of the aggressive warriors and explorers who during the Middle Ages influenced a large portion of the world, extending from Constantinople to America. Gwyn Jones's lively account makes learning the history enjoyable.

The History of the Danes is a 10-volume chronicle by the 13th-century monk Saxo, containing a fascinating mix of legend and history, and was where Shakespeare allegedly found the inspiration for his Hamlet character. *The Journey of Niels Klim to the World Underground* is probably Ludvig Holberg's most internationally recognized play. He is regarded as the father of Danish literature and created the Lille Gronnegade Theater at a time when Danish drama hardly existed.

The 19th century was the dawn of the Golden Age of Danish literature, marked mainly by the works of Søren Kierkegaard and Hans Christian Andersen. Kierkegaard was not really recognized in his own time, but re-discovered in the next century. Andersen is too often dismissed as simply a writer of fables, which were really aimed at an adult audience. His travel accounts, poems, plays, and other writings give a broader, and fairer, picture of who the man really was. The works of Karen Blixen (Isak Dinesen) are mostly set in Denmark and are excellent introductions to the country. A good starting point would be Blixen's debut *Seven Gothic Tales,* which was first published in the U.S. a year before its translation and Danish release in 1935. Blixen was like a literary Janus, simultaneously looking back at outdated traditions and gazing forward toward postmodern literature. The film *Out of Africa,* from Blixen's novel, has become her signature.

Pelle the Conqueror (volumes I and II) by Martin Andersen Nexø is a novel about a young Swedish boy and his father who work on a stone farm in Bornholm under hateful Danish landowners. Henrik Pontoppidan's *The Country of the Dead* is world literature at its finest. Pontoppidan won the Nobel Prize for Literature with another Dane, Karl Adolph Gjellerup, in 1917. Johannes V. Jensen is another Nobel Prize recipient. He is probably best known for his epic novel *The Long Journey,* but his *Poems* and the historical-mythical novel *The Fall of the King* demonstrate his outstanding use of language.

Laterna Magica is a novel of the Faroe Islands by William Heinesen, perhaps Denmark's greatest writer since Karen Blixen. Other excellent books on Denmark include: the satirical trilogy by Hans Scherfig—*Stolen Spring, The Missing Bureaucrat,* and *Idealists*; and Wallace Stegner's novel *The Spectator Bird,* which follows a man's exploration of his Danish heritage. Ib Michael's visits to foreign shores, especially Latin America, have a deep influence on his work. He brings this cultural inspiration back to Danish soil in his novel *Prince.*

Much of Carsten Jensen's prose is devoted to lovely travelogues drawn from numerous journeys throughout the world. A good starting point would be *I Have Seen the World Begin,* where he displays his uncanny eye for detail and insight into human behavior. Leif Davidsen was a foreign correspondent for the Danish media before becoming a potboiler best seller. His experiences abroad help draw settings for superb spy novels such as *The Russian Singer* and *Lime's Photograph.* For contemporary Danish poetry, try Jens Christian Grøndahl's collections *Silence in October* or *Lucca.*

In more recent children's literature, Bjarne Reuter's *Buster's World* tells an exciting tale with appeal for all ages. Peter Høeg's acclaimed novel *Smilla's Sense of Snow* is a compulsive page-turner that paints a dark and foreboding picture of Copenhagen and the waters around Greenland; the movie version debuted in 1997.

Fjord Press (Box 16349, Seattle, WA 98116, ☎ 206/935-7376, 🖷 206/938-1991) has one of the most comprehensive selections of Danish fiction in translation of any publisher in the United States. The Danish Literature Council's excellent Web site (www.literaturenet.dk) has a long list of books in translation and author profiles.

Movies

Babette's Feast, which won the Oscar for the best foreign film of 1987, was produced in Denmark. A year later Bille August won Danish cinema another Oscar for *Pelle the Conqueror* and launched his international career. Danny Kaye starred in the 1952 film *Hans Christian Andersen.* In fact, his crooning of "Wonderful Copenhagen" became Denmark's official tourism slogan. In 2005 Denmark will be celebrating Andersen's 200th birthday, and films related to the Danish storyteller are likely to be released. Disney's *The Little Mermaid* is a great way to get your kids interested in Andersen's fairy tales. A more recent film for youngsters is Pia Bovin's *Wallah Be* (2002), a humorous look at a suburban Danish boy who wants to be a Muslim. The film takes a comic approach to a political hot potato of the day.

Pusher (1997) has been called the Danish *Trainspotting* for its hard-driving tempo and director Niclas Winding Refn's portrayal of the drug culture. Refn takes a frightening and unique approach to the whodunnit mystery in *Fear X* (2003), starring John Turturro. *Let's Get Lost* (1997) was Jonas Elmer's film debut in which he effectively stages in black and white the laughter and tears of a group of young friends. Nils Malmros depicts 18th-century life on the Faroe Islands and the love affair between a minister and a young woman twice widowed in *Barbara* (1998).

Søren Kragh-Jacobsen, Lars von Trier, and Thomas Vinterberg co-founded the Dogma Manifesto, one of the boldest cinema experiments ever. The three wrote up a "vow of chastity" to make films with as few props and frills as possible. The results peel away layers of cinematic technique and leave the viewer with a raw view of the subject on screen. Vinterberg's *The Celebration* (1999) turns a family celebration into a nightmare; in *The Idiots* (1999) von Trier examines a perverse grass-roots experiment in human nature; and Kragh-

Jacobsen takes an off-center perspective of returning home to find love in *Mifune* (1998). Lone Scherfig's *Italian for Beginners* (2000) takes the Dogma concept into the romantic comedy genre. Scherfig stepped onto the international filmmaking stage with the English-language *Wilbur Wants to Kill Himself* (2002), a highly entertaining, warm comedy with a serious bent. Kragh-Jacobsen and Vinterberg both made English-language films in 2003. Kragh-Jacobsen's *Skagerrak* is part of what he calls the "Women's Trilogy" that started with *Mifune.* On their latest outing, two women spend their time pursuing men and liquor, but somehow end up finding direction and meaning for their confused lives. *It's All About Love* is Thomas Vinterberg's millennial fairy tale, a romance, with an unsettling dream-like atmosphere.

Susanne Bier's *The One and Only* (1999) provided audiences with hilarious romantic comedy that made it the best-selling picture in Danish history. In the same year Ole Christian Madsen gave viewers the stark realism of life for young non-ethnic Danes who step outside the law in *Pizza King.* Bier then made a real international breakthrough with her first Dogma venture *Open Hearts* (2002), a tear-jerker about personal tragedy and its effects on love. Lars von Trier revived the cinema musical, with a twist, in his *Dancer in the Dark* (2000), a work that won him a number of international awards and nominations. The film was a major victory for Danish cinema and an excellent follow-up to von Trier's *Breaking the Waves* (1997). In another trilogy in the making, director Per Fly investigates the class structure of Danish society and displays an amazing ability to get right down to eye level with the protagonist. *The Bench* (2000) examines the dark alcoholic underclass, and *Inheritance* (2003) follows with a view of upper-class life.

CHRONOLOGY

ca. 10,000 BC   Stone Age culture develops in Denmark.

ca. 2,000 BC   Tribes from southern Europe, mostly Germanic peoples, migrate toward Denmark.

ca. 1800–   The Bronze Age culture develops in Denmark. Metal tools and
500 BC   weapons are made, and trade with other European countries increases.

ca. 500 BC   Migration of Celts across central Europe impinges on Denmark's trade routes with the Mediterranean world. Trade becomes less economically crucial because of the growing use of abundant iron.

ca. 770   The Viking Age begins. For the next 250 years, Scandinavians set sail on frequent expeditions stretching from the Baltic to the Irish seas, and even to the Mediterranean as far as Constantinople and to North America, employing superior ships and weapons and efficient military organization.

811   The Eider River is declared the southern border of the Kingdom of Denmark. It remains there for nearly 1,000 years.

830   Frankish monk Ansgar makes one of the first attempts to Christianize Sweden and builds the first church in Slesvig, Denmark.

ca. 940–980   King Harald Bluetooth imposes Christianity on the people of Denmark. In less than a century, virtually the whole population has been converted.

1016–35   Canute (Knud) the Great is king of England, Denmark (1018), and Norway (1028). The united kingdom crumbles shortly after Canute's death in 1035.

1070   Adam of Bremen composes *History of the Archbishops of Hamburg-Bremen,* the first important contemporary source for Danish history.

ca. 1100–   The power of the Danish crown grows, and the country becomes
1200   dominant in the Baltic region.

1169   King Valdemar, who was acknowledged as the single king of Denmark in 1157 and undertook repeated crusades against the Germans, captures Rugen and places it under Danish rule, signifying the beginning of the Danish medieval empire. It culminates in 1219 when Valdemar marches to Estonia and builds a fortress at Ravel. In 1225, Valdemar, after being kidnapped by a German vassal, is forced to give up all his conquests, except for Rugen and Estonia, in exchange for his release.

ca. 1200   Saxo writes his history of Denmark, the first volume of Danish literature. It is an amazing source of history and legend, and is believed to have inspired Shakespeare to write about the fictitious Danish prince, Hamlet.

1282   At a meeting of the Hof, or Danish Parliament, Danish king Erik Glipping signs a coronation charter that becomes the first written constitution of Denmark.

ca. 1340   King Valdemar IV re-unites Denmark after a long period of civil unrest.

1370   The Treaty of Stralsund gives the north German trading centers of the Hanseatic League free passage through Danish waters and full control of Danish herring fisheries for 15 years. German power increases throughout Scandinavia.

1397   The Kalmar Union is formed by Queen Margrethe as a result of the dynastic ties between Sweden, Denmark, and Norway; the geographical position of the Scandinavian states; and the growing influence of Germans in the Baltic. Erik of Pomerania is crowned king of the Kalmar Union.

ca. 1417   The center of power shifts from Roskilde to Copenhagen, which becomes the capital of Denmark.

1479   The University of Copenhagen is founded.

1520   Christian II, ruler of the Kalmar Union, executes 82 people who oppose the Kalmar Union in an event known as the "Stockholm bloodbath." Sweden secedes from the Union three years later. Norway remains tied to Denmark and becomes a Danish province in 1536.

1528–36   The Reformation reaches Denmark. Lutheran clergy rapidly gain access to the royal court and spread the religious word. The Reformation brings on civil unrest culminating in The Count's War, in which the nobility wins power. King Christian III declares Lutheranism to be the official religion of the country. Catholic clergy are imprisoned, and Catholic properties and other assets are confiscated.

1534   Count Christoffer of Oldenburg and his army demand the restoration of Christian II as king of Denmark, initiating civil war between supporters of Christian II and supporters of Prince Christian (later King Christian III).

1563–70   Denmark wages war, but fails to reclaim Sweden.

1588–1648   King Christian IV sits on the throne in one of the longest and influential reigns in Danish history. Prosperity flourishes, despite an unsuccessful war against Sweden. Christian becomes known as the "Building King" for initiating huge construction projects, especially in Copenhagen, where many of the buildings still stand. His lavish spending brings the country to the brink of bankruptcy.

1611–16   During the Kalmar War, Denmark wages a campaign against Sweden in hopes of restoring the Kalmar Union.

1611–60   Gustav II Adolphus reigns in Sweden. Under his rule, Sweden defeats Denmark in the Thirty Years' War and becomes the greatest power in Scandinavia as well as northern and central Europe.

1660   The Peace of Copenhagen establishes the modern boundaries of Denmark, Sweden, and Norway.

1665   King Frederik III establishes an absolute monarchy.

1754   The Royal Danish Academy of Fine Arts is established.

1762   The Duke of Gottorp becomes czar of Russia and declares war on Denmark. Catherine, the czar's wife, overrules her husband's war declaration and makes a peaceful settlement.

1801–14   The Napoleonic wars are catastrophic for Denmark economically and politically: the policy of armed neutrality fails, the English destroy the Danish fleet in 1801, Copenhagen is devastated during the bombardment of 1807, and Sweden, after Napoléon's defeat at the Battle of Leipzig, attacks Denmark and forces the Danish surrender of Norway. The Treaty of Kiel, in 1814, calls for a union between Norway and Sweden despite Norway's desire for independence. The Danish monarchy is divided into three parts: the Kingdom of Denmark; the duchies of Schleswig and Holstein; and Iceland, Greenland, and the Faroe Islands.

1810–30 This is the Golden Age of Danish literature and art. Hans Christian Andersen and Søren Kierkegaard make their mark during this period. C. W. Eckersberg influences a generation of artists with his focus on nature.

1849 Denmark's absolute monarchy is abolished and replaced by the liberal June Constitution, which establishes freedom of the press, freedom of religion, the right to hold meetings and form associations, and rule by two chambers of Parliament, which are overseen by the king and his ministers.

ca. 1850– The beginning of the industrial age is heralded by the building of
1900 railroads in Scandinavia. The expansion of industrialism draws people to Copenhagen, which has a population of almost 1.5 million by the turn of the century.

1864 Denmark goes to war against Prussia and Austria; the hostilities end with the Treaty of Vienna, which forces Denmark to surrender the duchies of Schleswig and Holstein to Prussia and Austria.

1914 At the outbreak of World War I, Germany forces Denmark to lay mines in an area of international waters known as the Great Belt. Because the British fleet makes no serious attempts to break through, Denmark is able to maintain neutrality.

1917 Danish writer Henrik Pontoppidan is awarded the Nobel prize for literature.

1918 Iceland becomes a separate state under the Danish crown; only foreign affairs remain under Danish control. Sweden, Denmark, and Norway grant women the right to vote.

1920 Scandinavian countries join the League of Nations.

ca. 1930 The Great Depression brings unemployment to 40% of the organized industrial workers in Denmark. The age of the Social Democrats begins, and foundations are laid for the welfare state that still exists today.

1939 Denmark and the other Nordic countries declare neutrality in World War II.

1940 Germany occupies Norway and Denmark. Denmark trades basic cooperation with their occupiers in exchange for a degree of self-government.

1949 Denmark, Norway, and Iceland become members of NATO.

1952 The Nordic Council is founded to promote cooperation among the Nordic parliaments.

1973 Denmark becomes a member of the European Union. Queen Margrethe II ascends the throne of Denmark.

1982 Poul Schluter becomes Denmark's first Conservative prime minister since 1894.

1989 The Tycho Brahe Planetarium opens in Copenhagen, and Denmark becomes the first NATO country to allow women to join front-line military units. Denmark becomes the first country in the world to recognize marriage between citizens of the same sex.

1991   The Karen Blixen Museum opens in Rungstedlund, Denmark.

1992   Denmark declines to support the Maastricht Treaty setting up a framework for European economic union. Denmark wins the European Soccer Championships.

1993   Denmark is the president of the EU for the first half of 1993. In a second referendum, the country votes to support the Maastricht Treaty, as well as its own modified involvement in it. Tivoli celebrates its 150th year, Legoland celebrates its 25th birthday, and the Little Mermaid turns 80.

1996   Copenhagen is fêted as the Cultural Capital of Europe.

1997   Copenhagen's venerable Carlsberg Brewery, one of the largest supporters of the arts in Denmark, celebrates its 150th anniversary.

2000   In a national referendum, Danish voters reject full membership in the European Economic Union by voting against the euro to replace the krone as (inter)national currency. The Øresund Bridge linking Denmark to Sweden opens for rail and motor traffic, connecting Scandinavia to the Continent. Queen Ingrid dies at the age of 90. Swedish by birth and a beloved member of the royal family, her death is mourned throughout the country.

2001   Denmark gets a Liberal-Conservative coalition government after the ruling Social Democrats call for an election. Political campaigning generates a great amount of (sometimes critical) foreign interest as the focal topic of the election is limiting immigration.

2002   Prince Felix is born to Princess Alexandra and Prince Joachim. The first section of the Copenhagen Metro goes into operation. Denmark passes legislation to curb immigration. Denmark occupies the seat of the European Union presidency in the second half of the year. Danish prime minister Anders Fogh Rasmussen gets credit for successfully coordinating the planned expansion of the union from 15 to 25 member nations.

VOCABULARY

	English	Danish	Pronunciation
Basics			
	Yes/no	Ja/nej	yah/nie
	Thank you	Tak	tak
	Thank you	Mange tak	**mahng**er tak
	You're welcome	Selv tak	**sell** tak
	Excuse me (to apologize)	Undskyld	**unsk**-ul
	Hello	Hej	hi
	Hello/Good day	Goddag	go-day
	How do you do?	goddag	go-**day**
	May I introduce . . .?	å jeg presentere . . .	Mo yie pre-sen-teer
	. . . my friend	min ven	meen ven
	. . . my sweetheart	min kæreste	meen **care**-es-te
	. . . my son	min søn	meen sohn
	. . . my daughter	min datter	meen dat-ter
	. . . my mother	min mor	meen mor
	. . . my father	min far	meen far
	. . . my sister	min søster	meen **soes**-ter
	. . . my brother	min bror	meen bror
	. . . my wife	min kone	meen **ko**-neh
	. . . my husband	min mand	meen man
	. . . my boss	min chef	meen shayf
	Good morning (early)	godmorgen	go-**more**-en
	Good afternoon	goddag	go-**day**
	Good evening	godaften	go-**af**-ten
	Good night	godnat	go-nat
	Sleep well	Sov godt	sow gut
	Goodbye	Farvel	fa-**vel**
	See you later (casually spoken)	På gensyn Vi ses	pa **en**-sewn See you vee sees
	Today	I dag	ee **day**
	Tomorrow	I morgen	ee **morn**
	Yesterday	I går	ee **gore**
	Morning	Morgen	**more**-en
	Afternoon	Eftermiddag	**ef-tah**-mid-day
	Evening	Aften	**af**-dern
	Night	Nat	nat

Numbers

1	een/eet	een/eet
2	to	toe
3	tre	treh
4	fire	fear
5	fem	fem
6	seks	sex
7	syv	syoo
8	otte	**oh**-te
9	ni	nee
10	ti	tee
11	elleve	**el**-ver
12	tolv	tol
13	tretten	**tre**-tern
14	fjorten	**fyor**-tern
15	femten	**fem** tern
16	seksten	**sehgs**-tern
17	sytten	**soo**-tern
18	atten	**ah**-tern
19	nitten	**ni**-tern
20	tyve	**tyoo**-ver
30	tredive	**tred**-ver
40	fyrre	**few**-rer
50	halvtreds	hal-**trays**
60	tres	trays
70	halvfjerds	hal-**fyairz**
80	firs	feers
90	halvfems	hal-**fems**
100	hundrede	**hoon**-red-der
1000	tusind	**too**-sin
10,000	ti tusind	tee **too**-sin

Days of the Week & Months

Monday	mandag	**man**-day
Tuesday	tirsdag	**tears**-day
Wednesday	onsdag	**ons**-day
Thursday	torsdag	**tors**-day
Friday	fredag	**free**-day
Saturday	lørdag	**lore**-day
Sunday	søndag	**sin**-day
January	januar	**yan**-oo-are
February	februar	**feb**-oo-are
March	marts	marts

April	april	a-**breel**
May	maj	my
June	juni	yoo-**nee**
July	juli	yoo-**lee**
August	august	ow-**goost**
September	september	sep-**tem**-beh
October	oktober	ock-**toh**-beh
November	november	no-**vem**-beh
December	december	des-**sem**-beh

Useful Phrases

Do you speak	Taler	te-ler
English?	du engelsk	doo in-galsk
I don't speak . . . Danish	Jeg taler ikke . . . Dansk	yi tal-ler **ick** . . . Dansk
I understand	Jeg forstår	yi foh-stoh
I don't understand	Jeg forstår ikke	yi foh-stoh **ick**
I don't know	Det ved jeg ikke	deh **ved** yi ick
I am	Jeg er	yi ehr
American/British	amerikansk/britisk	a-meh-ri-**kansk**/bri-**tisk**
I am sick.	Jeg er syg	yi air **syoo**
Please call	Kan du ringe	can **doo** rin-geh
a doctor	til en læge?	til en **lay**-eh
Pharmacy	apotek	a-po-**teek**
Do you have	Har du et	har **doo** eet
a vacant room?	værelse?	varay-l-sa
How much does it cost?	Hvad koster det?	va cos-ta **deh**
It's too expensive.	Det er for dyrt	deh air **fohr** deert
That's inexpensive	Det var billigt	**day** vahr beeleet
How are you?	Hvordan har du det?	vore-dan **ha** do deh
I am fine/well	Jeg har det godt	Yie **ha** de gutt
I am very pleased to meet you.	Det glæder mig at træffe Dem.	Deh **glay**derr mig at **treh**fer dem
My name is . . .	Mit navn er . . .	mid nown air . . .
Where are you from?	Hvor kommer du fra?	Vore **com**-mer doo fra
I am from . . .	Jeg kommer fra . . .	Yie com-mer fra . . .
Where do you live?/ Where are you staying?	Hvor bor du hen?	Vore bore doo hen
How old are you?	Hvor gammel er du?	Vore gam-mel air **do**
Are you going to work today?	Skal du arbejde idag?	Skal doo **are**-buy-da ee-day
I am free	Jeg har fri	Yie har **free**
Beautiful	Smukt	smukt

I'm sorry. I don't like it.	Jeg synes ikke om det	yie **soo**-ners ick om day
Help!	Hjælp	yelp
Can you help me, please?	Vil De være så venlig at hjælpe mig?	vil dee **vay**-rer saw **ven**-lee ad **yel**-per my
Stop!	Stop	stop
I am lost	Jeg er faret vild	yi air **far**-rerd veal
How do I get to . . .?	Hvordan kommer yi til . . .?	vore-**dan** kom-merjeg til
. . . the train station?	banegarden	**ban**-eh-gore-en
. . . the post office?	postkontoret	**post**-kon-toh-raht
. . . the tourist office?	turistkontoret	too-**reest**-kon-toh-raht
. . . the hospital?	hospitalet	hos-peet-**tal**-let
Does this bus go to . . .	Går denne bus til . . .	**goh** den-na boos til
Where's the bathroom?	Hvor er toilettet	vor **air** toi-let-it
It's urgent	Det haster	day **hahs**-der
Where is the nearest bank?	Hvor er den nærmeste bank?	vor air den **nair**-mers-der bahnk
Where can I get a taxi?	Hvor kan jeg få en taxa?	vor kahn yie faw een **tahg**-sah
I would like to go to . . .	Jeg skal til . . .	Yie skal til
When?	Hvornår?	vor-**nawr**
On the left	Til venstre	til **ven**-strah
On the right	Til højre	til **hoy**-ah
Straight ahead	Lige ud	lee udh
North	nord	nor
South	syd	sudth
East	øst	ohst
West	vest	vest
What time is it?	Kan du sige mig hvad klokken er?	can do see my vadth **clok**-ken air
It is . . .	Den er . . .	Den air
one, two, three, etc.	et, to, tre, etc.	o'clock
quarter past . . .	kvart over . . .	kvart ower
quarter to . . .	kvart i . . .	kvart ee
half past (literally half before)	halv et, halv to, etc. (N.B. halv et = 12:30, halv to = 1:30 etc.)	hal . . .
big	stor	sdoar
small	lille	liller
early	tidlig	**tid**-lee
late	sen	sayn
It's (too) late	Det er (for) sent	de air (for) **seent**
It's (too) early	Det er (for) tidlig	de air (for) tid-lee
Sorry I'm late	Undskyld jeg kom for sent	**un**-skuld yie com for seent
Do you have time?	Har du tid?	ha do tid

How long will it take?	Hvor lang tid tager det?	vor lahng tid tah de
Would you like to go to the movies?	Skal vi i biografen?	Skal vee ee bee-o-grahf-en
I'd like to go to the movies	Jeg vil gerne i biografen	Yie vil gairn ee bee-o-grahf-en
What would you like to see?	Hvad kun du tænke dig at se?	Vadth koon doo tan-keh die at see
movie	film	feelm
It was a good movie	Det var en god film	de var een go **feelm**
Do you like music?	Kan du lide musik?	can du lee moo-**seek**
Would you like to dance?	Vil du danse med mig?	vil do dan-seh medth mie
I would like to	Det vil jeg gerne	de vil yie **gair**-ne
I like you	Jeg kan lide dig	yie can lee die
I love you	Jeg elsker dig	yie el-skah die
You are cute/pretty	Du er sød	do air **suhdth**
The same to you	I lige måde	ee **lee** mo-deh
Never	aldrig	**ahl**-dree
Maybe	måske	mo-**skee**
Always	altid	ahl-tid
Congratulations	Tillykke	til-**luk**-ka
I'm sorry to hear that (condolences)	Det gøre mig ondt	day goohr my unt
Weather	været	**vair**-it
It's raining/snowing	Det regner/sneer	day **rhine**-er/**snee**-er.
The sun is shining	solen skinner	sol-en **skin**-ner.
It's cold/hot.	Det er koldt/varmt.	day air kolt/varmt.
I'm cold.	Jeg fryser.	yie **froo**-ser.
Do you have an umbrella?	Har du en paraply?	har do een par-a-**ploo**
overcast	overskyet	ower-sku-et
It's windy	Det blæser	day **blay**-ser.

Dining Out

Would you like to have breakfast/lunch/dinner together?	Skal vi spise morgenmad/frokost/middag sammen?	skal vee **spee**-sa more en madth/fro-coast/mid-day sam-men
Are you hungry?	Er du sulten?	air **do** sool tan
I am hungry	Jeg er sulten	yie air **sool**-tan
I am thirsty	Jeg er tørstig	yie air **turss**-tee
What would you like to eat?	Hvad har du lyst til at spise?	vadth ha do loost til at **spee**-sa
Would you like a . . .?	Kunne du tænke dig en . . .?	coo-neh do tan-keh die een
Please bring me . . .	Må jeg få . . .	moh yie foh

Can I have . . .?	Kan jeg ffå . . .?	kahn yie faw
I'd like some . . .	Jeg vil gerne have . . .	yie vil **ger**-ner **hay**-fisk
Please pass the . . .	Kunne du række mig . . .	koo-neh do raik my
May I have a bit more, please?	Må jeg bede om lidt mere?	moh yie bee om lit meer
I'm a vegetarian	Jeg er vegetar	yie air ve-ge-**tar**
menu	menu	me-**nu**
fork	gaffel	gaf-**fel**
knife	kniv	ka-**new**
spoon	ske	skee
glass	glas	glass
cup	kop	cop
bowl	skål	skoal
plate	tallerken	tal-**air**-ken
napkin	serviet	ser-**veet**
bread	brød	brood
butter	smør	smoor
fish	fisk	fisk
vegetables	grøntsager	**grunt**say-er
salad/lettuce	salat	sal-**ate**
meat	kød	koodth
milk	mælk	malk
pepper	peber	**pee**-wer
salt	salt	selt
sugar	sukker	**su**-kar
water/bottled water	vand/Dansk vand	van/dansk van
ice cream	is?	ees
beer	øl	ohl
cup of coffee	kop kaffe?	cop **cah**-feh
wine	vin	veen
red wine	rødvin	**roadth**veen
white wine	hvidvin	**vidth**veen
assorted hors d'ouevre	forskellig hors d'oeuvre	fos-**geh**-lee or-**durvr**
sole	søtunge	**sur**-doanger
trout	ørred	**ur**-rerd
lobster	hummer	**hoa**-mer
crayfish	krebs	krebs
prawns	store rejer	**stoa**-rer **rig**-ger
steak	en engelsk bøf	een **eng**-erlsk burf
lamb	lammekød	**la**-mor-kurd
pork chop	svinekotelet	**sveen**-er-ko-ter-led
chicken	kylling	**kew**-ling

duck	and	ahn
It tastes good	Det smager godt	De smay-ya **gut**
Thank you for the meal (customary etiquette)	Tak for mad	tak for madth
You're welcome	Velbekomme	Vel-be-kom-men
Cheers	Skål	skoal
Thank you for the last time we were together (I had a good time)	Tak for sidste	tak for **seest**
It (the occasion) was/is pleasant/cozy.	Det var/er hyggeligt.	De var/air **hoo**-geh-lee.
The check, please.	Må jeg bede om regningen	mo yie bi om **ri**-ning
Is service included?	Er det med betjening?	air day med ber-**tyay**-ning

INDEX

A

Aalborg, 137–139
Aalborg Historical Museum, 138
Admiral ⊞, 37
Admiralen ✕, 120
Ærø Museum, 112
Ærøskøbing, 111–113
Åholm Automobile Museum, 88
Air tours, 158
Air travel, F24–F26
Bornholm, 156
Copenhagen, 60
Faroe Islands, 169–170
Greenland, 184–185
Jylland, 140
Sjælland, 90
Akademiet, 89
Åkirke, 156
Åkirkeby, 156
Allinge, 151
Almindingen, 156
Amager Museum, 56
Amalienborg, 12
Amalienborg Museum, 12
Amalienhaven, 14
Andersen, Hans Christian, 100
Andersen Nexøs Hus, 155
Anne Hvides Gård, 107
Arbejdermuseet, 17
Århus, 130–134
Århus Domkirke, 131
Århus Pass, 130
Arken, 58–59
Assens, 105
Assistens Kierkegaard, 17
Asummiut, 181
ATMs, F39
Avernakø, 106–107

B

Bakken, 57–58
Ballet, 46–47
Barometer, gilded, 10
Baroque Gardens, 75
Bars and lounges
Copenhagen, 41
Fyn and the central islands, 96, 103–104, 108–109, 113, 114
Jylland, 127, 133
Beaches, F18
Bornholm, 148
Copenhagen and environs, 47, 57
Faroe Islands, 169
Jylland, 127–128
Sjælland, 79, 87, 88
Beer and wine cellars, 138–139
Bellevue Beach, 57
Biking, F18, F26–F27, F44
Bornholm, 156

Copenhagen, 47–48, 60, 63
Faroe Islands, 170
Fyn and the central islands, 106, 115
Jylland, 124, 141
Sjælland, 90–91
tours, 63
Billund, 128–129
Bird watching, 74, 99, 106–107, 152, 166, 167–168
Bjørnø, 106–107
Boat and ferry travel. ⇨ See Ferries
Boat tours
Bornholm, 151
Copenhagen, 63
Fyn and the central islands, 99, 101
Greenland, 185–186
Jylland, 130
Sjælland, 92
Boating, F18
BonBon Land, 89–90
Books, 192
Børnekulturehuset Fyrtøjet, 100
Bornholm, F13, 145–158
arts and nightlife, 148, 150
children, attractions for, 151, 156
emergencies, 158
guided tours, 158
hotels, 147–148, 151, 152–153, 154–155
outdoor activities and sports, 149, 156
price categories, 145
restaurants, 146–147, 152, 154–155
shopping, 148–149, 153, 155
sightseeing, 149–156
transportation, 156–157, 158
visitor information, 158
Bornholm Museum, 146
Bornholms Kunstmuseum, 152
Børsen, 6, 7
Botanisk Have, 16, 17
Brandts Klædefabrik, F22, 101
Brattahlíð, 178
Bregninge Mølle ✕, F21, 110
Brewery, 19–20
Brøndums Hotel ✕⊞, 140
Bryggeriet Sct. Clemens ✕, F21, 132
Budolfi Kirke, 137
Bus tours, 63–64, 158
Bus travel, F28
Bornholm, 157
Faroe Islands, 170
Fyn and the central islands, 115
Jylland, 141–142
Business hours, F28
By Museum, 72

C

Café Nanas Stue ✕, 128
Cafés, 42, 96, 109, 120, 165
Camping, 77, 148, 151
Canoeing
Copenhagen, 48
Sjælland, 90
Car rental, F28–F29
Car travel, F29–F30
Bornholm, 157
Copenhagen, 61
Faroe Islands, 171
Fyn and the central islands, 115
Jylland, 142
Sjælland, 92
Carl Nielsen Museum, 100
Carlsberg Bryggeri, 19–20
Carlsberg Museum, 20, 21, 22
Carmelite Kloster, 72
Casinos, 42, 104, 129, 133, 139
Castles, F21, F22
Copenhagen and environs, 7, 12, 14, 18, 54
Fyn and the central islands, 95, 109, 110
Jylland, 131
Sjælland, 71–72, 73, 75, 76–77, 80, 81, 84, 85, 86
Charlottenborg, 12, 14
Charlottenlund, 54–55
Children, traveling with, F30
Christiania, 7
Christiansborg Slot, F21, 6, 7
Christianshavn, 6, 7–8, 23
Christianskirkjan, 167
Christiansø, 152
Churches, F21–F22
Bornholm, 153, 156
Copenhagen, 8, 10, 11, 14, 15–16, 19
Faroe Islands, 162, 164, 165, 167
Fyn and the central islands, 100
Greenland, 178, 179, 183
Jylland, 124–125, 129, 131, 136, 137, 139
Sjælland, 72, 75, 79, 80, 81, 83, 85, 86, 87, 89
Climate, F15
Club 42 ✕, 83
Convent, 72
Copenhagen, F12, 2–66
addresses, 59
arts and nightlife, 40–47
children, attractions for, 9, 22, 23
emergencies, 61
English-language media, 61–62
guided tours, 63–64
hotels, 33–40
money matters, 62
outdoor activities and sports, 47–49

price categories, 23, 33
restaurants, 9, 10, 15, 17, 18, 23–33
side trips from, 54–59
shopping, 49–54
sightseeing, 2–23
transportation, 62–63, 64–65
travel agencies, 65
visitor information, 65–66
Credit cards, F10, F39
Cruising. ⇨ *See* Boat tours
Customs and duties, F30–F32

D

Dancing and discos
Copenhagen, 42–43
Jylland, 127, 134, 139
D'Angleterre ⚏ , F20, 36
Danish design, F18, 53
Danish pastries, 188–189
Danish vocabulary, 198–204
Danmarks Akvarium, 55
Danmarks Grafiske Museum, 101
Dansk Arkitektur Center, 6, 8
Dansk Design Center, 19, 20
Dansk Jødisk Museum, 6, 8
Dansk Presse Museum, 101
De 7 Haver, 105
Den Fynske Landsby, 101
Den Gamle Arrest ⚏ , F20, 126
Den Gamle By, 131
Den Gamle Gaard, 105
Den Grimme Ælling ✕ , 103
Den Hirschsprungske Samling, 16, 17
Den Lille Havfrue (The Little Mermaid), 12, 14
Det Gamle Rådhus, 134
Det Kongelige Bibliotek(Royal Library), 6, 8
Det Kongelige Teater(Royal Danish Theater), 14–15
Disabilities and accessibility, F32–F33
Discounts and deals, F33
Dogsledding, 175, 182, 183, 185–186
Dominican monastery clock, 129
Domkirke (Roskilde), F21, 81, 83
Domkirke (Viborg), 136
Døndalen Forest, 151
Dragør, 55–57
Dragør Museum, 56
Drøhses Hus, 123
Dronningmølle, 69, 77
Duus Vinkjælder ✕ , 138
Dúvugarðar Museum, 166
Dyrehaven, 57–58

E

Ebeltoft, 134, 136
Ebeltoft Museum, 134
Egeskov Slot, F22, 109

Eiði, 166–167
Ekkodalen, 156
Electricity, F34
Emergencies, F34
Bornholm, 158
Copenhagen, 61
Faroe Islands, 171
Fyn and the central islands, 115
Greenland, 185
Jylland, 142
Sjælland, 91
Era Ora ✕ , 23
Eremitagen, 58
Erichsens Gård, 145–146
Esbjerg, 126–127
Esbjerg Kunstmuseum, 127
Esbjerg Museum, 127
Esrum Kloster, 75
Eventyrlandet, 89
Experimentarium, 54

F

Faaborg, 105–107
Faaborg Museum for Fynsk Malerkunst, 105
Falkonergården, 74
Falsled Kro ✕ , F20–F21, 105–106
Falster, 87–88
Fanefjord Kirke, 87
Fanø, 127–128
Fåreveile Kirke, 79
Faroe Islands, F13, 160–171
arts and nightlife, 165
emergencies, 171
guided tours, 171
hotels, 161–162, 164–165, 166–167, 168, 169
price categories, 162
restaurants, 164
shopping, 165
sightseeing, 162–169
transportation, 169–171
visitor information, 171
Ferries, F27–F28
Bornholm, 157
Copenhagen, 65
Faroe Islands, 170
Fyn and the central islands, 106
Greenland, 185
Jylland, 141
Sjælland, 91
Festivals and seasonal events, F16–F17
Fyn and the central islands, 96
Jylland, 123, 130, 131, 133, 135
Sjælland, 83
Film, 45, 46
Fishing, F41–F42
Bornholm, 149, 158
Fyn and the central islands, 111
Greenland, 175
Jylland, 121
Sjælland, 91
Fjords, 166, 180
Flaskeskibssamlingen, 112
Fodor's Choice, F20–F23

Folketinget, 7
Føroya Náttúrugripasavn, 164
Fortress of Hammershus, 149–150
Fredensborg, 73–74
Fredensborg Slot, 73
Frederiksborg Slot, 75
Frigate Jylland, 134
Frihedsmuseet, 12, 14
Frilandsmuseet, 58
Fyn and the central islands, F12, 95–116
arts and nightlife, 96, 103–104, 106, 108–109, 113, 114
children, attractions for, 100, 105
emergencies, 115
guided tours, 115–116
hotels, 96, 99, 103, 105–106, 108, 110–111, 112–113, 114
outdoor activities and sports, 104, 111
price categories, 95
restaurants, 96, 98–99, 101–103, 105–106, 108, 110, 112, 114
shopping, 97, 99, 104–105, 109, 111, 113, 114
transportation, 115, 116
visitor information, 116
Fyns Kunstmuseum, 100–101
Fyrtøjet ✕ , 146

G

Gardens
Copenhagen, F23, 16, 17, 18
Fyn and the central islands, 105
Sjælland, 73, 75
Gay and lesbian travel, F34
Gay bars and establishments, 43–44
Gefion Springvandet, 12, 14
Gilleleje, 69, 78
Glasmuseum, 136
Godt ✕ , 30
Golf, F42
Bornholm, 153
Copenhagen, 48
Fyn and the central islands, 104
Sjælland, 73, 74, 84, 88
Græsholmen, 152
Greenland, F13, 173–186
arts and nightlife, 179
emergencies, 185
guided tours, 185–186
hotels, 174, 176, 178, 179, 180, 181, 182–183, 184
outdoor activities and sports, 175–176, 181–182, 183
price categories, 176
restaurants, 174, 179, 182–183
shopping, 181
sightseeing, 176–184
transportation, 184–185
visitor information, 186
Gribskov, 74
Gudhjem, 151–153

Guided tours
Bornholm, 158
Copenhagen, 63–64
Faroe Islands, 171
Fyn and the central islands,
115–116
Greenland, 185–186
Jylland, 142
Sjælland, 92

H

H. C. Andersens
Barndomshjem, 100
Hærvejen, 136
Hagested Kirke, 80
Halsskov, 90
Hammeren, 150
Hammerichs Hus, 112
Hammershus, 149–150
Hans Christian Andersen Hus,
100
Hansen's Café, 76
Havnar Kirkja, 162, 164
Helligaandskirken, 6, 8
Helligaandsklosteret, 137
Helligdomsklipperne, 151
Helsingør, 69, 71–73
Hesselet ☒, F20
Hiking
Bornholm, 149, 156
Fyn and the central islands,
106–107
Greenland, 175
Hillerød, 69, 74–76
Himmelbjerget, 130
Hjejlen (paddle steamer),
130
Hjorths Fabrik, 146
Hjorths Røgeri, 154
Højbro Plads, 7
Højby Kirke, 79
Højerup Kirke, 86
Højesteret, 7
Holidays, F35
Holbæk, 80
Holbæk Museum, 80
Hollufgård, 101
Holmen, 9
Holmens Kirke, 6, 9
Hornbæk, 69, 76–77
Horseback riding, 49
Hos Grethe ✕, 112
Hospitalsdalen, 178
Hotel Dagmar ✕☒, F20, 126
Hotel Færgegaarden ☒, 106
Hotel Falster ☒, 88
Hotel Føroyar ✕☒, 164
Hotel Igloo Village ☒, 180
Hotel Marienlyst ☒, 72–73
Hotel Store Kro ✕☒, 74
Hotel Valle Slotskro ☒, F20,
85–86
Hotel Ydes ☒, F20, 103
Hotels, F20, F38. ⇨ *Also*
under individual islands
price categories, F36, 33, 68,
95, 118, 145, 162, 176
Humlebæk, 69, 71

Hvalsey Church, 178
Hviids Have, 105

I

Ida Davidsen ✕, F21, 31
Ilulissat/Jakobshavn,
182–183
Insurance, F35
Istedgade, 19, 20
Itineraries, F14

J

Jægerspris Slot, 81
Jazz clubs
Bornholm, 148
Copenhagen, 44
Fyn and the central islands,
104, 113
Jylland, 133
Jelling, 129–130
Jens Bang Stenhus, 137
Johannes Larsen Museet,
97–98
Jomfru Ane Gade, 137
Julianehåb Museum, 178
Jylland, F12–F13, 118–143
arts and nightlife, 120, 127,
129, 133–134, 138–139
children, attractions for,
128–129, 131
emergencies, 142
guided tours, 142
hotels, 120, 123–124, 125, 126,
127, 128, 129, 132–133,
136, 138, 139–140
outdoor activities and sports,
124, 142
price categories, 118
restaurants, 120, 123–124,
125–126, 127, 128, 130,
132, 136, 138, 139–140
shopping, 120, 124, 126, 134,
140
sightseeing, 118–139
transportation, 141–142
visitor information, 143

K

Kangerlussuaq/Søndre
Strømfjord, 180
Kastellet, 12, 14–15
Kerteminde, 97–99
Kirkjubøur, 165–166
Kirsten Clemann's Ceramic
Studio, 154
Klaksvík, 167
Klampenborg, 57–58
Klosterkirke, 89
Knud Rasmussens Fødehjem,
182
Knuthenborg Safari Park, 88
Københavns Bymuseum, 19,
20
Københavns Synagoge, 16, 17
Københavns Universitet, 16,
17
Køge, 84–86

Køge Museum, 85
Kolding, 118–120
Koldinghus, 118
Kommandanten ✕, F21, 26
Kommandørgård, 124
Kong Asgers Høj, 87
Kong Hans Kælder ✕, 26
Kongaminnið, 164
Kongelige Bibliotek, 6, 9
Kongelige
Repræsantationlokaler, 7
Kongelige Stald, 6, 9
Kongelige Teater, 12, 14–15
Kongens Have (Copenhagen),
18
Kongens Have (Odense),
100
Kongens Nytorv, 15
Konrad ✕, 26
Kronborg Slot, F22, 71–72
Kunsthallen, 101
Kunstindustrimuseet, 12, 15
Kunstmuseet Køge
Skitsesamling, 85
Kværndrup, 109

L

Ladby, 99
Ladbyskibet (Viking ship), 99
Landsbrugs Museum, 151
Landsmuseet, 179
Langeland, 111
Language, F35–F36
Larsen, Johannes, 97–98
Le Sommelier ✕, 30–31
Ledreborg Slot, 84
Legoland, F23, 128–129
Lejre, 69, 84
Lejre Forsøgscenter, F22, 84
Lindholm Høje, 137
Liselund Ny Slot ☒, 87
Liselund Slot, 86
Listasavn Føroya, 164
Lodging, F36–F39
Lolland, 88–89
Louisiana (museum), F22, 71
Lurblæserne, 6, 9
Lyø, 106–107

M

Madsebakke, 150
Magnus Cathedral, 165
Mail and shipping, F39
Maren Minors Hjem, 113–114
Marie Louise ✕, F21, 102
Marienlyst Slot, 72
Marmorkirken, 12, 15–16
Marsellisborg Slot, 131
Marstal, 113–114
Marstal Søfartsmuseum, 114
Meal plans, F36
Menesket ved Havet
(sculpture), 127
Michael og Anna Ancher's
Hus, 139
Middelaldercentret, 88
Miðvágur, 168

Missionhotellet Stella Marris
⌂, 108
Moesgård Forhistorisk
Museum, 131
Molskroen ✕⌂, 136
Mølsted Museum, 56
Monasteries, 75, 137
Monastery clock, Dominican,
129
Money matters, F39–F40
Møn, 69, 86–87
Møns Klint, 86
Møns Museum, 87
Møntergården, 100
Movies, 193
Museet for Fotokunst, 101
Museet for Moderne Kunst
(Arken), 58–59
Museums, F22–F23
Bornholm, 146, 151, 152,
155
Copenhagen and environs, 8, 9,
11, 12, 14, 15, 17, 18–19,
20, 22, 54, 55, 56, 58–59
Faroe Islands, 164, 166
Fyn and the central islands,
95–96, 97–98, 100–101,
104–105, 107–108, 110, 112,
113–114
Greenland, 178, 179, 181, 182,
183
Jylland, 118–120, 123, 124,
125, 127, 130, 131, 134,
136, 137, 138, 139
Sjælland, 71, 72, 75, 77, 80, 83,
85, 87, 88
Music, 46–47, 134, 139
Mykines, 169
Mykineshólmur, 169

N

Narsarsuaq, 176, 178
National Museum of
Photography, 9
Nationalhistoriske Museum,
75
Nationalmuseet, 6, 9
Neksø Museum, 155
Nikolaj Kirken, 6, 10
Nokken ✕, 68, 71
Nordjyllands Kunstmuseum,
138
Nordsjællands Sommerpark,
78
Nørrebro, 16, 29–30
Norse ruins, 178
Novo Latino ✕, 76
Nuuk/Godthåb, 179–180
Ny Carlsberg Glyptotek, F22,
19, 20, 21, 22
Nyboder, 16, 18
Nyborg, 95–97
Nyborg Museum, 95–96
Nyborg Slot, 95
Nyborg Tappenstreg, 96
Nyhavn, 12
Nyhavn 71 ✕, 37
Nylars Kirke, 156

O

Odense, 100–105
Odense Castle, 100
Odense River Cruises, 101
Odsherred, 78–80
Odsherreds Zoo Dryepark, 79
Oluf Høst Museet, 152
Opera, 46–47
Ordrupgaard, F22, 55
Østerlars, 153–154
Østerlars Kirke, F22, 153
Outdoor activities and sports,
F41–F42. ⇨ Also under
individual islands

P

Packing, F40–F41
Passports and visas, F41
Price categories, F33, F36
dining, 23, 68, 95, 118, 145,
162, 176
lodging, 33, 68, 95, 118, 145,
162, 176

Q

Qaqortoq/Julianehåb, 178
Qassiarsuk, 178–179
Qeqertarsuaq/Godhavn, 182
Queen Margrethe, 13

R

Råbjerg Mile, 139
Rådhus (Copenhagen), 6, 10
Rådhus (Jylland), 131
Rådhus Pladsen, 2, 6, 10
Radisson SAS Royal ⌂, F20, 38
Rebild Park, 137
Reinwalds ✕, F21, 27
Restaurants, F19, F20–F21,
F33–F34. ⇨ Also under
individual islands
price categories, F33, 68, 95,
118, 145, 162, 176
Ribe, 125–126
Ribe Domkirke, 125
Ribes Vikinger, 125
Ringsted, 69, 89–90
Riz Raz ✕, F21, 28
Rø Plantage, 153
Rømø, 124–125
Rømø Kirke, 124–125
Rønne, 145–149
Rock clubs, 44, 46, 165
Romsø, 99
Rosenborg Slot, F22, 16, 18
Roskilde, 69, 81, 83–84
Royal Court Theater, 11
Royal Hotel ⌂, 132
Roykstovan, 166
Rudolf Mathis ✕, 98
Rudolph Tegner Museum, 77
Ruins, 7, 178
Rundetårn, 16, 18
Runestener, 129
Rungstedlund, 68, 69, 71
Running, 49
Russiske Ortodoks Kirke, 16

S

Sailing, F18
St. Albans (church), 14
St. Olaf's Church, 165
SAK Kunstbygningen,
107–108
Saksun, 166
Sandur, 169
Saxildhus Hotel ✕⌂, 120
Schackenborg Slotskro ✕⌂,
F20, 123–124
Seafood ✕, F21, 132
Selsø Slot, 81
Senior citizen travel, F41
Seven Gardens, 105
Shopping. ⇨ See under
individual islands
Silkeborg Museum, 130
Sisimiut/Holsteinsborg,
180–182
Sisimiut Museum, 181
Sjælland, F12, 68–93
arts and nightlife, 73, 83–84, 86
beaches, 68, 76, 78, 79
children, attractions for, 71, 79,
88, 89
emergencies, 91
guided tours, 92
hotels, 72–73, 74, 76–77, 78,
80, 81, 83, 85–86, 87, 88–89,
90
outdoor activities and sports,
73, 74, 79, 84, 88, 90, 91
price categories, 68
restaurants, 68, 71, 72, 74,
75–76, 80, 81, 83, 85, 87,
88
shopping, 84, 90
sightseeing, 68–90
transportation, 90–92
visitor information, 92–93
Sjællands Odde, 79
Skagen, 139–140
Skagen Museum, 139
Skálafjørður, 166
Skansin, 162
Skansin Guesthouse ⌂, F20,
164
Skibby, 81
Skiing, 181–182
Skt. Bendts Kirke, 89
Skt. Knuds Kirke, 100
Skt. Nikolai Kirke (Køge), 85
Skt. Nikolai Kirke (Vejle), 129
Skt. Olai's Kirke, 72
Skipperhuset ✕, F21, 74
Skovshoved ⌂, F20, 37–38
Slættaratindur, 166
Slotshave, 73
Slotskirke, 75
Soccer, 49
Sommerland Sjælland, 79
Sønderho Kro ✕⌂, 128
Sorø, 89
Søstrup Kirke, 80
Sports and outdoor activities,
F41–F42. ⇨ Also under
individual islands